Current Issues in

Marriage

and the Family

Second Edition

P9-CBH-559

J. Gipson Wells

Mississippi State University

Macmillan Publishing Co., Inc.
NEW YORK

Collier Macmillan Publishers
LONDON

79-1327

Earlier edition copyright © 1975 by J. Gipson Wells

Macmillan Publishing Co., Inc.
866 Third Avenue, New York, New York 10022

Collier Macmillan Canada, Ltd.

Library of Congress Cataloging in Publication Data

Wells, J. Gipson, comp.
    Current issues in marriage and the family.

    Includes bibliographical references.
    1. Marriage—Addresses, essays, lectures.
2. Family—United States—Addresses, essays,
lectures.   3. Divorce—United States—Addresses,
essays, lectures.   4. Sex role—Addresses, essays,
lectures.   I. Title.
HQ536.W4   1979   301.42   78–7599
ISBN 0–02–425440–1

Printing: 1 2 3 4 5 6 7 8   Year: 9 0 1 2 3 4 5

Preface
to the Second Edition

It is certainly difficult to anticipate or predict the manner in which various social issues will change, particularly over a short period of years. For example, when the first edition of this book was published it was felt that the section on abortion reform might even at that time be out of date. This feeling was caused by the relatively recent U.S. Supreme Court decision which in effect nullified most state laws that had previously forbidden elective abortions. It appeared that the controversy was at last settled, and that the issue would simply disappear. But this has not been the case, since the various sides in this controversy are still battling as strongly as ever. The major focus of the antiabortion forces is now a constitutional amendment to ban abortions, which would override the Supreme Court decision. On the other hand, the major arguments used by both sides differ very little from the arguments used prior to the Court's decision. Thus, this edition has retained the section on abortion reform along with two of the articles from the first edition that exemplify those arguments.

Several of the issues that were newly emergent with the first edition have now been brought into slightly sharper focus in the last four years and have thus been treated a little differently in this revision. For example, the issue of having children has received a great deal of attention; two new articles have been added to that section. Many more states have now passed new and somewhat reformed divorce laws, so that the emphasis in that section now reflects those changes along with the need for additional reforms. The issue surrounding men's and women's changing roles has taken a turn more toward the problems of men, whereas earlier concern was more predominantly upon the situation of women. This shift is also reflected in this revision. Finally, a considerable amount of interest has been shown in the phenomenon of cohabitation. In the first edition this topic was included in the sections that were concerned with the questions of whether or not to marry and the alternative forms marriage might take. However, this increase in attention seems to justify treating cohabitation as an issue in its own right, and this is also done in the revision.

Some of the issues have not changed greatly since the first edition, so very little change has been made in the sections on marital fidelity and the future of marriage. However, the increased attention given to singlehood warranted some changes in the first section of the book, which is concerned with the question of marriage versus nonmarriage. Altogether, ten new articles have been included in this revision which either replace or supplement those included in the first edition.

J. G. W.

Contents

Part Four
Men's and Women's Roles

Part Five
To Have Children or Not?

Introduction

J. Gipson Wells

*I*T IS CERTAINLY no coincidence that most of the crucial social issues confronting American society in the current decade are also issues which are of central importance to the American family system as a basic social institution. These issues are also important for the individual families to which most people belong. The general society and the family face many common issues due to the fact that the threads of family life in our culture have been so thoroughly interwoven with the general fabric of the society as to be almost of one cloth. The family has always been seen as the backbone of the nation, and there has always been a strong belief that "as the family goes, so goes the nation." Of course, this has been true to some extent with almost every nation, from both an historical as well as a cross-cultural standpoint.

Almost any current social issue is also a family issue: the dermining of the family leading to the ultimate crumbling of the nation are certainly overblown, one can hardly deny that there is a close relationship between certain problems and issues of national significance and those problems and

1

issues which confront the family. Obviously, one reason for this close relationship is the fact that the family is one of the most basic institutions of any society, and this is certainly no less true in American society.

Almost any current social issue is also a family issue: the question of the efficacy of marriage itself; the question of whether or not to have children and if so, how many to have; the questions raised by the Women's Liberation Movement related to what the nature of women's roles should be; questions concerning legal reforms in the areas of divorce and abortion; and finally, even questions concerning the need or desirability of marital fidelity. The purpose of the articles in this book is to take a brief and objective look at each of these problems or issues, viewing them mainly from the perspective of the sociology of marriage and the family rather than as general social problems. That is, the issues will be approached primarily as concerns of marriage and family, both institutionally and individually, and secondarily as they might be related to the larger society.

Essentially, the plan of the book is to deal with specific issues that have emerged from the various viewpoints with respect to each issue. Within each of the first eight sections of the book, which represent what are felt to be the eight major issues facing marriage and the family today, there will be at least one article which attempts to take a neutral stance so as to give the reader a general understanding of the issue. There will then be several articles which present more specific, often opposing, points of view on the given issues. The editor's commentary which accompanies each section is also designed to increase the reader's overall knowledge and understanding of the issues and to aid in maintaining an objective stance as the reader approaches each issue. The final section (Part Nine) presents commentary along with two articles which aptly deal with the outlook for marriage and the family institution based upon the current trends with respect to the issues under scrutiny.

The 26 articles in this collection were gathered from a wide variety of sources, such as widely distributed popular magazines, the more esoteric professional journals, and a few lesser known national periodicals and reports. They present a wide range of points of view, and by studying the variety of arguments that surround each issue, the reader should be in a far better position to make an informed judgment about any of the eight major questions confronting the family today.

SOME BASIC CONCEPTS

The terms *marriage* and *family* will appear dozens of times throughout this book, and certainly everyone has a pretty good idea what these words mean. For most, however, the meanings are far too general, so that it is probably worthwhile to explore the meanings of these terms for the purpose of giving them more depth and precision. To better our understanding of marriage and family in American society, it should be helpful to use more universal cross-cultural definitions of these concepts as points of departure. In his book, *The Family in Cross-Cultural Perspective,* William Stephens presents relatively universal definitions of both of these terms. He defines marriage as "a socially legitimate sexual union, begun with a public announcement and undertaken with some idea of permanence; it is assumed with a more or less explicit marriage contract, which spells out the reciprocal rights and obligations between spouses, and between the spouses and their future children."[1] According to this definition, then, there are four basic components which go together to create a marriage: social legitimation, public acknowledgment, an assumption of permanence, and reciprocal rights and obligations. Marriages in almost every culture of the world, both preliterate and modern, appear to have most of these basic components.

Marriage is also a "rite of passage," that is, a status-changing event through which all who wish to create a family unit must go. As everyone knows, the marriage event is an integral part of families in particular and of the family institution in general. Thus, Stephens bases his definition of family upon his prior definition of marriage. He defines family as "a social arrangement based upon marriage and the marriage contract, including recognition of the rights and duties of parenthood, common residence for husband, wife, and children, and reciprocal economic obligations between husband and wife."[2] It is also useful to differentiate conceptually between conjugal family units and the family institution, and it should be pointed out that this definition of family applies essentially to the family unit as a special social grouping. However, some aspects of this definition might also apply to a definition of the family as a basic social institution in the same sense that business, government, schools, and churches are basic social institutions.

Basic social institutions are usually defined in terms of the common functions which they perform for most societies. Family might also be defined in this manner. In most societies the family is the institution which is given the responsibility of bearing and rearing children, for the purpose of maintaining the population. Childbearing usually requires and allows the legitimation of sexual activity, and the providing of a legitimate means of sexual satisfaction, unrelated to childbearing, also becomes a major institutional function of the family. In addition, there is also a wide range of economic functions assigned to the family such as the providing of food, clothing, and shelter for its members. Therefore, the family as an institution might be seen as something far more complex and comprehensive than the same term when applied to the conjugal family as a small group. Nevertheless, it is the individual family groups of a society which in turn embody the broader social institution.

Further discussions of the meanings of these terms, along with attempts to apply these definitions to varieties of actual kinship structures will be taken up in the commentary which precedes Part Three.

THEORETICAL VIEWPOINTS

A number of theoretical or conceptual frameworks have proved useful in the analysis of marriage and family issues.

Although some of the articles in this collection are more journalistic in nature, and thus do not reflect any particular theoretical orientation of sociology, the articles from the more scholarly sources do reflect one or more of the sociological frames of reference employed in family analysis. Additionally, the editor's commentaries which accompany each section will often rely upon one or a combination of these conceptual frameworks, although in most cases the frameworks will be implied rather than explicitly pointed out. In any event, it is felt that the reader should be aware, at least in a superficial way, of the various theoretical points of view upon which the articles and commentary rest.

Three such theoretical viewpoints or conceptual frameworks will be delineated here. The first is usually referred to as the "institutional approach" because it deals with marriage and family as a basic institution of any society. One of the definitions of family presented earlier dealt with it as an institution among other social institutions, and this type of definition coincides very well with the institutional approach. This viewpoint is reflected particularly in those parts of the book in which the issues of concern arise out of the relationship between the family and such other institutions as government, business, and church. For example, the family is required to relate to the government with respect to such issues as the control and registration of marriage, statutory sexual discrimination, and the legal aspects of abortion and divorce reform. The family institution and the religious institution encounter one another on such topics as the form and structure of marriage, whether or not to have children, abortion and divorce reform, and the moral aspects of marital fidelity. And finally, the relationship between family and the economy is of importance with such topics as marriage versus nonmarriage, men's and women's roles, having children, and to some extent divorce reform. Obviously, any analysis of the family and the various issues and problems which confront it must also concern itself with the other institutions with which the family is integrally related. (The family is also integrally related to the educational institution, but, with the exception of sex education, there are currently no crucial issues with respect to this relationship.)

The second conceptual framework might be very generally referred to as the "functional approach," and as used here, it is not precisely equivalent to structural-functionalism as found in general sociological theory. However, it does retain a few important aspects of structural-functionalist theory. Under this approach, the family is defined in terms of its functions, that is, what it does in and for the larger society. The assumption is made that all societal entities have certain functions to perform, and that when these functions are performed properly, society will operate in a reasonably well-organized fashion. Of course, this is an oversimplistic view of social organization based upon questionable assumptions about the nature of society, but it does serve as a useful analytical tool when dealing with the family, as well as with other social organizations and institutions.

Using this approach, one would define the family as that social grouping or organization which performs those functions or tasks that have been traditionally accepted as belonging to families. The circular nature of this definition is at once obvious, but the more complete discussion would go on to point out the particular functions which marriage and the family are expected to perform, such as the bearing and rearing of children to maintain the population and to give continuity and support to the culture, the provision of the basic physical necessities for its members, providing a center of affection and companionship for the individual, and providing a means for legitimate sexual satisfaction. There is a close relationship between the functional approach and the institutional approach, and it is made evident by the fact that institutions were also defined to some extent by their functions.

Using the functional approach, family-related issues or problems might be seen as occurring when something interferes with the organization or structure of the family so as to cause it to be unable to properly perform its functions. Furthermore, issues and controversies might arise when other institutions or organizations attempt to take away some of the family's functions, and in some cases, other institutions might try to force new functions upon it. This functional viewpoint might be utilized more specifically with such issues as abortion reform, where there is a move toward making such decisions a family matter rather than a legal one. Also, certain issues concerned with the legitimation of sex outside of marriage, for example, might be viewed within this framework as an erosion of a traditional family function.

The final conceptual framework which might be of use here are the basic elements of role theory. It attempts to analyze behavior, in this case male-female interaction, in terms of the manner in which people relate to each other through the various roles then enact. Social roles are the behavior that is expected of individuals as they move from one social situation to another, playing a slightly different but related role in each particular situation. The family unit might very well be analyzed and understood as a system or network of social roles, with each family member enacting one or more social roles both within and outside of the family. Sex roles—the concept of most importance here—refer to those roles which are defined or differentiated on the basis of the sex of the person attempting to enact the role. In the most basic sense, female children are taught to act like females "ought to act," while male children are taught "masculine" behavior. The result is that most children are raised to play only the sexually appropriate roles, and most social roles have built into them connotations as to which sex should be playing them. There is also a great deal of pressure placed upon members of society to play only roles sexually appropriate. Thus, the effeminate male is disdained, as is the female who attempts to hold a traditionally male occupation.

This application of role theory will be developed further in Part Four which deals with men's and women's roles and will also be indirectly applied in those sections dealing with divorce reform and marital fidelity.

The purpose of this very brief discussion of theoretical viewpoints is simply to alert the reader to the fact that many of the articles and most of the commentary rely upon one or a combination of them. However, these viewpoints are not always readily recognizable and the reader's prior awareness of them should aid in the understanding of the material.

SOCIAL PROBLEMS AND SOCIAL ISSUES

The concerns of this book might become even more evident by a demonstration of what is meant by the concept of *social issues*. In defining this term, it should also be useful to differentiate between social issues on the one hand, and the widely used concept of *social problems* on the other. Beginning with the latter term, a social problem might be defined as a social condition or situation that either directly affects or is thought to have some effect upon a significant number of people in ways which are thought by many to be undesirable or detrimental, either to those affected by the situation or to the society in general; furthermore, it is generally thought that something can and/or ought to be done to alleviate the condition through societal action.

There are at least two significant aspects to this definition. First, there are some conditions which have an actual or direct effect upon individuals or segments of the population, while other conditions are only thought or perceived to be detrimental. Thus, one type might be referred to as real social problems while the other might be termed *pseudo*-problems. For example, segments of most large cities have high rates of street crimes which certainly affect large numbers of people in an undoubtedly significant and direct way. Street crime would be considered a real social problem. On the other hand, many people believe that the sale and distribution of pornography is a serious social problem when in fact almost all research evidence and professional opinion supports the view that pornography is essentially harmless in most cases and may even be helpful to persons with certain kinds of sexual problems. This is an example of a pseudo-problem. However, whether problems are real or not, they nevertheless have an impact upon the society through their effects upon public opinion which in turn affect public policy.

The second significant aspect of the definition of social problems has to do with the number of people involved. There are, broadly speaking two categories of people related to any social problem: those who are directly involved in creating or receiving its ill effects and those who are simply aware of or concerned about the problem from a distance. In some cases, for example, the former group might be relatively small, while the latter segment of concerned citizens is quite large and their concern quite strong. Such would be the case with heroin addiction, which directly effects a comparatively small number of people, but about which there is great and widespread concern.

The opposite type of social problem would be the situation in which large numbers are directly affected, but about which there is comparatively little public concern. Such is the case with alcoholism and alcohol abuse, which is estimated to affect as many as 10 million people, but about which the general public fails to express anything near the degree of concern so often heard regarding other drugs.

The concepts of social problems and social issues are in some ways related, but a social issue is somewhat different in that it is a situation or condition which generates at least two conflicting points of view, both of which may be competing for public acceptance and support. In addition, the competing sides in the issue might be attempting to either bring about or impede change through legislation, court action, or other means. Some examples of social issues are divorce reform, abortion reform, and marital fidelity which, among others, are considered in this book. In many cases, the same condition might be a social problem as well as a social issue, but there are many situations that are clearly one but not the other.

There are some additional ways in which social problems and social issues might be related. First, some social problems often result in the creation of social issues, and this can occur in a number of ways. For example, the issue of marijuana legalization is a direct outgrowth of the problem of the abuse of marijuana and other drugs. From a conceptual standpoint, the problem and the issue may be seen as being separate from one another, although they do have a special relationship. Social problems also create social issues when heated differences of opinion arise among segments of the public, and perhaps among involved professionals, over the manner of treatment or resolution of the particular problems. An example of this situation is the differences of opinion which exist with regard to the best manner of dealing with various kinds of crime and criminals. Crime is the social problem, and how to deal with it becomes the social issue.

One final way in which social problems and social issues are related is that there is rarely ever complete agreement, either public or professional, over which conditions are social problems and which are social issues. Furthermore, many define some conditions as problems which others might define as issues, and still others may feel that a particular condition is neither a problem nor an issue.

Current Issues in Marriage and Family

The concern of this book is with certain social issues which have a direct bearing upon marriage and family in American society. Some of the issues considered here are related to social problems in one or more of the ways mentioned earlier, whereas others have developed as issues somewhat independently of any specific problems. Most of the issues dealt with throughout the book have already been referred to earlier in this introduction, but they will be more specifically delineated and organized in the book in the following manner:

1. *To marry or not*—This issue revolves basically around two questions. The first has to do with the viability of marriage as a major aspect of the family institution, and the second has to do with whether an individual should choose marriage or the single life.

2. *Marriage versus cohabitation*—With the increase in both the frequency of and the publicity given to couples living together without being married, the topic of cohabitation as it relates to marriage has now assumed the status of an issue in its own right.

3. *What form marriage*—The issues here are whether or not monogamy is still a functional form of marriage in the modern world, and the debate over altering our basic monogamous form of marriage.

4. *Men's and women's roles*—The focus of this issue is primarily on the effects of the Women's Liberation Movement on the family, but attention is also given to the effects of the movement on the roles of men and some of the changes in men's roles that may be occurring independently of that movement.

5. *To have children or not*—Questions raised by the new awareness of such problems as resource depletion, pollution and overpopulation, have caused young couples to give a great deal more thought about not only the question of family size, but whether or not to have children at all. Parenthood versus nonparenthood is the crux of this particular issue.

6. *Abortion reform*—This issue focuses upon the moral, religious, and legal aspects of the abortion question.

7. *Divorce reform*—The concern here is with the current reforms that are taking place in the divorce laws of many of the states, and the extent to which these reforms are adequate. Many states still need to begin the reform process and others are in need of still further reforms.

8. *Marital fidelity*—The recent increase in sexual candor in our society has created a great deal of alarm over the possible increase of infidelity, and the effects of such behavior upon marriage and the family. The crux of the issue is over the extent to which both individual spouses and society in general should tolerate this behavior.

More detailed development of the various positions and shades of opinion with regard to each of these issues will be found in the editor's commentaries which precede the groups of articles related to each issue.

REFERENCES

1. William Stephens, *The Family in Cross-Cultural Perspective* (New York: Holt, 1963), p. 5.
2. Ibid, p. 8.

Part
One

To Marry or Not?

ALTHOUGH THE BASIC ASSUMPTION underlying most of the articles in this book is that most people will choose to marry at least once, it seems logical to begin with the basic question as to whether or not one should marry. This issue, along with the questions of what form or structure intimate relationships should take, which are dealt with in Parts Two and Three, has been raised in recent years with increasing frequency by young people.

The question of marriage versus nonmarriage can be approached from two perspectives: from that of the society in general and from the standpoint of individual choice. On the one hand, the question might be raised as to the viability of continuing the institution of marriage in this or any other society; on the other hand, the issue may be viewed as dealing with the choice that each marriageable person faces as to whether or not he or she will choose marriage for himself or herself. Since marriage is currently, and will for the forseeable future be, the overwhelming choice of most persons in our society, it is likely to remain an important institution, if not a totally viable one. Therefore, the latter perspective, the question of personal choice about marriage, is dealt with here. Furthermore, the question of individual choice about marriage is in fact the real issue that is currently of concern to young people, especially in light of the increased concerns among the young about overpopulation, the increasing rate of divorce, and discrimination against women, and what each one as an individual might do to help alleviate some of these problems. An increasingly acceptable, and perhaps desirable, alternative which speaks directly to some of these concerns is to remain single.

The question of whether or not to marry, from the individual perspective, also has two sides; that is, does one choose the single life in the sense that he or she wishes to live alone or with someone of the same sex, or perhaps remain with the family of orientation (one's parents) ; or does one simply wish to avoid the legal and social bonds of matrimony while in fact living in a quasi-married state usually referred to as cohabitation. The basic issue here is whether or not cohabitation is a total rejection of marriage or rather an attempt to alter its traditional form. Part Two deals with the question of marriage versus cohabitation and Part Three deals with the issue of altering the currently accepted form of marriage. The fourth article in this section, however, is also concerned in part with the question of the form of marriage.

As we have stated, the vast majority of people in this country, as well as other countries, choose marriage over the single life. In the United States, over 95 per cent of all people will marry at least once during their lifetimes. As long as records have been kept and statistics compiled on marriage rates, the rate of marriage has remained relatively high. Beginning in the 1860's, the marriage rate fluctuated between 8.5 and 9 per 1,000 population, with a slight but steady increase in the rate. This slow increase continued until 1920 when the marriage rate reached 12.0. A sharp decline in the marriage rate then occurred which reached bottom in 1932 with a rate of 7.9. Thereafter, several rapid rises and falls followed with the highest historical rate of 16.4 occurring in 1946, which incidentally was also the year of the highest divorce rate in American history until the 1970's.[1] The marriage rate again declined to 8.4 for 1958, but has generally been on the rise again until more fluctuations appeared in the 1970's.[2]

Marriage rates for selected years

Year	1966	1968	1970	1971	1972	1973	1974	1975	1976	1977
Rate	9.5	10.4	10.7	10.6	11.0	10.9	10.5	10.1	9.0	10.1

Source: National Center for Health Statistics, U.S. Department of Health, Education and Welfare.

The decline in the marriage rate from 1972 through 1976 was thought by many to indicate a general decline in marriages that would become a major trend.[3] However, the most recent data for 1977 show another increase in the rate.[4] About the only thing the experts in this area can agree upon is that there is no clear trend and no clear interpretation of recent data with regard to whether or not marriage is on the decline.

One element that may be having some effect upon the marriage rate is the average age at which people marry. There is evidence that young people, particularly those entering their first marriage, are doing so at a later average age than in previous years. For a number of years the age at marriage gradually declined, but around 1955 this trend reversed so that the average age at first marriage in 1975 was 21.1 for females and 23.5 for males.[5] But this trend has been in effect much longer than the recently declining marriage rate, and has probably had only a slight effect on the marriage rate.

Another demographic change that has probably had some effect upon the marriage rate is the declining proportion of young people of marriageable age in the total population. There are also indications that more divorced people are choosing not to remarry.[6] Any changes in the marriage rate are likely the result of the combination of numerous factors, many of which are unaccounted for. The important point is that in our society most people still do marry, as is the case with the members of every society around the world. Although fluctuations do occur, the marriage rate is still quite high.

Some years ago John Sirjamaki stated that in American society marriage was a dominating life goal. His implication is that Americans are unusually concerned with the development and maintenance of man-woman relationships, which are within the context of marriage or at least having the potential for marriage.[7] This idea is also basic to Bernard Farber's model of "universal, permanent availability," which he uses to describe dating, courtship, and marriage behavior in our culture. In short, Farber said that people were always in the marriage market, even those who were already married.[8]

Additional evidence of our preoccupation with marriage can be seen in the high rate of second, third, and subsequent marriages found in American culture. About 20 per cent of all marriages are second or subsequent marriages involving either widowed or divorced persons.[9]

Thus, it is fairly clear that Americans have traditionally desired the married state and continue to do so, even to the point of looking with scorn or suspicion upon the unmarried or never-married members of society. Bachelors and spinsters were once thought either to have some idiosyncrasy that made them unmarriageable, or to be homosexual. Single people are still seen as being somehow different or strange, although the stigma attached to the single state seems to be losing strength among younger, especially college-educated, people. However, it is still difficult to find people expressing the desire to remain single, and when such opinions do emerge, those holding them continue to find it difficult to enact their desires because of a number of very strong social pressures.

The pressures against the single life and in favor of marriage come not only from our cultural traditions but also in a much more direct and personal form from one's family and friends. Most parents of marriageable young people hold with many of the traditional views toward marriage, and more specifically, they have a strong desire for grandchildren. Moreover, in most cases one's own friends are themselves probably already married or are getting married. From the married couple's point of view, continuing friendships with single people presents a number of problems that are mainly related to a divergence of interests but are also related to the feeling that the single person might represent a threat to the member of the couple of the same sex or to the marital relationship itself. Additionally, most entertainment in our culture is based upon couple participation or interaction, and this tends to put the single person in the position of being somehow out of place.

In spite of the tremendous pressures brought to bear upon young people to seek marriage, a movement is afoot that is beginning to bring to light a number of negative aspects of marriage along with some positive reasons for not marrying. This movement is having at least two results. It is providing those who are either unmarriageable or who have already chosen not to marry with an increasingly acceptable rationale for their choice and it is encouraging other as yet unmarried young people to take a second look at their own choices in this matter and to consider alternatives to marriage that may carry less stigma than in the past.

The four articles in this first section approach the question of marriage versus nonmarriage from several points of view and reach or lead to a variety of possible conclusions. The first article "In Defense of Traditional Marriage" reports the results of a *Life* magazine survey of 62,000 of its readers concerning the status of their own marriages and some of their attitudes and feelings about the new trends and practices related to marriage. The overall tone of the article is optimistic, with most of the respondents reporting that their own marriages are happy and successful. The respondents, however, also demonstrated a remarkable tolerance for other points of view, about divorce, living together, and trial marriage. The reader should bear in mind that these findings are very much the product of the type of sample from which the findings are drawn. That is, the majority of *Life* magazine readers were most likely to be members of that group which is loosely termed the middle class. This is the segment of the population that is more likely to have successful and happy marriages in contrast to the working and lower classes which account for the vast majority of the broken homes in our society. However, one certainly should not discount the findings of this survey altogether on the basis of the sample used, since this middle class is the largest segment of society in terms of socio-economic similarity, and the norms, values, and attitudes are probably most representative of the society as a whole. The findings of this survey do reflect to some extent what might be called the middle-class bias. One conclusion drawn from the article is that things might not be as bad as some would have us believe them to be, and that a lot of happy marriages are still around that operate within the so-called traditional style.

The second article of this section presents a unique point of view. Caroline Bird, the author of "Women Should Stay Single," is active and well known in the Women's Liberation Movement, although she would probably not be classified as a radical within that movement. Her article views the good and bad points of marriage and points out a number of advantages that might accrue to the woman who remains single. Although one might legitimately disagree with her main premise, that people marry basically for sex and that increased sexual freedom is responsible for some women not marrying, many of Bird's ideas are both valid and thought provoking. Ultimately, her view is that women no longer have to marry for security and that a woman's major needs and satisfactions of life can be gained without her having to sacrifice the advantages of the single life.

Singlehood is often viewed as an undesirable life-style in our society, and as acceptable only as a period of transition between the attainment of adulthood and the entering into marriage. In the third article, Roger Libby challenges this point of view with the notion that singlehood can and should be a positive option for many individuals. Furthermore, this option should not be a lifetime choice but rather one that can be chosen or rejected several times during the course of one's life, and for a variety of legitimate reasons. As the title of the article implies, the emphasis is upon the creative aspects of singlehood and the advantages that may result from this life-style for those who choose it.

The final article in this section, "Marriage: The Traditional Alternative," could just as easily have been placed in either Part Two or Part Three, since it is concerned not only with the question of whether or not to marry but also addresses the issue of cohabitation as well as the various forms that marriage may take. The authors of this article look at several of the arguments used in opposition to marriage and give particular attention to the importance and the nature of commitment.

REFERENCES

1. Ruth S. Cavan, *The American Family* (New York: Crowell, 1969), pp. 539–541.
2. *Monthly Vital Statistics Report Annual Summary for the U.S., 1972.* U.S. Department of Health, Education, and Welfare, National Center for Health Statistics, p. 1.

19

3. *Monthly Vital Statistics Annual Summary for the U.S., 1976*. U.S. Department of Health, Education and Welfare, National Center for Health Statistics, p. 1.

4. *Monthly Vital Statistics Report*. U.S. Department of Health, Education and Welfare, National Center for Health Statistics, Vol. 26 (January 6, 1968).

5. *Current Population Reports*. U.S. Depart of Commerce, Bureau of the Census, Series P-20, No. 287.

6. Paul C. Glick and Arthur J. Norton, "Marrying, Divorcing, and Living Together in the U.S. Today," *Population Bulletin,* Vol. 32 (Population Reference Bureau, 1977), pp. 8–9.

7. John Sirjamaki, "Cultural Configurations in the American Family," *American Journal of Sociology.* Vol. 53 (1947–48), pp. 464–470.

8. Bernard Farber, *Family: Organization and Interaction* (San Francisco: Chandler, 1964), pp. 103–134.

9. *Marriages Trends and Characteristics*. U.S. Department of Health, Education, and Welfare, Vital and Health Statistics—Series 21, No. 21, p. 17.

1.

In Defense of Traditional Marriage

Tom Flaherty

M arriage, like God, is not dead," declares Mrs. Robert Scrafford of Franklin Lakes, N.J. "True, marriage is not always blissful after the honeymoon bloom wears away. But it fulfills our most basic human needs as nothing else can. I predict that during the '70's the pendulum will swing back toward a deeper awareness of the advantages and good sense of the strong, dedicated marriage."

Mrs. Scrafford was responding to a LIFE questionnaire that asked readers to express their views on the trends and challenges in marriage today. 62,000 answered the questionnaire. Group responses came from churches and Sunday schools, college and high school sociology classes, from guests at a dinner party and from people working in offices. Some married couples answered jointly, as did some unmarried couples who live together. Six hundred readers wrote letters to expand on the answers they had checked. Though there were some important exceptions, the responses, taken together, amount to a sober, often enthusiastic, sometimes angry defense of traditional marriage in America.

The 62,000 readers are a general but not precise cross section of the U.S. Three out of five are presently married. More than 70 per cent have attended college. 45 per cent, the largest age group, are under 30.

The questionnaire they answered appeared in a special section of LIFE (April 28) devoted to experiments in marriage: a collective family, unmarried parents, a frontier-style partnership, a troubled couple in therapy and another that had drawn up a formal contract for sharing household responsibilities.

Many readers were incensed that the survey overlooked the religious status of matrimony as a holy institution. They quoted liberally from the Bible in asserting (1) that the bond of marriage is indissoluble and (2) that woman's role in it is subservient to man's. "If this nation doesn't begin living the way God intended us to, we are lost," warned a Port Angeles, Wash. reader. "Religion may not be important to many people nowadays," wrote an Oak Park, Ill. woman, "but I feel that our Christian faith has made all the difference between a 'blah,' mediocre marriage and a thing of real beauty." A mother of four children in Winona Lake, Ind. says, "We've had plenty of problems. But the daily influence of Christ in our hearts and in our home has made the difference."

Other readers considered LIFE's discussion of changing attitudes toward marriage to be dangerously immoral, a threat to the foundations of society itself. "You are tempting thousands of young people to experiment with sin," wrote a charter subscriber in Grand Rapids who said that he had burned his copy of the issue—after cutting out and answering the questionnaire.

But an overwhelming majority of the 62,000 were willing, even eager, to scrutinize their own marriages and the institution itself. Though not exactly starry-eyed, almost half of them rate their own marriage as "very happy." Another one-third called it "happy." "I checked 'happy' instead of 'very happy,'" said a Texas wife of seven years' standing, "because I believe that as we grow older and more mature together on this lifetime adventure we will become even closer. After we've been married 50 years, God willing, I hope I will be able to say 'very happy.'"

Indeed, the happiest group were those over 50. The least satisfied —though not drastically so—were those between 30 and 49. Looking around, the respondents were not so sanguine about the marriages of their families and friends. Almost half thought the other marriages they are familiar with are generally either "all right" or plain "unhappy." Only 12 per cent thought other people were "very happy."

One person in three said he, or someone close to him, had sought marriage counseling from a clergyman or other professional. (Among those who are separated or divorced, 70 per cent had sought counseling.) A majority (including 85 per cent of those who have split up) said that counseling had *not* been helpful in keeping couples together. But some were convinced that counseling had helped the individual, if not the marriage.

"It is possible to obtain more satisfaction and happiness out of marriage and the rearing of a family than from any other undertaking," wrote a husband in Everett, Wash. "Both of my parents give love unselfishly not only to each other but to their children," adds a college senior from South Carolina. "This is what I consider a successful marriage and what I hope mine will be like." A Plano, Tex. woman who just celebrated her 25th anniversary advises, "The survival of marriage, that tender structure on which our civilization is built, depends upon the decency of each human being and our concern for each other." A Cabot, Vt. wife and mother married 26 years adds simply: "I know that to my family I'm a very special person. What more can any woman ask?"

Effort, trust, and tolerance are the credo of many who consider their marriages the happiest. "Granted that marriage is made in heaven, and has to be lived down here," argues an Ogden, Utah reader, "it's still the only worthwhile commitment two human beings can make." From a Belleville, Ill. reader: "The key to the whole thing is, you have to think about somebody besides yourself." And from North Highlands, Calif.: "Marriage means forgiving when need be, smiling when you'd really like to swear, and, once you've cooled off, feeling secure enough in your love to talk about your hurts and disappointments. A sense of humor is a help in any situation; it's a must in marriage."

A 60 per cent majority of both men and women said they believe that a husband should help his wife with housework and caring for their children. Most of the rest agree that a husband should help out if his wife works. And one reader in three believes that the basic change in the marriage of the future will be a more equal sharing of all responsibilities. "Most husbands who really want to partake of marriage enjoy performing duties that children require," says a Nashville reader. "I believe in doing the chores together," writes a Ridgewood, N.J. man. "My earliest memories are of my father helping with the laundry so that he and my mother could go off and play tennis together." A Ravenna, Ohio woman adds, "He helps me, I help him. In our house, no one keeps count."

But the readers were overwhelmingly opposed (87 per cent nay) to the idea of a formal contract spelling out the household duties of each partner. "In the time consumed filling out a contract, the whole ruddy house could be cleaned!" exclaims a pediatrician's wife in Kingston, N.Y. "Marriage is not a cold-blooded contract," writes a Ridgecrest, Calif. reader whose response was echoed by others. "In a true marriage, based on love and trust, you do things for each other because you want to, not because there is a contract."

Almost half the respondents think women devote too much of themselves to their children, at their husbands' expense. Those who are separated or divorced think this way by a two-to-one margin. Women, surprisingly, are much more apt than men to consider this a problem. One wife, however, suggested that the survey should have included a companion question: "Do husbands devote too much of themselves to their jobs at the expense of their wives and children?"

By a seven-to-one margin the readers voted that, if possible, couples should get away from their children for a period each year. "I think the rate of nervous breakdowns and divorces could be halved," writes a Bakersfield, Calif. mother of two small children, "if parents could get away from their children for even three days a year to renew their sense of 'self' and to SLEEP LATE."

Several Long Island couples wrote that they have devoted week-end "vacations" to a movement called Marriage Encounter. In it, a husband and wife, with the guidance of other volunteer couples, "take an honest look at themselves and their marriage, assess the goods and the bads, and set a positive course toward the goals they hope to attain."

From the daughter of a "disastrous" marriage in Oakland, Calif. comes a different point of view on vacations: "It's not so much that couples should get away from their children, as that the children should get away from their parents."

Though an overall majority says No to husbands and wives taking vacations apart from each other, 30 per cent of those who rate their marriage "happy" or "very happy" think it is a good idea, as do 60 per cent of those who aren't particularly happy. Only 30 per cent of the married readers have ever tried separate vacations. "We're apart too much as it is," was one typical response. Another was, "Never again. I missed him too much."

Though LIFE readers' approach to marriage is anything but frivolous, their attitude toward divorce is remarkably tolerant. Only 2 per cent hold that divorce should never be permitted. ("Marriage is eternal. What God has joined together . . .") Another 22 per cent believe divorce is acceptable only in very limited circumstances ("Adultery is the only just cause"). But 43 per cent believe divorce should be readily available if both partners want the marriage to end. An additional 33 per cent approve divorce if only one partner wants it. "What good is the marriage if one partner wants out?" asks a New York reader. "It's already kaput." The over-50 generation is only marginally more conservative on the divorce issue (35 per cent say never or only *in extremis*) than the under-30's. And readers in mid-America are only a step more conservative than those from the mid-Atlantic or West Coast.

To be unhappy and not get a divorce can be painful. "I have remained married for 20 years because I felt an obligation to honor my vow," wrote one reader who specifically asked not to be identified. "My own wasted life is my fault, but maintaining this weird limbo has also impaired my children's potential." On the other hand, to be divorced late in life "can almost destroy you," according to one reader who has been through it. "What do you do with a used Mommy?" she asks.

Despite her loneliness, the "used Mommy" has concluded that it is a lovely thing to be free." Her experience parallels that of a New Mexico reader who wanted to figure out why her first husband had deserted her. She finally decided, "The poor guy was just bored to death by my sanctimonious goodness."

Another indicator of the readers' tolerance for new forms of marriage is that 40 per cent, evenly spread along age lines, approve of "collective" families in which several couples share everything except sex. But approving collective marriage for others doesn't necessarily mean one would choose it for himself. "I couldn't stand the population," writes one (noncollective) wife. "Privacy is a dear, dear commodity."

Group marriage in which several couples share everything *including* sex received very little support: 10% overall, 13% of those under 30. "If that's what you want," one reader asks, "why get married in the first place?"

The question of unmarried couples living together sharply divided the readers. 22 per cent approve. 28 per cent do not. Perhaps most important, an even 50 per cent chose LIFE's third alternative: the decision is up to the couples themselves—"it's *their* business."

Living together out of wedlock, say some, is "plain sinful" and "a disgrace to our community." More typical was the comment of a divorcée in Boulder, Colo.: "Living together without marriage won't work. It's too much fun and games. There has to be a commitment for a relationship to be real." A mother of five in Valatie, N.Y. adds: "The only thing that unmarried couples solve is that they don't take each other for granted. But in a good marriage, one never takes the other for granted." A Florida physician says, "It's a couple's own business if they choose to live without a license. The trouble is most of them tend to flaunt it before the public as if to say, 'See this—if you don't like it, tough.' "

An unmarried partner in Michigan says poignantly: "I dig living with my friend because I worship the ground he walks on. But more than anything in the world, I want to be Mrs." A young Connecticut woman disagrees: "The reason we have never gotten married is plain: marriage simply frightens us."

In their letters, a substantial number of readers recommend living together as a premarriage "trial." From Salt Lake City: "We lived together for a year before marrying and would have had it no other way." From Glendale, Calif.: "I lived with my husband for two years prior to our marriage, to make absolutely certain we knew what we were getting into. We are married five years and are extremely happy." And from a divorced mother in Providence: "I would rather see my daughter live with a man before marriage than to go through the tragic years her father and I did."

The question of unmarried couples having and rearing children brought the sharpest division of all. Married readers and those over 30 strongly reject the idea; single persons, and most of those under 30, approved. Overall the vote was 48% No, 38% Yes, with the rest offering no opinion. "My 'husband' and I have lived together for 12 years without marriage," writes a mother of four in Chicago whose children use their father's name. "I think our union is happier than a lot of our friends'." A Long Beach, Calif. couple adds: "We've been together for five years and are expecting our second child soon. We're the happiest couple we know."

Those opposed are concerned mainly with the fate of children born out of wedlock. "Please advise caution," urges a West Jordan, Utah reader. "The child is a potential victim if one or both parents decide the responsibility is too great." An anonymous reader warns of the consequences: "I hope someday there will be no such thing as an 'illegitimate' child. However, I am one, and no human being should wish such a stigma on another. Make no mistake! The stigma of illegitimacy is still alive and well in the good old U.S.A."

The trial marriage is one trend that some readers see for the future. In-depth counseling *before* marriage is another. "Counseling should be as mandatory as the blood test," insists a Pasadena woman whose own marriage failed. Others suggest making marriage more expensive to get into. "Elevate the license fee to several hundred or even $1,000," suggests a San Francisco reader. "Divorce is costly. Marriage should be too."

Statistically, only a minority on either extreme forecasts that marriage will remain totally unchanged or that it will become totally obsolete. The large consensus in between believes the thorny old institution will survive, basically because so many people want it to.

As Mrs. Jenny South of Los Angeles says, "In our rootless society, it is great to know that two people are happy to stand beside each other, to love and give of themselves freely, whatever lies ahead."

2.

Women Should Stay Single

Caroline Bird

Since world war II, most American women have married and had their babies in their early twenties. In 1960, for instance, only 28 per cent of the women ranging from 20 to 24 were single. But in 1970, 36 per cent of the women in the marrying ages were single.

At graduation, Barbara Ballinger, Barnard '71, was introduced by her friends as the only member of her class who was getting married. The distinction may have been exaggerated; but breakdowns from the 1970 Census available about that time were a surprise even to those who knew that getting married the year of graduation was no longer important to women college students.

The increase was dramatic. Young, unattached women are highly visible. They are a lush market for everything from hair curlers to airline tickets. And since the population grew during the 1960's, the increase in absolute numbers meant that there are now more than twice as many of them running around the country.

Why didn't they marry? Most people—and particularly most men —say, "Why of course, it's the pill. Kids don't have to get married anymore." The reflex explanation is refreshing because it cuts out what my nine-year-old son calls the "gooey stuff," and goes to the heart of the matter: people marry primarily in order to have sex handy. Logically, they ought to welcome the pill for making available the good thing (sex) without the inextricable bad thing (marriage). Instead, the whole idea makes mothers and most men uneasy.

"What's to become of them?" a man-about-town between marriages asked me rhetorically. "New York is full of bright, beautiful, expensively dressed young women. All of them are desperately willing, and some of them are damn nice girls."

"What's to become of *you?*" I countered. "When are *you* going to get married again?"

He took the question as evidence of hostility. "Oh, I'll probably marry again soon enough," he replied. "I'm tired of entertaining in restaurants. But I'm in no hurry."

"Well, maybe that's the way the single girls feel," I pursued. "New York is full of bright, attractive single girls. They like men. They like sex. But do they really want to entertain your business contacts? Do they really want to get married?"

"Sure say they do!" he retorted.

It's hard for men to grasp the notion that women may not want to be wives. If a girl is attractive and single, they figure that she's hung up on sex or men, or at the best, has had abysmally bad luck. A great many middle-aged men still believe that women don't get ahead in business because only the lemons are left to compete in the business world: the brightest and the best are removed from the competition to rear babies in the suburbs. You can even find women who believe this.

The fact of the matter, of course, is the other way around. Single women over 30 are brighter, better-educated, healthier, and happier than single men over 30. Bachelors are worse off than spinsters in every way except salary. Age for age, single men are more apt to be mentally ill, three times as apt to say they are unhappy, four times as apt to say they don't like their work. They are more apt to get sick. They die younger—by their own hand as well as from other causes. And so far as happiness can be measured, they lose out this way. On the Happiness Scale devised by Norman Bradburn of the National Opinion Research Corporation in Chicago, single men score less happy than single women.

The reason is obvious as soon as you think about it a moment. As long as women try to marry men better than themselves, the *best* women (on any scale that matters) will be precisely those who will lose out on the marriage market and enter the career market. There are as many gifted women as gifted men, but the men don't mind—and some even prefer—marrying their inferiors; but women are reared to prefer a man they can look up to. The losers in this game are the top women and the bottom men; so inevitably, bachelors are the stupidest, poorest, least competent jerks from the wrong side of the railroad tracks; while the single women, who are frequently derided as "spinsters," are in real life apt to be bright, beautiful, wellborn creatures who literally can't find men good enough for themselves.

This is the Marriage Gradient. It has always been around. What is new is that there are now so many exciting alternatives to marriage—alternatives that include sexual relationships—so many alternatives that the brightest women no longer have as much incentive to play dumb. Many more women have been to college; and it doesn't matter that they went just because that's "where the boys are." The mere fact that they have gone to college has raised their aspirations, particularly their aspirations for self-expression.

Talk to the graduates of 1971 and you find them full of unfinished personal business. The best of them are surprisingly unworried about the decline in trainee jobs. "There is so much I want to do," they'll say. "I want to travel. I need to grow up. I want to find myself before I settle down."

Young people of former times postponed serious thought of marriage because they "wanted to have a good time." Now they postpone marriage because they don't think they are ready for it. Marriage sounds too hard. Because they don't have to get married to have sex, young people of the 1970's can be much cooler-headed about the kind of marriage they demand. As the urgency declines, the standards rise to clearly impossible levels.

The new Puritanism demands that the "gooey stuff" be examined not as decoration or lubrication for a relationship—difficult at best —but with the literal eye of a child. In the past, the hypocrisy of the wedding ceremony has been endured with help from corny jokes, and a ritual nervousness on the day itself.

But the brides of the 1970's won't say what they don't mean. These new brides are even rewriting the ceremony. Linda Bird Johnson faced her groom, rather than the minister. Many marry themselves, Quaker style. They read favorite poems, or make up the vows they pledge, or insist on being married in bare feet, or even naked. Parents are sometimes excluded; or the mother, as well as the father of the bride, stands at the altar. It's a way of saying, "Our marriage is not for society. It's for us."

Another expression of the new Puritanism is the refusal to marry a mate on the ground that you can't be sure how you are going to feel about anything next year. Far from being promiscuous, these openly declared arrangements are actually conscientious objections to marriage. In practice as well as in theory, the young people of the 1970's are developing a two-step marriage: (1) living together; (2) then, if children are desired, legal marriage. Many of the couples who have formalized their marriage after living together for years buy the whole traditional package, including a church wedding and sterling silver.

Young people are waiting to have children, and the demographers studying the abrupt drop in the fertility rate of women 20 to 24 no longer think that the babies will come later. It's not like the Depression of the 30's or World War II, when deeply desired babies were postponed for practical reasons. Many young women now frankly say they don't like taking care of children; or more often, that they simply aren't up to rearing them, even if adding to the population were desirable. Increasingly, too, they have other things they want to do.

Are young women staying single because they have been "corrupted" by Women's Liberation? Maybe. But I'm inclined to think that the casual relationship is the other way around. It wasn't until a critical mass of young women remained single in their twenties that it was politic to admit out loud that marriage isn't essential to happiness. Feminism was never deader than it was during the 1950's, when the marriage rate hit a new high, and the age of first marriage, a new low. The ideal of universal, compulsory marriage boomed marriage counseling—and psychiatric therapy.

A half century ago, when a fifth of our women never married, marriage itself was psychically undemanding for those who entered it. But in midcentury, marriage became the thing that all but eight per cent of women tried at some time in their lives to do. Everyone was led to expect a marriage that was a great personal achievement, like the celebrated love affairs of history. Everyone was required to improve his sexual performance to virtuosic standards on pain of neurosis. Married couples expected their marriage to grow; and a marriage that served as a means to any other end was snubbed as mean-spirited, if not actually immoral.

Rising divorce rates and disillusion with domesticity were the inevitable result; and thoughtful sociologists were beginning to lay the blame not on the frailties of human beings, but on impossible standards for marriage.

"I sometimes wonder where we would be now if the Standard American Marriage had been enforced in the past," Dr. Leslie Koempel, Professor of Sociology at Vassar College, wrote in a popular article "Why Get Married?" Medieval monks, explorers, immigrants, schoolteachers, and women like Florence Nightingale and Clara Barton were necessarily unmarried, she pointed out, as were many of the greatest of our great men. She wrote:

> The faculty of Princeton once named the 10 biggest contributors to the advancement of human knowledge. Of the 10, Plato, Newton, and Leonardo da Vinci never married; Socrates couldn't make a go of it; Aristotle and Darwin married long after embarking on their work; and domesticity does not seem to have made many demands on Galileo, Shakespeare, Pasteur, or Einstein. Similarly, Michelangelo and Keats never married. Milton, Lincoln, Edgar Allan Poe, and Shelley were 'failures' at marriage. How many self-respecting modern American girls would excuse Nobel scientist Irving Langmuir who fell into shoptalk on his way to pick up his wife and walked by her, tipping his hat to her vaguely familiar face?

The Saturday Evening Post printed Dr. Koempel's views in its St. Valentine's Day issue of 1965 as a "Speaking Out" column devoted to opinions not necessarily shared by the editors, and blurbed the title "Why Get Married?" on the cover, just above a luscious pink heart framing a woman contemplating roses, who was obviously happy to be a sex object. Her answer was obviously that of the management: "For love, of course!"

The media were not, however, hitting young women where they lived, as the rising average age of the readership of major women's magazines attested.

All through the 1960's, each college generation of women differed so radically in its outlook from those in college just before them, that seniors complained that they were as out of touch with the freshmen as with their own parents.

The economic base of traditional marriage was eroding much faster than its ideological base. Men no longer had to marry to get sex. Women no longer had to marry to get financial or even social support. Meanwhile, more young people went to college, remaining single or contracting companionate-style marriages in which the wife was more likely than the husband to bring home the money. As the decade wore on, it was easier and easier for women to get a job of some kind: two-thirds of the *new* jobs created during the decade—13.8 million in all—were jobs employers regarded as women's jobs. This meant that while more and more women worked— and virtually all young women *had* to work—fewer of them could hope to rise up the promotional ladder. Although nine out of ten women worked at some point in their lives, only one percent ever made the five-figure salaries required to support a family in middle-class, suburban style.

Young women couldn't help feeling gypped. Far from getting it both ways, as critics of aspiring women have alleged, young women of the early 1960's couldn't get it either way: they couldn't get the good jobs themselves, and they had to work to help support the style of living to which college and television told them they were entitled. In 1970, 41 per cent of the wives of professional men— ideal husband timber—were out earning money.

Women's Liberation fell like a spark on this dry tinder. It is probably accidental, but the first women's caucuses withdrew from the Civil Rights Movement in 1968, the year of "the great marriage squeeze," a term coined by Dr. Paul C. Glick of the U.S. Bureau of the Census to describe a statistical wrinkle in the marriage market which demographers warned would make 1968 a bad year for brides.

The marriage squeeze arises because the most popular age for women to marry is 20, and the most popular age for men, 22. These ages are now a bit higher. The age gap between the average bride and groom has tended to become less; but the changes are in terms of decimal points per year. The point is that women like to marry men older than themselves. Ordinarily, it doesn't matter, since usually there are as many men of 22 as there are women of 20. But for the women who were 20 years old in 1967, this was not the case.

In 1947, we had a big baby crop. Returning soldiers settled down and the next year there were a million more babies born than the year before. That meant that little girls born in 1947 had to find husbands from the relatively thin baby crop of 1945.

Thus in 1967, the squeeze was on. It was a year when women of dating age began to complain that "there just aren't any men around," and only the demographers realized that they were speaking the literal truth. Some, of course, married men their own age, speeding the collapse of the age gap between brides and grooms. But since about half the college age young people were in college of some kind, a great many of the girls waited to marry. Many stayed on in college or devoted themselves wholeheartedly to their jobs. The squeeze gave many of them a year or two of adult mobility to find themselves. One way or another, a critical mass of educated young women got a chance to taste the satisfactions of being single and on their own and they were encouraged, if only by sour grapes, to view the joys of married life more suspiciously than would have been comfortable for them to do as brides.

Women's Liberation did not invent the facts, but it spread them with the explosive force of repressed material surfacing to attention. The fact, long known by sociologists, is that Standard American Marriage is not a good status for women. The case against marriage is getting its day in court. Some of the evidence:

1. *Health* The health of the married is generally better than that of the single, but the difference is nowhere near as great for women as for men. Careful breakdowns by age, sex, and marital status suggest that there are many ways in which single women are better off than married women.

This is the surprising finding of a U.S. Public Health Service inquiry into symptoms of psychological distress which was published in August, 1970. The researchers asked a cross section of the population whether they were troubled with nervousness, inertia, insomnia, trembling hands, nightmares, perspiring hands, fainting, headaches, dizziness, and heart palpitations.

Contrary to expectations, old maids simply aren't the nervous nellies they're made out to be. Never-married people reported fewer symptoms than the married; never-married white women were strikingly free of nervous symptoms, in spite of the fact that women as a sex were twice as apt to complain as men. It certainly looks as if the institution of matrimony was harder on the nerves of women than men; and the suspicion is confirmed by the further finding that housewives report more psychological symptoms than wives who have jobs. The investigators discerned a new disease, "housewife syndrome."

2. *Happiness* Studies of mental health made in midtown Manhattan and in New Haven, as well as elsewhere, report the same relationship between mental health and marriage. Married people are better off than single people. They have fewer neurotic symptoms, are less likely to be admitted to mental hospitals, are more likely to score high on the Bradburn Happiness Scale. But marriage

makes a much bigger difference for men than for women; and in some ways, old maids are stabler, less anxious, and happier than married women. Married men are happiest, followed at some remove by married women, single women, and single men straggling far behind. Studies of happiness in marriage find that men are more satisfied with their marriages than women.

3. *Money* There's a persistent myth that "women own the country" and that "women have it better because men work to support them." But the myth is usually repeated with a wink or a giggle that indicates the speaker knows he is mythologizing. The fact of the matter, of course, is that married or single, women never get their hands on as much money at any point in their lives as men do. By last count of the New York Stock Exchange, 49 per cent of the shareholders of stock in listed corporations are females, but they own less than 20 per cent of the shares, and are less likely than male shareowners to make decisions on buying or selling their holdings, let alone affecting the policies of their corporations.

While no one pities rich women, wives of men with capital may have less control over family finances than working-class women who frequently bring in a lion's share of the family income. Clare Booth Luce is one of the richest widows in America. As the wife of Henry Luce, the publisher of *Time, Life,* and *Fortune,* she has always lived lavishly and been able to buy anything she wishes for herself or her many homes. But she says that the only money that she has really been able to invest in enterprises and causes of her own choosing has been the money she herself earned.

Marriage subjects wives to disabilities as credit risks and candidates for job promotion. A woman lawyer I know who has worked herself up to a senior position with a Federal agency recently married a man who earns less. As a single woman, she had been paying much less rent than she could swing; but as a married woman, landlords refuse to count her income because she is not the "head of the house." When she was a single woman, department stores were delighted to give her credit; but when she went to open an account after her marriage, she found that the store insisted on going by the credit available to her as the wife of a man who was temporarily unemployed. Her long and favorable credit rating as a single woman didn't count.

The most serious disability, of course, is the custom as well as the law which decrees that the domicile of a married couple shall be the place in which the husband resides. This means that wives cannot move to new job opportunities as easily as husbands. A wife who seeks a promotion must give information about her family plans that clearly amount to an invasion of privacy.

4. *Social Life* Marriage was regarded as insurance against loneliness; and in the regimented life of the 1950's, this was frequently true. Except in the bohemian quarters of the big cities, parties were given by and for couples, and even bachelors found themselves handicapped by their lack of a party-giving wife. But that advantage

is beginning to fade. Even in the 1950's, the ritual round of suburban parties was boring to many of those who participated in them, and was frequently blamed for a rise in alcoholism.

Parties in which men talked shop in one corner of the room while women talked shop in the other corner were the inevitable result of social life based on couples rather than individuals. Young people are sensitive to the sterility of living roles. "I hate to go to a party as half of a pair," one young woman writer complained. "People in Ann Arbor think it's odd, but my husband and I have taken to splitting up social engagements. We go together only when we both want to go."

If I've made the case against marriage from the point of view of wives, it is only because most people believe with Dorothy Parker that "Men in single state should tarry, while women, I suggest, should marry." But in really egalitarian marriages, husbands can make the same case against marriage as wives. More husbands than is generally realized, for instance, resist transfers that would disemploy their wives.

The fact of the matter, of course, is that the old deal of sex-for-support has long been a dead letter. Marriage is no longer the only way to fulfill any basic human need. It is still the most satisfactory as well as the easiest way to do a great many things, such as rearing children; but it is no longer the *only* way to make a success even of that. The Israeli kibbutz and communal child-rearing experiments in the United States turn out acceptable human products.

Wives can no longer do as good a job of catering, cooking, baking, butchering, nursing, teaching, sewing, child-training or decorating as the specialists their husband's money can buy. Nor can a wife expect to be as good a dancer, hostess, sounding board, business adviser, sexual partner, or showpiece as some women he can find to specialize in one of these feminine roles. So women who are modestly affluent through their own nonbedroom efforts are finding that one man is not necessarily the best partner for chess, sex, camping, partygiving, investing, talking, plumbing, vacationing, gallery-going, and all the other activities which the city offers. *No husband or wife can supply the full satisfaction a single person may derive from a love affair, a sex affair, a job, friends, a psychiatrist, or even, at the end, a top-flight trained nurse.*

Traditionalists who subscribe to the sex-for-support theory assume that marriage will break down if women can support themselves. One sociologist thinks the sex-support deal can be salvaged as long as working in the bedroom is easier for women than jobholding. But what happens when sex is divorced from pregnancy, and when women want it as much as men? What happens when sexual intercourse occupies the same role in the life of a woman as it does in the life of a man?

There remains, of course, love. Love may be grand, but it was never the original purpose for which marriage was intended; and it now has to compensate for a growing list of inequities and inconveniences. At the risk of spoiling St. Valentine's Day, it is relevant to ask exactly what love does for people and whether Standard American Marriage is any more essential to love than it is to sex.

The answer is long, but to put the question is to suggest that love and marriage may not be as inseparable as the horse and carriage of the popular tune. If love is a commitment between persons which provides emotional support, then it is obvious that traditional marriage is not the only institutional framework which can nurture it. If love, mutual support, face-to-face daily relationships are essential or desirable—and I am sure that they are—wouldn't we do better to start from scratch and design an institution specifically to evoke and produce these desirables?

Work groups, play groups, the "gang," the "outfit" in the armed forces, friends, colonies, collectives, communes—all are doing this work now. Some of these relationships have advantages over traditional marriage. Not the least of these is the frankly experimental and informal character of the group which encourages exploration of the psyche and dispenses with sanctions which shrivel mutuality.

This is not to say that marriage won't survive. The most probable future is going to be the most difficult social situation of all. Many life styles will co-exist. Young people will choose what they prefer, and as they grow, choose again and again. Traditional marriage will satisfy many men and women, but it will never again command the prestige of the "one right way" to live. When traditional marriage is a matter of choice, it will never again confer the security it carried when traditional marriage was the only respectable choice.

3.

Creative Singlehood as a Sexual Life-Style: Beyond Marriage as a Rite of Passage

Roger W. Libby

Single people have received little attention in research, theories, and scholarly analysis of social scientists. Family sociologists have either ignored singles or relegated them to boring, out-of-date discussions of dating, courtship, and mate selection as steps toward marriage and parenthood. The neglect is blatant in that the number of adults between twenty-five and thirty-four who have never been married increased by 50 percent between 1960 and 1975 (U.S. Bureau of the Census, 1960, 1975). About half of those aged eighteen to thirty-nine are unmarried, and typically about a third of a woman's adult life is spent as a single person (U.S. Bureau of the Census, 1970). There are more women than men who are single at any given time, but as will be seen in this paper single men appear to be less happy as a group than single women. Since most writing on singles has been journalistic or descriptive social science unrelated to any well-developed theory, little is understood about singlehood as a sexual life-style.

The stereotype of the Joe Namath kind of swinging single and the opposing stereotype of the frustrated and miserable single person (as in George Gilder's *Sexual Suicide* and *Naked Nomads*) obscure the realities of singlehood. These polarized images which surface in the mass media and in everyday interaction blind social scientists and others to the range of life-styles being lived or contemplated by singles. Furthermore, the bulk of descriptive research on premarital sex and on cohabitation among college students has not informed social theory concerning singlehood. This is because the college years are too early to identify singlehood as an active choice rather than a premarital stage in the monogamous model. The same may be true of the post-college singles subculture which has received attention in the mass media.

Computer dating, singles' bars, career orientations in urban areas, and even a singles' church (*Newsweek,* June 12, 1972) offer opportunities for single people to socialize and work together; but in many if not most singles social functions, the end goal is still to find a partner to live with or to marry. We are socialized in a couple-oriented society where at least 90 percent are expected to (and in fact do) marry.

However, at any one time about a third or more Americans are unmarried, separated, or in some way "unattached." Census figures do not allow for a precise delineation of living arrangements such as cohabitation, but the high divorce rate, the rise in the average age of first marriage, and the apparent longer period between divorce and remarriage (when remarriage occurs) provide a demographic basis for speculation about the dissolution of couples and emergence of singlehood as a life-style. It is also important to take into account divorced, separated, and widowed people when discussing singlehood as a sexual life-style. It may be significant, for example, that widowhood is increasing more for women than for men. This is because men are older when they marry than are women, and women tend to live longer; this creates stiffer competition among women for marital partners (Glick, 1976, personal discussion).

Singlehood is beginning to emerge as a positive option to marriage and other couple images. Social and ideological support for singlehood as a choice, rather than as a residual category for the unchosen and lonely, has come from the women's liberation movement, from the alternative life-styles and human potential movements, and from such groups as Zero Population Growth (ZPG), Planned Parenthood, and the National Organization for Non-Parents (NON). In addition, discrimination against singles in the tax structure has lessened (1972 Tax Reform Act, Dullea, 1975).

Ira Reiss (1973) has noted a trend toward increased legitimacy of choice of sexual life-styles and toward greater permissiveness in attitudes and behavior in heterosexual relationships prior to and after marriage. Murray Straus (letter to author, November 1975) has proposed the hypothesis that the more sexually restrictive a society, the more singleness will be defined in negative ways (because marriage is necessary to make sex legitimate). And yet, family sociology has not investigated singlehood as an important life-style or satisfactorily analyzed various social sanctions for and against singlehood.

This article will attempt to bring us one step nearer to a clear conceptualization of the costs and rewards of choosing singlehood as a sexual life-style. The focus will be on the roles and position of single people over their sexual lives or "careers." I will discuss definitional issues first; then review the available literature; present some theoretical models; and finally suggest questions for future research.

DEFINITIONS: WHO IS SINGLE

In both the professional and popular literature, single people have been inconsistently defined. While some researchers would simply limit singles to never marrieds, others include divorced, separated, and widowed people who are not cohabiting with a sexual partner. Others incorporate legal, social, and personal dimensions into the definition, such as age, intention to remain single or to marry, acceptance or nonacceptance of multiple sexual and emotional relationships, living arrangement, means of financial support, involvement in primary (even if not exclusive) sexual relationships, and the budgeting of time between one or more people and other obligations. Some distinguish between the labels *unmarried, single,* and *unattached.* Others simply state that singlehood, like marriage, is a state of mind rather than a legal status or a label conferred by others. Some define singlehood in terms of marriage (thus the stages "premarital" and "postmarital"), while others view singlehood as a choice rather than a stage. Although the definition of "single" may seem obvious to some, the definitional issues are complex.

Rather than defining singlehood in any narrow way, I will consider the whole range of sexual life-styles that potentially fall within the single category. In this context, singlehood might be a choice for some, or a stage leading to marriage or remarriage for others. It might also be a stage leading to cohabitation, which could in turn lead to marriage. On the other hand, marriage may be seen as an interim stage, with divorce and singlehood emerging as choices at later stages. My emphasis is on the *process* and on the concept of a sexual career involving different choices made at different stages in the life cycle. *Yesterday's choice could be today's stage in transition to tomorrow's new choice.*

To go further with this conceptualization of sexual career choices, there are costs and rewards involved with any choice. Those who *choose* to be single do so after evaluating the relative costs and rewards of other life-styles which are realistic options. The existence of a theoretical choice is not the same as having the option to make that choice, or to openly act on one's preferences. For example, one may want to have multiple sexual partners, and one may visualize this as a choice, but unless there are partners available and willing, along with a network of people and social institutions to support such a life-style, the option does not actually exist.

√ Before continuing to define singlehood, perhaps it would help to say what a single person *is not. For the purposes of this paper, "creative singlehood" is not legal marriage or cohabitation. A creatively single person is not emotionally, sexually, or financially dependent on one person; psychological and social autonomy are necessary to be defined as single* (Margaret Adams, 1971). If one person allows another to monopolize the majority of his or her time to the near exclusion of others as sexual partners, that person would not be considered single. A single person is committed to various leisure and occupational relationships, but does not make an exclusive commitment which precludes other emotional and sexual experiences.

Singlehood is a state of availability. This definition rules out those who are totally or mostly dependent on a relationship which demands conformity to the monogamous model, but it could include separated and divorced people, regardless of whether they are parents. This definition, then, goes beyond legal categories to focus on self-definitions and on the social identities acquired through labeling.

Although a person may be single either by choice or from the lack of opportunity to find a suitable partner, I will stress those creative singles who choose to remain single, and who choose not to cohabit or limit sexual behavior to one person. A single person may be eighteen or seventy-five, but this paper will emphasize the upper-middle-class college graduates in urban areas who are involved in professional careers and have a rather open opportunity structure for relating sexually with multiple partners. Although single people may change their life-styles at any point after reevaluating their particular situations, I will emphasize those who have chosen creative singlehood instead of cohabitation, sexual celibacy, marriage, or communal living. Being single need not mean being alone, but some time alone is assumed here. Furthermore, having primary and/or coprimary (equally primary) intimate relationships, as well as secondary and transitory relationships, would not necessarily conflict with singlehood.

There are *degrees* of singlehood, as I will illustrate later. One may be more single one month than another but still not move outside the single status. Or, one may be single, choose to cohabit or marry, and perhaps choose to later divorce and become single again. In this sense singlehood and other choices are *reclaimable* statuses or identities. One has the option of repudiating a current identity or reclaiming an earlier status.[1]

The strong emphasis on marriage as the final outcome of the dating-courtship script has essentially made singlehood a "deviant" choice. In spite of increased acceptance of premarital and non-marital intercourse, for many *marriage is a rite of passage to legitimize sexual expression.* The emerging legitimization of singlehood as a sexual life-style flies in the face of the traditional view of premarital relationships leading to marriage. In Part Three of this book, Roy and Roy identify reasons for the emphasis on marriage and offer a suggestion for social policy. They state:

> It is principally because of the fear of sexual involvement that the singles are excluded from married society. In the new dispensation, a much more active and aggressive policy should be encouraged to incorporate single persons wtihin the total life of a family and a community.

The fear of intimate or sexual relationships with married people is an underlying factor which contributes to the isolation of many singles from community life. A single person's availability to others is a critical factor affecting his or her identity.

Singlehood can change along various dimensions as one moves through the life cycle. A single person's role responsibilities and rights depend on familial, economic, and other considerations; commitment may shift from singlehood to some form of coupling and back again in response to other factors in one's life (Gilbert Nass, letter to author, October 1975). Roles shift in that they are defined by the self and by various reference groups and significant others. As social acceptance of singles increases and a social support system evolves, the roles attached to the single position will multiply. Institutionalized support for the sexual conduct of available single people may be minimal currently, but it is growing, particularly in large cities where the proportion of singles is high.

This brings me to some basic concepts which underlie creative singlehood and other multiple relationship life-styles. The social scripting of sexual and sex role behavior (or alternative sexual life-styles) is based on the following assumptions.

1. There is an eternal, erotic, emotional attraction between people, and a permanent availability of people to each other for emotional and sexual expression regardless of marital or living arrangements or sex. Bernard Farber (1964) predicted a trend away from the orderly replacement of marriage partners (lifetime monogamy) toward a more free-floating permanent availability. He stated: "Permanent availability implies that the basic needs of the individual may change . . . and that meeting personality needs at an early age may not suffice to maintain the marriage" (1964, p. 168).
2. There is an emerging autonomy of sexual expression apart from marriage, the family, and reproduction, so that the individual, not the couple or a larger entity, is the lowest common denominator when considering the meaning of sexual conduct (Jetse Sprey, 1969).
3. There is increasing visibility and viability of sexual life-styles (called the legitimacy of sexual choice by Ira Reiss, 1973); the full range of choices is receiving increased social support so that realistic options are increased.
4. We live in a secretive society where people can do as they wish

without negative social sanctions if they are relatively discreet (open opportunity structure).

5. Change in one aspect of a culture or in one stage of a sexual career (such as increased sexual intercourse before marriage) affects change in other institutional arrangements or stages (such as the ground rules for sexual behavior for married partners). New definitions of coupling (such as sexual friendships outside a primary relationship as in sexually open marriage) force a new look at singlehood.

6. Sexual behavior cannot be isolated or compartmentalized from the rest of a relationship. Nonsexual motives for sexual behavior and sexual motives for nonsexual behavior make compartmentalization of sex from various emotions, desires, expectations, and fantasies impossible.

The above assumptions give support to creative singlehood, and they encourage multiple sexual and emotional relationships for all categories of single and coupled people. The assumptions also feed into the social scripts for two contrasting sexual life-styles described in Table 1 (Libby, 1976).

A SELECTIVE REVIEW OF THE LITERATURE ON SINGLES

The purpose of this review is to present the essence of what is now known or suspected about singles. Demographic data on age trends for first marriage, divorce rates, and similar descriptive information will be briefly covered. Then the few relevant empirical studies of singlehood as a chosen life-style will be described, and some journalistic literature will be discussed.

DEMOGRAPHIC DATA

Paul Glick (1975) and Jessie Bernard (1975) have presented some of the most current statistics on the delay in marriage and the increase in divorce, single parenthood, and various living arrangements for never married and other unattached people. It is difficult to predict whether marriage rates will continue to decline. We do know, though, that the average age of first marriage for women increased from twenty to twenty-one between 1960 and 1974, and the age increase for men during that period was from about twenty-two plus to twenty-three. Single men and women are delaying marriage and choosing to remain single longer. The proportion of women aged twenty to twenty-four remaining single has increased from 28 percent in 1960 to 40 percent in 1974 (U.S. Bureau of the Census, 1974). The figures for men are obscured by the movement of men in the armed forces.

Glick notes several reasons for the increase in age at marriage for women. About three times more women were enrolled in college in 1972 compared to in 1960, and the increase in employment for that period was greater for women than for men. Also, women at their

TABLE 1   *Two Social Scripts for Sexual Relationships*

	"Primrose Path" of Dating	Branching Paths of "Getting Together"
Fifth to Sixth Grade	Structured heterosexual activities; spin the bottle type of activity; having one boyfriend or girlfriend.	Unstructured activities, with no emphasis on marriage or relating to one member of the opposite sex. Interest-orientation rather than obsession with one opposite sex person.
Seventh to Ninth Grade	Group dating and dating with parents as chaperone figures. Parents drive car, etc. Sneaking around with opposite sex. Emphasis on meeting personal needs and acceptance from peers by conforming to their expectations.	No parental imposition of monogamous expectations. Nonpossessive, equalitarian relationships with no emphasis on dichotomy of sexual and nonsexual relationships.
High School	Double dating and single dating in cars with exclusive expectation once one dates a person a few times (going with one person, or "going steady").	"Getting together" *rather than* dating, with female initiating relationships as much as male and paying and driving car as much as male does.
After High School	Work and continue monogamous dating, or date more than one person, or go to college and do same, or marry monogamously. Static, rigid role expectations for female and male. Stress physical levels of intimacy as a basis for sexual morality. Sex viewed as economic ownership, meeting one's personal security needs, and as exclusive. If live together, it is sexually exclusive. Divorce, tolerate unhappy "marriage," or for a minority, live happily ever after in a sexually and emotionally exclusive monogamous marriage.	Stress qualities and common interests in relationships as a basis for decision making about sex and other relationship concerns. Touching and sensuality encouraged. Sex only in mutually appropriate and mutually discussed situations. Sex as one language in some relationships with a range of symbolic meanings—from mutual pleasure (or horniness), to love (love not seen as exclusive but as multiple following Robert Rimmer in *The Harrad Experiment*, and other novels.)

Remarriage and divorce, or a repeat of the above (serial monogamy with "cheating" on the side by both spouses).

Emphasis on the weakness of the participants in marriage when unhappiness or divorce occurs, rather than questioning the monolithic image of marriage as "the answer" for anyone who chooses to marry.

Disillusionment with marriage for many. Searching for the "good life," but confused as to how to find it. Conflict between images in the mass media and what the local minister is preaching. Enter the therapist . . . who may or may not help. . . . What next?

If live together, relationship is sexually and emotionally nonexclusive.

Creative singlehood, or if marriage, some similar kind of open-ended arrangement such as the alternatives described in this book.

A *decision* to be open or closed in various areas of marriage, with the ongoing process of renegotiation of the marital contract. Marriage as a process rather than a static set of promises.

Various open marriages with comarital or satellite relationships viewed as supportive of the pair bond rather than as a threat to it.

Swinging—from recreational to utopian.

Group marriage.

Communal living with or without sexual sharing.

Compartmentalized marriage—with "night off" from marriage.

If divorce, joy rather than sadness (creative divorce).

Synergy: $1 + 1 =$ more than 2. (See O'Neill & O'Neill, 1972.)

NOTE: It is not uncommon for those socialized in the traditional script to later decide to take on different roles and to adopt one of the emerging alternatives to the monogamous image or the cheating reality . . . so some switching back and forth between scripts prior to and after marriage(s) is common. The above scripts are two *ideal types* on a continuum rather than actual dichotomies. However, many people still fit the traditional extreme of the "primrose path."

peak marrying age (twenty-one) have outnumbered men at their peak marrying age (twenty-three) in any given year. Because the peak is about two years earlier for women than for men born the same year, there is a younger but larger group of women competing for partners from the smaller and older group of men. This situation, which Glick calls the "marriage squeeze," will probably exist until the average age of marriage for men and women equalizes.

As Margaret Adams (1971) explained, the economic autonomy that college degrees and employment provide is critical to the emergence of singlehood as a life-style for women.[2] Both Glick (1975) and Adams (1971) consider the women's liberation movement to be a contributing social force supporting singlehood for women. Glick concludes that the postponement of marriage and childbearing by women appears to be part of a trend toward choosing alternatives to marriage, and he feels women may both try and like alternatives, including singlehood (Glick, 1975, p. 4).

The census data make it difficult to reflect on singlehood as a sexual life-style because living arrangements are not precisely delineated. "Living alone" and "living with nonrelatives" does not distinguish singlehood beyond a legal status; one might be cohabiting, monogamous, or creatively single. Since a sexual career may include frequent changes in living arrangements, more frequent data collection and/or accurate biographical information on individuals is necessary to chart role transitions. Although Jessie Bernard (1975) used census data to describe changing life-styles from 1970 to 1974, she admittedly could only speculate about their meaning and trends in sexual and living arrangements. Nevertheless, Bernard's and Glick's data tentatively indicate that marriage is becoming less popular.

The decreasing popularity of marriage appears dramatic when one observes the linear increase in divorce rates. There were over one million divorces in 1975 in the U.S.—6 percent more than in 1974. In contrast, the marriage rate dropped 4 percent that year, to roughly 2.1 million (U.S. Bureau of the Census, 1976). Glick and Norton (1977) estimate that one in three marriages for women thirty years old has ended or would end in divorce. After comparing marriage and divorce rates over a seven-year span, Ivan Nye (personal discussion with author, February 1976) predicted that national statistics on divorce will soon reach the levels of such states as California and Washington, where about 50 percent of first marriages, and even more remarriages, end in divorce. Since divorce is more prevalent among the remarried (Nye & Berardo, 1973, p. 529), it would appear that people will be spending more of their adult lives in some single status.

Furthermore, we cannot assume that those who do not divorce are happily married. The marriage and family literature (including longitudinal studies) reveals that only about 10 to 20 percent of marriages are self-reported as happy throughout most of the marriage, and wives report less satisfaction than husbands. Also, more men than women remarry; five-sixths of divorced men and three-fourths of women aged thirty-five to forty-four remarry (Glick, 1975). Apparently the double standard of aging, whereby women tend to be considered less attractive sooner than men (Susan Sontag, 1972), and the larger proportion of women to men with increasing age account for such a sex differential in remarriage rates. Since women tend to be less satisfied with marriage, it may also be that they are less anxious to remarry. The relaxation in divorce laws (although many so-called "no-fault" laws are not as the label implies, Weitzman, 1974) and the decreasing social stigma of divorce make singlehood a more viable alternative for both sexes. In spite of the increased economic independence of women through increased employment, women still appear to have more liabilities such as children and fewer assets to bargain for remarriage. Finally, it appears that the period between divorce and remarriage is increasing for young people of both sexes.[3] Even though most divorced people still remarry, an increase in the time interval after divorce, which has been about three years, may indicate a trend toward postmarital singlehood without remarriage for a growing population.

EMPIRICAL STUDIES

In addition to demographic statistics, studies of attitudes about marriage contribute to predictions about future life-style choices. Although the social psychology literature indicates that attitudes alone are not very accurate predictors of behavior, when considered with behavioral intention and selected situational, reference group, and social support variables, attitudes do contribute to the prediction of behavior (Fishbein & Ajzen, 1975; Acock & DeFleur, 1972). Peter Stein (1973) collected data on a population of college students (N of nearly 500, with a response rate of 75 percent of the college's class of 1973). He found that 3 percent of freshman women did not expect to marry as compared to 8 percent of senior women. Most impressive was his finding that 40 percent of senior college women did not know whether or not they should marry, and 39 percent of seniors felt that traditional marriage is becoming obsolete (Stein, 1973). Yankelovitch (1972) has noted a similar increase in disillusionment with marriage among college student samples over the years.

Whitehurst (1977) and White and Wells (1973) have also studied university students' attitudes toward various life-styles. These investigators concluded that some changes were in the making but that dramatic, widespread changes in life-style choices should not be expected. Twelve percent of Whitehurst's three hundred non-randomly selected students felt that monogamy is dying; of these 88 percent were single. Whitehurst found that 58 percent agreed it is possible to love (including sexually) more than one person at a time, but more marrieds than singles felt this way.[4] The implications of such beliefs for extramarital and comarital sex, as well as for eventual divorce and choice of singlehood or remarriage, are obvious. Furthermore, less than half intended to have conventional marriages like those of their parents, and nearly a fifth would be willing to try group living arrangements. Generally, then, Whitehurst's student subjects perceived some need for change in conventional monogamous marriage.

In the past few years, some research directly concerned with singlehood and sexuality has been undertaken. Stein (1975) conducted in-depth interviews with ten women and ten men (median ages of thirty-five and twenty-nine, respectively). All but two subjects had been married or involved in some type of exclusive sexual relationship prior to choosing a nonexclusive single life. Stein purposefully limited his sample to those who were nonexclusive, who did not plan to marry in the near future, and who did not hope to live with one person in an exclusive relationship in the near future. Thus, singles in this sample were defined as those who were sexually available to multiple partners after having experienced exclusivity. This is an obvious bias; one would expect such a sample to strongly endorse singleness, due in part to their previous unhappiness in exclusive relationships. Not surprisingly, Stein's sample felt that exclusive and/or marital relationships restricted human growth. One wonders what would be reported by other types of singles including those who had never experienced an exclusive relationship, or those who had been involved in an open marriage, communal living, group marriage, or some other alternative to traditional monogamous marriage or exclusive cohabitation.

Stein identifies some of the pushes and pulls toward and away from singlehood and monogamous marriage. Stein rightly points up the need for an ideology to make singlehood more viable as an option to marriage, and he identifies the lack of control which single people have over their existence (due to economic exploitation by such businesses as singles' bars, for instance). Stein's list of pulls toward singlehood (which might more precisely be called rewards from an exchange theory view) includes career opportunities, variety of experiences, self-sufficiency, sexual availability, exciting life-style, freedom to change and experiment, mobility, sustaining friendships, and supportive relationships such as men's and women's groups, group living, and specialized groups. Pushes toward singlehood (or costs associated with other life-styles) include suffocating one-to-one relationships, obstacles to self-development, boredom, unhappiness and anger, role playing, and conforming to expectations of others. Some other pushes toward singlehood could be poor communication with a mate, sexual frustration, lack of friends, isolation and loneliness, limitations on mobility and possible experiences, and influence of or participation in the women's movement (Stein, 1975, pp. 493–4). Stein also lists pulls and pushes toward marriage, most of which involve economic, emotional, and sexual security, and the influence of parents.

While Stein's study does offer some insights into one segment of the singles population, it also has several limitations. First, Stein did not present his findings in the context of any well-developed theoretical framework. In addition, he refers to singlehood as an emerging social movement (a response to sources of discontent, a set of goals, and a program to implement the goals, as defined by Killian, 1973). This claim is not justified; it would be more accurate to conceive of singlehood as one of several intimate life-styles receiving increased social and legal support from the human potential, women's liberation, and population control social movements. A more comprehensive treatment of Stein's study is available in his book, *Single In America* (1976). Stein's ideas for future research, presented in his article and book, are likely to spur more systematic and theoretically based empirical investigations into singlehood.

Fishel and Allon (1973) carried out an extensive ethnographic study of singles' bars. They utilized participant observation and open-ended interviews with one hundred people in eight singles' bars in New York City. Their conceptualization of single people was consistent with those of Stein and of such singles' publications as *Single Magazine*. Being single meant not being married or living together and not being engaged, pinned, or going steady. Taking the self-definitions of the participants in the bars, a "constant, steady relationship" implied attachment and not singlehood. There were some who were married or suspected of being married who frequented the singles bars. For these people, the researchers concluded that singlehood was situational—that one could appear single and behave according to that social image. Actual interaction patterns were stressed and a situational definition of singlehood used. However, coupling was found to be a primary goal of participants in the singles' bars—success was often measured by achieving coupling and leaving singlehood behind. In this sense, singlehood as choice or stage is a critical research question.

Fishel and Allon's research is based in social theory, largely drawing on Georg Simmel's sociability theory of interaction patterns and Irving Goffman's analysis of interaction. The researchers concluded that singles' bars were full of those seeking companionship as an answer to their self-estrangement and isolation from others. The picture was one of disillusionment with self and others, dissatisfaction with the prescribed role playing in the singles bar, and a sense of boredom which the participants hoped to replace with excitement, ego support for being attractive, and some semblance of intimacy with others.

Fishel and Allon's findings are consistent with another study of singles in Chicago by Starr and Carns (1973). A nonrandom availability sample of seventy single people was interviewed in 1970 and 1971; all in the sample were college graduates in their early to mid-twenties who had done graduate work and then moved to the big city to work. None had been married and most had no previous conception of the singles scene. The relative ease in meeting people during college had not been experienced in the urban single life.

The frequency with which the subjects went to singles' bars dropped off the longer they lived in the social context of urban singlehood; this was particularly true of women. Single men were often in search of instant sex, and many had sex with women of lower social status. Men were more sexually oriented, while women tended to be interested in friendship and permanent relationships. Starr and Carns found that singles' bars, neighborhood apartment living complexes, and parties did not offer much in the way of companionship or satisfactory ways to meet people. The majority of cross-sex friendships resulted from having been introduced to someone when at work (usually to someone who did not work in the same office). The researchers viewed the work world as the most significant context in which singles could develop a strong sense of self. The carefree swinging singles image was not supported. The contrast between the relatively happy singles in Stein's select sample in New York City and those in the samples collected by Starr and Carns and by Allon and Fishel is suggestive of the broad range of life-styles and degrees of singlehood.

The process of adjusting to a new single life includes relating to old and new friends and meeting companions for intimacy and sex. Yet the traditional sociological research on friendship patterns fails to include sexual expression as a dimension of some friendships. For example, Booth and Hess (1974) failed to deal directly with the issue of sex in friendship in their data collection on eight hundred middle-aged and elderly urban residents. Booth and Hess apparently assumed that friendship by definition excludes sex. Ramey and other investigators have shown this to be false. Friendship studies should consider the full range of friendship types rather than narrowing their observations to conform with their narrow world views (implications for the sociology of knowledge are rampant).

Research on personality characteristics and adjustment to marital or nonmarital life gives some clues to the viability of singlehood for women as compared to men. Spreitzer and Riley (1974) carried out a secondary analysis of a sample of 2454 applicants for social security benefits. The median age of the sample was fifty-five, and less than 3 percent were under thirty-five (1974, p. 534). They found that higher intelligence, education, and occupation were associated with singlehood for females, while single males tended to have poor interpersonal relations with parents and siblings (1974, p. 541).

Several other studies compare singlehood and marriage in terms of relative adjustment and happiness for men and women. Genevieve Knupfer, Walter Clark, and Robin Room (1966) found that single men were more antisocial and maladjusted than married men. They also concluded that single women aged thirty and over were less depressed, neurotic, passive, and maladjusted than their married counterparts. In agreement with the conclusions of Knupfer et al., Jessie Bernard (1972) summarized four studies and concluded that single men were less happy than married men.

Luther Baker's (1968) results similarly supported those of Knupfer et al. He found that never married women without children had above average personal and social adjustment based on the national norms established for the California Test of Personality. Finally, Lenore Radloff's (1974) study of depression indicated that single women were less depressed than divorced or separated women, but that single men were more depressed than divorced or separated men.

In contrast to the above, Norval Glenn (1975) found that married persons of both sexes reported greater global happiness than any category of unmarried persons, and that the difference in happiness between marrieds and unmarrieds was greater for females than for males. The Glenn study utilized self-report data from 1972, 1973, and 1974 social surveys of the U.S. conducted by the National Opinion Research Center. Glenn's study suggests that the data from the above researchers should be cautiously interpreted; however, as Bernard (1975) has noted, the self-reported global happiness of the married women in Glenn's study may be suspect, partly due to the social desirability of reporting greater happiness than is actually felt. Bernard concludes that such data tend to obscure "the dismal picture of the mental health of married women so convincingly documented in the research literature" (1975, p. 600).

The conclusion to be drawn from most available data is that marriage is probably better for men than it is for women. Existing studies of the relative adjustment and happiness of single women and men do not warrant sweeping conclusions about the dire state of single men as argued by journalists such as George Gilder, but it does seem that single women are happier than single men.[5] Perhaps this pattern will change as more men become independent and liberated; male dependency on mother and then on wife as pseudo-mother may account for the greater unhappiness of single men.

JOURNALISTIC REPORTS

Journalists, on the other hand, have carried out some more thorough (though not methodologically precise) investigations of singlehood than have social scientists. One journalistic investigation of singlehood is the now classic study of the world of the formerly married by Morton Hunt (1966). In that study Hunt identified a broad range of life-styles for formerly married people—from the "abstainers" to the "addicts." It is significant that Hunt's book is still in print ten years later, and that he has been asked to carry out a new study to update his earlier book. For the updated study, Morton and Bernice Hunt collected questionnaire data on a non-random, availability, mail-in sample of separated and divorced people in order to compare parents with nonparents. They looked at the process of adjusting to a new single life, including relating to old and new friends, meeting companions for intimacy and sex, and planning to remain single or to remarry.

Studies on increased premarital and extramarital sex, though only indirectly relevant to singlehood, indicate support for Sprey's (1969) argument that there is an increasing autonomy of sex from marriage, the family, and parenthood. Daniel Perlman's (1974) study, for example, documents the rise in sexual activity among unmarried college students. He found that his liberal sample reported both high self-esteem and more coital partners when compared with subjects of earlier studies by Stratton and Spitzer (1967) and by Reiss (1966). It remains for future research to identify how much of what is commonly called premarital or extramarital sex is really nonmarital and thus part of the single life.

Between the extreme images of the swinging and always elated single and the desperately lonely, suicidal single lies a continuum of single people with joys and sorrows similar to those of people electing other life-styles. Since Martin Panzer's article, "No World for a Single," appeared in *Coronet Magazine* (April 1955), singlehood as a choice rather than a residual category of undesirables has become a reality for some. As the article suggests, it may be that most single people are not happy; this is the view of George Levinger who notes that more do not opt for singlehood because they "need deep attachments that go beyond the 'modular man' [or woman] syndrome implied as normative by Toffler" (letter to author, November 1975). Levinger noted that his research with University of Massachusetts students "indicates that almost none would look forward to a future in which he or she remains permanently single." Of course, the attitudes expressed by a sample of college sophomores may not be adequate predictors of the later behavior of this same group.

Similarly, Jeanette Ames McIntosh and Gilbert D. Nass (1975) studied 109 females at Wheelock College, and it was found that 5 percent were willing or very willing to remain unmarried throughout their lives. As Wheelock has a fairly conservative student body, it might be hypothesized that more liberal samples would yield larger minorities who desire lifelong singlehood. Furthermore, it is possible that the proportion of women selecting singlehood along with careers will increase over time.

We are left, then, with the impression that singlehood (like marriage) is not a lifelong commitment for most people. Choices are usually replaced by new choices. After all, singlehood could not be a binding choice, for to whom would one be bound by such a choice? To oneself? Perhaps theoretical choices vary more than real options, but we will not really know the range of either choices or options without more comprehensive, theoretically grounded research. In the meantime, social scientists leave speculation and descriptive studies to journalists, for the most part, just as they previously left the study of sex to Kinsey, a zoologist. One wonders how long social scientists will wait to study the realities of the twentieth century.

One journalist (Phyllis Raphael, 1975) has argued that twentieth century woman's dilemma is whether to marry or not, but that she need not worry about sex since it is available to the single person who wants it. Raphael feels that most people want to be married and that they attempt to act on that want. Furthermore, she argues that people are what they *do* rather than what they *say* they do. As simple as this may seem, it indicates the importance of comparing attitudes, behavioral intentions, and reported behavior with actual interactive behavior. Such comparison is essential if we are to determine how satisfied people really are with various life-styles.

A THEORETICAL APPROACH TO SINGLEHOOD

It will be helpful to consider singlehood within a theoretical framework. Four figures have been developed as aids in presenting theoretical models of different aspects of singlehood. The first figure presents various dimensions of singlehood and a continuum of degrees of singlehood. The second figure depicts the transitions in relationships over time. The third and fourth figures describe the process of evaluation and reevaluation of life-style decisions. The theoretical approach taken here integrates elements from symbolic interaction, role, and exchange theories.

The degrees and dimensions of singlehood presented in Figure 1 are some of the many considerations that enter into decisions made about sexual life-styles and role transitions. They help define the relative rewards and costs associated with decisions. However, and exchange transactions over a sexual career. (These factors are Figure 1 is limited in that it does not identify the process of role dealt with in the remaining figures.) Before explaining Figure 1, the relevance of exchange theory will be discussed.

As Libby and Carlson (1976) indicate, the relative costs and rewards of any relationship or decision in a relationship include not only observable rewards and punishments, but inner feelings, motives, and other less tangible but extremely important emotional and cognitive states. For example, one factor which contributes to a person's perception of fairness in relationships is the relative degree of interdependence (with reciprocity) or dependency. Usually dependency entails an unbalanced interaction with one person both incurring greater costs than the other person and being less satisfied with the relationship. As will be explained, such a lack of reciprocity usually results in a reevaluation of the relationship (see Figure 3), although some people remain in relationships with little apparent profit.

There are several ways to conceptualize a sequence of interactions and decision making in terms of exchange theory. Thibaut and Kelley (1959) used reward-cost matrices to depict the possible outcomes of social interaction. Outcomes are evaluated through comparison levels (CL) which are "the lowest level of outcomes a member will accept in the light of available alternative opportunities" (such as other more attractive people to relate to), and by comparison level for alternatives (CL alt.), which is "the standard the

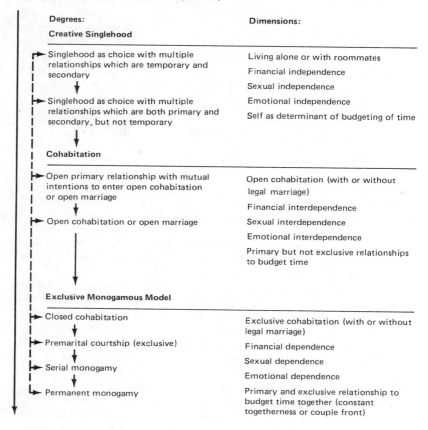

Decentralized commitment and interdependency

Degrees:

Creative Singlehood

Dimensions:

Singlehood as choice with multiple relationships which are temporary and secondary

Living alone or with roommates

Financial independence

Sexual independence

Singlehood as choice with multiple relationships which are both primary and secondary, but not temporary

Emotional independence

Self as determinant of budgeting of time

Cohabitation

Open primary relationship with mutual intentions to enter open cohabitation or open marriage

Open cohabitation (with or without legal marriage)

Financial interdependence

Open cohabitation or open marriage

Sexual interdependence

Emotional interdependence

Primary but not exclusive relationships to budget time

Exclusive Monogamous Model

Closed cohabitation

Exclusive cohabitation (with or without legal marriage)

Premarital courtship (exclusive)

Financial dependence

Serial monogamy

Sexual dependence

Emotional dependence

Permanent monogamy

Primary and exclusive relationship to budget time together (constant togetherness or couple front)

Centralized commitment and dependency

FIGURE 1. Degrees and dimensions of sexual life-styles. (Note: *The dotted lines with arrows indicate feedback loops to other life-styles if one chooses to or is forced to leave a particular life-style. The continuum from creative singlehood to the exclusive monogamous model does not assume a regular progression. People do not necessarily go from top to bottom of the figure; one may stop at any point, or skip life-styles (they may begin with traditional premarital courtship and end with serial monogamy or permanent monogamy, skipping cohabitation). The arrows indicate the entry points into the various life-styles.*)

member uses in deciding whether to remain in or leave the relationship" (or, when comparing other relationships or potentials for relationships with current relationships) (Thibaut & Kelley, 1959, p. 21). Decisions are based on the assumption that people enter and remain in relationships (or life-styles) only as long as the relationships and life-styles are evaluated by the interactants to be profitable (profit in exchange terms is rewards minus costs) .

Secord and Backman (1974) have pointed out that changes occur in the perception of rewards and costs for any given relationship:

> Rewards and costs may change as a function of (1) past exchanges which shift reward-cost values of current behaviors, (2) changes in the characteristics of the dyad members occurring through training, education, or other experiences, (3) changes in external circumstances that introduce new rewards and costs or modify the values of old ones, (4) sequential factors in the relation itself, such as the augmentation of satisfaction in current relations as a result of previously rewarding experiences in the dyad, and (5) associations with other behaviors having different reward-cost values (Secord & Blackman, 1974, p. 234) .

Reward-cost benefits in one's relationships are illustrated by the categorization of sexual life-styles in Figure 1. Reading down from "singlehood" to "permanent monogamy" one can see the lessening degrees of autonomy from others. Choosing singlehood may include multiple relationships of a transitory nature, or more intense and enduring bonds (such as primary relationships) . The "Dimensions" section of Figure 3 identifies some of the costs and rewards associated with various sexual life-styles. The range of life-styles is collapsed into three major prototypes: creative singlehood, cohabitation, and monogamy. These three prototypes are useful in comparing the partitioning of one's time, money, emotions, and sexual expression in various life-styles. Many people, of course, are in gray areas outside these prototypes involving some different combination of the dimensions.

Figure 2 was created to illustrate the sequential effects of rewards and costs in relationships over time. The reevaluation of the relative costs and rewards of relationships over time is central to the exchange theory conceptualization used as a basis for explaining and predicting transitions in relationships. Thibaut and Kelley (1959) and others have published various interpretations of exchange theory (sometimes called interpersonal attraction or equity theory) which have recognized the importance of the sequential effect of past decisions on present and future decisions about relationships. Without considering sequential effects from past exchanges in a matrix of relationships, one cannot identify satiation of a given stimulus situation (for example, when one is bored with the same person doing the same things) . A researcher must be aware of present and past exchanges as well as the matrix of likely outcomes for a particular exchange. In the sexual realm this means one must be aware of past and present exchanges with sexual, emotional, and ego values. To do this we need a biographical and current analysis

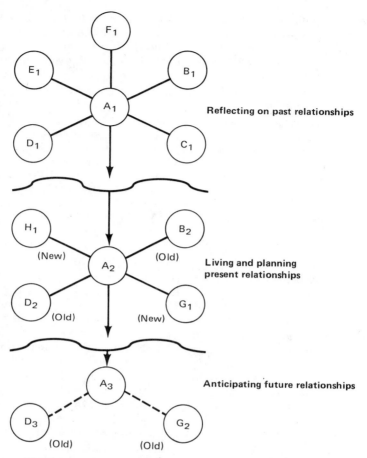

FIGURE 2. Transitions in relationships over time. (Note: Person A_1 (past) is traced to the present (A_2) and the future (A_3). Person A forms relationships with Persons B-G at one stage or another. The biography of relationships can be used to reflect on one's past, to analyze the present configuration of old and new relationships, and to hypothesize about future relationships. Some relationships might be primary, coprimary, secondary, transitory, or simply acquaintanceships. According to exchange theory, reflecting on past relationships, living with present relationships, and anticipating future relationships all influence the perception of relative costs and rewards of relationships.)

of the relative costs and rewards associated with the myriad of relationships in each person's life. Such data could be collected over time, or from retrospective accounts (Libby & Carlson, 1976). It is imperative to carry out a sequential analysis in order to explain—let alone predict—the nature of decisions leading to role transitions.

The implications for exchange outcomes for competing sexual choices appear in Figure 2, where a sample overview of the development and demise of a person's relationships over time is provided. The costs and rewards associated with each relationship change as the individual's personal and social situations, expectations, needs, and desires change; this affects whether the person maintains or abandons various relationships. Some patterning of role expectations and behaviors can usually be identified through such a natural history analysis of one's relationships over time, and projecting into the future may be possible.

Figure 3 illustrates the reevaluation of current relationships. A person in the reevaluation stage of potential "unbonding" must consider the rewards and costs of the various life-style options. When and if a person selects singlehood, there are both pulls and pushes which affect the new single identity. The process of coupling, dissolution of coupling (or unbonding), and identification of "crucial events" and "turning points" (Turner, 1970, pp. 12–13) resulting in role transitions and transformations in choices of life-styles appears in Figure 3. As can be seen in the figure, ongoing decisions about roles, needs, and self-identities involve a series of role bargains where discrepancies between actors' sexual and emotional expectations and behavior contribute to perceived costs and rewards for various role behaviors.

When there are discrepancies and crucial events concerning identities, needs, or role definitions in a relationship, the actors typically consider hypothetical alternative relationships or life-styles. Hypothetical comparisons may be complemented by actual comparative experiences with others serving as role models to consider alternative roles and ways of interacting and making commitments. After reentering the interactional space of the troubled relationship, the actors (Persons A and B) must decide whether to leave the relationship, change it, or continue living with unfulfilled needs. The hypothetical process of role-need-identity-taking with peers and significant others as models or mirrors of the self aids in weighing the costs and rewards of putting energy into the troubled relationship. For example, Figure 3 would allow us to hypothesize that Person A and Person B have a primary relationship (it might be two cohabiting people, two single people, or a married couple). Due to various crucial events, one or both people may be unhappy enough to reevaluate the worth or the nature of the relationship. The evaluation line indicates that Person A is exposed to others who can serve as role models. These role models (possibly close friends or even movie stars) provide a basis to compare the costs and rewards being experienced in the relationship with Person B, with the costs, rewards, and role expectations connected with the roles of the models.[6] The reevaluation line leading back to the primary relationship symbolizes the comparison of alternative relationships (as shown by the role models) with the present troubled primary relationship. Person A and Person B then decide whether to continue

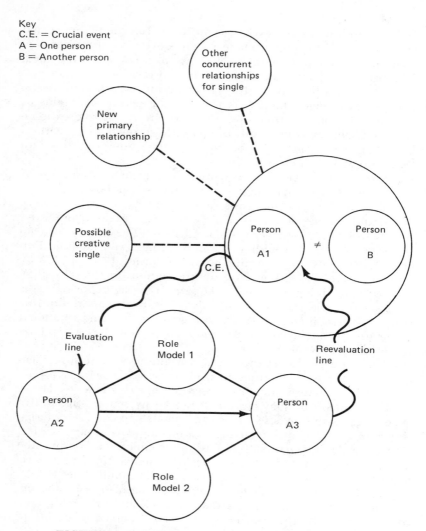

FIGURE 3. *Reevaluation of role expectations for a relationship.* (Note: *Here we can see Person A's evaluation of needs and possible roles and future identities prompted by difficulty in the relationship with Person B. Among the options are to stay in the present relationship or to become creatively single. Person B may go through an evaluation process similar to that illustrated for Person A.*)

their relationship as it is, to change their role expectations, or to uncouple. The outcome could be other primary relationships, or a series of secondary relationships. Uncoupling may lead to creative singlehood or to recoupling with another person or the same person. The lack of a set of static role expectations forces continual reevaluation of the relative costs and rewards in all relationships. But whatever the outcome, the reevaluation process occurs after crucial events lead to comparisons with role models.

If the outcome of someone's reevaluation of a relationship results in a possible single, that person has further role choices for relationships in his or her sexual career, as shown in Figure 4. The person can move into the status of a single and then become a cohabitor after meeting someone. Or the person can marry someone after orbiting (searching) for a partner. A third alternative is to meet several people and become a creative single. These three major types of role choices in a transitional stage are depicted in Figure 4.

Key
P.S. = Possible single
A = One person
B = Another person

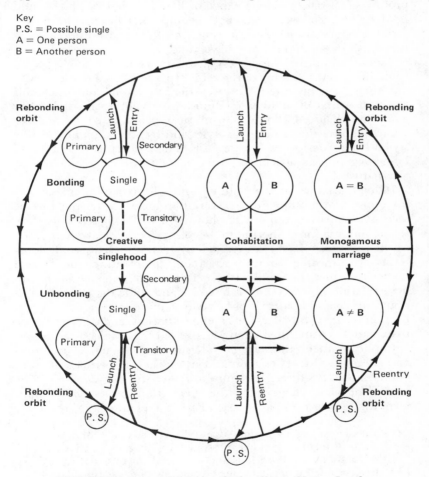

FIGURE 4. *Transitions in role bonding.* (Note: *In the lower half of the circle, the single person may launch into orbit seeking a new bond after losing a primary relationship; the cohabitors may launch into orbit because they have grown apart; and the married couple may seek new bonds because of dissatisfaction with their relationships.*)

Figure 4 illustrates bonding and unbonding and transitions to various sexual life-styles. Satisfactory bonding is illustrated in the top half of the figure, while the dotted vertical lines to the bottom half show the weakening of bonds in a given life-style (the unsatisfactory state as with Person A in Figure 3) and how one may launch into another life-style after breaking the previous bond (s).

The possible *transitions* (through orbiting) in role bonding (or coupling) over a sexual career are shown in Figure 4. Individuals may select singlehood, cohabitation, or monogamous marriage at various times. The three life-styles in Figure 4 (creative singlehood, cohabitation, and monogamous marriage) are only examples (or prototypes) from the larger range of life-style choices which could be described. For example, single people don't have to have four separate bonds at one point in time; some may have three bonded relationships, and others may have none.

As one example of the process of role transitions, a single person could orbit and enter any of the three types of life-styles (or bonds) and then (possibly due to bad experiences) launch out into orbit again in search of another relationship or another life-style. Any entry into a given choice may in turn be followed by another launching into the orbit of life-styles and reentry into another life-style with greater promise of rewards. The nature of the entry and launching process depends in part on one's comparison level for alternatives.

Individuals vary in their ability and willingness to tolerate an unhappy relationship. Further variation between people can be seen by comparing those with short-term and long-term (career) sexual orientations. Short-term people typically make more frequent role transitions and live mainly in the present, while long-term career people carefully chart out their future and have a higher tolerance threshold for costs in everyday interaction in intimate relationships. People learn habits, and while these can change, it appears that old patterns of behavior tend to reemerge. Such patterns influence future decisions and negotiations and can contribute to explanations and predictions of role and life-style choices.

Implications for the nature and length of dyadic relationships and alternative life-styles abound. Farber's (1964) permanent availability model has direct relevance to the continuing demise of lifelong monogamous marriage as the *only* option in everyday commitment and interaction patterns. As Farber explains:

> . . . depending as it does upon the tentativeness of interpersonal relations, permanent availability suggests that family relationships are capricious and as a result of this capriciousness, people cannot have much confidence in long-run plans. Short-run planning in family life is more consistent with the view of marriage as a voidable relationship and remarriage as a perennial possibility than is long-run planning. To have confidence in long-range planning, individuals must regard their social relations as relatively stable and orderly. Career

orientation implies that family relations are predictable over long periods of time. Career [i.e., long-term] orientation is therefore more consistent with orderly replacement from one generation to the next than is role orientation (1964, p. 306).

Farber's model leads me to the conclusion that people will launch out of both monogamous marriage and cohabitation arrangements increasingly more frequently. Even though creative singlehood cannot be viewed as a lifelong choice for most, it appears to offer an attraction for an increasing proportion of people who are dissatisfied with other more traditional choices involving sexual exclusivity and other restrictions often in conflict with the need to be free. Figure 4 represents the entry and launching process; it may be that more people will be in orbit (far out?) as they make short-term commitments to a life-style and then seek happiness through quick role transitions to other choices. Toffler (1970) predicted that we would move toward a series of transitory and casual sexual relationships or encounters; these could be illustrated in Figure 4, as could the option to remain in a given life-style such as cohabitation or monogamy for longer periods of time. Future research may reveal that the pleasure of new sexual and emotional experiences, along with the comfort and affection of long-term love relationships which are minus the hassles of cohabitation, will be a strong "pull" toward creative singlehood in the future.

SOME RESEARCH QUESTIONS

Currently there are many more questions than answers about singlehood as a sexual life-style. Some examples of research questions include:

1. How do the happiness, adjustment, and interaction-commitment patterns of singles vary by size of city; by ratio of women to men; by marital status, such as never married, separated, or divorced; by parenthood or nonparenthood; by education, occupation, and income; and by migration patterns?
2. How do those who select singlehood make such a choice? Who are their role models? How do variant time periods affect modeling effects and role transitions? How do specific reference groups, attitudes, situations, significant others, and various mass media affect the choice and relative viability of singlehood? What are the key social supports and negative sanctions for singlehood?
3. What is the interrelationship between the various dimensions of singlehood (financial, sexual, emotional, time budgeting, career orientation, etc.)?
4. What are the proportions of people who either select or "fall into" the various life-styles in Figure 1? What is their relative happiness, controlling for sex and age?

5. To what extent do various samples of people from all marital categories view creative singlehood as moral, appropriate, or as a threat to marriage? How do social labels mesh with self-definitions of singles?

6. What are the crucial events and turning points which lead to role transitions and changing commitments as one moves in and out of various social situations, occupations, cities, new social contacts, etc.? How does the single experience vary by sex, age, biographical history, and current social situation? How does the opportunity structure vary in terms of meeting and maintaining relationships? Who is best and worst suited to creative singlehood and why?

7. What are the correlates leading to high self-acceptance as opposed to high self-esteem? Do singles commonly distinguish between these two self-concepts? Why are some single by choice and others by default? How do these two groups differ?

8. What interpersonal experiences (such as encounter groups) are helpful in maintaining emotional stability and personal happiness and combating anomie?

9. When one chooses singlehood, is the choice binding to anyone? To the self? What is the nature of personal commitments to singlehood? Is singlehood viewed as a temporary state or as a commitment for an extended period of time? What differences are there between those who see singlehood as a temporary state and those who have no intention of changing their life-style?

10. To what extent is singlehood a state of mind? Do married and cohabiting people consider themselves to be at least part-time single? On what basis? How do their claims relate to their actual interactive behavior?

11. When comparing what singles say they feel and do with what they really do, are they honest with others and with themselves about their happiness?

12. What are the differential experiences of those who have primary, coprimary, secondary, and transitory sexual relationships as singles? How are short-term and long-term commitments defined in various kinds of friendships and other sexual and nonsexual relationships? If distinctions are made between commitments to sexual and nonsexual friends or acquaintances, on what basis are such distinctions made, and what are the implications for intensity and permanence of these relationships?

The questions could go on, but the challenge before social scientists is to pose more theoretically grounded questions, to develop theoretically based hypotheses, and to carry out studies that will indicate how theories should be modified in light of data. Retrospective life histories (as recommended by Stein, 1975), combined with longitudinal and cross-sectional studies should yield valuable data on what it means to be single in urban and suburban America. In-depth interview studies of single people with a broad range of personal, family, and social backgrounds, and engaged in a variety of personal and professional pursuits should provide a basis for comparisons, explanations, and ultimately for some predictions about the future of creative singlehood. Interview studies will have to be complemented by participant observation studies carried out in the single's work world, restaurants, bars, hotels, and clubs, as well as in other social settings which cater to a mixture of single and married people. Analyses of attitudes, feelings, and behaviors in such a range of public settings with the use of multiple research methods such as interviews and participant observation should yield results which have some theoretical value. Large attitude and opinion surveys (such as that by *Psychology Today* on happiness, October 1975) could also contribute to knowledge, if not theory, about the costs and rewards associated with the single life as compared with marriage.

Perhaps in the end we will find that single people are not as different in their goals as many would contend. It may be that most people, regardless of life-style or marital status, really just want to be happy and seek pleasure. Creative singles may be saying that they don't need marriage or cohabitation to find sexual and emotional happiness. For those who choose creative singlehood, marriage is not a necessary rite of passage for legitimizing one's sexual identity.

REFERENCES

Acock, A. & M. DeFleur. A Configurational Approach to Contingent Consistency in the Attitude-Behavior Relationship. *American Sociological Review 37* (1972) : 714–726.

Adams, M. The Single Woman in Today's Society: A Reappraisal. *The American Journal of Orthopsychiatry 41* (1971) : 776–786.

Baker, L. The Personal and Social Adjustment of the Never-Married Woman. *Journal of Marriage and the Family 30* (August 1968) : 473–479.

Bernard, J. Infidelity: Some Moral and Social Issues. In J. H. Masserman, ed. *The Psychodynamics of Work and Marriage,* 1970.

Bernard, J. *The Future of Marriage.* New York: World Publishing Co., 1972.

Bernard, J. Marriage: Hers and His. *MS. 1,* No. 6: December 1972.

Bernard, J. Comments on Glenn's Paper. *Journal of Marriage and the Family 37* (August 1975) : 600–601.

Bernard, J. Notes on Changing Life Styles, 1970–1974. *Journal of Marriage and the Family 37* (August 1975) : 582–594.

Booth, A. & E. Hess. Cross-Sex Friendship. *Journal of Marriage and the Family 36* (February 1974) : 38–47.

Dullea, G. "Marriage Tax": It Has Couples in a Rage (and Even Divorcing). *The New York Times* (March 27, 1975) : 26.

Farber, B. *Family: Organization and Interaction,* San Francisco: Chandler Publishing Co., 1964.

Fishbein, M. & I. Ajzen. *Belief, Attitude, Intention, and Behavior.* Reading, Mass.: Addison-Wesley, 1975.

Fishel, D. & N. Allon. Urban Courting Patterns: Singles' Bars. Paper presented at the American Sociological Association Annual Meeting, Summer 1973.

Gilder, G. *Sexual Suicide.* New York: Bantam Books, 1973.

Gilder, G. *Naked Nomads.* New York: Quadrangle, 1974.

Glenn, N. D. The Contribution of Marriage to the Psychological Well-Being of Males and Females. *Journal of Marriage and the Family* *37* (August 1975) : 594–600.

Glick, P. A Demographer Looks at American Families. *Journal of Marriage and the Family 37* (1975) : 15–26.

Glick, P. Some Recent Changes in American Families. *Current Population Reports.* Bureau of the Census, Special Studies, Series P-23, No. 52, U.S. Government Printing Office, 1975.

Glick, P. Personal discussion with Roger Libby, March 1976.

Glick, P. & A. Norton. Marrying, Divorcing, and Living Together in the U.S. Today. *Population Bulletin.* Vol. 32, No. 5. Population Reference Bureau (1977).

Hunt, M. *The World of the Formerly Married.* New York: McGraw-Hill Book Co., 1966.

Killian, L. Social Movements. *Society Today, 2nd ed., Del Mar, Cal.: CRM Books, 1973.*

Knupfer, G., W. Clark, & R. Room. The Mental Health of the Unmarried. *American Journal of Psychiatry 122* (February 1966) : 841–851.

Libby, R. W. & J. Carlson. Sexual Behavior as Symbolic Exchange: An Integration of Theory. Unpublished manuscript, 1976.

McIntosh, J. & G. Nass. Career Orientation and Heterosexual Autonomy Attitudes of Wheelock Students. Paper presented at Wheelock College Colloquium, May 1975.

Newsweek. First Singles' Church. (June 12, 1972).

Nye, I. & F. Barardo. *The Family: Its Structure and Interaction.* New York: Macmillan, 1973.

O'Neill, N. & G. O'Neill. Open Marriage: A Synergic Model. *Family Coordinator 21* (1972) : 403–409.

Panzer, M. No World for a Single. *Coronet Magazine 37* (April 1955).

Perlman, D. Self-Esteem and Sexual Permissiveness. *Journal of Marriage and the Family 36* (August 1974) : 470–473.

Radloff, L. Sex Differences in Mental Health: The Effects of Marital and Occupational Status. Paper presented before the American Public Health Association. October 1974.

Raphael, P. Twentieth Century Woman's Dilemma. *Female Forum (Penthouse* Special Edition), 1975.

Reiss, I. L. The Sexual Renaissance in America. *Journal of Social Issues* 22 (April 1966).

Reiss, I. L. *Heterosexual Relationships Inside and Outside of Marriage.* Morristown, N.J.: General Learning Press, 1973.

Secord, P. & C. W. Backman. *Social Psychology,* 2nd ed. New York: McGraw-Hill, 1974.

Sontag, S. The Double Standard of Aging. *Saturday Review* (September 23, 1972): 29–38.

Spreitzer, E. & L. Riley. Factors Associated with Singlehood. *Journal of Marriage and the Family 36* (1974): 533–542.

Sprey, J. On the Institutionalization of Sexuality. *Journal of Marriage and the Family 31* (1969): 432–441.

Starr, J. & D. Carns. Singles in the City. In *Marriages and Families.* H. Lopata, ed. New York: D. Van Nostrand Company, 1973.

Stein, P. Changing Attitudes of College Women. Unpublished study, Rutgers University, 1973.

Stein, P. Singlehood: An Alternative to Marriage. *Family Coordinator 24* (October 1975): 489–505.

Stein, P. *Single.* Englewood Cliffs, N.J.: Prentice-Hall, 1976.

Stratton, J. & S. Spitzer. Sexual Permissiveness and Self-Evaluation: A Question of Method. *Journal of Marriage and Family 29* (August 1967): 434–442.

Thibaut, J. & H. Kelley. *The Social Psychology of Groups.* New York: John Wiley and Co., 1959.

Toffler, A. *Future Shock.* New York: Bantam Books, 1970.

Turner, R. H. *Family Interaction.* New York: John Wiley & Sons, Inc., 1970.

U.S. Bureau of the Census. *Census of Population, 1960: Persons by Family Characteristics.* Vol. II., 4B, U.S. Government Printing Office, 1964.

U.S. Bureau of the Census. *Census of Population, 1970: Persons by Family Characteristics.* Vol. II., 4B, U.S. Government Printing Office, 1973.

U.S. Bureau of the Census. *Marital Status and Living Arrangements: Current Population Reports,* Series P-20, No. 271, U.S. Government Printing Office, March 1974.

Weitzman, L. Legal Regulation of Marriage: Tradition and Change. *California Law Review 62,* July-September 1974: 1169–1288.

White, M. & C. Wells. Student Attitudes Toward Alternate Marriage Forms. In R. Libby & R. Whitehurst, eds., *Renovating Marriage: Toward New Sexual Life Styles.* Danville, Calif.: Consensus Publishers, 1973, pp. 280–295.

Whitehurst, R. Youth Views Marriage: Awareness of Present and Future Potentials in Relationships. In Libby, R. & R. Whitehurst. *Marriage and Alternatives.* Scott, Foresman and Company, 1977.

Yankelovich, D. *The Changing Values on Campus.* New York: Washington Square Press, 1972.

FOOTNOTES

1. The concept of reclaimable identities was arrived at with Ronald Mazur (letter to author, October 1975).

2. Also, as Gordon Clanton has suggested to the author (letter, January 1976), we may find that with greater affluence more people will choose to remain single. There may be an economic threshold operating; as a society we can only sustain single people to the extent that we have the housing, jobs, and social support for singlehood.

3. This is not yet a demonstrated fact (Paul Glick, discussion with author, 1976), but I believe this trend will be documented in the near future.

4. Jessie Bernard's (1970) discussion of younger couples stressing exclusivity and older couples opting for permanence without exclusivity is relevant here.

5. Commenting on this article, Gilbert Nass offered a contrasting point of view. He stated: "Single life may not be better for single women than single men. In fact, given society's bias in favor of men, the male bachelor has much more going for him. However, in a world in which the advantages lie with married men, the man who is single is more likely to be among the population who can't take advantage of this good deal because of personal handicaps (there are exceptions of course). Thus, it is probably the better selection of single women over single men that causes them to function better despite an environment geared toward men. As Knupfer, et al. (1966) point out, a well-adjusted woman may be unmarried because no one asks her— the same cannot be said for single men.

6. Elizabeth Havelock and Bob Whitehurst have suggested (letter, January 1976) that married people view single people as role models, too. Their observation is that marrieds both vicariously identify with the "swinging singles" image, and at the same time pity singles for their isolation and assumed loneliness. The married may find the freedom of the single person appealing, but at the same time the single person may view the married person as happy because of the companionship of the marital partner. These contrasting images of the costs and rewards associated with both singlehood and marriage perpetuate the existence of both as choices.

4.

Marriage: The Traditional Alternative

Don Sloan
Lillian Africano

M arriage has traditionally been the most binding ritual involving men and women, and there was a time when neither a
man nor a woman was considered "complete" without it. Now all
that is changing, and "till death us do part" is translated into "as
long as we both shall love" or "as long as it's no hassle." Couples
often choose the latter description, thinking it's the freest and
easiest kind of relationship—and then find themselves falling into
an emotionally expensive trap. They may buy the myth that marriage is "just a piece of paper," and then find themselves coping
with all the problems of marriage without its social, legal and
emotional safeguards. For despite its difficulties and limitations,
marriage has proven itself to be a uniquely productive, protective
and enduring framework for a stable, committed relationship.

WHY NOT MARRY?

When you consider a living-together arrangement, you should be
careful to make the decision on the basis of your own values and
on a realistic assessment of your wants and needs. Quite often,
women today reject marriage because it is tied up in their minds
with an old, unliberated stereotype: the perfect wife who bakes
bread, raises perfect children and caters to her husband's every

whim (and who, if abandoned, falls apart, with no life or identity of her own) .

Instead, women choose a lifestyle on the basis of a new stereotype: the independent careerwoman who relates to men in the same exploitative way the "macho" male relates to women. And in doing so, women exchange one limiting role for another and overlook the fact that real equality between the sexes comes from mutual trust and sharing. Knowing that you can make love and walk out doesn't automatically liberate you sexually or psychologically. In fact, it may trap you. Today's woman doesn't need to follow any one pattern; she can be an independent individual without rejecting the human need for belonging, for experiencing commitment.

But since sex without marriage is so much in vogue, many women are afraid it's not sophisticated or contemporary to admit that they want to be married, even when they know they do. It's easier, particularly if the men they're involved with say they're "not ready" for matrimony, to let the relationship drift.

In the past, mating rituals followed a more or less predictable progression: a period of dating, with kissing and various kinds of sex play, and with intercourse restricted to "serious" or married couples. Presumably, the degree of commitment grew naturally as a couple took each step; by the time they had reached the point of sharing a roof, they were deeply committed to each other.

Today, with an accelerated pace of living and a desire for "instant togetherness," a couple may opt for living together as a form of engagement: "We'll get married if this works out." They may also say nothing at all but mean, "I love you, I want to be with you, but I honestly don't know where we go from here" or "I don't like living alone, so I may as well move in with you until something better comes along."

PROBLEMS

Let's say, however, that a couple begins living together because they're in love and they want their relationship to be free, completely voluntary. They are still going to come up against many of the problems that arise in marriage. Problems involving money (who pays for what) will surface, and may well be touchier in an unmarried set-up because the feeling of "mine" and "yours" tends to be stronger than the concept of "ours." There may be "in-law" problems with families who disapprove of the lifestyle. The pains of jealousy are also common, especially when the couple, having chosen "freedom" rather than commitment, feel they don't have the right to verbalize their feelings and to ask for the reassurance and security they would have in a marriage.

And sooner or later, what happens in many "just-living-together" arrangements is that one of the pair wants to get married and the other doesn't. This can lead to a tug of war that is draining and demoralizing to both. The one who wants "more" may become tense, worried and preoccupied with strategies to convince the other. Whatever insecurities exist will probably become exaggerated, because the basic question is: "Why doesn't he/she want me in the same way I want him/her?" And the answer can be: "He/she doesn't care enough," or, worse yet, "I'm not good enough, smart enough, attractive enough, etc." Meanwhile, the reluctant partner starts to feel worried and guilty, and the "easy" part of the relationship evaporates. In fact, the relationship itself will probably fall apart, but not before it causes pain and emotional damage to both.

Of the reasons couples give for not getting married, only one is sound—genuine contentment with the situation. Most couples give other excuses: "Sex is easier." "It's simpler if we keep our lives (and checking accounts) separate." "There's an ex-spouse in the picture and I don't feel like taking on any more responsibilities." "It's easier to split if things don't work out." All of these are the worst kinds of reasons not to make a commitment because they are mechanical rather than human. In addition, most of them aren't even true.

SEXUAL DYSFUNCTION

Take the concept of "easier sex." Lack of commitment can actually inhibit sexual response instead of improving it. For among couples seeking sex therapy, about twice as many unmarried women report orgasmic difficulties as married women.

Psychological orgasmic problems among women are often partly the result of our still male-dominated culture. Traditionally, women have been powerless and dependent, and they respond to this situation negatively, with hostility. They may throw dishes or shoot their lovers, but most often these angry feelings surface during sex and result in a lack of orgasm. In the living-together arrangement, these underlying pressures combine with the uncertainties of non-commitment.

And the woman is usually aware, on some level, that she is taking the greater risk. For example, if a couple start living together in their 30s and then split up in their 40s, the man is in a better position to find a new partner. He is still considered extremely eligible, a bachelor with the added attraction of not paying alimony or child support. A woman in her 40s, unfair as it may be, has her choice narrowed by custom and prejudice.

But men also have sexual problems caused in part by casual, no-commitment living situations. The most typical occurs when the man wants to get married and the woman doesn't. He may want her to agree to commitment, as he defines it, because he wants the security of a permanent relationship. When she won't, he can become fearful of rejection. He may experience feelings of sexual inadequacy, a "fear of performance" in bed which can cause episodes of impotence and other problems. He may even worry that his partner wants other sexual experiences. Ultimately, he may not trust her emotionally any more, and when this subtle trust breaks down, it can lead to a vicious circle of sexual dysfunction: His sense of rejection leads to impotence, causing her to have a negative reaction, which reinforces his feelings of inadequacy.

Although both sets of problems can be treated, the sex therapist relies on commitment as a critical factor for success.

Another variation on the sexual theme is the theory that sex is better, more exciting, in an unmarried relationship. "Why spoil it?" the reasoning goes. "Why risk sexual boredom by getting married?" One case that at first glance seems to support this premise concerns a couple who reported that sex had been satisfactory until they married, at which point the husband became impotent. He then began an affair with his secretary which started out on a fairly intense level sexually, but after awhile he became impotent again. The man tried still another partner, and the problem recurred after just a few encounters. His was a problem caused not by marriage or commitment but by the machismo concept of "scoring." Once the conquest was made, he lost interest sexually.

And it's almost as common to see a woman, whose active sex life is all tied up with role-playing, suddenly lose interest in sex after marriage. She has achieved the "reward" she was after, and the role-playing is no longer necessary.

Cases like these coexist with others in which sex remains the same or even improves after marriage. Because sexual dysfunction is a defense, a way of hiding, it is not caused by a married or committed situation per se, but by the underlying problems of the people involved.

VULNERABILITY

As for the standard argument that it's easier to break up when you're not married, this is true only in a legal sense. When any emotionally involved couple thinks of splitting up, there's a lot of negative energy aroused in feelings of guilt, insecurity, anxiety. "What's going to happen to me?" "Will I ever find someone else?" "Can I take the chance of ending up alone?" When the break-up is handled through the institutionalized channels of divorce, many of these negative feelings can be dissipated through rituals, in the mechanics of dealing with papers and judges and lawyers. There's time to sort through anger and hurt and start to heal. But when there is no marriage, "good-by" can be as quick and simple as packing a bag—and as overwhelming as a death in the family. When it's all over in a day, there is no transition, no ritual for dealing with all the pain.

There is, finally, one other important reason why couples choose not to marry, and that is fear of vulnerability. Being vulnerable is an integral part of commitment, and crossing the line into a socially structured way of life makes you legally, economically and emotionally vulnerable. In choosing commitment, you put yourself in a position where someone can really get at you. Becoming so emotionally exposed is frightening, but it offers enormous rewards. To take that step means that you trust each other, and as a wise man once said, "To be trusted is a greater compliment than to be loved."

ARE YOU COMMITTED?

The dictionary defines commitment as "the act of pledging or engaging oneself," but the actual ingredients that bind a relationship can vary. They may be economic ("two can live as cheaply as one"), social ("what would we tell our friends if we broke up?"), emotional ("we're in love and we want to be together").

Whatever your particular motivation is, you may sometime find yourself at a critical point where your relationship must either move to a new stage or end. When this happens, a few guidelines might help chart a direction.

Ask yourself what attracted you to your partner, what made you agree to each step you've taken so far. Now consider your answers (whether they be "intelligence," "kindness," "nice smile," "good sense of humor," "nice face," "great body") and ask yourself: "How do I feel about all those characteristics now?"

If the points of appeal are still strong, you're off to a good start toward developing a deeper level of commitment.

Step 1: Check your level of determination. Unless you both agree to devote a certain amount of energy to making your relationship one that satisfies your needs, it will deteriorate and fall apart.

Step 2: Examine your expectations, asking if they are realistic. For example, if you have been uncommitted because you want to live in the city and he wants to put down roots in the country, is it possible for one of you to compromise?

Step 3: And this is crucial! Establish good communications so that the messages from Steps 1 and 2 can be given and received in an ongoing way. If a commitment is to grow and survive, you both must maintain verbal, non-verbal and sexual contact to keep in close touch with each other's feelings and needs.

Part
Two

Marriage Versus Cohabitation

A T LEAST TWO ISSUES are involved in most discussions of the relationship between marriage and cohabitation. One is the issue of personal and social morality, and the other is the issue of the meaning of cohabitation in the sociological sense. From one standpoint, there is concern over the rightness or wrongness of nonmarital sexual relationships, and over such relationships being practiced openly, at least with some limited degree of openness. These might be termed issues of general societal concern.

The major issue from the standpoint of the social scientist is reflected in such questions as the part played by cohabitation in either facilitating or inhibiting marriage, or the question as to where cohabitation fits into the dating-courtship-mate selection process. More particularly, those studying this behavior wish to know whether cohabitation is simply a new phase or stage being added to the courtship process, or whether it is actually becoming a substitute for marriage itself.

Although some aspects of cohabitation are a new social phenomenon, generally speaking this practice has been around for some time. In fact, the term *cohabitation* was commonly used to refer to common-law marriage only a decade or two back. But recent usage has brought about a meaning in the term that specifically indicates that the couple living together is *not* married in any form, common law or otherwise. For some there is even an open declaration that marriage is to be avoided and that cohabitation is a means of avoiding it. Even with this change in meaning, the type of behavior under scrutiny is still not so new. For example, divorced people who are considering remarriage often live together for a period of time to see if they can get along. This is likely a result of their not wanting to remarry too hastily with the possibility of making another mistake. Cohabitation has also been practiced among older and retired persons who have been widowed or divorced, but who desire not to jeopardize their retirement income or inheritance arrangements by entering into a legal marriage. The really new aspect of cohabitation is its emergence among never-married college students as an alternative housing arrangement.

The practice of cohabitation among college students and other young people arose as a consequence of several significant changes in the living arrangements of students with a simultaneous change in the general atmosphere of more openness in sexual relationships and other sexual matters. Specifically, the abolition of dormitory curfews for women, greater freedom in living arrangements on campus (coed dormitories), and the sudden increase in apartment living by students, along with the increase in sexual freedom of recent years facilitated the development of the alternative of cohabitation as a desirable living arrangement for some students.

A typical pattern has been for a female to drift into a cohabitation arrangement while still maintaining a dormitory room for the sake of appearances.[1] As the couple spends more and more time together at the male's apartment, it is easy to fall into the pattern of simply not returning to the dormitory at night or for the entire weekend, since dormitory rules of the past no longer exist. The reverse process also occurs with the male spending more and more time at the female's apartment, but males are more likely to live off campus than are females.

The problem that most concerns marriage and family professionals is to determine just what cohabitation is. That is, what precisely does cohabitation mean to the people involved and to the marriage institution? There are a number of possible answers to this question, each of which may have some relevance for particular relationships.

Is cohabitation a trial marriage? For some it may be. In the case of young and middle-aged divorced persons who live together for a time, many want to try a marriage-like relationship before they remarry. For these individuals, cohabitation would certainly have to be considered as a trial marriage. The picture, however, is less clear with college students. An early study of cohabitation in the late 1960's indicated that most of the couples surveyed intended to get married to each other at some later date.[2] However, later studies have shown less of a relationship between cohabitation and marriage, with most of those questioned and particularly the males indicating that they had not entered the cohabitation arrangement with marriage in mind.[3] Also, there was a high rate of "breaking up" for many of the cohabiting couples.

Is cohabitation a substitution for marriage? In the more recent studies, living together seems to be more a matter of convenience and practicality than a marriage-type arrangement.[4] This is not to indicate that these relationships are not based upon strong emotional attachments, because most of them are. Sharing a living situation does have certain practical advantages which are often recognized by those participating in it. Some liaisons were begun with the knowledge and understanding that they would be temporary in nature, such as the sharing of quarters while traveling on an extended tour of Europe, the United States, or on a vacation during the holidays. Since most couples who live together do not present themselves to the public as being married, cohabitation cannot be considered the same as common-law marriage. Reiss states that since most cohabiting couples make every effort not to become pregnant and plan to resort to abortion if pregnancy occurs, these relationships, therefore, lack some of the requirements that are necessary to meet the definitions of an ordinary marriage.[5]

Is cohabitation another form of exploitation? There is some evidence that whereas one member of a cohabiting couple is entering a "meaningful relationship," the other member may be exploiting the relationship very much in terms of the traditional double standard. One study found, for example, that many of the female partners expressed a desire for, and a high prospect of, getting married, whereas their male partners expressed no such desire.[6] Another study indicated that the female ultimately did most of the household chores such as cooking and cleaning, much like the traditional division of labor found in the average marriage.[7] It appears that some males are taking advantage of

74

the new ideology of "meaningful relationships without the necessity of marriage" to further exercise the sexual double standard to their advantage, with little investment by way of long-term commitment on their part.

Is cohabitation a new form of courtship? It should be clear at this point that cohabitation serves different functions and purposes which vary not only from one couple to the next but also by sex. In our view this new and limited practice represents for most young people who engage in it an additional development in the more ordinary courtship process. In the past it was not unusual for a limited proportion of couples to engage in premarital sex prior to marriage, and in some cases without a marriage following. The only thing different about cohabitation now may be that it is done more openly, with more interaction being compressed into a briefer time frame. Just as some premarital sexual relationships in the past led to marriage whereas others did not, the same is true of cohabitation relationships. They may also be viewed as a more serious or concentrated form of going steady, with a more open sexual element.

Although cohabitation has received a great deal of attention, it is still a pattern of behavior that involves only a small minority of young people, especially young people attending colleges and universities. Cohabitation is probably more widely practiced among those not involved in higher education or who are beyond that age group.

Since the phenomenon of cohabitation is relatively new and since a great deal of research is currently being undertaken regarding it, the issues involved have not yet emerged in a coherent form. In other words, no one is sure just yet what "sides" in this issue will come into focus. Thus, the articles in this section take a more general look at this behavior pattern, attempting to throw light on some of the questions that have been raised. The first article, "Shacking Up: Cohabitation in the 1970's," is based upon a nationwide representative sample of young men, aged 20 to 30 years. It seeks to ascertain the nature and extent of their experiences in living with females in a nonmarried state.

The second article, "Cohabitation: The Tender Trap," takes a more practical or applied approach in that it seeks to point out some of the pitfalls, legal and otherwise, in cohabitation. The article also makes some suggestions as to ways of avoiding some of these pitfalls.

REFERENCES

1. Ira L. Reiss, *Family Systems in America,* 2nd ed. (Hinsdale, Ill.: The Dryden Press, 1976), p. 88.

2. Michael P. Johnson, "Courtship and Commitment: A Study of Cohabitation on a University Campus," unpublished master's thesis, University of Iowa, 1969; cited in Reiss, op. cit., p. 87.

3. Judith L. Lyness, Milton E. Lipetz, and Keith E. Davis, "Living Together: An Alternative to Marriage," *Journal of Marriage and the Family,* 34 (May 1972), 305–311.

4. Eleanor P. Macklin, "Heterosexual Cohabitation Among College Students," *The Family Coordinator,* 21 (October 1972), 463–473; Charles Lee Cole, "Cohabitation in Social Context," in Roger W. Libby, and Robert N. Whitehurst, *Marriage and Alternatives: Exploring Intimate Relationships* (Glenview, Ill.: Scott, Foresman and Company, 1977), pp. 62–79.

5. Reiss, op. cit. p. 88.

6. Lyness et. al., op. cit.

7. Macklin, op. cit., pp. 463–473.

5.

Shacking Up: Cohabitation in the 1970s

Richard R. Clayton
Harwin L. Voss

In recent years, social scientists have shown considerable interest in alternative or variant life styles. The many books, articles, conferences, and special issues of journals devoted to this topic attest to the scope and intensity of that interest. Because of its implications for marriage and the future of the family as an institution in American society, specialists in the family have been intrigued by cohabitation.

The term *cohabitation* is used to describe nonmarital heterosexual living arrangements (see Macklin, 1972). In some ways cohabitation appears to be an entirely new practice. Yet, in other ways it seems to be merely an extension of what formerly was known as "shacking up"—semipermanent or permanent heterosexual relationships initiated without benefit of clergy.

Cohabitation is similar to, but different from, marriage. The commitment of the partners may be similar in marriage and cohabitation (Johnson, 1969; Lewis, 1973; Lewis, Spanier, Storm and Lehecka, 1975). Furthermore, there may be little or no difference between marriage and cohabitation in the way the partners perform their respective roles. However, marriage is socially sanctioned and involves legal obligations, whereas cohabitation does not. Cohabitation also does not appear to be a perfect analogue of common-law marriage because the participants generally acknowledge that they are *not* married.

Scholars have questioned whether cohabitation is a substitute for or merely a new stage in the courtship process or whether it constitutes an alternative to marriage as the basis for relatively permanent heterosexual relationships. While relevant, questions about the long-range effects of cohabitation on the participants' entry into, and the stability of, marital unions presuppose extensive cohabitation in American society. One may inquire legitimately: how many young (or old, for that matter) people have ever lived with a partner of the opposite sex outside the bonds of matrimony? how many are currently cohabiting? In other words, before the effects of cohabitation on marital and familial behavior in the future can be assessed, it is imperative to determine the *extent* of cohabitation.

At the present time information regarding the prevalence of cohabitation in the general population is not available. The studies reported thus far have been limited to small nonrandom samples, to random samples in which the response rate has been too low to determine prevalence accurately, and to samples largely restricted to white college students. In fact, knowledge of the characteristics that distinguish those who have cohabited from those who have not is essentially based on two studies, both of which were published in 1974. The first was conducted by Henze and Hudson (1974) at Arizona State University but included only 27 males and 14 females who had cohabited. In the second study, Peterman, Ridley and Anderson (1974) analyzed mailed questionnaires completed by 473 male and 626 female students at Pennsylvania State University. These investigators selected a random sample from the student population, but the response rate was only 38 percent for males and 50 percent for females. Consequently, it is questionable whether or not one can generalize, even to the students at Pennsylvania State University, on the basis of this study.

The purposes of this paper are: (a) to present data about the lifetime and current prevalence of nonmarital heterosexual cohabitation that were obtained between October 1974 and May 1975 in personal interviews with a nationwide random sample of 20 to 30 year old men; and (b) to compare the characteristics of those who have formed a nonmarital heterosexual union with those who have not done so. The data presented in this paper are descriptive, but they provide an estimate of the prevalence and correlates of cohabitation in a nationwide sample.

THE SAMPLE

The sample was a multi-stage, stratified random sample drawn from Selective Service records of the men who registered in the years 1962 through 1972 in the 48 coterminous states. With minor exceptions, registration occurred within a month of a man's 18th birthday. Consequently, the sample represents the population of males born in the years 1944 through 1954 who survived to the age of 18. While a few men failed to register in this period, there is no evidence suggesting that their number was sizable. There certainly is no equally complete listing of young men from which a sample could be drawn.

The first step in drawing the sample was completed by Temple University's Institute for Survey Research prior to the initiation of this study. Their sampling framework consisted of 100 primary sampling units selected to represent the continental United States. Alaska and Hawaii were excluded because of the added costs which would result from fieldwork in these states. Within each primary sampling unit, two Selective Service Boards were chosen randomly. Within each board, men were selected individually for each of the 11 registration years in such a way that the number selected would be proportional to the number of registrants in each year. A board in a populous area had a greater chance to be selected than a board in a less populous one, but an individual who registered with the latter type of board had a greater chance of selection than one in the former type. Thus, the sample was selected to give all young men in the continental United States an equal chance to be chosen. The procedures used in selection of the sample are described more fully elsewhere (O'Donnell, Voss, Clayton, Slatin and Room, 1976).

Of the 3,024 men in the target sample, 36 were deceased, and seven were incompetent and incapable of being interviewed. As a result there were 2,981 potential interviewees. Of these, 2,510 (84 percent) were interviewed; 174 (6 percent) were located but refused to be interviewed; and 263 (9 percent) of the respondents could not be located. For 34 men (1 percent) locations were known, but interviews were not obtained, largely because the men resided outside the United States, and their addresses were discovered after the overseas interviews were completed.

A comparison of the 2,510 interviewees with the 471 men who were not interviewed revealed that a somewhat higher proportion of the older men and those who had registered in large metropolitan areas were not interviewed. However, nonresponse bias was minimal, and the men who were interviewed are representative of the target population—men born in the years 1944 through 1954, inclusive.[1]

DEFINITIONS

While the primary focus of the study was on nonmedical drug use, it was possible to make inquiries in addition to the traditional survey item regarding current marital status in which the response categories are single, married, separated, divorced, or widowed. Specifically, questions concerning marriage, experience in nonmarital heterosexual relations, and current living arrangements were included.

The dependent variables examined in this paper were derived from the responses to four questions. To determine the respondent's current living arrangements, each man was asked: (1) "At present, are you (a) married, and living with your wife; (b) living as a partner with a woman you are not married to; or (c) are you *not* now living with a wife or partner?" As this question was phrased, the first two responses could refer to relatively long-term unions or to ones formed shortly before the date of the interview. Just as classification of a man as currently married does not imply that the marriage existed for any particular length of time, in this paper we will use the terms *current cohabitation* or *currently cohabiting* in reference to the men who, at the time of the interview, were living with a woman outside matrimonial bonds. The men who were not living with a wife or partner were classified as either living with their parents or living independently on the basis of a question posed earlier in the interview regarding whether the respondent still resided with his parents.

Regardless of the answer provided to the question about current living arrangements, each respondent was asked two additional questions: (2) "How many times have you been married?" and (3) "How many times have you lived as a partner for six months or more with a woman you were not married to at the time?"[2] Answers to the question about number of marriages will be used to assess the relation between multiple marriages and cohabitation, whereas responses to the latter question reflect the *lifetime prevalence* of cohabitation. In this question the six-month time period was specified to avoid inquiry about short-term liaisons. It should be noted that these data refer to the nonmarital heterosexual sharing of living accommodations at some period in the respondent's life, and only relationships that existed for six months or more are included, regardless of whether or not they existed at the time of the interview. Consequently, 14 men who were currently cohabiting were not included in the figures for the lifetime prevalence of cohabitation because they reported a current relationship that, at the time of the interview, had been in existence from one to five months.

FINDINGS

LIFETIME PREVALENCE

Of the 2,510 young men in the sample, 2,066 (82 percent) have never cohabited for six months or more. Included among those who have never cohabited are 821 men who have never married, 1,176 men who have been married once, and 69 men who have been married two or more times. These men comprise 33 percent, 47 percent, and less than 3 percent, respectively, of the sample. In short, the life style of approximately 80 percent of the men has been traditional with respect to serious heterosexual relationships. Yet, 444 (18 percent) of these young men reported that they had cohabited, or lived with a woman outside the bonds of matrimony for a period of six months or more. The data regarding lifetime prevalence suggest that cohabitation is neither widespread nor is it a rare occurrence among the men born in the years 1944 through 1954. The conclusion that most of the young men have followed traditional heterosexual lives also may apply to many of those who have cohabited in view of the fact that two-thirds of them have only had one nonmarital relationship of this kind.

Examination of the rows in Panel A in Table 1 reveals that 14 percent of those who have been married once, also have cohabited. In comparison, 21 percent of those who have never married have cohabited, as have 35 percent of the men with multiple marriages. Inspection of the columns in Panel A shows that a higher percentage of those who have never cohabited have been married once, whereas the men who have cohabited are more likely to report either that they have never married or have been married two or more times.

It should be noted that only 107 (4 percent) of the men in the sample have been married more than once. It may be that cohabitation eventually will be experienced by a larger proportion of the men if they experience marital disruption. As shown in Panel C in Table 1, 30 percent of the men who currently were cohabiting had been married one or more times. It may be noted that in Panel A in Table 2 the proportion of men in each age group who were married is higher in each successive category. Stated differently, a sizable proportion of the 821 men who had neither cohabited nor married were 20 or 21 years of age at the time of the interview, and these men may enter nonmarital heterosexual unions in the future. Thus, the lifetime prevalence of cohabitation may be substantially higher than 18 percent; in an epidemiological sense, there are still numerous men "at risk." This is also true for marriage; presumably some of the 1,033 men who had never married will do so in the future. As previously noted, the definition of lifetime prevalence of cohabitation employed in this study required some degree of stability or continuity—only relationships of six months or longer duration were included. Consequently, the prevalence figure of 18 percent is a conservative estimate of the extent to which young men have been partners in a nonmarital relationship.

The association between cohabitation and current living arrangements is shown in Panel B in Table 1, and these data are also relevant to the concept of "at risk." Twelve percent of the men who were currently married had cohabited one or more times. Of the 796 men living independently, 22 percent had cohabited. In addition, 273 men who had never cohabited were still living in their parental home. Thus, a sizable portion of the sample is "at risk" insofar as the possibilities of marriage and cohabitation are concerned.

Another important point in Panel B in Table 1 is that only 120 (5 percent) of these 20 to 30 year old men were, at the time of the interview, living with a woman to whom they were not married. Thus, the extent of existing nonmarital heterosexual unions or current cohabitation is substantially lower than the lifetime prevalence

TABLE 1 *Cohabitation, Marriage, and Current Living Arrangements*

Number of Cohabitations

Panel A: Number of Times Married	None			One			Two or More		
	Column %	N	Row %	Column %	N	Row %	Column %	N	Row %
None	40	(821)	79	49	(140)	14	45	(72)	7
One	57	(1176)	86	41	(118)	8	48	(76)	6
Two or More	3	(69)	65	10	(27)	25	7	(11)	10

Number of Cohabitations

Panel B: Current Living Arrangements	None			One			Two or More		
	Column %	N	Row %	Column %	N	Row %	Column %	N	Row %
Married	56	(1152)	88	37	(104)	8	33	(53)	4
Cohabiting	1	(14)	12	22	(63)	52	27	(43)	36
Independent	30	(627)	79	38	(109)	14	38	(60)	8
Living with Parents	13	(273)	96	3	(9)	3	2	(3)	1

Number of Marriages

Panel C: Current Living Arrangements	None			One			Two or More		
	Column %	N	Row %	Column %	N	Row %	Column %	N	Row %
Married	—	(——)	—	89	(1215)	93	88	(94)	7
Cohabiting	8	(84)	70	2	(32)	27	4	(4)	3
Independent	65	(668)	84	9	(120)	15	7	(8)	1
Living with Parents	27	(281)	99	*	(3)	1	1	(1)	*

An asterisk (*) denotes less than one percent.

of cohabitation. This suggests that cohabitation is *not* a permanent form of heterosexual union: these relationships either terminate or the partners marry. The fact that only 5 percent of the men were currently cohabiting is consistent with the recent survey of sexual behavior among 100,000 American women in which it was found that only 3 percent were "living with a man" to whom they were not married (Levin and Levin, 1975). However, more than 90 percent of the women in Levin and Levin's sample were married, and the age range in their study was considerably broader than in this investigation.

The number of times the men were married is shown in relation to current living arrangements in Panel C in Table 1. While 70 percent of the men who were cohabiting had never married, they comprised only 8 percent of the "never married" males; 65 percent of these men were living independently, and 27 percent were still living at home.

There were 168 men who reported that they had been married but were not currently living with their wives. Of these, 76 percent were living independently. An additional 21 percent were cohabiting. This percentage is substantially higher than the comparable figure for the men who had never married, as only 8 percent of them were cohabiting. Four of the men who had been married had returned to their parental home. In contrast, 12 of the men who had cohabited currently resided with their parents (Panel B). The numbers are small, but one possible interpretation is that marriage signifies a greater degree of independence from parents than does cohabitation.

One crude indication of the stability of marital and cohabiting relationships may be derived from these data. Of the total sample, 1,477 men had married, and 1,309 (89 percent) were currently living with their wives. Almost identical percentages, 89 and 88 percent, respectively, of the first and later marriages were intact at the time of the interview.[3] In contrast, 444 men had cohabited, but only 106 of these men currently were cohabiting. As previously noted, 14 of the men who were cohabiting did not meet the six-month criterion included in the question used to define the lifetime prevalence of cohabitation, as these unions, at the time of the interview, had existed for periods ranging from one to five months. In other words, three-fourths of the cohabitations had terminated, either through dissolution of the union or through marriage.

As noted earlier, detailed information was not obtained about each heterosexual union a man had entered. Consequently, it is possible to determine if cohabitation led to marriage only for those men who reported one marriage and one cohabitation. As may be seen in Panel A in Table 1, there were 118 men who reported such a pattern of heterosexual relationships. Twenty-two of these men were living independently, and 17 were cohabiting. Six of these 39 men described only one relationship; therefore, it may be inferred that cohabitation led to marriage, although these marriages were no longer intact. The remaining 79 men currently were married: of these, 38 described only one heterosexual union and, again, it may be inferred that cohabitation led to marriage. In other words, for 37 percent of the men with one experience in cohabitation and one marriage, cohabitation led to marriage. Obviously, some of the men who had cohabited more than once may have married their partner. In addition, some of those who are currently cohabiting may marry.

SOCIAL AND DEMOGRAPHIC ANTECEDENTS

Implicit in many sociological analyses is the assumption that a number of social and demographic factors influence a person's predisposition to engage in unconventional activities. The applicability of this assumption to cohabitation will be examined with reference to age, size of city of residence in the formative years, social class background, and ethnicity.

Age. Year of birth or age at the time of the interview is related to current cohabitation and the lifetime prevalence of cohabitation, as may be seen in Table 2. The figures for lifetime prevalence of cohabitation and for the various kinds of current living arrangements are quite similar for the two older age categories. Furthermore, the figures for the 22 to 24 year old men more closely resemble those for the older men than the percentages for the youngest age category. Specifically, 21 percent of the 25 to 27 year old men had cohabited, and this figure is not substantially different from the ones for the adjacent age categories. However, among the 20 and 21 year old men, only 12 percent reported having ever cohabited. In the terminology of Campbell and Stanley (1963), this reflects a lack of exposure to maturational forces for the younger men. This point is also relevant with regard to the percentages of men in these age categories who currently are cohabiting. Furthermore, it is apparent that the "risk" of marriage is related to age—three times as many men in the oldest age category, in comparison with those in the youngest category, were married. The younger men were more likely to be living independently or with their parents. Again, one may infer that the figures for the lifetime prevalence of cohabitation and marriage, particularly for the 20 to 24 year old men and especially for the 20 and 21 year olds, would be higher if the men were contacted at the age of 40 and asked about heterosexual relationships.

City size. Size of city of residence to age 18 also is related to cohabitation. These data support the idea that persons who grow up in a metropolitan area are more likely to engage in unconventional activities than others. A higher percentage of those who lived in cities of one million or more while they were juveniles have cohabited than men who resided in smaller communities. In fact, the percentages decline regularly from the largest cities to the

TABLE 2 *Cohabitation and Current Living Arrangements by Social and Demographic Antecedents*

Number	Total 2510	Ever cohabited		Current living arrangements			
		Yes 444	No 2066	Married 1309	Cohabiting 120	Independent 796	Living with parents 285
	Number			Percentages			
A. *Birth Year—Age in 1974:*							
Before 1947—28 to 30 years old	541	17	83	72	6	20	3
1947–1949—25 to 27 years old	692	21	79	63	5	27	5
1950–1952—22 to 24 years old	740	19	81	48	5	35	11
After 1952—20 to 21 years old	537	12	88	24	3	45	28
B. *Place of Residence to Age 18:*							
1 million or more	187	28	72	41	7	36	16
100,000–999,999	610	20	80	49	5	32	13
25,000–99,999	466	18	82	51	5	33	12
2,500–24,999	730	14	86	52	5	33	10
Less than 2,500	456	16	84	61	3	27	9
Outside United States	61	18	82	61	3	30	7
C. *Father's Education:*[a]							
Less than high school	1053	15	85	60	3	25	11
High school	740	19	81	52	4	33	11
College	505	19	81	36	8	44	12
D. *Ethnicity:*							
White	2103	16	84	54	4	31	10
Black	303	29	71	36	8	38	17
Other	104	18	81	58	6	23	13

[a] Missing information = 212.

85

rural areas, with only one minor reversal. While the differences are not as dramatic, there is a similar linear relationship among those currently cohabiting. This finding conflicts with the conclusion of Peterman and his coworkers that city size is not related to cohabitation.[4]

Social class. Another antecedent variable that sociologists would expect to be predictive of cohabitation is social class. The father's education is used as an indicator of the respondent's social class background. The men whose fathers had not completed high school were somewhat less likely to have ever cohabited. There was a stronger relationship for current cohabitation: 8 percent of the men whose fathers had a college education were cohabiting in comparison with 3 percent of the men whose fathers had not completed high school. Thus, the data do not confirm the conclusion based on studies of college students that parental education is unrelated to cohabitation.

Ethnicity. Of the blacks, 29 percent reported that they had cohabited. This is a substantially higher figure than is found among whites (16 percent) or those from other racial or ethnic backgrounds (18 percent). Similar differences exist for current cohabitation—8 percent of the blacks in comparison with 4 percent of the whites were cohabiting at the time they were interviewed. There is also a sizable difference in the percentages of blacks and whites who were married. The black respondents were more likely to be living independently or in the parental home than were whites or the men from other ethnic groups.

CURRENT SOCIAL AND DEMOGRAPHIC STATUS

Education. In the first two sections of Table 3 the respondents are classified according to their enrollment in school and their educational attainment. The men who were not attending school and those who had less than a high school education were more likely to have cohabited or to be cohabiting than their counterparts. Only 15 percent of the men currently attending college were cohabiting. This finding is inconsistent with the assertion of Peterman, Ridley, and Anderson (1974:344) that: "Cohabiting, or heterosexual unmarried 'living together,' seems to be a form of relationship highly popular among young adult Americans, particularly college students." While cohabitation may be more common among today's college students than it was a generation ago, it is apparent that this phenomenon is less common than previous studies of small samples of college students had suggested. Further, it is evident that investigations restricted to college students cannot be used to estimate the prevalence of a particular form of behavior in the general population.

In some of the studies of cohabitation it apparently has been assumed that innovative life styles are initially adopted by affluent

TABLE 3 Cohabitation and Current Living Arrangements by Social and Demographic Characteristics

Number	Total 2510	Ever cohabited		Current living arrangements			
		Yes 444	No 2066	Married 1309	Cohabiting 120	Independent 796	Living with parents 285
	Number			Percentages			
A. *Currently in school:*							
Yes	547	15	85	39	3	44	14
No	1963	18	81	56	5	28	10
B. *Educational attainment:*							
Less than high school	394	23	77	57	6	24	12
High school	933	17	83	58	4	25	13
College	1183	17	83	46	5	39	10
C. *Size of city of current residence:*[a]							
1 million or more	146	29	71	36	8	36	19
100,000–999,999	631	19	81	48	6	37	12
25,000–99,999	573	18	82	50	5	35	10
2,500–24,999	754	14	86	58	3	28	11
Less than 2,500	352	14	86	59	3	25	13
Outside United States	43	33	67	49	9	42	0
D. *Region of current residence:*[b]							
Northeast	459	20	80	45	6	31	17
North Central	706	15	85	53	4	32	11
South	840	15	85	57	4	29	11
West	461	22	78	50	6	35	8
Outside United States	43	33	67	49	9	42	0
E. *Church attendance:*							
Weekly	430	7	93	58	1	26	14
Monthly	471	12	88	56	2	30	13
Less than monthly	798	19	81	54	5	30	10
Never	811	26	74	45	8	37	10

[a] Missing information for 11 cases.
[b] Missing information for 1 case.

persons. An alternative possibility is that cohabitation is new to affluent whites who are unaware of the history of common-law marriage, and that "shacking up" has not been unknown among lower-class members of society. Cohabitation of college students in recent years may constitute an independent discovery of an alternative life style that has existed for some time in other sectors of society. It is possible, of course, that the motives underlying and the meaning attached to cohabitation may differ for college students and those from the less affluent sectors of society.

City size and region. There is a strong relationship between the size of the city in which the men were currently residing and both the lifetime prevalence of cohabitation and current cohabitation. This finding supports the view that innovative life styles are more readily adopted in larger cities. Of the men who were living in cities with more than one million in population, 29 percent had cohabited, and 8 percent currently were cohabiting. As size of city of residence decreases, the percentage who have ever cohabited or who were cohabiting decreases. Relatively few of the respondents currently reside outside the United States, but 33 percent of these men had cohabited, and 9 percent currently were cohabiting. In addition, higher percentages of the men living in the more densely populated Northeastern region and in the Western region had cohabited or were cohabiting than was the case for men living in the Southern and North Central regions. To some extent, these differences may reflect the migration of more innovative men into larger cities and toward the Northeast and West. Another possibility is that the sociocultural milieu of the larger cities and these regions is more tolerant of "unconventional" behavior or alternative life styles.

Church attendance. The frequency of church attendance is also related to cohabitation. Only 7 percent of the men who indicated that they attend religious services once a week had ever cohabited, and only 1 percent of them were cohabiting. In contrast, 26 percent of the men who never attend church had cohabited, and 8 percent were cohabiting at the time they were interviewed. Furthermore, those who attend church with some degree of regularity were more likely to be married and less likely to be living independently than those who never attend religious services.

BEHAVIORAL CORRELATES

The associations between cohabitation and 11 kinds of behavior (some of which may be considered unconventional) are shown in Table 4. Two of the items—voter registration and political campaigning—clearly reflect conventional activities. The respondents have not been mere passive observers of the political scene: 72 percent have registered to vote, 22 percent have participated in

TABLE 4 *Behavioral Correlates of Cohabitation and Current Living Arrangements*

| Number | Total | | Ever cohabited | | Current living arrangements | | | |
	N	%	Yes 444	No 2066	Married 1309	Cohabiting 120	Independent 796	Living with parents 285
					Percentages			
Have You Ever:								
a) Lived in a commune?	129	5	14	3	3	16	8	3
b) Attended an outdoor rock concert or festival?	1173	47	69	42	34	70	62	52
c) Meditated, or explored an eastern religion or philosophy?	396	16	27	13	10	24	25	13
d) Joined a street gang?	273	11	17	10	11	15	10	11
e) Registered to vote?	1795	72	68	72	71	67	74	67
f) Followed a vegetarian, macrobiotic, or organic diet?	200	8	17	6	4	20	12	8
g) Campaigned or worked for a political candidate, issue, or cause?	553	22	27	21	18	29	29	19
h) Taken part in a political demonstration?	368	15	24	13	10	26	21	15
i) Studied astrology, ESP or the occult?	406	16	25	14	10	26	25	14
j) Bummed around the United States or elsewhere?	399	16	35	12	11	41	23	10
k) Thought pretty seriously about committing suicide?	211	8	15	7	6	16	12	6

some kind of political campaign, and 15 percent have taken part in a political demonstration.

Almost one-half of the respondents have attended an outdoor rock concert or festival. Approximately one of every six respondents has meditated, or explored an Eastern religion or philosophy; studied astrology, ESP, or the occult; and "bummed around" the United States or elsewhere. On the other hand, relatively few of the men have ever belonged to a street gang; followed a macrobiotic diet or organic diet; contemplated suicide; or lived in a commune.

There is a consistent relationship between participation in these kinds of activities and both the lifetime prevalence of cohabitation and current cohabitation. With the exception of voter registration, the percentage of men who report each of the other kinds of behavior is always higher for those who have cohabited than for those who have not. Similar differences are observed between those who were cohabiting and the married men. The men living independently are more similar to those who were cohabiting than to the married men. In contrast, the percentages for the respondents still living with their parents are strikingly similar to those of the married men. The differences, then, are not merely a function of age. Rather, cohabitation is a relatively unconventional form of behavior, at least at this point in time, and those who have ever cohabited or were cohabiting are more likely to have engaged in other kinds of behavior that are considered unconventional according to current social standards.

NONMEDICAL USE OF DRUGS

Another form of unconventional behavior is nonmedical or illicit drug use. The relationships between cohabitation and drug use are shown in Table 5. Drug use refers to the lifetime prevalence or "ever use" of these substances, and two licit drugs, tobacco and alcohol, are included for comparative purposes. For the licit drugs, the differences between those who have and have not cohabited are minimal. However, the men who have ever cohabited are more likely to have used each of the other substances than are those who have not cohabited. With the exception of heroin, the differences in terms of percentage points range from 22 to 30. Similarly, higher percentages of the men who currently were cohabiting report use of each of the illicit drugs than those with other living arrangements. With one minor exception, the percentages are lowest among the married men. For example, 7 percent of the married men, in comparison with 41 percent of those who were cohabiting, have used cocaine. Although not shown in tabular form, these patterns were also observed when comparisons were made in terms of current use as well as heavy or extensive use of these drugs.

The data presented in Tables 4 and 5 suggest that cohabitation is correlated with other behavior that is defined as unconventional. The reader is cautioned not to draw unwarranted causal inferences because the temporal order of these forms of behavior has not been

TABLE 5 *Cohabitation and Current Living Arrangements by Use of Nine Drug Classes*

			Ever cohabited		Current living arrangements			
Number		Total 2510	Yes 444	No 2066	Married 1309	Cohabiting 120	Independent 796	Living with parents 285
	Number	Percentage				Percentages		
Ever Used:								
Tobacco	2211	88	93	88	91	91	87	78
Alcohol	2434	97	100	96	97	100	97	94
Marihuana	1382	55	79	50	46	83	68	51
Psychedelics	550	22	46	16	13	52	34	20
Stimulants	581	23	47	17	16	48	34	15
Sedatives	409	16	34	12	9	41	26	12
Heroin	148	6	16	3	3	18	9	6
Opiates	493	20	41	15	13	44	28	16
Cocaine	352	14	35	9	7	41	23	12

established, nor have controls for antecedent variables been instituted to test the relationships for spuriousness (see Hirschi and Selvin, 1973).

AGE AT FIRST SEXUAL INTERCOURSE

Cohabitation refers to nonmarital heterosexual living arrangements, and with few exceptions, sexual intercourse constitutes one facet of these relationships. The extent of nonmarital sexual activity is known to be correlated with the age at which intercourse first occurs (Zelnik and Kantner, 1972; Levin and Levin, 1975). The data in Table 6 show the relationship between age at first intercourse and cohabitation.

Twenty-seven percent of the respondents indicated that they had engaged in intercourse by the age of 15. The comparable figures for those who have and have not cohabited are 48 and 23 percent, respectively. Only 172 (7 percent) of the men reported that they had never experienced sexual intercourse. In terms of current living arrangements, 25 percent of the married men, in comparison with 47 percent of those cohabiting, reported that they had initially engaged in intercourse by the age of 15. These data suggest that men who have sexual intercourse at an early age are more likely to enter nonmarital heterosexual unions than those who first experience intercourse at a later age.

SUMMARY AND CONCLUSIONS

The current and lifetime prevalence of heterosexual cohabitation, as well as some correlates of cohabitation, are examined in this paper on the basis of data obtained from a nationwide random sample of 2,510 young men. Eighteen percent of the respondents had lived with a woman for six months or more outside the bonds of matrimony, but 65 percent of these men had done so with only one partner. Furthermore, at the time of the interviews, only 5 percent of the men were cohabiting. The data indicate that in terms of serious heterosexual relationships most young men in the United States are conventional.

While some differences were observed according to age, size of city of residence to age 18 and social class background, the antecedent variable that yielded the greatest difference in cohabitation was ethnicity. Twenty-nine percent of the blacks had cohabited in comparison with 16 percent of the whites; and 8 and 4 percent, respectively, of the blacks and whites currently were cohabiting. The men who were not enrolled in school and those who were high school dropouts were more likely to have cohabited or to be cohabiting than others. Cohabitation also was related to residence in large cities and in the Northeastern and Western regions, as well as such unconventional activities as studying an eastern religion or philosophy, using illicit drugs, and experiencing sexual intercourse at an early age.

TABLE 6 *Cohabitation and Current Living Arrangements by Age at First Sexual Intercourse*

Age at first sexual Intercourse	Total	Ever cohabited		Current living arrangements			
		Yes	No	Married	Cohabiting	Independent	Living with parents
Number	2510	444	2066	1309	120	796	285
				Percentages			
13 or younger	10	21	8	8	22	12	10
14–15	17	27	15	17	25	16	17
16–17	26	26	26	28	24	24	20
18–19	22	18	23	24	16	22	18
20 or older	17	8	19	22	13	15	8
Never	7	1[a]	8	1[b]	0	11	26

[a] This figure represents 5 of the 444 men who had ever cohabited. While these respondents said they had lived as a partner with a woman, it is possible that these men only shared living accommodations and did not have sexual relationships.

[b] A total of 15 of the 1,309 men who currently were married and living with their wives reported that they had never had sexual intercourse. The question about the year in which intercourse initially occurred was included in a self-administered questionnaire. It is possible that these men interpreted the question in reference to premarital intercourse. It also is possible that they answered the question accurately.

It would appear that neither cohabitation nor marriage has reached a peak in terms of prevalence among the young men born in the years 1944 through 1954. A sizable proportion of the men are "at risk" to cohabit or marry. It is noteworthy that 21 percent of the men who formerly were married were cohabiting, whereas only 8 percent of the men who had never married were doing so. This suggests, but certainly does not demonstrate, that some of the men who are currently married may, if they experience marital disruption, establish a nonmarital heterosexual union. On the other hand, it was inferred that for 37 percent of the men with one experience in cohabitation and one marriage, cohabitation had led to marriage. Thus, cohabitation may be a prelude to marriage for some persons. For others, especially those who have experienced an unsatisfactory marriage, cohabitation may be a temporary or permanent alternative to matrimony. These are suggestions, not causal inferences and, indeed, it would be inappropriate to draw causal inferences from the descriptive data presented in this paper.

A number of questions about cohabitation remain unanswered. One of these concerns lifetime prevalence, and in subsequent research older persons should not be ignored. Although no systematic data are available, anecdotal reports indicate that Social Security requirements have resulted in extensive "shacking up" among retired persons. Efforts should be made to examine both historical and maturational effects in future studies. Additional data are also needed regarding: (a) the incidence of new cases of cohabitation each year and the age at which cohabitation occurs; (b) the demographic, attitudinal, personality, and behavioral characteristics of persons who cohabit; and (c) the influence of significant events—for example, full-time employment, college graduation, divorce, and retirement—on cohabitation.

REFERENCES

Campbell, Donald T., and Julian C. Stanley
    1963 Experimental and Quasi-Experimental Designs for Research. Chicago:Rand McNally.

Henze, Lura F., and John W. Hudson
    1974 "Personal and family characteristics of cohabiting and non-cohabiting college students." Journal of Marriage and the Family 36 (November) :722–727.

Hirschi, Travis, and Hanan C. Selvin
    1973 Principles of Survey Analysis. New York:Free Press.

Johnson, Michael P.
    1969 "Courtship and commitment: A study of cohabitation on a university campus." Unpublished master's thesis, University of Iowa, Iowa City.

Levin, Robert J., and Amy Levin
    1975 "Sexual pleasure: The surprising preferences of 100,000 women." Redbook 145 (September) :51–58.

Lewis, Robert
1973 "A logitudinal test of a developmental framework for premarital dyadic formation." Journal of Marriage and the Family 35 (February) :16–25.

Lewis, Robert, Graham B. Spanier, Virginia Storm, and Charlotte Lehecka
1975 "Commitment in married and unmarried cohabitation." Paper presented at meetings of the American Sociological Association, San Francisco, August.

Macklin, Eleanor D.
1972 "Heterosexual cohabitation among unmarried college students." The Family Coordinator 21 (October) :463–472.

O'Donnell, John A., Harwin L., Voss, Richard R. Clayton, Gerald T. Slatin, and Robin G. W. Room
1976 Young Men and Drugs: A Nationwide Survey. National Institute on Drug Abuse. Washington, D.C.: U.S. Government Printing Office.

Peterman, Dan J., Carl A. Ridley, and Scott M. Anderson
1974 "A comparison of cohabiting and noncohabiting college students." Journal of Marriage and the Family 36 (May) :344–354.

Zelnik, Melvin, and John F. Kantner
1972 "Sexuality, contraception and pregnancy among young unwed females in the United States." Pp. 355–374 in Charles F. Westoff and Robert Parke, Jr. (Eds.), Demographic and Social Aspects of Population Growth. Washington, D.C.: U.S. Government Printing Office.

FOOTNOTES

1. Further analysis of the data is needed. Specifically, interviewer effects have not been assessed.

   While the interviews could not be conducted anonymously in view of the fact that the subjects were drawn from Selective Service listings, the respondents were assured that they would never be identified. Each respondent was informed that the study was being conducted under a grant of confidentiality obtained from the Attorney General of the United States according to provisions in the Comprehensive Drug Abuse Prevention and Control Act of 1970. The grant of confidentiality provided the investigators with authority "to withhold the names and other identifying characteristics of persons who are the subjects of research conducted pursuant to and in conformity with this research project. You may not be compelled in any Federal, State or local civil, criminal, administrative, legislative, or other proceeding to identify the subjects of such research."

2. The men who had cohabited or married were asked an additional series of questions—when the relationship began, the age of the partner, drug use of the partner, her educational attainment, and whether or not she worked all or most of the time—regarding their latest or only relationship and, if applicable, their first relationship. In the analysis this information is utilized to assess whether cohabitating partners subsequently married.

3. The "later" marriages were almost all second marriages. Of the 107 men who reported multiple marriages, 104 had been married twice, and 3 had been married three times. The marriages of 2 of the latter 3 men were intact.

4. It should be noted that the relationship between city size and cohabitation may reflect the concentration in large cities of blacks who, as will be noted, were more likely to have cohabited.

6.

Cohabitation: The Tender Trap

Emma Stevens
Stephen Holmes

Are you living with a lady? Thinking about maybe living alone or moving in with a different lady? Before you tell your roommate to start checking the apartment listings, you'd better study the new rules of the cohabitation game.

For example, you probably don't know that you may have to give her half of everything you accumulated while she was living with you. You may even find that you owe her alimony. How about this for a surprise: You may have to pay her a "salary" for all the time she was with you.

You think the business world is rough? Wait until she files for divorce. You may end up trying to prove that you were never married—your word against hers.

Are you married—officially, that is? Do you keep a companion on the side? You may be an unwitting bigamist. Your wife could sue you, your ladyfriend could also sue you and the state could finish you off with a criminal prosecution.

Are you married but living with someone else? The "else" could be accumulating the same rights your wife has. Possibly more.

Hold on, you say? We've got you in shackles already and you haven't even committed a crime (at least none you know of). As they say, ignorance of the law is no excuse. Let's start from the top. If you're single and want to enjoy a lovely roommate, the courts are now proclaiming that she has a right to some of the money and property you acquire during the time she lives with you. A judge may also decide that you have to pay her money for the value of her time spent as your cook, housewife and companion.

Perhaps an example will help: A few years ago, you met Michelle and so enjoyed her company that you asked her to move in with you. You came to depend on having her around all the time. One night, as you were falling asleep, blissfully drained, you mumbled something about her going along on your next business trip. She couldn't get away from her job, she said. You vaguely remember saying, "To heck with your job. I'll take care of you." There followed those peaceful years when she took care of your house, traveled with you, entertained your business associates and generally enhanced the tranquillity of your life. But you change and inevitably you met another lady who better suited your needs at the time. Exeunt Michelle. Enter the new lover. Michelle asked for help while she reentered the wage market. You gave her a little money until you thought she had had enough time to find a job. And that should have ended that chapter of your life, right?

Wrong. Change the facts a little and you have the case involving Lee Marvin and Michelle Triola. Lee was married for the first two years that he lived with Michelle, but he didn't marry her after his divorce. Nevertheless, Michelle found it more socially convenient to have her last name changed to Marvin. After six years, Lee married his high school sweetheart. He gave Michelle support money for over a year, during which she found it impossible to resume her lapsed career as a singer-entertainer. Then Michelle filed suit, claiming half of everything Lee had earned while they'd been living together. She also wanted permanent support payments. Lee, she said, had promised her everything if she would just be his lady.

At first, she couldn't find an attorney to take her case; when she did, she ran into the unsympathetic trial and appellate courts. Her final appeal was to the most prestigious state court in the land—the California Supreme Court. Armed with brilliant briefs, attorney David M. Brown argued for the rights of all unmarried couples who live together. On December 27, 1976, Michelle won. The old rules of the living-together game were blown apart.

Here are the new rules:

1. Sin, morality and adultery are out.
2. The gender of your roommate is unimportant.
3. If you and your lady have agreed that she has any rights to your property, the courts will enforce the contract.
4. If the courts can infer from your conduct that you two have any kind of implied or tacit agreement, they will enforce that, too.
5. If an unmarried couple has no express, tacit or implied agreements, it is up to judges to examine the expectations of the

parties and then equitably divide property acquired during the relationship.

6. If you lead her to believe that she is not just donating her time working in your home or in your business, the courts will probably award her a reasonable salary.

7. Judges may also infer that you are obligated to support her after she moves out.

8. The courts will not enforce any agreement for payment of sexual services—that's prostitution.

When do the rules apply to you? When you cross the line between "just dating" and "being involved," not a very clear distinction.

You're at the *disco*. There's a lithe female animal spinning sinuously in the strobe lights. Soon you're dancing with her. Afterward, at a table, you're both laughing and chatting. Later, you intertwine those perfect bodies in love. That's a casual encounter; no legal problems.

You go to work the next day, but your mind keeps focusing on her. You go out with her again. She's tall and sensuous and, my God, you can talk with her for hours. How did you get so lucky? And now it has to be weekends away, playing with her, listening to her, loving with her. You're not seeing much of your home anymore (or she's not seeing much of hers). You're doing everything together. You may have crossed the line.

Generally, you're all right in a straight dating situation. But if you start making promises to each other concerning shared goals, if you begin investing time and money together for a common purpose, that's not just dating. The courts will treat you like any two people who have made an agreement. That is contract law.

Here's an example of conduct that may amount to a contract while you're still dating:

You find that "almost" dream investment, a run-down apartment house with tremendous potential. All it needs is a little paint and plumbing and landscaping. She may or may not put some money into it, but you two spend all your spare time fixing it up—painting stairs, with dirty hands, big smiles, eating cheese sandwiches while you lie on the floor. You never talk about the implications of what you're doing, but you can't say that she's just donating her time. She may have some expectations, may be entitled to the reasonable value of her services in helping you renovate the building. Or she may have a right to some percentage of the profits from the increased rental income. This sort of thing normally happens after you're cohabiting, but it doesn't matter that you're not. At least with respect to this project, the courts may see your conduct as indicating an implied partnership, joint venture or the like.

What happens when you move in together? One thing is clear: All the cases concerning cohabiters say that neither party acquires any rights from the mere fact of their living together. If they live together in a vacuum: They don't speak to each other. Each pays his own way. Each does his own dishes and laundry and buys and cooks his own food. Each does *nothing* for the benefit of the other.

Well, if that's cohabitation, you can have it. No two people live together without having some expectations even before they move in. You can't spend much time with a lady who's sharing your home before you have tacit, implied or expressed agreements concerning the conduct of your joint lives. She helps you—you help her. It's a way of life. You have definitely crossed the line. What the *Marvin* case did was recognize human nature and the fact that we all live in an economic world. It said that a court must analyze all the circumstances involved in each cohabitation relationship and then, with respect to money or property, equitably fulfill the expectations of the couple. The male (and it's still usually the man) can no longer keep all of the union's property when the inevitable breakup comes.

So, you see, the new rules become applicable not because you live with that lady but because of *how* you two share your lives. You can have two, ten or just one home. You can be married to someone else. The *Marvin* ruling applies because of the expectations of the partners. If she structures her life to fit in with yours— either because you want her to or because you allow her to—they apply.

Let's explore what that means in economic terms. Michelle and Lee represent the normal factual setting of the living-together couple: The man works for wages and the woman works at home for the man. When the sweetness ends, the property and income accumulated during the alliance will probably be divided equally between you (absent a contract to the contrary); you may have to support her until she can re-enter the job market; or you may *just* owe her about $13,000 for each year that she was your housemate, companion and general factotum.

Now, you may be thinking that because you earn $25,000 and she brings in merely $12,000 and you have a pooling contract, you are entitled to receive twice as much as she does when the property is divided. Not so. To the court, she's been assuming the role of a housewife also. Economists estimate the value of a homemaker's services in excess of $13,000 a year. The total of her income and services puts her up there in the 50–50 situation.

The reason a housewife's services are so valuable is that they free you from expenses for a maid, driver, cook, hostess and party caterer, to name a few. Also, the lady's services are seen as a direct contribution to your career and income capacity—a man living with a woman in a stable relationship is less suicidal, less criminal and healthier physically and mentally.

Of course, if the two of you are sharing the homemaking chores, you merely add one half of the value of those services to your respective incomes and divide the property according to the percentages you arrive at that way.

Naturally, these examples don't cover all situations. Apply the basic principles to your own setup. But if you have a written contract, it will govern.

Contracts. Percentages. Reasonable value of services. Good God, all you want is to have an extended sexual encounter with the fringe benefit of having her live with you. If that's all there is to your relationship, you may be all right for a while; but when the relationship goes on and you set up "housekeeping," the new rules will apply to you.

And the *Marvin* guidelines *will* apply to you. Don't think that you're safe just because you don't live in California. Michelle and Lee weren't the first couple to live together and California isn't the first state to recognize the rights of unmarried women. Quietly, beginning in 1909, state after state has been enforcing all sorts of oral and written contracts between cohabiters—even where the relationship itself has been illegal, immoral or adulterous.

Several decades ago, couples held themselves out as man and wife because of social pressure. But to the courts, it makes no difference whether or not the couple have been known as Mr. and Mrs. when a division of property is at issue.

In 1909, Margreth Williams strode in front of the justices of the Texas Supreme Court, declaring that her old man had said that if they combined their labor, skills and earnings and bought a ranch, she would own half. She admitted that she was the backup while he went out and earned the actual bread to buy the place, and she said she had never actually contributed a cent to the purchase price. She stared them straight in the eyes and said, "A promise is a promise and I want half of that ranch." Margreth got her half. Even back then, a woman's services were equal to a man's when the parties agreed to pool their efforts. Does that remind you of the *Marvin* ruling? It should. That case was brought to that court's attention.

In the years that followed, many other states enforced those oral promises that nobody thought he had to keep: Arkansas (1911), Minnesota (1921), South Dakota (1927; in that case, they also gave the woman temporary "alimony"), Tennessee (1932), Delaware (1934), California (1943), Florida (1947), Wisconsin (1947), New York (1950), Arizona (1952), Idaho (1955), Washington (1957), Vermont (1960), Louisiana (1966), North Carolina (1969). In 1975, the Michigan Supreme Court even went so far as to give a female workman's-compensation survivor benefits just because she had been living with a man.

But wait, you say, don't a large number of states that find cohabitation either illegal or against public policy still refuse the lady any interest in your property? Yes, that's true.

States such as Louisiana have statutes that deny, in effect, *only the female* any rights arising from nonmarital unions (however, in 1966, one court found a way around the statutes). But by 1969, law-review articles began to attack the validity of those statutes because they discriminate against a woman who chooses an alternate lifestyle. David Brown's briefs collect the United States Supreme Court's constitutional decisions on the subject. Those cases make it clear that statutes such as Louisiana's will fall under constitutional attacks.

For example, Michelle's petition said:

> The distinction made by California between married and nonmarried relationships raises serious constitutional questions. The United States Supreme Court has stated on more than one occasion that family life is a uniquely private area in which individual decisions are protected against governmental intrusion. The nonmarried family can be presumed to have all of the characteristics that make the married family unit constitutionally protected: They involve fundamental decisions which determine the character of a person's life; they are of a uniquely personal nature; they often implicate profound human relationships; and they generally center around the home. If an individual has a fundamental right to structure his own home life and decide with whom he wishes to live, governmental action or inaction which seeks to place unnecessary burdens upon the exercise of such right would appear to require compelling justification.

Couples recently have been found to have constitutionally protected rights to privacy and freedom of association with which neither the Federal nor the state government may interfere. These rights are embodied, among other places, in the due-process and equal-protection clauses of the U.S. Constitution. And while it is true that the present U.S. Supreme Court is somewhat retarded in its thinking, reliance need not be placed on it. Most states will follow the reasoning and example of California and find "independent" state grounds for giving cohabs protection in order to prevent the Federal Supreme Court from having a say in the matter.

Nobody knows how many people in the U.S. are cohabiters holding themselves out as man and wife. What *is* known from Census Bureau statistics is that between 1970 and 1976, there was a 100 percent increase in the number of people who were openly cohabiting and retaining their individual identities. A reasonable extrapolation of the cases and the statistics suggests that the present number of people involved in nonmarried relationships in the U.S. alone is in the millions.

But there are also compelling economic reasons for the states to step in and protect the expectations of couples living together. It used to be that a woman had to and could depend upon a man to support her. Today there are more women than men and there aren't enough wealthy men to support them all. Women have to be able to take care of themselves or go on the public dole. If a lady forgoes her earning capacity to live with and help a man, it's going to take her time to become an adequate income producer again. The case being made more and more often is that there is no reason why the male who's responsible for her being temporarily unable to provide for herself should not bear the burden of her support until she gets back on her feet. Otherwise, she becomes a public charge. Divorce laws provide the dependent spouse with a re-entry vehicle to society—alimony. And the courts are now saying that cohabitation is a kissing cousin to marriage. That's why they're creating judicial remedies to provide unmarried spouses with the means to sustain themselves until they are economically self-sufficient.

So either you protect yourself or it's a good bet that the courts will start distributing your cash as if you were a philanthropic organization.

How *do* you protect yourself? Either before you cohabit or early in the union, you must enter into a written contract that covers both of your expectations. (No, you don't have to make her sign a contract before you spend that second joyous night together, but have her sign it if she has lived with you for a month and has moved her belongings in.) Generally, whatever you put in the contract will be enforced by the courts, if necessary.

The agreement may be as simple as a release, on her part, of any and all interests in your income and property acquisitions during the union and of any anticipations that she may have of your support when she leaves. Or it may be as complicated as necessary. You don't need an attorney. Just jot down what property rights each of you thinks are involved, date the paper and sign it. "We are a partnership," dated, signed. Easy.

It's also a good idea to make a new memorandum of your mutual understandings every so often. If your contract is old, either of you can claim that it has been changed by oral agreement and you may be shocked to learn what your partner thinks the new understanding is: Making note of the changes is the only way you can be certain you won't be in for some big surprises.

This may all sound tedious, but you should actually be pleased with the *Marvin* decision. Its benefits far outweigh its disadvantages. It's true that you may have to contract for your economic survival, but without those tangible written promises, the lady might go into court and prove that you are married.

Married?

You remember that little business trip the two of you took when you signed in at all the hotels as man and wife? Has she been using your charge cards and signing your name with a Mrs. in front? Did you file a joint tax return in order to be in a lower income bracket? Can you say for sure whether or not your neighbors think you're married? Do you have any children living with you? Do they call you Daddy? If you're married and you keep a lady in a condominium you own or in an apartment you rent, is your professional business card on the door or the mailbox? All that's required in the District of Columbia and 13 states (Alabama, Colorado, Georgia, Idaho, Iowa, Kansas, Montana, Ohio, Oklahoma, Pennsylvania, Rhode Island, South Carolina and Texas) is a private oral agreement between the two of you that you are married—*and you are married.* This is known as common-law marriage and if you have ever resided with your lady in one of those states, the wedlock will be recognized and enforced there and everywhere else in the world. It's your word against hers. This legal union may be proved in law by the mere fact of cohabitation coupled with reputation as man and wife. New York lets you marry by private written agreement, but even if that's lost, you're still a husband. Even if you already have a wife, the courts of these states may find that you've entered into a second, bigamous, common-law marriage and may divide your property between your two wives while you spend the next ten years in jail. If you have lived with a woman for three years in New Hampshire, you are married. In Virginia, you will have to prove that you aren't married. And in over half of the states, for many purposes, even if you can prove you aren't married, you will still be treated as if you were. That's not common-law marriage; that's judicial shotgun marriage.

Here's a case you're going to love: *Warner vs. Warner*—Supreme Court of Idaho (common-law marriage state) —decided in 1955. The man and a married woman started off as simple cohabiters. When she got that final decree of divorce from her legal husband, she told Warner, the man she was living with, she wanted to leave him, too. He said, "Pleeeeease don't go. Live with me as my wife." She did. Nine months later, she split anyway and filed for divorce from him. He went into court and said, "Hey, we were merely cohabiters and because that relationship is illegal, she has no rights." The court said he was trying to deny her property rights. He got it with both barrels.

First the court said that during the initial, illicit period of cohabitation, while she was married to another man, she acquired permanent rights to her lover's property. "A court of equity will protect the property rights of the parties in such cases, either according to their agreement in respect to property or according to principles of equity and justice."

While he was reeling, the court hit him again. It said that he *must* have made some promises to make her stay with him. Therefore, the court would not allow him to deny the validity of the nine-month marriage. It then granted her a divorce *and divided his property a second time.* Beware of those glib promises; she may be carrying a tape recorder.

Have her sign that contract tonight. "OK," you say, "what should it include?" (See the sample documents at the end of this article.) Start with your names. End by dating and signing it. Everything in between is up to you. You shouldn't wait too long after she moves in before you do it, though. If she's been living with you for a while before you contract or when you make changes and she does go to court, the judge may decide that you were involved in a "confidential relationship." This means that she reposed trust and confidence in you and you are obligated to deal openly and fairly with her. A grossly unfair contract dated late in your union would be deemed a result of your "undue influence" and would be set aside. A written release when she moves in is fine. But don't be greedy later. If after you cohabit for a while and you contract to pool your mutual earnings and you are to take everything—she gets nothing, not even reasonable value of her services as perhaps your bookkeeper—that's an extreme example of unfair dealings.

The Mutual Release and the Cohabitation Contract are models only. Do not automatically use them in your situations. The language of each is unfortunately legalistic and you may not fully appreciate all the implications of either without first seeking the advice of an attorney. Both are best used as forms to be followed by you as guidelines in the areas that you want to cover for your own purposes. You should write your own release or cohabitation contract in plain, clear and ordinary language, so that the rights and obligations undertaken by both signators will be easily understood.

On the other hand, couples with a stable relationship who want to be certain that their bargains will be carried out should have their attorney prepare a contract in the form of a business agreement. Make yourselves a partnership, a joint venture or a corporation. Many married couples do exactly that so that they can obtain all the benefits allowed under the Federal tax laws. The tax consequences of such contracts are complicated (for example, you have to have the intention of doing business for a profit), but, generally speaking, you can split income just as married couples do when they file a joint return. You will be entitled to greater deductions from income. Reduce your total personal income. Lower your tax bracket and still take the singles' deductions. If you decide that you want to have all of these advantages, employ a tax attorney to structure your transactions and prepare your contract. He will know what to do.

You may save thousands of dollars. Of course, on paper, your alliance looks very complicated, but nothing in your life has actually changed. It is far easier for two single people than for marrieds to structure their economic lives in order to legally avoid tax liability. The Internal Revenue Service has an obstacle course of regulations designed to prevent wedded spouses from taking many deductions that are readily available to singles acting in alliance.

Courts are used to enforcing business contracts. Cohabitation agreements are new. The former will be readily upheld, while the latter might not be automatically acceptable. Pick the pact that best suits you. But do express your bargains in writing. The new rules of the living-together ball game will be applied to you. Turn them to your advantage.

You will want your contracts or releases to specify that they are governed by California law and that all disputes arising out of them must be resolved through binding arbitration in front of an arbiter instead of a judge. Business contracts normally specify what state's law is to be applied, so that they can get the maximum contractual benefits allowed. You know that California has decided that living-together contracts are valid and binding. You get the maximum benefit by making its law applicable. An arbitration hearing can be set, had and all disputes resolved within a matter of months, instead of the two to five years it normally takes in any civil case. As for costs, an arbitration hearing is like buying at Woolworth's instead of Saks. The arbiter should be given a copy of the *Marvin* decision, along with the contract.

SAMPLE DOCUMENTS TO MAKE LIVING TOGETHER LESS PAINFUL IN THE END

MUTUAL RELEASE

This mutual release agreement is entered into this _____ day of _____, 19_____, by and between _____ _____ and _____.

We are desirous of entering into a cohabitation relationship but do not desire to acquire any rights or obligations with respect to property, income, support that might otherwise accrue to either of us by reason of this temporary union.

We therefore give these, our mutual and complete releases, each to the other. We hereby waive any and all rights or interest in the property or income of the other that might in any manner arise by reason of our cohabitation or the rendition of services one to the other. We specifically waive any and all rights, additionally, to support, maintenance, child custody or child support that may arise in any manner from our association.

We further agree that we are not now married nor shall we ever claim that we are legally married unless subsequent to the date of execution by us of this instrument we enter into a duly licensed formal marriage.

In the event that any dispute or legal cause of action arises between us relating to this or any subsequent agreement between us, we hereby agree that the same may be determined only by an arbitrator selected by the American Arbitration Association. We each hereby relinquish any right we may have to have any other person whomsoever represent either of us at any hearing before such arbitrator. The arbitrator's decision, it is hereby agreed, shall be binding, final and nonappealable. The arbitrator shall not have the right or the power to award as part of his determination of any dispute any fee, cost or expense incurred by either of us relating to the dispute or the hearing before the arbitrator, except the arbitrator's fees and a hearing reporter's fees.

DATED: _____ SIGNED: _____

(man)

_____

(woman)

COHABITATION CONTRACT

This agreement made this _____ day of _____, 19_____, by and between _____ and _____, who presently reside in the state of _____.

Whereas we wish to enter into a state of cohabitation similar to matrimony but do not wish to be bound by the statutory or case-law provisions relating to marriage:

It is hereby agreed that we shall cohabit for an indefinite period of time subject to the following terms:

1. That we agree that we are a partnership for all purposes;
2. That any children born of us shall have the surname _____;
3. That any real or personal property acquired during the relationship shall be deemed to be owned equally;
4. That all income of either of us and all our accumulations during the existence of the cohabitation shall be one fund from which all our debts and expenses arising during the existence of this union shall be paid and each of us shall have an equal interest in the sum thereof, and equal right to the management and control thereof, and an equal entitlement to the excess remaining after satisfaction of all such debts and expenses;
5. That if the man is desirous of an abortion of any embryo caused to be created by us but the woman is desirous of bearing the child, the woman hereby releases the man from any and all legal obligations of any nature whatsoever that he might otherwise have by reason of the birth of such a child; and the man must express his disapproval of the birth in writing, signed and notarized and given to the woman at least five months prior to the birth;
6. That the woman shall have the exclusive right to determine whether or not she may obtain an abortion;
7. That if both of us are desirous of having and do have a child by our union, such child shall be maintained and supported from the aforesaid fund for as long as we shall cohabit and we both shall be equally obligated for the support of said child upon termination of our relationship; and that we shall, upon termination, be equally obligated to expend not less than one fifth of our respective incomes for the maintenance and education of such child until it reaches the age of its majority is deceased, whichever first occurs;
8. That our cohabitation may be terminated at the sole will and election of either of us expressed by a written notice thereof given one to the other;
9. That this agreement may be modified in any manner by any agreement in writing signed by both parties, except that no modifications may decrease the obligations that we have agreed to undertake with respect to any children born of our union;

10. That both of us shall have joint custody of any children and the woman shall have their care and control unless otherwise agreed;

11. All property listed on the pages attached hereto and that are made part of this agreement by this reference, and are signed by both of us, is the separate property owned by the one under whose name it is listed prior to the making of this agreement. All listed property is and shall continue to be the separate property of the party now owning it;

12. All property received by either of us by gift or inheritance during the duration of our cohabitation shall be the separate property of the one so receiving it;

13. If either party fails or refuses to perform any obligation required by this agreement, that one shall be responsible for and hold the other harmless from any and all legal fees, expenses and costs incurred by the other in obtaining such performance or in securing the rights of the other, including those incurred in seeking damages for the breach of this agreement;

14. That the validity of this agreement shall be determined solely under the laws of the State of California as they may from time to time be changed;

15. Upon termination of this agreement by either party, the real and personal property acquired and owned as aforesaid shall be sold and the proceeds of such sale or sales shall be divided equally between us unless both of us agree otherwise in writing, signed by both of us; and,

16. In the event that any dispute or legal cause of action arises between us relating to either this or any subsequent agreement between us, we hereby agree that the same may be determined only by an arbiter selected by the American Arbitration Association. We each hereby relinquish any right we may have to have any other person whomsoever represent either of us at any hearing before such arbiter. The arbiter's decision, it is hereby agreed, shall be binding, final and nonappealable. Both parties shall equally bear the arbiter's fees.

DATED: _____ SIGNED: _____

_____
(man)

_____
(woman)

The execution of this agreement was witnessed by _____
_____.

The parties acknowledge that they have signed this agreement and said acknowledgment is notarized by _____.

Part
Three

What Form
Marriage?

*I*F MARRIAGE IS HERE TO STAY, which is one of the cautious conclusions reached in the commentary for Part One, then the question of what forms marriage might possibly take should be considered. Discussions of marriage alternatives have been given increased attention in marriage and family literature as well as in the media. The phrase *marriage alternatives* actually has two usages. On the one hand, it refers to living arrangements which would be alternative to, in the sense of taking the place of, what is now commonly called marriage. On the other hand, it might refer simply to the possible variety of forms which could be attained within the arrangement which could still be called marriage.

In the editor's "Introduction," the position was taken that any living arrangement which served what we generally call family functions could theoretically and realistically be called a family. Along this same line, any persons involved in carrying out these same functions cooperatively might be said to be married to one another or at least to form a family. Thus, the only alternative to marriage within this meaning would be nonmarriage, that is, choosing to live either alone or in some arrangement which performed none of those basic functions.

Since nonmarriage was dealt with in Part One, the focus here will be upon marriage alternatives in the second sense, that is, upon the varieties of possible living arrangements which create families and perform family functions. More specifically, we are concerned here with the current status and the future of traditional monogamy as the common and currently the only legal marriage form in America.

Young people tend to be interested in the prospect of trying out new forms of marriage, but the fact is that, at least with respect to marriage forms, there is "nothing new under the sun." Humans have at one time or another tried every possible type of structural arrangement for carrying out family functions. These experimental forms have not been limited to preliterate or non-Western cultures; they have taken their place in United States history with such well-known groups as the Oneida Community and the Mormons, as well as à number of other less famous attempts. Needless to say, none of these organized attempts to restructure the family has ever succeeded for any appreciable length of time.

With respect to the possible alternatives which family or marriage structure might take, there are several limitations which not only affect the number of available possibilities, but also influence their chances of success. These limitations may be categorized as biological on the one hand and sociocultural on the other. Of course, one of the aims of those proposing or attempting new forms is the overcoming of these limitations, especially the sociocultural ones.

Biological limitations are those placed upon humans and social institutions by their physical makeup and environmental requirements. In the first place, the bearing of children requires at least one male and one female who are sexually mature and fertile. Thus, any arrangement which could be called marriage must have at least one male and one female member. (Some homosexuals have attempted to "marry," but since this arrangement could not carry out the major marital function of procreation, it would be difficult to label it a marriage in the sense in which the term is used here.)

An additional biological limitation is found in the fact that one man may serve as the mate to several women for procreational purposes, but the obverse is not true, since men cannot carry and bear children. This is probably the reason why *polygyny,* the marriage of one man to several women, is more prevalent than is *polyandry,* the marriage of one woman to several men. The former is conducive to much more reliable population maintenance than is the latter. Of course, monogamy rather than any of these multiple forms is by far the most prevalent form throughout the world both currently and historically.

There does exist the biological possibility of a group marriage in which several men and several women are all commonly married to each other. The possibility has been the basis of a number of the recent experiments in this country, but most have been unable to maintain the required total sexual availability and monogamous relationships tend to emerge. In a "group family" in which there are more men than women, as is often the case, the emergence of monogamous relationships tends to create conditions such that the maintenance of total sexual availability, and thus the group nature of the family, becomes highly problematic. At this point the experiment usually either breaks up or develops into a community of monogamous conjugal units not greatly unlike the normal marriage form of our culture.

The problem of experimental group families actually reflects some of the social and cultural limitations placed upon marriage forms. In this particular case, the young experimenters are simply unable to overcome, in spite of their great desire to do so, the habitual ways of viewing man-woman relationships which were socialized into them as children and adolescents. Sexual possessiveness is one of these habitual views, probably one of the strongest extant in Western culture.

Additional social and cultural limitations have to do with norms concerning the legitimacy of children as well as those which regulate, to some degree, the sexual conduct of people both premaritally and within marriage. These limitations are often tied in with legal norms, which also form a part of the cultural limitations placed upon marriage.

Legal norms define which persons may marry at all and to which specific other persons one may become married to if legally eligible. For example, persons must be of a certain age to marry, and they may not marry persons who are too close kin to themselves. In most states, monogamy is legally sanctioned either directly or by statutes which state that a marriage is not legal if one or both parties is married at the time to someone else. There are further legal norms which define the various responsibilities with respect to care, maintenance, and support which bear upon persons who marry.

A complete discussion of the biological, social, cultural, and legal limitations placed upon marriage forms could fill an entire book, but suffice it to say that within these various limitations with their varying degrees of strength there is not as great a possibility for differing or altering the structures or forms of marriage as might at first be assumed. However, a number of experts in family-related fields have advocated variations of marriage forms which would require less alteration of the norms than those changes advocated by the bolder experimenters. For example, a psychiatrist, concerned with the special problems of retired and widowed persons, has suggested that they be allowed to form polygamous marriages for a number of definitely practical advantages.[1] Some of the advantages offered include the consolidation of scarce economic resources, the greater ability to meet the variety of sexual needs of older persons, and the increased ability of this arrangement to meet a variety of physical care needs.

On a number of occasions, Margaret Mead has advocated a two-step type of marriage in which young people could take the first step as a sort of trial marriage. Only when the couple decided that they wanted to make the bond permanent and to have children would they go on to the second step, which would be a regular marriage.[2] To a great extent, this is precisely what some young couples are doing who are living together, as described in the previous section. However, this type of arrangement has in no way been formalized or accepted as yet in our culture as a legitimate institution.

Another innovative view of marriage alternatives, one which calls for no alteration or violation of current social norms, is that offered by Sidney Jourard. He suggests that currently married couples might "re-invent" their own marriages—they might revitalize their marriages by introducing radically new ways in which to relate to each other, still within the framework of monogamy.[3]

The basic question raised by all of these proposals, as well as by the current criticisms of marriage and the family, is the question of the continued workability and usefulness of traditional monogamy. The first two articles in this section deal directly with the viability of monogamy, and the third article looks at a wide variety of patterns for innovation in marriage which are emerging.

One important caution is offered with respect to those who are advocating alterations and innovations in traditional monogamy, because of a significant discrepancy or contradiction which emerges from much they suggest. Many of the advocates of change say that the basic fault of monogamy is that there is not enough sexual input or variety in most marriages, and so the changes they propose usually involve some method of increasing the number of sexual partners available to a given spouse, either through multiple spouses or through some form of acceptable adultery. The basic contradiction of this position lies in the fact that only a small minority of marriages which fail do so because of sexual problems or dissatisfactions. Most marriages disintegrate over problems other than sexual ones. Thus, there is an attempt to cure the ills of marriage by dealing with only one rather minor marital problem while ignoring a multitude of other more crucial ones. On the other hand, the view might be taken that marriage is simply not in as bad a shape as we have been led to believe. The article which began this book supported that position.

In the opening article of this section, Herbert Otto asks the question "Has Monogamy Failed?" After a review of the now-waning commune movement, along with a presentation of some of the less radical proposals regarding alternative marriage styles, he presents his own view of the status and potential of monogamous marriage. Here the key word is *potential*, since Otto feels that in spite of the experiments going on, monogamy is here to stay, at least for the foreseeable future. The basic monogamous structure still has great potential as an institution for the development of human growth and satisfaction, and the final portion of this article presents some of the writer's suggestions for attaining this potential.

The second article, "Is Monogamy Outdated?" offers an opposing point of view. It does not totally reject monogamy as much as it takes to task what might be termed the *culture* of monogamy. The authors of this article feel that, because of recent social changes which we have undergone, many of the customs and attitudes which accompany monogamy in our culture have brought monogamy to the point of crisis. Monogamy, as it has operated in our culture, has failed to modify itself in order to deal with changes in sex norms and values. Furthermore, it has failed to make adequate provisions for those in the society who do not marry, along with the widowed and divorced. And finally, say the authors, monogamy has not yet found a way to humanely terminate marriages.

The article goes on to suggest a number of rather radical changes which the authors feel would make monogamy a more workable form of marriage. However, they are rather pessimistic about the acceptance of their proposals and about the future of monogamous marriage.

The final article of Part Three, "Emerging Patterns of Innovative Behavior in Marriage," by James Ramey, is a rather lengthy and sometimes complicated one. However, both the length and the complexity are necessary because the author is attempting to bring together into one conceptual model a variety of marriage-related behaviors which at first seem to be only loosely related. As the list of references for this article indicates, the topics of swinging, communal living, and group marriage have been dealt with extensively; however, no previous writer has attempted to analyze these phenomena by means of a single conceptual model.

The model which Ramey develops views these varieties of behavior as constituting a continuum of which the basic dimension is the "depth and complexity of commitment" of the individual involved to the marriage unit. At one end of the continuum is free love, which involves no commitment. Then come dyadic marriage, mate swapping (swinging), open marriage, intimate friendship, evolutionary commutes, and group marriages, which demand the most commitment. The article discusses all of these types of arrangements and shows how a particular "pair-bonded" couple might move through the continuum by increasing their commitment to themselves and to others.

The article concludes with a discussion of the possible impact these types of experiments might have upon contemporary marriage and family structure, as well as upon our society in general.

REFERENCES

1. Victor Kassel, "Polygyny After Sixty," *Geriatrics*, 21:214–218 (April 1966).
2. Margaret Mead, "Marriage in Two Steps," *Redbook*, 127:48 (July 1966).
3. Sidney M. Jourard, "Reinventing Marriage: The Perspective of a Psychologist," in Herbert A. Otto, ed., *The Family in Search of A Future* (New York: Appleton, 1970), pp. 43–49.

7.

Has Monogamy Failed?

Herbert A. Otto

Never before in the history of Western civilization has the institution of marriage been under the searching scrutiny it is today. Never before have so many people questioned the cultural and theological heritage of monogamy—and set out in search of alternatives. The American family of the 1970's is entering an unprecedented era of change and transition, with a massive reappraisal of the family and its functioning in the offing.

The U.S. statistic of one divorce per every four marriages is all too familiar. Other figures are even more disquieting. For example, a recent government study revealed that one-third of all first-born children in the United States from 1964 through 1966 were conceived out of wedlock, thereby forcing hasty marriages that might not have occurred otherwise. Some marriage specialists estimate that anywhere from 40 to 60 per cent of all marriages are at any given time "subclinical." The couples involved could materially benefit from the help of a marriage counselor, but they never reach a clinic. Divorce is still the most widely accepted means of coping with a marriage beset by problems. Relatively few couples having marital difficulties are aware of available marriage counseling services or utilize them. Divorce today is very much a part of the social fabric, and some sociologists refer to a "divorce culture." It is safe to say that most men, women, and children in this country have been touched by the divorce experience—either in their own families, or among friends and close acquaintances.

The other day a good friend, senior executive of a large company and in his early forties, dropped by for a visit. He told me he had been thinking of divorce after sixteen years of marriage. The couple have a boy, twelve, and two girls, one of whom is ten, the other eight. "We've grown apart over the years, and we have nothing in common left anymore other than the children. There are at least twenty years of enjoying life still ahead of me. I was worried about the children until we discussed it with them. So many of their schoolmates have had divorced parents or parents who had remarried, they are accustomed to the idea. It's part of life. Of course, if the older ones need help, I want them to see a good psychiatrist while we go through with this. My wife is still a good-looking woman, younger than I, and probably will remarry. I'm not thinking of it now, but I'll probably remarry someday." This situation illustrates an attitude and the climate of the times. Divorce has become as much an institution as marriage.

Paradoxically, the high divorce rate can be viewed as both a symptom of the failure of monogamy and an indication of its success. A large majority of men and women remarry within four years after their divorce. As Dr. Bernard Steinzor points out in his latest book, *When Parents Divorce*, "divorce has become an expression of the increasing personal freedom afforded the average citizen." It is a fact that the average citizen continues to pursue personal freedom within the framework of marriage. Serial monogamy or progressive monogamy is today so widespread that it has arrived as an alternative structure. According to one analyst, we are close to the day when 85 per cent of all men and women reaching the age of sixty-five will have been remarried at least once. I am reminded of a cartoon that appeared in *The New Yorker* some time ago: A young couple is shown leaving what is identified by a sign as the home of a justice of the peace. The bride, dressed in the latest mod fashion, turns brightly to her young man and says, "Darling! Our first marriage!"

The full-scale emergence of serial monogamy has been accompanied by an explosive upswing of experimentation with other alternative structures. Begun by the under-thirty generation and hippie tribal families, the 1960's have seen the growth of a new commune movement. This movement has started to attract significant segments of the older, established population. For example, I recently conducted a weekend marathon in Chicago—under the auspices of the Oasis Center—that was open to the public. Seven out of thirty-six participants were members of communes. Three of the seven were successful professional men in their mid-forties. Another participant, a college professor in his early thirties, mentioned that he had been a member of a commune composed of several psychiatrists, an engineer, a teacher, and a chemist. When I visited New York following the Chicago weekend, a senior editor of a large publishing house casually mentioned that he and some friends were in the process of organizing a commune. They were looking for a large brownstone close to their offices.

The commune movement even has its own journal, *Modern Utopian*. Issued by the Alternatives Foundation of Berkeley, California, it is in its fourth year of publication. In 1969, this journal published the first comprehensive directory of intentional or utopian communes in the United States and the world. The addresses of close to 200 intentional communities in this country are given. (It has been estimated that there are four to six times this number of communes in the United States.) California leads the *Modern Utopian* directory with more than 30 listed. New York has 28 and Pennsylvania 13, with communes listed from 35 other states. Half a dozen books that I know of are currently in preparation on the commune movement.

Communes of various types exist, varying from agricultural subsistence to religious. To provide a base for economic survival, many of the communes furnish services or construct marketable products such as hammocks or wooden toys for preschoolers. Others operate printing presses or schools. Most communes not located in cities raise some of their own food. Relatively rare is the commune that is self-supporting solely on the basis of its agricultural operation. Sizes vary with anywhere from 12 persons or fewer to 100 persons or more as members of an intentional community. The educational and vocational backgrounds of members also vary widely. The young people and school dropouts are currently being joined by a growing number of "Establishment dropouts." Many of these are people who have made successful contributions in their chosen vocations or professions and have grown disillusioned, or who are seeking to explore new life-styles.

Communes often have their beginnings when several persons who know each other well, like each other, and have similar values decide to live together. Sometimes a commune is formed around a common interest, craft, or unifying creative goal. Political views or convictions may also play a role in the formation of a commune. There are a number of peace-movement and radical communes; sometimes these are composed of political activists, and sometimes of people who see the commune movement as a "radical approach to revolution." Members of one such group, the Twin Oaks community in Virginia, think of themselves as a post-revolutionary society. As detailed in *Modern Utopian,* this "radical commune" was organized as the result of a university conference:

> Twin Oaks was started by a group of people who met while attending an "academic" conference during 1966 at Ann Arbor, Michigan, on the formation of a Walden II community. One of the Twin Oakers related how this conference resulted in a very elaborate, academic type plan on how to get a Walden II community going. But when the conference was over, the professors all returned to their teaching posts, and

nobody had any idea where they could get the several million dollars that the plan called for to start the thing. So eight people decided to start right away with whatever resources they could get together. . . .

For while Twin Oaks was designed to be a living experiment in community, it also aims to stimulate others to do the same. As one member said, "We generally hold to the opinion that people who *don't* start communities (or join them) are slightly immoral." It's all part of the revolution being over— they define revolution as a "radical restructuring" of society, both economic and, more important, cultural. (But maybe you can't really separate the two.) One member summed up a desirable post-revolutionary society as: "A society that creates people who are committed to non-aggression; a society of people concerned for one another; a society where one man's gain is not another man's loss; a society where disagreeable work is minimized and leisure is valued; a society in which people come first; an economic system of equality; a society which is constantly trying to improve in its ability to create happy, productive, creative people."

The personal property a member brings to a commune remains his, although he may be expected to share it when needed. Some purists object that, since members do not donate personal property for the benefit of the group, the current social experiments should not be referred to as "communes." Obviously, the term has acquired a new meaning and definition. The emphasis today is on the exploration of alternate models for togetherness, the shaping of growing dynamic environments, the exploration of new life-styles, and the enjoyment of living together.

A number of communes are deliberately organized for the purpose of group marriage. The concept of group marriage, however, differs widely. Some communes exclusively composed of couples having a living arrangement similar to the "big family" or group family that originated in Sweden in 1967. These married couples share the same home, expenses, household chores, and the upbringing of the children. Infidelity is not encouraged. Other group-marriage communes tolerate or encourage the sharing of husbands and wives. On the other end of the group-marriage continuum are communes such as The Family near Taos, New Mexico. This group of more than fifty members discourages pairing—"Everyone is married to everyone. The children are everyone's."

The life-span of many communes is relatively short due to four major disintegrative pressures that fragment intentional communities. Disagreement over household chores or work to be performed is a major source of disruption. When members fail to fulfill their obligations, disillusionment and demoralization often set in. Closely related are interpersonal conflicts, frequently fueled by the exchange of sex partners and resultant jealousy. Drugs do not seem to create a major problem in most communes, as there is either a permissive attitude or drug use is discouraged or forbidden. A small number of religious/mystical communes use drugs for sacramental purposes and as a means of communion.

The problems associated with economic survival generate considerable pressure. A final strong force that contributes to the collapse of communes stems from the hostility of surrounding communities. There are innumerable instances of harassment by neighbors, strangers, civil authorities, and police. The persistent and violent nature of this persecution is probably traceable to deep-seated feelings of threat and outrage when the neighboring communities discover a group in their midst suspected of having unorthodox living arrangements. These pervasive feelings of resistance and anger (which may be partially subconscious) are conceivably engendered in many persons by what they perceive to be a threat to the existing family structure.

Another highly promising field of inquiry is the area of family strengths. Little or no research and conceptualization had been done in relation to this area until the work of the Human Potentialities Research Project at the University of Utah, from 1960 through 1967. Paradoxically, family counseling and treatment programs have been offered for decades without a clearly developed framework of what was meant by family strengths, or what constitutes a "healthy family." In spite of extensive efforts to obtain foundation or government support for this research, no financial support was forthcoming. Ours remains a pathology-oriented culture saddled with the bias that the study of disorganization, illness, and dysfunction is the surest road to understanding the forces that go into the making of health and optimum functioning.

The emergence of alternative structures and the experimentation with new modes of married and family togetherness expresses a strong need to bring greater health and optimum functioning to a framework of interpersonal relationships formerly regarded as "frozen" and not amenable to change. There is no question that sex-role and parental-role rigidities are in the process of diminishing, and new dimensions of flexibility are making their appearance in marriage and the family. It is also evident that we are a pluralistic society with pluralistic needs. In this time of change and accelerated social evolution, we should encourage innovation and experimentation in the development of new forms of social and communal living. It is possible to invent and try out many models without hurting or destroying another person. Perhaps we need to recognize clearly that the objective of any model is to provide an atmosphere of sustenance, loving, caring, and adventuring. This makes growth and unfoldment possible.

It is in this light that the attention of an increasing number of well-known humanistic psychologists has been drawn to the institution of marriage. A new recognition of the many dimensions and possibilities of monogamy is beginning to emerge. For example, Dr. Jack Gibb and Dr. Everett Shostrom have each been conducting a series of couples groups at Growth Centers designed to revitalize and deepen love in the marital relationship.

Another eminent psychologist and author, Dr. Sidney Jourard, suggests that we "re-invent marriage" by engaging in "serial polygamy to the same person." He points out that many marriages pass through a cycle of gratifying the needs of both partners, and are experienced as fulfilling until an impasse is reached. One partner or the other finds continuation in that form intolerable, and the marriage is usually legally dissolved at that point. He believes it is possible for the couple at this juncture to struggle with the impasse and to evolve a new marriage with each other, one that includes change, yet preserves some of the old pattern that remains viable. This is the second marriage that, whatever form it takes, will also reach its end. There may then again be a time of estrangement, a period of experimentation, and a remarriage in a new way—and so on for as long as continued association with the same spouse remains meaningful for both partners.

One of the originators of the group marathon technique, Dr. Frederick Stoller, has another interesting proposal to add new dimensions to marriage and family relationships. He suggests an "intimate network of families." His intimate network consists of a circle of three or four families who meet together regularly and frequently, share in reciprocal fashion any of their intimate secrets, and offer one another a variety of services. The families do not hesitate to influence one another in terms of values and attitudes. Such an intimate family network would be neither stagnant nor polite, but would involve an extension of the boundaries of the immediate family.

The weight of tradition and the strong imprinting of parental and familial models assure that for some time to come the overwhelming bulk of the population will opt for something close to the family structures they have known. In view of this strong thrust, it is all the more surprising that preventive programs (other than didactic approaches) that center on the strengthening of the family are almost unknown. Also sadly lacking is massive federal support for programs designed to help marriages and families beset by problems. A network of federally supported marriage-counseling clinics making marital and premarital counseling services available throughout every state in the union could accomplish a great deal toward reducing marital unhappiness and divorce.

Present-day medical science widely recommends that we have an annual physical check-up as a means of prevention. In a similar manner, annual assessment and evaluation should be available to couples interested in developing and improving their marriages. The goal would be to identify, strengthen, and develop family potential *before* crises arise, with the main focus on helping a family achieve an even more loving, enjoyable, creative, and satisfying marriage relationship. The plan of a marriage and family potential center was developed in 1967 and 1968 by a colleague, Dr. Lacey

Hall, and myself during my stay in Chicago. The project was supported by the Stone Foundation, but, owing to a number of complex reasons, the program was never fully implemented. As a part of the work in Chicago, and also under the auspices of the National Center for the Exploration of Human Potential, a number of "More Joy in Your Marriage" groups and classes have been conducted and have shown considerable promise as a preventive approach.

Another possibility to introduce new elements of growth and creativity to monogamy is contained in my own concept of the "new marriage," i.e., marriage as a framework for developing personal potential. This concept is based on the hypothesis that we are all functioning at a small fraction of our capacity to live fully in its total meaning of loving, caring, creating, and adventuring. Consequently, the actualizing of our potential can become the most exciting adventure of our lifetime. From this perspective, any marriage can be envisioned as a framework for actualizing personal potential. Thus, marriage offers us an opportunity to grow, and an opportunity to develop and deepen the capacity for loving and caring. Only in a continuing relationship is there a possibility for love to become deeper and fuller so that it envelops all of our life and extends into the community. However, growth, by its very nature, is not smooth and easy, for growth involves change and the emergence of the new. But growth and the actualization of personal potential are also a joyous and deeply satisfying process that can bring to marriage a *joie de vivre,* an excitement, and a new quality of zest for living.

There are a number of characteristics that form a unique Gestalt and distinguish the new marriage from contemporary marriage patterns:

1. There is a clear acknowledgment by both partners concerning the *personal relevance* of the human potentialities hypothesis: that the healthy individual is functioning at a fraction of his potential.
2. Love and understanding become dynamic elements in the actualization of the marital partners' personal potential.
3. Partners in the new marriage conceive of their union as an evolving, developing, flexible, loving relationship.
4. In the new marriage there is planned action and commitment to achieve realization of marriage potential.
5. The new marriage is here-and-now oriented and not bound to the past.
6. There is clear awareness by husband and wife that their interpersonal or relationship environment, as well as their physical environment, directly affects the actualization of individual potential.
7. There is clear recognition by spouses that personality and the actualization of human potential have much to do with the

social institutions and structures within which man functions. The need for institutional and environmental regeneration is acknowledged by both partners as being personally relevant, leading to involvement in social action.

8. Husband and wife have an interest in exploring the spiritual dimensions of the new marriage.

Since it is often difficult for two people to actualize more of their marriage potential by themselves, participants in the new marriage will seek out group experiences designed to deepen their relationship and functioning as a couple. Such experiences are now being offered at Growth Centers that have sprung up in many parts of the United States. Extension divisions of institutions of higher learning and church organizations are also increasingly offering such group experiences. Based on my many years of practice as a marriage counselor, it has long been my conclusion that every marriage needs periodic rejuvenation and revitalization. This is best accomplished in a couples group that focuses on the development of greater intimacy, freedom, joy, and affection.

The challenge of marriage is the adventure of uncovering the depth of our love, the height of our humanity. It means risking ourselves physically and emotionally; leaving old habit patterns and developing new ones; being able to express our desires fully, while sensitive to the needs of the other; being aware that each changes at his own rate and unafraid to ask for help when needed.

Has monogamy failed? My answer is "no." Monogamy is no longer a rigid institution, but instead an evolving one. There is a multiplicity of models and dimensions that we have not even begun to explore. It takes a certain amount of openness to become aware on not only an intellectual level but a feeling level that these possibilities face us with a choice. Then it takes courage to recognize that this choice in a measure represents our faith in monogamy. Finally, there is the fact that every marriage has a potential for greater commitment, enjoyment, and communication, for more love, understanding, and warmth. Actualizing this potential can offer new dimensions in living and new opportunities for personal growth, and can add new strength and affirmation to a marriage.

8.

Is Monogamy Outdated?

Rustum Roy and Della Roy

MONOGAMY: WHERE WE STAND TODAY

The total institution of marriage in American society is gravely ill. This statement does not apply to the millions of sound marriages where two people have found companionship, love, concern, and have brought up children in love. But it is necessary in 1970 to point to the need for *institutional* reforms, even when the personal or immediate environment may not (appear) to need it. Yet many refuse to think about the area as a whole because of personal involvement—either their marriage is so successful that they think the claims of disease exaggerated, or theirs is so shaky that all advice is a threat. Is the institution then so sick? For example:

> Year after year in the United States, marriage has been discussed in public print and private sessions with undiminished confusion and increasing pessimism. Calamity always attracts attention, and in the United States the state of marriage is a calamity.

These are the words with which W. H. Lederer and D. Jackson open their new book *The Mirages of Marriage*. Vance Packard in *The Sexual Wilderness* summarizes the most recent major survey thus: "In other words, a marriage made in the United States in the

This article first appeared in *The Humanist,* March/April 1970 and is reprinted by permission.

late 1960's has about a 50:50 chance of remaining even nominally intact."

Clifford Adams concludes from an Identity Research Institute study of 600 couples that, while numerically at 40 per cent in this nation and in some West Coast highly-populated counties, the *real* divorce rate is running at 70 per cent, that in fact "75 per cent of marriages are a 'bust'." And Lederer and Jackson report that 80 per cent of those interviewed had at some time seriously considered divorce. So much for the statistics. Qualitatively the picture painted by these and 100 others is even bleaker but needs no repeating here.

There is no doubt then about the diagnosis of the sickness of marriage taken as a whole. Yet no person, group, magazine, or newspaper creates an awareness of the problems; no activist band takes up the cause to *do* something about it. Some years ago, we participated in a three-year-long group study and development of a sex ethic for contemporary Americans, and we found this same phenomenon: that serious group study and group work for change in the area of sex behavior is remarkably difficult and threatening, and hence rare. Thus, we find an institution such as monogamous marriage enveloped by deterioration and decay, and unbelievably little is being done about it on either a theoretical basis or detailed pragmatic basis.

For this there is a second major reason: marriage as an institution is partly governed by warring churches, a society without a soul, a legal system designed for lawyers, and a helping system for psychiatrists who almost by their very mode of operation in the marriage field guarantee its failure. Consequently, marriage is rapidly losing its schizophrenic mind, oscillating between tyrannical repression and equally tyrannical expression.

By the term *traditional monogamy,* we refer to the public's association with the word, i.e., marriage to one person at a time, the centrality of the nuclear family, and the restriction of all overt sexual acts, nearly all sexually-tinged relationships, and heterosexual relations of any depth to this one person before and after marriage, expectation of a lifetime contract, and a vivid sense of failure if termination is necessary. John Cuber and Peggy Harroff in *The Significant Americans* have called this "the monolithic code," and it is based on precepts from the Judaic and Christian traditions. All working societies are structured around such codes or ideals, no matter how far individuals may depart from the norms and whether or not they accept the source of such "ideals."

How does a change in a code or ideal come about? When the proportion of the populace living in conflict with their own interpretation of the monolithic code, and "getting away with it," reaches nearly a majority, then *new* ideals must evolve for the social system to remain in equilibrium. We are convinced that although no *discontinuous* change in the ideals of a culture is possible, "traditional monogamy" as an ideal may be altered *in a continuous fashion* in order to respond to the needs of men and women today.

Traditional monogamy was *one* interpretation of the Judaeo-Christian tradition. We are convinced that for widespread acceptability any *new* ideals must be interpretable in terms of Judaeo-Christian humanism, the basic framework of mainstream "Americanism," and the most explicit humanism so far developed. Such an interpretation is neither difficult nor likely to encounter much resistance from the many other contemporary American humanisms which have not swung far from the parent Protestant humanism. But the importance of such an interpretation for continental middle-class America is crucial, as the tenor and very existence of the Nixon administration bring home to those who live in the more rarified climes of East or West coast. If a new monogamous ideal is to evolve, it must be acceptable to middle America, liberated, affluent, but waspish at heart.

CAUSES OF THE CRISIS

Social institutions are the products of particular social environments, and there must be a finite time lag when an institution appropriate for one situation survives into a new era in which the situation has changed drastically. It is clear that traditional monogamy is caught precisely in this overlap of two radically different situations. It is important to identify precisely the particular problem-causing elements of change in the environment.

1. *The sexual revolution has made it infinitely more difficult to retain monogamy's monopoly on sex.* We live in an eroticized environment which is profoundly affecting many institutions. The change towards greater permissiveness and its effect on the sexual climate can be summed up in the aphorism, "What was a temptation for the last generation is an opportunity for this." Underneath it all are the measurable, real physical changes: the advent of prosperity, mobility, and completely controlled conception.

Parallel to physical changes are vast social changes. The eroticization of our culture oozes from its every pore, so much so that it becomes essentially absurd to expect that all physical sexual expression for a 50-year period will be confined to the marriage partner. Moreover, this eroticization escalator shows no sign of slowing down, and its effect on various institutions will be even more drastic in the future. Following are some illustrations.

The influence of the literature, the arts, the media, and the press on the climate for any institution is profound, and marriage is no exception. Caught between the jaws of consumer economics in a free-enterprise system and the allegedly objective purveyors of accurate information (or culturally representative entertainment), human sexuality has become the most salable commodity of all. Perform, if you will, the following simple tests: examine the magazine fare available to tens of millions of Americans; spend a few hours browsing through *Look,* and *Life,* and try *Playboy;* work up to something like *Cosmopolitan.* If you are serious, visit a typical downtown book shop in a big city and count the number of pictorial publications whose sole purpose is sexual titillation. Next try paperbacks available to at least 100,000,000 Americans—in every drugstore: *Candy,* Henry Miller, *Fanny Hill,* the complaining Portnoy, valleys of dolls, and menchild in promised lands, carpetbaggers at airports, couples and groups. Does *one* speak of the beauty and wonder of uniting sex to marriage? Go see 10 movies at random. Will *The Graduate, I Am Curious,* or *La Ronde* rail against sexual license? Thus the mass media have had a profound effect on the American people's marriage ideals. They especially confuse those to whom their traditions, speaking through emasculated school, bewildered church, and confused home, still try to affirm a traditionally monogamous system. Yet some have mistakenly denied that there is a causal relationship between the media and our rapidly changing value systems. Worst of all, very few of those who urge the freedom of access to more and more sexual stimuli work to legitimize, socially and ethically, a scheme for increased sexual outlets.

2. *There is a vast increase in the number and variety of men-women contacts after marriage, and no guidelines are available for behavior in these new situations.* Of the sexual dilemmas which our present-day culture forces upon the ailing institution of traditional monogamy, premarital sexual questions now appear very minor. For all intents and purposes premarital sexual play (including the *possibility* of intercourse) has been absorbed into the social canon. We foresee in the immediate future a much more serious psychological quandary with respect to extra- or co-marital sexual relations of all levels of intensity. The conflict here is so basic and so little is being done to alleviate it, that it is only surprising that it has not loomed larger already. Traditional monogamy as practiced has meant not only one spouse and sex partner at a time but essentially only one heterosexual *relationship,* of any depth at all, at a time. We have shown that our environment suggests through various media the desirability of nonmarital sex. Further, our culture is now abundant in opportunity: time, travel, meetings, committees, causes, and group encounters of every stripe bringing men and women together in all kinds of relationship-producing situations. Our age is characterized by not only the opportunity but by the necessity for simultaneous multiple relationships. One of the most widely experienced examples is that chosen by Cuber and Harroff in their study of the sex lives of some "leaders" of our society. They noted the obviously close relationship of such men with their secretaries, with whom they work for several hours a day. But the same opportunity now occurs to millions of middle-class housewives returning to work after children are grown. They too are establishing new heterosexual friendships and being treated as separate individuals (not to mention as sex objects) after 10 or 15 years.

3. *Traditional monogamy is in trouble because it has not ad-*

justed itself to find a less hurtful way to terminate a marriage. From the viewpoint of any philosophy that puts a high value on response to human need and the alleviation of human suffering, the mechanisms available for terminating marriage are utterly unacceptable. Traditional monogamy involves a lifetime commitment. Anything that would necessitate termination short of this must, therefore, be a major failure. Divorce American style demands so much hurt and pain and devastation of personalities that it is imperative that we attempt to temper the hurt caused to human beings. We must take as inescapable fact that about half of all marriages now existing will, and probably should, be terminated. The question is how best this can be done to minimize total human suffering, while avoiding the pitfall that the relief of immediate pain of one or two persons is the greatest and single good. Full consideration must always be given to all the significant others—children, parents, friends—and to the long-range effects on society. The institution of traditional monogamy will increasingly come under attack while it is unable to provide a better means to terminate a contract than those now in use.

4. *Traditional monogamy does not deal humanely with its have-nots—the adult singles, the widowed, the divorced.* Statistically speaking, we in America have more involuntarily single persons above age 25 or 30 than those who had no choice about a disadvantageous color for their skin. The latter have had to bear enormous legal and social affronts and suffered the subtler and possibly more debilitating psychological climate of being unacceptable in much of their natural surroundings. But this disability they share with voiceless single persons in a marriage-oriented society. Our society proclaims monogamy's virtue at every point of law and custom and practice, as much as it says white is right. Biases, from income tax to adoption requirements, subtle advertisements, and Emily Post etiquette all point to the traditional monogamist as the acceptable form of society. Unbelievably, this barrage goes on unopposed in the face of some tens of millions of persons outside the blessed estate. Monogamy decrees that the price of admission into the complex network of supportive relationsips of society is a wedding band. Yet it turns a blind eye to the inexorable statistical fact that of those women who are single at 35 only $\frac{1}{3}$, at 45 only $\frac{1}{10}$, and at 50 only $\frac{1}{20}$ will *ever* find that price. Is access to regular physical sexual satisfaction a basic human right on a plane with freedom or shelter or right to worship? For effective living in our world every human being needs individuals as close friends and a community of which he or she is a part. Traditionally, monogamous society has ruled, ipso facto, that tens of millions of its members shall have no societally approved way of obtaining sexual satisfaction. Much worse, because sexual intimacy is potentially associated with all heterosexual relationships of any depth, they must also be denied such relationships.

Here, surely, every humanist must protest. For it is *his* social ideal

—that the greatest good of human existence is deep interpersonal relationships and as many of these as is compatible with depth— that is contravened by traditional monogamy's practice. Moreover, there is less provision today for single women to develop fulfilling relationships than there was a generation or two ago. The larger family then incorporated these losers in the marital stakes into at least a minimal framework of acceptance and responsibility.

A Theory for Change

Any vision of a better future for society presupposes, consciously or unconsciously, a value system and basic assumptions about the nature of man. A theory of man and life must precede a theory of monogamy. Our view of the nature of man is the Judaeo-Christian one. Man was meant to live *in community*. The normative ideal for every man is that he live fully known, accepted, and loved by a community of significant others. In this environment his individual creativity and his creative individuality will be realized to the maximum extent, and he can serve society best.

MAN—COMMUNITY—SOCIETY

In this spectrum we have, as yet, not even mentioned marriage, and instructively so. There is a crucially important hierarchy of values, in which the individual's needs and the community's good are vastly more important than the laws or preferred patterns of marital behavior. Indeed, these laws must be tested empirically by the criterion of how well they have been found to meet the individual-community-society needs most effectively. It is important to see that the humanist is not committed, prima facie, to *any* particular pattern of men-women relationships.

Marriage, monogamous or polygamous, fits somewhere between the individual and community levels of social organization. Unfortunately, in many cultures the institution of marriage and the stress on the family has generally militated against, and sometimes destroyed, the community level of relationship.

This has not always been so—not even in America. The larger family of maiden aunts and uncles and grandparents, and occasional waifs and strays, has been a part of many cultures including that of the rigidly structured joint-family system in India and the plantation system of the American South. Tribal cultures abound. In the Swiss canton or settled New England town the sinews of community are strong enough to make them fall in between the extremes represented above and lying, perhaps, closer to the former. There is an inverse correlation between the complexity of a highly developed society and the strength of community channels and bonds. It is in the technology-ruled society where we find men and women turning to the intimacy of marriage to shield them from future impersonalization when the second level of defense—the community level—has disintegrated through neglect. But monogamous marriage is altogether too frail an institution to carry that load also. A typical marriage is built frequently of brittle and weak members held together by a glue of tradition rapidly deteriorating under the onslaught of a half-dozen corroding acids—mobility, prosperity, permissiveness, completely controlled conception, and continuously escalating eroticization.

There is no question that the first and essential step in the evolution of monogamy is the recovery of the role of community in our lives. It appears to us, however strange a conclusion it seems, that precisely because our world has become so complex, depersonalization is an essential, ineradicable fact of our lives in the many public spheres. This requires then a radical structuring of the private sphere to provide the supports we have found missing in the traditional monogamy pattern. To know and accept ourselves deeply we need to be known and accepted. And most of us are many-sided polyhedra needing several people to reflect back to ourselves the different portions of our personality. With changing years and training and jobs this need grows instead of diminishing. Thus, it comes about that the humanist has a great deal to contribute to his fellows.

Our proposed modification of monogamy, then, has the re-emphasis of community as one of its primary goals. This is hardly novel, but it has been the conclusion of every group of radical Christian humanists trying to reform society for hundreds of years. And it was the New World which provided for them a unique opportunity to attempt the radical solutions. Hence, we have dotted across America the record and/or the remnants of hundreds of experiments in radical community living.

Today we believe that society's hope lies in working at both ends of the game—the basic research and the development. We need to become much more active in optimizing or improving present marriage in an imperfect society: changing laws, improving training, providing better recovery systems, and the like. But alongside of that, we need to continue genuine research in radically new patterns of marriage. This can only be carried out by groups or communities. Further, we need not only those groups that seek solutions withdrawn from the day-to-day world, but those that are willing to devise potential solutions which can serve as models for its eventual reform within the bourgeois urban culture.

Basic Research in Marriage Patterns

We cannot here do justice to a discussion of possible models for radical new patterns of marriage-in-community. Instead, we wish only to emphasize the importance of such experimentation and its neglect, in our supposedly research-oriented culture, by serious groups concerned for society. It is hardly a coincidence that the yearning for community should figure so prominently in all utopian schemes for remaking society. The contemporary resurgence is described in B. F. Skinner's *Walden Two* or Erich Fromm's *Revolution of Hope* and Robert Rimmer's *Harrad Experiment.* It is being attempted in groping, unformed ways in the hippie or other city-living communes and is being lived out in amazingly fruitful (yet unpublicized) models in the Bruderhof communities in the United States and Europe and the Ecumenical Institute in Chicago. And in rereading the details of the organization of the hundreds of religious communities, we find that they have an enormous amount to teach us on many subjects, from psychotherapy to patterns for sexual intercourse.

Probably the most important lesson for contemporary America, however, is that communities survive and thrive and provide a creative framework for realizing the human potential if their central purpose is outside themselves and their own existence. The second lesson is one taught by the complex technology: wherever many persons are involved, *some* discipline and order are absolutely essential.

Were it not for the sheer prejudice introduced by a misreading of Judeao-Christian tradition and its bolstering by the unholy alliance of state-and-church Establishment, we may well have learned to separate potential from pitfall in various patterns of communal living. The Mormon experience with polygamy is not without its value for us, and Bettelheim has helped shake the prejudice against nonparent child-rearing, drawing on data from the kibbutzim. Rimmer, perhaps, through his novels *The Rebellion of Yale Marratt* and *Proposition 31,* has reached the widest audience in his crusade for a variety of new marital patterns. He has dealt sensitively and in depth with the subtle questions of ongoing sexual relations with more than one partner—the threat of which is perhaps the most difficult taboo against communal life for most educated Americans. From some dozens of histories in personal and marathon encounter situations, we believe that Rimmer's portrayal of typical reactions is remarkably accurate. Most middle-class, educated Americans above 35 have been so schooled into both exclusivity and possessiveness that no more than perhaps 10 per cent could make the transition into any kind of structured nonexclusivity in marriage. But for the younger group, especially those now in college, the potential for attempting the highly demanding, idealistic, disciplined group living of some sort is both great and a great challenge. It is here perhaps, by setting up contemporary-style communities of concern and responsibility, that young humanists can make one of their greatest contributions to society at large.

MODIFYING TRADITIONAL MONOGAMY

No company survives on its fundamental research laboratory alone, although many cannot survive long without one. Each needs also a development group that keeps making the minor changes to its existing products in order to eliminate defects in design and to meet the competition or the change in customer needs. So too with marriage. While far-out research *must* proceed on new patterns, we must simultaneously be concerned with the changes that can modify traditional monogamy to meet its present customer needs much more effectively—that is to say, humanely.

Our society is pluralist in many of its ideals. The first and most important change in society's view of marriage must also be the acceptance of the validity of a range of patterns of behavior. The education of our children and of society must point to ways and points at which, *depending on the situation,* it is right and proper to make this or that change. Indeed, we can doubtless describe the era we are entering as one of *situational monogamy*—that is, traditional monogamy can still be upheld as the ideal in many circumstances, but in specific situations modifications are not only permitted but required.

INSTITUTIONALIZING PREMARITAL SEX

Premarital sexual experience is now rather widely accepted, covertly if not overtly, throughout our society. Especially when we use the word *experience* instead of *intercourse,* the studies from Kinsey to Packard support a very substantial increase in necking and petting, including petting to orgasm. The new rise in keeping-house-together arrangements in college and beyond is spreading like wildfire. We see an opportunity here for a simple evolution of the monogamous ideal within relatively easy reach. Almost all analysts believe that postponing marriage by two or three years and making it more difficult—with some required period of waiting or even waiting and instruction—would be very beneficial. Traditional marriage in its classical form enjoined a "decent" (six months to two years) engagement period partly for the same reason. One of the main drives toward early marriage is that there is no other way to obtain regular sexual gratification in a publicly acceptable manner. By one simple swish of tradition, we can incorporate all the recent suggestions for trial marriages, baby marriages, and so forth, and cover them all under the decent rug of the engagement. Engagements with a minor difference: that in today's society they entitle a couple to live together if they desire, and sleep together—*but not to have children.* Thus, engagement would become the final step that entitles one to legal sex—publicly known sex with contraceptive devices. By no means need this become the universal norm. Pluralism of marital patterns should start here, however. Many parents and various social groups may still urge their members to restrict engagements to a noncoital or nonsexual level of intimacy; but even here they would do well to legitimize some advanced level of sexual activity, and by so doing they would probably protect their marriage institution more effectively. Our very spotty feedback from student groups would suggest that "everything-but-coitus"— which is a lot more sex than the last generation's "little-but-coitus" —has some value as a premarital maxim. The humanist must also affirm that quintessential humanness is choice against one's immediate desires. He must point to the loss by this generation of perhaps the most exquisite sexual pleasures, when it comes as the culmination of long-deferred desire of the loved one. We mourn the loss of Eros in a day when Venus comes so quickly, for it is Eros who is human, while Venus reminds us that we are *human* animals. Well may we paraphrase the Frenchman and say, "In America we tend to eat the fruit of coital sex green."

Along with the engagement-including-sex concept could be introduced the idea of training for marriage. Everyone falls for the training gimmick. Driver education, often taken after three years of driving, is still useful, and is induced by the lower insurance rates. Similarly, if society required a marriage-education course before granting a license, another important step in improving the quality of marriage would have been achieved.

EXPANDING THE EROTIC COMMUNITY
IN THE POST-MARITAL YEARS

With the engagement-including-sex, we have broken the pre-marital half of monogamy's monopoly on sex. It is our judgment that for the health of the institution it will become necessary in America in the next decade to break the second half also—post-marital sexual expression. (Recall that our theory demands that we seek to maximize the number of deep relationships and to develop marriages to fit in with a framework of community.) To do this we are certain that the monopolistic tendencies of relationships must be broken, and hence the question of sexual relations cannot be bypassed. We believe that in the coming generation a spectrum of sexual expression with persons other than the spouse is certain to occur for at least the large majority, and possibly most persons. If monogamy is tied inextricably with post-marital restriction of all sexual expression to the spouse, it will ultimately be monogamy which suffers. Instead, monogamy should be tied to the much more basic concepts of fidelity, honesty, and openness, which are concomitants of love of the spouse, but which do not necessarily exclude deep relationships, possibly including various degrees of sexual intimacy, with others. In the studies and counseling experience of many, including ourselves, there is no evidence that all extramarital sexual experience is destructive of the marriage. Indeed, more and more persons testify that creative co-marital relationships and sexual experience can and do exist. But most persons need guidelines to help steer them from the dangerous to the potentially creative *relationships,* and to provide help on the appropriateness of various sexual expressions for various relationships. A few practices are crucial:

1. *Openness:* Contrary to folklore, frank and honest discussions at *every stage* of a developing relationship between all parties is the best guarantee against trouble. We know of husbands who have discussed with their wives possible coitus with a third person, some to conclude it would be wrong; others, un-

wise; others to drop earlier objections; and still others to say it was necessary and beautiful. We know of wives who have said a reasoned "no" to such possibilities for their husbands and kept their love and respect, and many who have said "yes" in uncertainty and have found the pain subside. Openness is not impossible.

2. *Other-centeredness:* Concern for *all* the others—the other woman or man, the other husband or wife, the children—must be front and center in reaching decisions on any such matters.

3. *Proportionality:* Sexual expressions should be proportional to the depth of a relationship. This leads, of course, to the conclusion that most coitus and other intimate expressions should only occur with very close friends: a conclusion questioned by many, but essential for our theory.

4. *Gradualism:* Only a stepwise escalation of intimacy allows for the open discussion referred to above. Otherwise such openness becomes only a series of confessions.

It is important to discover the value of self-denial and restraint. It is incumbent on them to demonstrate, while accepting other patterns, their ability to maintain loving, warm relationships with both single and married persons of the opposite sex and of limiting the sexual expression therein in order, for example, to conserve psychic energy for other causes.

PROVIDING A RELATIONSHIP NETWORK FOR THE SINGLE

It is principally because of the fear of sexual involvement that the single are excluded from married society. In the new dispensation, a much more active and aggressive policy should be encouraged to incorporate single persons within the total life of a family and a community. She or he should be a part of the family, always invited —but not always coming—to dinner, theaters, and vacations. The single person should feel free enough to make demands and accept responsibility as an additional family member would. The single woman, thus loved and accepted by two or three families, may find herself perhaps not sleeping with any of the husbands but vastly more fulfilled as a woman. No couple should enter such relationships unless the marriage is secure and the sexual monopoly not crucially important; yet all concerned couples should be caused to wonder about their values if their fear of sexual involvement keeps them from ministering to such obvious need. The guidelines for decisions, of course, are the same as those above. We know of several such relationships, many but not all involving complete sexual intimacy, that have been most important in the lives of the single persons. Recently, we have observed that our present society makes it very difficult for even the best of these relationships to continue for a lifetime. And we see the need for developing acceptable patterns for altering such relationships creatively after the two-to-five-year period which often brings about sufficient changes to suggest reappraisal in any case. The dependent woman often becomes confident and no longer needs the same kind of support; the independent one becomes too attached and becomes possessive enough to want exclusivity. The mechanisms we discuss under divorce should no doubt operate here as well.

LEGALIZING BIGAMY

It may appear as a paradox, but in keeping with the theory above and the pluralist trend of society, it is almost certainly true that contemporary-style monogamy would be greatly strengthened if bigamy (perhaps polygamy-polyandry) were legalized. This would provide a *partial* solution to the problems dealt with in the last two sections; moveover, it would do it in a way that is least disturbing to the monogamous tenor of society. The entire style—contract and living arrangements of most persons—would be unaffected if one woman in 20 had two husbands in the house or one man in 10 had two wives—sometimes in different cities and frequently in different houses. There is a substantial unthinking emotional resistance to legalizing bigamy based partly on a supposed, but incorrect, backing from Christian doctrine. There is, however, no Biblical injunction sanctifying monogamy; the Christian humanist is not only free to, but may be required to, call for other patterns. Indeed, after World War II the Finnish church is reported to have been on the verge of legalizing bigamy, when the great disparity in women:men ratio, which stimulated the inquiry, was found to have improved beyond their expectations.

In the next decade, this ratio is expected to get as high as 7:5 in this country, and it is higher in the highest age brackets. Various gerontologists have suggested the legalization of bigamy for the aged, and the capacity for social change in our society is so weak that perhaps bigamy will have to be legalized first under Medicare! It is indeed difficult to see why bigamy should not be legalized, once the doctrinal smokescreen were to be exposed for what it is.

MAKING DIFFICULTIES AND DIVORCE
LESS DESTRUCTIVE OF PERSONALITIES

A reform of the total system of marriage *must* provide for a much less destructive method for terminating one. The first change required in our present ideal is to recognize that a good divorce can be better than a poor marriage. We can continue to affirm the importance of the intention of the lifelong commitment, but we must begin to stress the quality of the commitment and the actual relationship as a higher good than mere longevity. Early detection of trouble makes repair easier and surgery less likely. If we take our automobiles to be inspected twice a year to be safe on the highways, is it too much to expect that the complex machinery of a marriage could be sympathetically inspected periodically to keep it in the best working condition? Here the church and the university can help by showing the need for and providing such inspections. Conceivably a biennial or triennial marriage marathon or week-long retreat utilizing the newest insights of encounter groups could be made normative for all marriages. Such checkups would in some cases catch the cancer early enough and in others indicate the need for surgery. In any case, a failing marriage needs to be treated by a person or persons who are neutral on the value of divorce itself, committed to the goal of maximizing human potential, and not determined to preserve marriage for its own sake. We believe that a team of a marriage counselor and, where appropriate younger clergymen or another couple who are close friends can, over a period of several months, help the husband and wife arrive at a wise decision most effectively. The use of a fixed-length trial for either separation or continuance, after specific changes, with an agreed-upon evaluation at the end of the period, has proved its real value in all the cases where we have seen it used. Our own experience has been that many of the worst situations are avoided if the couple can keep channels open to their closest friends—always working with them together. Two helpful changes need to occur here. First, it should be made much more acceptable to talk openly and seriously about marital tensions with close friends; and second, we should all learn the principle of never giving any personal information about absent *third* parties except when we think it can specifically do some positive good.

For ordinary divorce, it is difficult to see what the professional psychiatrist or lawyer-as-adviser can contribute; indeed it appears axiomatic that with traditional Freudian psychiatry there can be no compromise—it is simply incompatible with the rational approaches to helping even irrational persons. In most instances, its result is the introduction of wholly unnecessary polarization (instead of a reconciling attitude, even while separating) between two persons who were the most important in the world to each other. This we find tends to undercut the faith that such persons can ever have in any other person or cause. The price of so-called self-understanding is the mild cynicism which extinguishes the fire of the unlimited liability of love and drains the warmth and color from two lives. Neither paid psychiatrist nor loving friend can avoid the tragedy in the kind of situation when John married to Mary has become deeply attached to Alice. But this tragedy need not be compounded by bitterness, anger, and self-justification in the name of helping. We do know of couples divorcing and parting as friends, persons who *love* each other to the best of their ability and yet, after sober, agonizing months of consideration, decide to separate. We know that that is the way it must happen in the future.

CONSERVING IDEALS: CHANGING THE MARRIAGE SERVICE

Because our psychological conditioning is affected even by every minor input, we can help preserve the monogamous *ideal* by bringing in honesty at the high points in its symbol life. This would mean, for instance, minor alteration of the traditional marriage service, and not necessarily to water down its commitments. Thus, everyone recognizes the value of a lifelong commitment. But to what should that commitment be? To preserving a marriage when we know that half will fail and make all involved guilty over it? Why not, rather, a lifelong commitment to loving and speaking the truth in love? One can be true to this even if separation occurs. Why should not the marriage service make the closest friends—best man, maid of honor, who have essentially trivial roles in the ceremony—take on a real commitment to become the loving community for the couple, covenanting to communicate regularly, stand by them always, but also to speak admonition in love whenever they see it needed. Even such a small beginning would symbolize the fact that each couple enters not only into a marriage but also into a much-needed community.

Disease Diagnosed; Prognosis: Poor

The rebellion of the young reflects only intuitively their alienation from a science-technology-dominated world which they have not the discipline to understand. The need for new and revitalized institutions that would provide every kind of support to individuals could not be greater. Inexorable logic points to the centrality of community in any such attempts. Yet no American, indeed Western, sociologist or psychologist of any stature (always excepting Skinner) has paid any serious attention to their structuring. We attribute this largely to their ignorance of the primitive Christian costs of their own heritage, and see it in the great loss to contemporary humanism of the insight and *experimental data* from those bold humanist experimenters of the last century. However, it is unlikely that in the permissive society it will be possible to demand the minimum discipline required for a community to cohere. What changes can we really hope for on the basis of present observations? On the basis of emotional reactions and capacity for change in attitudes to men-women relationships, sexual patterns, or marriage, which we have observed even in the most secure and highly motivated persons, we can only be discouraged and pessimistic. Always here and there the exception stands out: concerned persons acting out love and new ways demanded by new situations. We agree with Victor Ferkiss when he says in *Technological Man:*

> There is no new man emerging to replace the economic man of industrial society or the liberal democratic man of the bourgeois political order. The new Technology has not produced a new human type provided with a technological world view adequate to give cultural meaning to the existential revolution. Bourgeois man continues dominant just as his social order persists while his political and cultural orders disintegrate.

Bourgeois man will persist and along with him, traditional monogamy. But for humanists, there is no release for the mandate to try to alter traditional monogamy to make it better serve human needs, for "we are called upon to be faithful, not to succeed."

9.

Emerging Patterns of
Innovative Behavior in Marriage

James W. Ramey

T he mass media are replete with sensational stories of free love, swinging, communes, and group marriages; usually implying ruptured standards, moral decay, and threats to the institution of marriage. Moralists point with alarm to one out of four marriages ending in divorce, freely circulating swinger ad magazines, campus orgies, and flourishing communes. Here is their proof that the minions of hell are fast taking over. Fortunately there is another, more positive, explanation for these phenomena. Viewed in the context of diffusion of innovation, we are witnessing the realignment of traditional marital relationship patterns rather than deviations from the norm. As Beigel (1969) indicated, this is a supportive development aimed at reforming monogamous marriage.

Diffusion of innovation refers to the process of change and the generally accepted means of determining which of many possible changes is actually taking place. It has been found that no matter how long a particular practice has been accepted by small groups, such changes do not move into the mainstream of society until approximately seven to ten per cent of the population adopts them. (Pemberton, 1936) Once this level of saturation is reached, general acceptance rapidly follows, so that within a few years the vast majority of people can be expected to accept ideas or activities that may have been the norm for a small percentage of the population

Reprinted from *Family Coordinator,* Vol. 21 (Oct. 1972), pp. 435–456. By permission of the National Council on Family Relations.

for decades. As an example of this kind of change, some women were smoking more than a generation ago, but it was not until World War II that this activity was accepted generally as proper behavior. When acceptance did come, it happened almost overnight —in just less than a decade. (Ramey, 1963)

This paper presents a paradigm, or model, for research in the area of evolutionary sexual behavior in marriage. This model serves three purposes. First, it provides a basis for systematic classification of current research on alternative sexual life-styles for pair-bonded couples, particularly free love, swinging, communal living, and group marriage. Some of this research will be examined and analysis of this material will be organized in respect to the paradigm. A more critical look will be taken at current research findings and gaps in present research knowledge identified. Second, the paradigm is designed to foster further inquiry, to suggest fruitful lines of endeavor for new research. It should not be conceived as a complete theory of evolutionary marital sexual behavior, but is offered merely as a proposal that ultimately may lead to the development of a useful theory. Third, the model provides marriage partners with a cogent way of conceptualizing their relationship, and hence affords them a guide for analyzing their pair-bond behavior and evaluating their own degree of commitment and effectiveness as partners in a union of equals.

Before introducing our definitions of the behaviors with which this paper is concerned, the scope of the inquiry will be defined, the point of view from which it is being undertaken, and the limits imposed upon it. Initially an attempt is being made to link together, as part of a composite whole, several types of marital behavior generally considered to be deviant. Reasons will be presented for believing that these behaviors are in fact evolutionary, stemming from two basic changes in our society: the shift toward a *temporary systems* society and the shift toward regarding women as people with equal rights, privileges, and responsibilities, rather than as chattel. We do this as a means of clarifying the growing number of contradictory statements, many of which claim to be based on actual participant-observer experience, with regard to swinging, group marriage, and communes. We hope and believe this approach will help to focus research in the field on the gaps and overlaps that would seem to have the highest payoff potential in increasing our understanding of what is happening. We do not propose to critique and/or relate all of the previous research in the field. It would seem much more important to sketch in the broad picture as we see it, leaving more detailed analysis to later efforts. We hope the sketch will prove sufficiently interesting to tempt others to do likewise.

It seems appropriate to begin with several definitions.

1. *Free love* is open-ended sexual seeking and consummating without legal or other commitment of any kind.

2. *Swinging* generally involves two or more pair-bonded couples who mutually decide to switch sexual partners or engage in group sex. Singles may be included either through temporary coupling with another individual specifically for the purpose of swinging or as a part of a triadic or larger group sexual experience.
3. *Intimate friendship* is an otherwise traditional friendship in which sexual intimacy is considered appropriate behavior.
4. When individuals agree to make life commitments as members of one particular group rather than through many different groups, they may constitute a *commune*. The number of common commitments will vary from commune to commune, the critical number having been reached at the point at which the group sees itself as a commune rather than at some absolute number.
5. In a *group marriage* each of three or more participants is pair-bonded with at least two others.

The term *pair-bond* is used to reduce ambiguity. A pair-bond is a reciprocal primary relationship involving sexual intimacy. A pair-bonded couple see themselves as mates. This is not necessarily the case in a primary relationship, which can be one-sided and need not include sexual intimacy. The term pair-bond is preferred rather than *married couple* for another reason—not all pair-bonded couples are married.

Four basic definitions deal with a range of behavior that is increasingly complex. They are interrelated and often sequential. They stem from the human propensity to become involved in ever more complex relationships, a propensity based on the fact that humans are problem-solving organisms. Today's world is increasingly inundated with evidence that this is so—that man seeks to increase the complexity of his interactions. Toffler (1970) has added a new word to our lexicon—future shock. Yet somehow one of the age-old institutions, marriage, has resisted this trend. Why should this be?

There appear to be two interrelated causes. First is the existence of male dominance in society, with all that it implies. Unequals tend not to form complex relationships. Second, in the past, and indeed in many subcultures and in much of the lower-middle- and working-class levels of society today, two married persons in a stable and permanent social context need to seek little from each other. Psychological and interpersonal needs can be satisfied in a variety of ways through kin, neighbors, and friendship. Husband and wife literally live in two different worlds. As Bott (1957) pointed out:

> Couples in close-knit relational networks maintained a rigid division of labor, were deeply involved in external bonds, and placed little emphasis on shared interests, joint recreation, or a satisfying sexual relationship. Couples in loose-knit networks, on the other hand, show little division of labor, emphasize marital togetherness, and are highly self-conscious about

child-rearing techniques. The transition from working class to middle-class status and from urban villager to suburban environment tends to bring about a loosening of relational networks and is therefore usually associated with an increase in the intensity and intimacy of the marital bond, and a decrease in marital role differentiation.

Marriage did not change much, over the ages, until the pair-bond was composed of peers. As long as the woman was considered chattel, the relationship was not one of equality. Such terms as "doing wifely duty," "marriage rights," and "exclusivity," literally meant, and for most people still mean, that the pair-bond is male dominant. Little wonder, then, that marriage has so long resisted the universal human urge to intensify the complexity of relationships. Komarovsky (1962) and Babchuck and Bates (1963) have strongly supported the thesis that both husband and wife maintain close relationships with same-sex peers and that the marital relationship tends to be male-dominated in both blue-collar (Komarovsky) and lower-middle-class couples. (Babchuck and Bates)

It is possible to point to attempts by some, at various times and places, to free marriage to some degree from the restraint of male domination and by thus proclaiming equality of the sexes, to permit the emergence of alternatives to exclusivity in marriage. These efforts always failed or were tolerated only in certain special, small, restricted, and segregated groups, because in the larger society women were not yet peers. Bird (1970) shows how, in a patriarchal society, conditions at a physical or economic frontier may, of necessity, produce equality of the sexes, but as soon as the period of consolidation and stability is reached, it becomes a mark of status to keep an idle woman. The emergence of free love in conjunction with revolutionary movements is noted time and again, only to see the return of male-dominated pair-bond exclusivity as soon as the revolution succeeds or fails. Indeed, free love can be considered a revolutionary tool, for it quickly sets apart and isolates the in-group from family and friends, both symbolically and literally.

In this context it is important to understand that "revolutionaries" or dissidents can be political, social, religious, economic, cultural, or a combination of these. Often the combination is called utopian, hippie, or anarchistic without regard to the actual goals or beliefs involved. A few of these people are regarded as the lunatic fringe and are tolerated by the larger society because they are amusing and sometimes even productive, especially the cultural radicals such as musicians, artists, or theatrical types. Others have been less tolerated, typically driven out or underground, and often persecuted, no matter what the stripe of their dissident bent. The survival factor in such groups appears to be strong patriarchal and/or religious orientation and considerable structure. Almost invariably they have eased away from sexual experimentation in favor of exclusive male-dominated marriage bonds. This happens in spite of the fact that, in theory at least, any alternative to pair-bond exclusivity could be practiced in a closed group, provided the group was willing to accept joint child-rearing and nurturing responsibility.

Nevertheless, until the society as a whole began to accept the right of the female to be a peer, such excursions into marriage alternatives could only fail. A woman who is dependent on her husband must grant his requests, including the demand for sexual exclusivity, even though she may know that he is not practicing the same exclusivity. If she has no skills to sell, no viable means of support without him, she can hardly demur. An economically emancipated wife is in a much better position to insist on equality because she is self-sufficient, a factor that may also increase her social self-sufficiency. Thus the stage is set for pair-bonding between equal partners, each able to sustain a life outside marriage, so that both enter into the relationship voluntarily on the assumption that the anticipated benefits will be greater than would be available in a non-pair-bonded state. Furthermore, survival of the marriage depends on each continuing to place a higher value on maintaining the pair-bond than on reverting to their previous state. In other words, a continuing relationship depends on each continuing to extend to the other the privileges of open marriage in the O'Neill (1972) sense. Osofsky (1971) has characterized this as a form of parity or androgeny where each partner has an equal number of options for roles outside the marriage. Consensual sexual activity outside the pair-bond would be among these options but should not be construed as a determinant characteristic of a pair-bond. The final touch to this new equal status in the pair-bond is female control over conception for the first time in history. Pregnancy is no longer a viable threat to the female. The advent of the pill has removed the last major physical weapon in the male arsenal.

In the 1950's trends toward increased geographic and career mobility and toward greater social and economic freedom for women began to come together for the emergence of the new life-styles in marriage. Academic, professional, and managerial people became increasingly mobile, leading William H. Whyte, Jr. (1956) to write *The Organization Man* and Russell Lynes (1953) to coin the term *Upper Bohemian* to describe these people. The United States Bureau of the Census pointed out that 20 per cent of the population moved to a new location outside the county in which they had been living, and much of this movement was accounted for by the aforementioned academic, professional, and managerial groups. Riesman, Glazer, and Denny (1955) pointed out that this is an *other-directed society* and identified these same types of individuals as typifying the new breed which must be capable of self-restraint while recognizing that groups vary in what is considered desirable and undesirable behavior. As Slater (1968) tells us, they saw the other-directed individual as one who must be acutely sensitive and responsive to group norms while recognizing the essential arbitrariness, particularity, and limited relevance of all moral imperatives. Pity the inner-directed conformist, therefore, the throwback who was programmed from birth to display a limited range of responses in all situations, regardless of environmental variation, which, while possibly heroic, is excessively simpleminded.

As Slater develops the temporary systems theme, following in the footsteps of Bott, Komarovsky, and others cited earlier, he says:

> Spouses are now asked to be lovers, friends, mutual therapists, in a society which is forcing the marriage bond to become the closest, deepest, most important, and putatively most enduring relationship of one's life. Paradoxically, then, it is increasingly likely to fall short of the emotional demands placed upon it and be dissolved.

The end point of Slater's argument is that people can and must press toward the full exploitation of their talents, since in a truly temporary society, everyone would have to be a generalist, able to step into any role in the group to which he belongs at the moment. This is in marked contrast to the present situation, in which the upper bohemians tend to specialize in certain roles (which is one of the reasons they are mobile) both on the job and in social situations. Consequently, each time they move to a new geographic location they must search for groups that need their roles.

It is these several reasons that have caused some of the results in the sexual area of shifting from ritualistically determined marriages based on rights to self-determined ones based on privilege. Highly mobile pair-bonds who are here today and moved tomorrow cannot depend on formal or ritual structure because they are perpetually in a time-bind. They must turn to each other and evolve a much more complex relationship to replace kin, neighbor, and friendship relational structure that is no longer available on a long-term basis. They must also develop means of getting informally plugged in quickly whenever they move. When Lynes coined the upper bohemian label, it was for the purpose of describing just such informal networks, although he did not describe their sexual overtones. It is interesting to find Farson (1969) and Stoller (1970) advocating various forms of intimate networks as a means of dealing with the interpersonal intimacy impoverishment of the isolated nuclear family. It is rather surprising that recognition of the existence of such systems has been so late in coming.

The temporary systems strata is the group in which women are most likely to be treated as peers. This group is augmented by others with sufficient education and exposure to ideas to be strongly influenced by current trends. (Gagnon and Simon, 1968; McLuhan and Leonard, 1967; O'Neill and O'Neill, 1970; Ramey, 1972; and Smith and Smith, 1970) Already many of the college-age young people have the same attitudes toward peer relationships in the pair-bond that exist among some of the better educated upper middle-class members of the depression generation. A surprising number of people in the general population seem to believe that, indeed, it is the young people who should be blamed for giving birth to the idea that men and women are equals!

The current forays into sexual alternatives to monogamy are seen as attempts to build a more complex network of intimate relationships that can absorb some of the impact of the new-found complexity of the pair-bond by short-circuiting the process of developing ancillary relationships in the usual ritualistic manner. It is believed that this occurs for two reasons: 1. Because there is not time to go through a long process of finding a group that needs the roles the couple can fill, and 2. because using sexual intimacy as an entry role guarantees the couple that, other things being equal, they can fill the role. Particularly if such ties are to take up the slack of the unavailable kin-neighbor-friendship relational systems, as well as relieve some of the pressure on the newly complex pair-bond interaction, they must begin on a much deeper, more intimate basis than the ties they replace. Both time and emotional press will allow nothing short of this. The relationship must cut through the ritual layers quickly in order to be of any help, and indeed, as Brecher (1969) indicates, the entire courting sequence is often telescoped from several weeks or months to as little as an hour. What better way to insure that this will happen than to attempt to relate in a taboo area? Everyone has had the discouraging experience of pursuing a friendship for many months, only to discover suddenly an emotional block to further progress toward meaningful interaction, which was not apparent when the relationship first began. Usually there is no means of discovering what the other person's taboos will be until one comes up against them. While the assumption that those without sexual taboos will have a minimum of other taboos to intensive interaction on the gut level is not a valid one, it seems to hold up well for many people in many situations, perhaps because sexual inhibitions are among the deepest rooted.

Entry into free love or swinging relationships typically takes place from this set of circumstances. A less typical set will be described later. Entry into communes and group marriage sometimes takes place without going through either of these stages, but more typically proceeds from them, especially among the 30-and-over age group. (Ramey, 1972)

Given the societal conditions that have made it necessary for couples living in a temporary-systems world to find new ways to function as a couple that are more complex than have been necessary in the past, and given also that women are more likely to be peers at such a societal level than formerly, it does not follow that all couples in this situation will react by becoming involved in one of the alternative life-styles under discussion. But these conditions do foster such behavior on the part of some people, and for them it will be a more successful adaptation than for those whose pair-bond is not a relationship of peers. It is evident that this behavior is also emulated by others who are neither in the temporary-systems strata nor peers in the pair-bond, as well as by a few who may be part of the working class. (Ramey, 1972; Smith and Smith, 1970; Symonds, 1970; Bartell, 1970)

THE MODEL

Much of the confusion in discussions of swinging, communes, and group marriage relates to the difference between committed and uncommitted relationships. For heuristic purposes, this embraces Kanter's (1968) three types of commitment: *cathectic,* or commitment to the individual; *cognitive,* which involves weighing the value of continuing in a group or leaving it; and *evaluative,* which involves belief in the perceived moral rightness of group ideology.

The following hypotheses are proposed:

1. Nonconsensual adultery and swinging are free love activities which involve no commitment or minimal commitment.
2. Intimate friendship, evolutionary communes, and group marriage involve considerable individual commitment, and in the case of the communes and group marriage, commitment to the group as well.
3. Swinging may constitute a transitional step between minimal individual commitment and growth of such commitment between spouses.
4. Once husband and wife have begun to experience the joy and satisfaction of individual growth through joint dialogue and commitment, they may find their newfound responsiveness to one another so satisfying that they drop out of swinging.
5. As the marriage takes on more and more aspects of a peer relationship, the couple may consensually agree to increase the complexity of their relationship through the development of intimate friendships with other individuals or couples, through which the sense of commitment to the individual is extended to these significant others.
6. A significant portion (apparently about 50 per cent, Ramey 1972) of the couples who become candidates for evolutionary communes or group marriage come from among those who have developed intimate friendships.
7. Group marriage, which combines commitment to the group with multiple pair-bonding among the members of the group, is the most complex form of marriage.
8. These various marriage alternatives can be placed on a continuum that ranges from dyadic marriage with minimal commitment (in which there may be nonconsensual adultery), to swinging, to peer marriage, to intimate friendship, to evolutionary commune, to group marriage.

In general, by *commitment* we mean a relationship involving dialogue, trust, and responsibility. Within the pair-bond, we accept Kanter's definition of cathectic commitment, "willingness to accept unlimited liability for."

Neither of these profiles concerns intelligence, income level, or formal education, although it is unusual to find the committed person lacking money or education unless he has deliberately chosen to renounce them. Extreme pictures have been drawn in order to sharpen the contrast. Some people have insight in some areas and not in others, but it is nevertheless possible to clearly distinguish between those who seek to relate to others and those who do not find it possible to do so. This differentiation is necessary to comprehension of the diffusion process to be described, but it should be emphasized that these are normal, average people. Although their religious commitment tends to be low, they range politically from radical to conservative, are better educated than most of the population, and are of high socioeconomic status, so that they hardly fit popular conceptions of deviant individuals. (Smith and Smith, 1971) In fact, one recently completed study employed the MMPI and found the subjects "disgustingly normal." (Twitchell, 1970, as reported by Smith and Smith, 1971)

Figure 1 indicates the relationship between the degree of complexity of the commitment individuals are willing to make and the type of pair-bond relationship one is likely to find them enjoying. The figure reads in one direction only; not all individuals with deep and complex levels of commitment will necessarily join a group marriage, but individuals in a group marriage can be expected to have such a commitment within their relationship. The pair-bond involving peers is deliberately indicated to be at a level above the zero point on this figure.

The first thing that is apparent from Figure 2 is that free love activities such as affairs, adultery, or swinging are treated differently from intimate friendship, evolutionary communes, or group marriage. Free love is an uncommitted activity (open-ended sexual seeking and consummating without legal or other commitment of any kind) that is widespread among both single and married individuals. It may occur between the marriage partners within some mar-

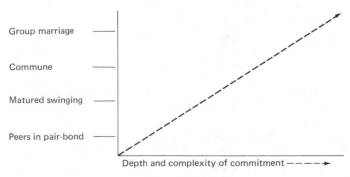

Figure 1.

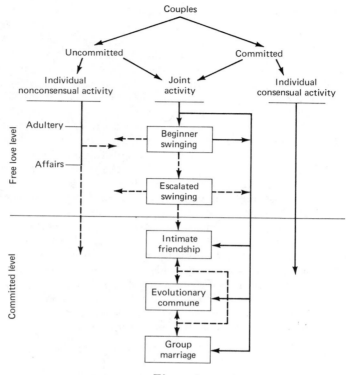

Figure 2.

riages, and is the type of activity which Bell and Silvan (1970) refer to as "activity which usually involves guilt and dishonesty and often does not include any notion of fun and recreation." It is easy to understand that people caught up in the stereotype of high drama, jealousy, and tragic romance as part of their cultural expectation about a one-sided relationship outside the pair-bond would not only not have fun, but would neither invest nor receive enough pleasure from the relationship to make it a joyous exchange rather than a contest-chase, tragic loss, or terrible trap.

There is a crossover between the free love and committed levels through swinging. Most uncommitted couples never manage to get beyond the two stages of swinging, since their activity remains strictly on a free love basis, even though it involves joint activity. Such a couple may decide to legitimize individual nonconsensual activity by becoming jointly involved in swinging. The reverse is also possible.

It is possible, though unlikely, that an uncommitted couple may become temporarily involved in intimate friendship, group marriage, or a commune. Intimate friendship, which will be more fully defined later, can be distinguished from free love swinging in terms of Martin Buber's (1955) distinction between collectivity and community:

> Collectivity is not a binding but a bundling together: individuals packed together, armed and equipped in common, with only as much life from person to person as will enflame the marching step. But community . . . is the being no longer side by side but with one another of a multitude of persons. And this multitude, though it also moves toward one goal, yet experiences everywhere a turning to, a dynamic facing of, the other, a flowing from I to thou. . . . Collectivity is based on an organized atrophy of personal existence, community on its increase and confirmation in life lived toward one another.

If such involvement results in the removal of blocks to the ability to develop and sustain complex relationships, well and good. In many instances, however, such attempts are indeed temporary and may be disastrous for the intimate friendship group, commune, or group marriage involved. There is a great deal of evidence to support this contention. (Kanter, 1970; Nordhoff, 1961) Many reports of communes and group marriages that have not succeeded indicate that the group was unable to deal with uncommitted people who had not been recognized as unable to deal with complex relationships before they were accepted into the group. It is usually easy for the intimate friendship group to simply drop the couple. (Palson, 1970; Breedlove, 1964)

Some uncommitted couples manage to grow sufficiently to graduate to either intimate friendship or consensual individual sexual activity that is based on more than simple sex. While this does not seem to be the case for most of the uncommitted, the potential is always present, and it is not unreasonable to conjecture that, given time, greater numbers will move into the ranks of the committed. Considering the degree to which this has occurred over the past two decades, it may not take as long as expected. While most of these people continue to operate at the free love level, many seem to be progressing from individual excursions outside the pair-bond to joint swinging. Even if they never move to a more complex relationship than this, they will have taken a significant and rewarding step toward ability to relate in their marriage, for the one spontaneous response interviewers frequently hear is the vast improvement experienced in ability to talk to one another, not only about sexual matters, but in general. (Brecher, 1969; Denfield and Gordon, 1970; O'Neill and O'Neill, 1970; Palson, 1970; Smith and Smith, 1970)

Turning to the committed side of Figure 2, one finds that in a union of equals, both persons are free to explore, on a consensual basis, any and all forms of complex relationship that seem interesting. In the O'Neills' terms (1972), this activity can be termed *open marriage*. Those who practice open marriage often develop intimate friendships. Some couples begin moving toward more complex experiences in this manner and progress to making multiple life commitments through the same group (generally identified as a commune) or to the most complex type of marital commitment—establishing more than one pair-bond simultaneously (group marriage). Other couples skip the intimate friendship stage and move directly into the communal or group-marriage stage. How many will ultimately be satisfied to relate at which level is not known.

Since there are so many new recruits swelling the ranks of swingers, communalists, and group marriages, and there is also constant turnover of those who are interested but uncommitted who find such activity too threatening once they have tried it, it is difficult to assess the degree of diffusion as well as the level of complexity at which most people ultimately establish relational system homeostasis. One cannot guess how long the process will take for the average couple.

Sometimes one or more group marriages can be found in a commune. Members of communes and group marriages almost always feel free to swing or engage in individual sexual activity outside the group with complete acceptance of such activity by the group. Also, while many committed couples enter swinging activity at the intimate friendship stage via personal introduction by friends who are already intimate, some go through the beginner stage first, especially if they live in a new neighborhood or a socially limiting situation that forces them to use surreptitious means, such as a blind ad in a swinging magazine, to gain entry into the swinging scene. A few of these people might pass through the escalated stage.

SWINGING

Swinging was defined at the beginning of this article as:

> Generally involving two or more pair-bonded couples who mutually decide to switch sexual partners or engage in group sex. Singles may be included either through temporary coupling with another individual specifically for the purpose of swinging or as part of a triadic or larger group sexual experience.

To say that swinging generally involves two or more pair-bonded couples may seem inexact. Actually, swinging may involve adding only one person of either sex to the pair-bond. Some couples find it easier to relate to one person than to two. Some find it easier to locate one person who is compatible with both than to find another couple in which both the male and the female are compatible with both husband and wife. Singles are thus involved in swinging directly. It is surprising that this point has been disputed by some reporters on the swinging scene (Breedlove, 1964) especially since many acknowledge that it is the swinging singles who sometimes give the total swinging scene a bad name. Palson (1970) points out that:

To singles, swinging looks more like a long time of sexual encounters with no attempt to form the "proper" kind of personal union, whereas married couples, secure in their own union, can experience friendly sex with others, knowing that they have achieved a permanence with one mate as morality ordains, and that sex with others can actually enhance this relationship.

Many researchers have interviewed threesomes (Smith and Smith, 1970; O'Neill and O'Neill, 1970) and it would appear that more stable threesome relationships exist than any other type. The author recently analyzed ads in four major swinger magazines and found that the second most looked-for situation, whether the advertiser was a couple, a single male, or a single female, was "couples or single females desired." The third-ranked desire was for "couples or singles, male or female." Bartell (1971) reports similar results.

The implied threat to the pair-bond of accepting a single into a sexual union, even temporarily, obviously is a problem for the committed couple. More couples swing with single women than with single men. In a male-dominate pair-bond, the male has little to gain from swinging with a single male, along with the threat of direct competition in the swinging situation with his wife, unless he happens to enjoy sexual contacts with other men. Even in the latter case, he would be unlikely to expose such inclinations to his wife. Such activity would be more likely to occur if the couple regarded themselves as equals, free to explore all kinds of multiple sexual relationships.

Some people, especially therapists, have characterized swinging as a male-dominated activity that serves largely to actualize male fantasies. The recent report of the President's Commission on Obscenity and Pornography (1970) suggests that women are just as likely to have such fantasies, as did Masters and Johnson (1966). It has often been pointed out that men are most likely to suggest swinging, but less often remarked that men are also most likely to suggest getting out of swinging. This seems to occur because swinging is a great equalizer which appears to promote female independence due to the markedly different capacity of the female for prolonged sexual involvement and the newfound sense of self-worth that many wives find in swinging. This is one of the reasons that many couples reevaluate their own pair-bonding relationship as a result of their involvement in swinging.

Our definition emphasized that swinging does not necessarily involve mate switching. It simply may involve participation in group sex, as defined by the O'Neills (1969). Some swingers who will not swing with a single are quite willing to involve singles in group sex, as at a party. Singles may also form temporary couples for the purpose of swinging with those couples who will not swing with a single alone or because the single is a married person whose mate refuses to swing.

Symonds' (1970) definition of swinging suggests that this is an activity involving strangers. Brecher (1969) has pointed out, however, as have others, that the same sort of courtship occurs in swinging that occurs between two people on a conventional date, but that this courtship is more likely to be truncated than among the unmarried.

Swinging has been separated into a beginner and escalated stage, both of which are uncommitted in nature and are linked to intimate friendship, to which many swingers graduate.

Couples become involved in swinging for many reasons. They want to make out, they seek an alternative to clandestine individual adventures outside the pair-bond, they see other people doing it, or one partner, usually the husband, forces the other into it often to assuage guilt or to "save the marriage." They make an issue of swinging without any emotional involvement, at least at the beginning. "It is just a sex thing."

The committed couple, by contrast, becomes involved in intimate friendship because they wish to expand their already joyous relationship by joint investment in other people at the sociosexual level in responsive, responsible relationships. In either case, the societal pressures outlined earlier will have contributed greatly to developing the climate in which such activity can be expected to flourish.

Many committed couples grow into intimate friendship naturally with friends of long standing. Others are introduced into intimate friendships by mutual friends, where the person-to-person interaction is more important than the genital-to-genital interaction and the object is to form relationships that may include sexual involvement as one part of a much larger and more complex level of interaction. The complexity depends on the people involved. Some find that developing a close union with one or a few couples is sufficient to meet their needs. Others form looser bonds with a greater number of people. The nature of the involvement varies much the same way as the involvement between mates in a pair-bond.

How does one become a swinger? An essential ingredient is to see oneself as a swinger. Many people who switch partners occasionally do not consider themselves swingers, although others might say they are. Some who do not actually swing like to believe they are swingers, although they would not be so classified by others. Many would-be swingers try it once and decide it is not for them. Little is known about this group because it is hard to identify. No one can even say how large it is. While it may be relatively unimportant, there are those who are keenly interested because they are concerned about just how many swingers there are in the population. The percentage varies with the definition of swinger, not to mention the other difficulties with establishing it. In terms of the diffusion of innovation, however, it is of interest to know whether current saturation is nearing the critical eight to ten per cent level at which one would look for rather rapid and overwhelming acceptance of swinging by the society.

Once the decision is made to try swinging, one must find the swingers. Many nonswingers think swinging is a made-up fantasy created by journalists and others with something to sell. Many swingers are convinced that the whole world swings! If the potential swinger does not have swingers among his friends that he knows about, he may attempt to seduce friends to try it. This can be risky business, especially in the eyes of the neophyte, who may turn next to public entry points. Apparently only about five per cent are forced to do this (Breedlove and Breedlove, 1964), although Bartell claims it is the most-used method. A number of public swinging institutions have parallels in the singles world, such as swinging bars, socials, magazines, personal columns in underground papers, and the Sexual Freedom League. The uncommitted seem much more likely to use these public entry points than the committed, who find it much easier to relate to others in a meaningful way.

The second swinging stage, called *escalated swinging*, is avoided by most swingers. Those who get there may do so because they made a poor decision. It may take some time for the uncommitted couple to arrive at this decision. She may begin to feel like a prostitute. He may become impotent. Having sex with people with whom one does not relate gets stale pretty quickly for most people.

Some people drop out at this point, deciding that swinging is not for them after all. Others realize that they must invest in people if swinging is to continue to have meaning for them. These people may graduate to intimate friendship. The sharing of intimacy not only has been working on them as a couple, it has also given them a bridge to other people. A few make the third choice—they escalate. They restore potency by upping the ante, experimenting with more and more way-out behavior. Ultimately this path must form a closed loop, for such escalation cannot be continued indefinitely. Eventually they must drop out or begin to relate to people as people and not as sex objects.

Swingers do not appear to handle their swinging relationships on a different basis than other friendships. On the contrary, it would appear that most swinging couples simply add swinging to the list of criteria they use for selecting friends, just as the sailing crowd and the mah jong group choose most of their friends from among those who share this common interest. Reports that swingers compartmentalize swinging apart from otherwise ordinary lives appear to confuse the common tendency of some swingers to hide swinging from their business associates or others in straight society with having two social worlds. Time constraints alone would argue against this. As Paul Goodman said in a recent interview (1971):

> In the instances where I have been able to make a contact I have almost invariably found a friend and in many of these cases these friendships have gone on for 30 or 40 years, even though they rapidly become non-sexual relationships. . . . St. Thomas Acquinas has pointed out the chief use of human sexuality, aside from procreation, is getting to know another

> person—in other words, you don't love somebody and then have sex with them. You have sex with them and then love them.

Many couples indicate that they were quite active when they began swinging but tapered off as soon as they found people with whom they shared the same norms and standards that they had previously used to select friends. The decision to largely confine their circle of friends to those people, they explain, is because relationships with these people are more honest and open on all levels and not just in relation to swinging. In a significant number of these relationships there is only occasional swinging, or no longer any swinging, and it is not unusual to find that these couples are no longer actively looking for new swinging partners.

No one knows, at this juncture, how many of the uncommitted get beyond the free love levels we have been discussing. So many newcomers are joining the scene that the issue is quite confused. It may be some time before we can say with any assurance how many of the uncommitted are able ultimately to relate to others well enough to be graduated to the intimate friendship classification.

Symonds (1970) classified swingers as either recreational or utopian, whereas Bartell (1969) claimed that the chief characteristic of all couples in his sample was their inherent normality. We believe Symonds may have failed to differentiate between those beginners who constitute the extremist fringe at the lower edge of the spectrum and those swingers who are in academic, professional, and managerial strata and tend to exhibit more of the attributes of her utopians than of her recreationals (Brecher, 1969, Ramey, 1972, O'Neill and O'Neill, 1970). Also there is the possibility that she failed to distinguish between this group and the beginners who are still overwhelmed with the idea of swinging and even more with relating to people on a more complex level. Most swingers exhibit *some* of the attributes she identifies with recreationals, while few, if any, exhibit all of her utopian attributes and none of the recreational. This may be especially important in California, where knowledge of swinging has permeated many layers of society that are not usually involved in complex pair-bond relationships.

An important distinguishing characteristic of the intimate friendship, commune, or group marriage is the open problem-solving and relating they favor. Carl Rogers said in 1951 that people resist experience which might force them to change through denial or distortion of symbolization. Thus the uncommitted swinger must either drop out or ritualize the swinging experience. Recognizing this, those who wish to help the uncommitted bridge the gap must relax the situation and reduce the threat. As Rogers went on to say:

> The structure and organization of self appears to become more rigid under threat; to relax its boundaries when completely free of threat. Experience which is perceived as inconsistent with the self can only be assimilated if the current organization of self is relaxed and expanded to include it.

The committed appear to recognize this. Their striking emphasis on openness, sensitivity to feelings, and acceptance of differences is not uncharacteristic of some other in-groups where there is a marked perceived difference between the in-group peers and "other" (Ramey, 1958).

Observers of the swinging scene have been consistently impressed by the degree to which swingers accept people as they are, allowing them to express their feelings and attitudes freely and nonjudgmentally, and operating in a generally democratic manner, treating males and females as peers (Brecher, 1969; Lewis, 1969; Kanter, 1970). The basic rules seems to be responsiveness to the other person's needs and desires; the next most basic: "do your own thing." It is this atmosphere of permissiveness and understanding that provides a situation free of threat in which the beginners can work out their own internal frame of reference and reach responsible interpretations and insights. The resulting self-acceptance generally leads to observable improvement in the individual's interpersonal relations. This fits Rogers' thesis well. It also facilitates graduating from swinging to intimate friendship.

COMMUNES

Many people seem to equate *commune* and *intentional community* without realizing that a commune is only one of many different types of intentional community. A commune is an expression of the desire to make the dyadic pair-bond a subset of one, rather than many mediating groups between it and the society at large. Most people make life commitments through a number of groups: work groups, play groups, special-interest groups, hobby groups, health groups, religious groups, economic groups, social groups, political groups, cultural groups; in fact, as Alexis de Tocqueville is alleged to have said, every time four or five Americans get together they form a new group. The critical point is that most persons do not make a large percentage of their commitments through one single group. Marks (1969) has defined commune in terms of:

> Joint or common ownership and function and specifically sharing dining and sleeping quarters.

This definition seems more restrictive than necessary. Huxley (1937) claimed that:

> All effective communities are founded upon the principle of unlimited liability. In small groups composed of members personally acquainted with one another, unlimited liability provides a liberal education in responsibility, loyalty, and consideration. . . . Individual members should possess nothing and everything—nothing as individuals and everything as joint owners of communally held property and communally produced income. Property and income should not be so large as to become ends in themselves, not so small that the entire

energies of the community have to be directed to procuring tomorrow's dinner.

At all times and in all places communities have been formed for the purpose of making it possible for their members to live more nearly in accord with the currently accepted religious ideals than could be done "in the world." Such communities have devoted a considerable proportion of their time and energy to study, to the performance of ceremonial acts of devotion and, in some cases at any rate, to the practice of "spiritual exercises."

From . . . the salient characteristics of past communities we can see what future communities ought to be and do. We see that they should be composed of carefully selected individuals, united in a common belief and by fidelity to a shared ideal. We see that property and income should be held in common and that every member should assume unlimited liability for all other members. We see the disciplinary arrangements may be of various kinds, but that the most educative form of organization is the democratic. We see that it is advisable for communities to undertake practical work in addition to study, devotion, and spiritual exercises; and that this practical work should be of a kind which other social agencies, public or private, are either unable or unwilling to perform.

Definitions of commune are difficult to find but many of the elements are in this lengthy quote from Huxley. In order to encompass all of the groups that claim to be communes today, however, it is necessary to devise a less restrictive definition, such as the one at the beginning of this paper:

When individuals agree to make life commitments as members of one particular group rather than through many different groups they may constitute a commune. The number of common elements will vary from commune to commune, the critical number having been reached at the point at which the group sees itself as a commune rather than at some absolute number.

Although some communes do share dining and/or sleeping quarters and some espouse joint ownership, income, and function, this is not the case for all communes. Quite a few communes have separate quarters, either in a jointly owned apartment building or in separate houses, for example. The type and range of common commitments is such that "being a commune" is almost a state of mind. Some groups, which have many more of the kinds of commitments in common usually associated with communes, call themselves co-ops.

Which of the many life commitments are most commonly met through a commune? Creating goods and services, worshiping in a specific manner, merchandising, purchasing, property ownership and management, farming, travel, educating and rearing children in a specific manner, study, friendship, and social or political action are some of the common attributes of communes. The world has always functioned through interest groups. The most common of these through the ages has been the tribe and its components, the families. One of the most-often-cited reasons for the current upsurge of interest in communes is the desire to return to an extended family or tribal grouping. Indeed, many communes refer to themselves not by name, but simply as "the family."

It is not by accident that the successful communes, those that have survived, have not been extended families but have instead been groups with a strong unifying and motivating drive and a strong leader. In many cases this unifying factor has been religious. Currently, in addition to the religious drive, there are a substantial number of successful communes built around the desire to optimize coping capacity in a quasi-capitalistic society; these are people who establish a commune in order to do better that which they are already doing well.

There are three major varieties of communes and one trial variety. They can be classified as the religious communes which have existed in America since 1680, if not earlier; the utopian communes; and the new breed of evolutionary communes mentioned above. What distinguishes this latter group is that they are not about to drop out of or attempt to change the existing society. They simply seek to increase their ability to work effectively within the system. The fourth type of commune is the student commune, which will be handled in a separate section because of its two unique characteristics—it is temporary and it is a learning situation.

Utopian commune	Evolutionary commune	Religious commune
Drop-out orientation	High achievers	Highly structured
Do your own thing	Highly mobile	Authoritarian leader
Loosely organized	Straight jobs	Work ethic
Usually subsidized	Upper middle class	Usually self-sustaining
Youth oriented	Opinion leaders	Withdrawn from society
Sometimes revolutionary	Most over 30	Family oriented
Usually short-lived	Many post-children	

Religious communes have enjoyed the highest survival rate among all United States communes, probably due to their strong patriarchal, highly structured, and fervently goal-directed orientation. Although some have loosened up a bit over the years, others have survived with little change. The most successful group, the Hutterites, have grown from three original colonies in 1874 to over 170 colonies today, each averaging about 150 members. Most of these groups are in the provinces of Alberta, Saskatchewan, and Manitoba, Canada, but approximately 50 colonies are scattered through South Dakota and Montana. A religious group of more recent origin, the Bruderhof, came from Germany to the United States in the 1950's, by way of England and Paraguay because of persecution that began in the 1930's. Already the original settlement in Rifton, New York, has spawned two other groups, one in Connecticut and the other in Pennsylvania. Religious communes are not the concern of this paper, but for those who wish to pursue the subject, see Carden, 1969; Hostetler, 1968; Krippner and Fersh, 1970; Nordhoff, 1961; Kanter, 1970; and Redekop, 1969.

The utopian communes have suffered unreasonably at the hands of the press. Many are unjustifiably called "hippie communes" while others actually fit this designation. The most successful of these new drop-out groups are highly structured, centering around the leadership of strong, charismatic individuals, or deliberately submerging leadership in a consensual format that seeks to elevate all group members to the level of generalist. Some groups have strong political overtones, either in the revolutionary sense or in terms of complete withdrawal from society. These are the back-to-the-land, organic-food, vegetarian, hand-labor groups who typically seek to become completely self-sustaining without recourse to the rest of society. Still other groups are "do your own thing—when the spirit moves you" groups. Some of these are heavily involved in the drug culture. Most utopian groups espouse the values of rural living, although few of them are found in the country.

Just as the religious communes cluster at the highly structured end of a continuum, so do many of the utopian communes cluster at the unstructured end of the continuum, but the failure rate is extremely high among these groups. Other utopian groups can be found at points on the continuum, and many of them seem to be slowly migrating toward the more highly structured end. All of the utopian groups located in the country labor under the handicap of high visibility, which makes survival especially difficult in the light of sensational headlines in the mass media. A significant recent development among the utopians is the emergence of collectives of communes. There are at least a dozen of these collectives already and more are being set up all the time. Free Vermont, for example, is a collective of sixteen communes which already sponsors a number of joint projects, such as a children's commune, a traveling medical test service, and a peak-load work-sharing system. The Powelton Village Association of Communes in Philadelphia, which includes 30 communes, operates a flourishing food-purchasing co-op, a baby-sitting service, and a free garage for fixing communal automobiles at cost. They are now considering alternative ways of dealing with banks and insurance companies and setting up a car pool. As in the case of religious communes, the focus of this paper is elsewhere and the reader is directed, for further information, to Collier, 1969; Houriet, 1969; Hine, 1953; Kriyanada, 1969; *Modern Utopian,* all issues; Kanter, 1970; and Spiro, 1963.

The new breed among communes, those the author calls *evolutionary communes,* is the least known. They are springing up across metropolitan areas without fanfare, going out of their way to avoid publicity in most cases, realizing that if they attract attention they will be diverted from their goals. There is particular concern about evolutionary communes here because they appear to be the most attractive to those academic, professional, and managerial people who make up the temporary-systems strata, assuming they elect to continue working within the present society. Those who do not choose to do so can be expected to go in the direction of the utopian commune rather than the religious commune in almost every case. For this reason, many of the things said about evolutionary communes will also apply to some of the more highly structured utopian communes.

While there may be those who are enamored with the back-to-the-land movement, most evolutionary communalists have no intention of abandoning either their careers or their middle-class comforts. The basis for establishing such a commune is the desire of a group of committed people to cope with our present-day society in a more successful manner than they can manage as couples or individuals. This coping can take many forms, depending on the particular group. The desire to provide better schooling for their children, to pool resources for investment, shelter, purchasing, and to provide access for luxuries otherwise unavailable are among the reasons for this movement. One group may be especially concerned about providing the buffer of group security against extended unemployment so that members can be free to stay in a particular geographic area without suffering career setbacks because they refuse to move physically in order to move up the career ladder. Few couples have sufficient resources of their own to take a chance on waiting, perhaps for several months, until an appropriate job can be found in the city. A related concern in many groups is the desire to provide educational opportunities for group members or their children that are beyond the resources of a single couple.

The most basic reason for becoming involved in an evolutionary commune, however, is the desire to expand the complexity of inter-relationships beyond the possibilities inherent in the pair-bond itself. In the widest sense, the key term is propinquity, for communal living makes possible a person-to-person intimacy on both sexual and nonsexual levels that goes far beyond even the most closely knit intimate friendship group. It simply is not possible to sustain the same level of interaction among intimate friends that one has in the pair-bond unless members of the group are in close proximity to one another much of the time. The level of interaction falls short of multiple pair-bonds (in most cases), however. While group marriages have been found in communes, most communalists are not yet ready to go so far as to consider themselves married to several people at once. The size of most communes argues against such intimacy if the readiness state of the members does not, for evolutionary communes range in size from ten to 130 individuals.

As mentioned earlier, man is a problem-solving organism, happiest when he is solving problems of an ever-increasing degree of complexity. It is at the level of commune or group marriage that one most often hears couples speak about the joy of interrelating on a more complex basis. They speak with excitement and animation about personal growth in the shared context of a group larger than two, which seems to provide a different and more stimulating critical mass for personal development, often in directions the couple do not share in common and therefore cannot develop on their own.

An overriding external factor that may contribute to the predisposition of many people toward more complex interrelationships is the current swing of family life to its lowest common denominator—the barely viable nuclear family. Leaving aside the political and economic forces that have promoted this move, the lack of viability remains sadly evident, since the norm of working father, housekeeping mother, and children actually exists in less than fifty per cent of American families. The vast majority of Americans have had personal experience with the sense of aloneness that comes with growing up in or being a marriage partner in a nuclear family that must cope alone with the vicissitudes of life. Many know the burden of life in a nuclear family that proved not to be viable and became less than the norm—a single-parent family or a two-working-parent family. Childless couples or couples with grown children also experience great difficulty when problems threaten the viability of the family. The extended family is remembered as a less vulnerable lifestyle for the family because the larger size of the group made it more viable. Communes and group marriages are seen as a way of moving back toward that more viable group size and doing so, moreover, with *chosen* individuals.

Before discussing evolutionary communes further, two important points about communes in general must be made: first, with respect to how they get established, and second, with regard to how they handle sexual intimacy.

Some communes are started with almost no preplanning or attention to the basic questions that should be answered in order to avoid almost certain failure. This is the case especially with so-called hippie communes, where the word of the day is "Action! Let it all hang loose and it will all come together." This kind of simple faith in miracles is pathetically common and the communes that begin this way are almost certainly doomed to failure. Others engage in talk marathons that may go on for months, without ever discussing the basic questions that must be resolved, or without resolving them. Again, the end result is usually failure. The religious commune groups usually seem to avoid this problem because they are typically led by a strong man who makes all the decisions and will not brook dissension and because they are united in religious fervor—the strong leader is expressing God's will. The evolutionary communes are most likely to have approached the decision to establish a commune by establishing a consensual process for working through structure and process as the first step in moving from being talkers to becoming doers (Ramey, 1967).

Five distinct types of sexual intimacy prevail in communes, some of which are so destructive that, everything else being equal, the commune is still very likely to fail because of the sexual structure. One of these patterns is celibacy. A commune that practices celibacy can last only one generation unless it is able to attract enough recruits to replace those who die. The Shakers were one such group that did not succeed. Exclusive monogamy is another sexual stance; in most religious communes exclusive monogamy is practiced with extreme prohibitions against the transgressor, who may even be expelled from the group. Free love is sometimes the sexual mode of the commune, but this is less often the case than is generally imagined. Free love groups seem to be very short lived; probably a group that is uncommitted sexually is uncommitted in general and thus unable to sustain the level of cooperation necessary to the survival of a commune. A few communes claim to practice free love on a committed basis; the group consists of "brothers and sisters" who are all one family and the family takes responsibility jointly for child rearing and nurturing. Since they practice free love only within the group, albeit without pair-bonding, they are enjoying the best of two worlds. Their responsibility is to the group, not to the individual, but they are not a group marriage because no one is pair-bonded. The author knows of at least one such group that has survived for more than two years and appears to be getting stronger. It is too early to speculate about the long-range effects, however, even though one is strongly tempted to draw parallels with the early days of the kibbutzim, many of which began this way.

The most generally practiced intimacy pattern is intimate friendship, especially in the evolutionary commune but also in many utopian communes. Group marriages can sometimes be found in a commune, usually involving three to six individuals out of the total population. A commune that involves both group marriage and intimate friendship is not likely to break up over sexual problems. On the other hand, a commune that includes both exclusive monogamy and any kind of sex outside the pair-bond is a good candidate for trouble (*The Modern Utopian,* all issues). Combinations of exclusive monogamy and free love, exclusive monogamy and group marriage, or celibacy and free love are very unlikely to occur. Swinging or group marriage and celibacy in the same group would seem an unlikely combination, but not necessarily a fatal one, although such combinations would seem to lower the survival factor. The combination of either intimate friendship or group marriage with free love is unlikely, but if it did occur, survival of the group would probably depend either on weeding out the uncommitted or helping them work out their inability to relate to others on a responsible level. Examples of the problems discussed in this paragraph are most numerous in *The Modern Utopian,* vol. 1, nos. 1–6; vol. 2, nos. 1–6; vol. 3, nos. 1–3; and vol. 4, nos. 1–4, which contain many articles about the life and death of communes, written by participants.

The evolutionary commune appears to be a comparatively recent development on the commune scene. It is clearly distinguishable from the utopian commune because its members are not reacting against the system. They come together out of the desire to do better that which they are already doing well. In an economic sense, the lesson of the co-op movement is not lost on these people. But in general, especially if they have already explored the possibilities inherent in intimate friendships, they are aware that there is a tremendous exhilaration in pushing the limits of interaction potential. They know that involvement at higher levels of complexity is more demanding on the individual than staying within the limits of the pair-bond. Also, they are aware that it is more rewarding, the degree of pleasure equalling the amount of investment in these relationships. As mentioned earlier, the committed pair-bond does not necessarily go through the transitional or experimental stage of intimate friendship along the route to the more complex communal or group-marriage situation. Some couples develop friendships to a degree of interaction that transcends the usual taboos on gut-level dialogue and makes possible direct exploration of the possibilities inherent in communal sharing of life commitments. This paper has concentrated on the swinging stage of this development because at this time, more people seem to be at this stage of growing into more complex interrelationships than are possible within the exclusive framework of the pair-bond.

GROUP MARRIAGE

Group marriage involves an even greater degree of complexity of interaction than communal living. The Constantines (1971) have defined this type of union admirably. They state:

> A multilateral marriage is one in which three or more people each consider themselves to have a primary relationship with at least two other individuals in the group.

The definition at the beginning of this paper is a restatement of the Constantines' definition which simplifies and clarifies the nature of the relationship:

> In a group marriage each of the three or more participants is pair-bonded with at least two others.

The term *pair-bond* is more explicit than *primary relationship* for the reason stated earlier; pair-bonded individuals are mates.

Group marriage may involve a couple and a single, two couples, two couples and a single, three couples, or three couples and a single. As far as is known to the author, no group marriage consisting of more than seven individuals has been verified as existing, and the likelihood that such a group might exist is doubtful. The addition of one individual greatly increases the number of possible pair-bonds in the group. In a triad, each individual has twice as many pair-bonds as in a dyad. Six pair-bonds are possible in a group of four people, ten are possible in a group of five, fifteen are possible in a group of six, and twenty-one pair-bonds are possible in a group of seven people. The odds against developing all possible pair-bonds rises rapidly with additional group members, yet a fully developed group marriage would presumably be one in which all possible pair-bonds did in fact exist. Thus adding an eighth person would add seven more possible pair-bonds, for a total of 28. Triads and two-couple group marriages are the most popular types.

The suggestion was made that triads and pentads (Ramey, 1972) should prove more stable than tetrads or hexads because they start out with odd numbers, and indeed, the Constantines have found more triads than any other size group, half of which involved two males and half involved two females. The argument is based on the somewhat negative assumption that couples may decide to form a group marriage on the basis of much less initial talking-through than would be likely with odd-sized groups. This assumption is based on personal knowledge of several group marriages that were started on very short notice and lasted only a few weeks or months. In fact, one of these, involving three couples, began on the basis of three weeks of discussion among couples who were hitherto strangers! One would expect a great amount of soul-searching among three or five people before they entered into a group marriage. Of course one would hope most couples would investigate thoroughly, but with the basic pair-bond relationship to fall back on, this might not occur.

Implicit in any serious discussion of group marriage is an examination of reactions to same-sex pair-bonds. Same-sex pair-bonds are most common among females in group marriages. The Constantines have found same-sex bonds between males both less frequent and much more critical to the success of the marriage. The author also knows of other instances in which incipient development of a male-male relationship broke up the marriage. It would seem relatively safe to say that a group marriage in which everyone is ambisexual will have higher survival potential, all other things being equal, than one involving one or more monosexual individuals.

For some people the idea of being married to two or more individuals at once is overwhelming. But establishing a dyadic marriage involves a growing together, not a spontaneous happening. The same is true for a group marriage which begins with a set of potentials that are developed fully only over time. To begin, all that is necessary is the assurance that everyone in the group can sustain multiple pair-bonding. This is why the definition specifies that each individual in the group have at least two pair-bonds before the group can be called a group marriage. Many groups that first appear to be group marriages do not meet this qualification, especially in the case of threesomes, in which two people are pair-bonded with the same person, usually of the opposite sex, but not with each other. There are many such relationships, and a number of people are led to believe that the number of group marriages in existence is much greater than it really is because they assume these relationships to be group marriages. As a matter of fact, upon confirming such relationships, it would appear that there may be one hundred threesomes for each triad. Such a union might be considered an intermediate step between dyadic marriage and group marriage, but it is clearly two dyadic marriages with one common partner rather than a group marriage.

The complexity of interaction that must be faced upon establishing a commune or group marriage is greater than that faced upon moving from pair-bond exclusivity to intimate friendship. The situation is further complicated by the fact that each group must work out its own ground rules. Premarital courting at the dyadic level occurs within an understood structure that is already well defined by society. Each couple makes major and minor decisions in terms of already internalized givens and expectations about marriage, and what is appropriate and permissible within the framework of marriage. Since society has not prescribed norms, standards, and activities for group marriages or communes, a great deal more preplanning and exploration must be undertaken to work through expectations and structure behavior than is the case upon entering into dyadic marriage.

A representative list of the types of problems that must be dealt with will quickly indicate the magnitude of the task. The following list is not definitive, nor are the decision areas listed in order of importance, since there are matters that each group will have to decide for itself:

> Decision-making procedures, group goals, ground rules, no-no's, intra- and extra-group sexual relationships, privacy, division of labor, role relationships, careers, relationship with outsiders, degree of visibility, legal jeopardy, dissolution of the group, personal responsibilities outside the group (such as parent support), urban or rural setting, type of shelter, geographic location, children, child-rearing practices, taxes, pooling assets, income, legal structure, education, trial period.

Many decisions can be put off until after the group embarks upon their new adventure, but most of those listed above must be worked out in the planning stage.

Age appears to be a prominent earmark of success in both communes and group marriages. The complexities to be faced are such that personal hang-ups, pair-bond hang-ups, and career hang-ups should have been solved before a couple takes this step, since a tremendous investment of time, effort, and emotional energy will be required to achieve success in the new undertaking. It follows that one would expect to find people over 30 most often involved in a successful group, and indeed, this is the case. In fact, the Constantines have not found a group marriage with participants under this age level still extant, while there is knowledge of only one tetrad in which one individual is 28 and another is 25 and the group is still extant.

The two areas of concern that are most frequently discussed in group marriage, money and the division of labor, are the least worrisome in actual practice. Developing a viable decision-making pattern is much more involved, because consensus takes an inordinate amount of time, and until the group develops the degree of trust necessary to be comfortable with differentiation of function and concomitant delegation of routine decision-making, there will necessarily be many hours spent in deciding as a group. Once sufficient trust has developed to assign functional responsibility, the group will only have to consider major or policy decisions, just as in a dyadic marriage or any other organization. Although a set of ground rules will probably be established initially, they will become less and less important as the marriage develops informal norms, standards, and activities. It has been suggested that a rough measure of the current stability of a group marriage is the degree to which they persist in clinging to the formal rules and contracts set up at the beginning of the marriage.

A trial period of some sort is essential to the success of dyadic marriage in the eyes of many people. This is an even more important factor in working through the developmental stages of a group marriage and of a commune as well. This can become a problem if it is not handled on a reasonable basis. A recent advertisement in the *Village Voice* placed by a group of would-be communalists led to the interesting discovery, upon talking to the initiators, that they wished to start the commune with ten couples and that a prerequisite to beginning would be for all the individuals in the group to live with each other for one week in pairs first. A quick count reveals that 190 pairs are involved here, so that for 19 weeks every individual would be separated from his own mate while living with all the others. Yet these people were surprised when the impracticality of this plan was pointed out to them. It had not occurred to them that they were talking about a 19-week project! Nevertheless, however it is arranged, some kind of physical sharing is an important step in the planning stage. Many people handle this trial stage by planning a joint vacation or renting a summer house together. Others may join one of the communal work brigades that are becoming an important part of the utopian rural commune scene. This mechanism not only provides the work brigade with a taste of working together as a communal group but also provides existing farm communes with essential seasonal labor.

It is important to remember that a group marriage is a hothouse situation which generates intense pressure on all its members to grow. In such a situation relaxation, quiet time, and personal privacy assume much greater importance than in the dyad. Also, the group marriage should not lose sight of the need to have fun together. The old saw, "the group that plays together stays together," is not far wrong—remembering that pleasure and happiness are major goals of any kind of marriage.

Visibility is a special problem for both communes and group

marriages, but particularly for the latter, since in most states, group marriage is not legal. Especially if there are children involved, the marriage is vulnerable to attack on the basis of contributing to the delinquency of minors, if not the basis of fornication, adultery, immoral conduct, or operating a bawdy house. How will the group handle interaction with relatives, friends, neighbors, tradesmen, and the like? Will visitors or tourists be allowed, and on what basis? Will the group maintain secrecy about its existence, and how much secrecy? Location will affect the answers to these questions. Rural locations have high visibility, so rural groups must be particularly careful to build bridges to the neighborhood. For example, Franklin Commune in Vermont was "hassled" by all kinds of official and unofficial groups for the first six months of its existence. They assumed that the work ethic of Vermont farmers was best for establishing peaceful coexistence with the community and they devoted much of their energy to this end, which corresponded with their desire to make the farm self-sustaining. Soon these efforts began to pay off. In their second summer they brought in 2700 bales of hay, plus 1300 bales for their neighbors, which they did out of neighborliness and not for pay. This is only one example of their effort to be good neighbors. It is not surprising that they have earned the respect and admiration of their community, which is now willing to go to bat for *them* when the need arises.

Groups with children in public school have higher visibility than those with no children in school, but there seems to be no pattern of problems associated with this factor. Teachers and other children tend to see and hear what they expect to see and hear rather than the reality (Ramey, 1968).

Perhaps the most deep-rooted difference that can develop in a group marriage regards child rearing. Deciding about parentage is easy, and agreement on having children and on what to do about the children if the marriage breaks up can be settled beforehand. Groups that start with babies or no children find it much easier to work out a joint child-rearing agreement than those who come into the marriage with older children. Not only must the parents work out a mutually agreeable program that is also agreeable to the non-parents, there is also the problem of compatibility and adjustment among the children themselves. Finally, there is the incipient problem which many swingers avoid, that of deciding how developing children should fit into the sexual interrelationship of the marriage.

Uncommitted swingers almost universally hide their swinging activities from their children (how successfully is a matter of question), whereas many individuals involved in intimate friendships are as open with their children about their interfamily relationships as they are about all other aspects of life. Some of the successful communes (Oneida, for example) initiated the children into full sexual participation in the life of the commune at puberty. This is such a taboo area today that there is little or no data about current practices. Some swinging groups include unmarried teenagers and/or married children and their spouses. The author has heard of at least one group involving a three-generation swinging family. How widespread such practices might be is unknown, since only very recently has it been discussed. The author has knowledge of one group marriage that consisted of a widow, her son and daughter, and their spouses. This group broke up over an incipient sexual relationship between the two males because one was unable to handle the possible implication that he would be deemed homosexual if he allowed the union to develop.

The types of problems we have raised as examples of issues facing a group marriage have had to do largely with the group-maintenance aspects of marriage. There is also goal-directedness to be dealt with. Goals have not been discussed at length here because it is believed that those people who undertake to add a more complex dimension to marriage are not in basic conflict with the goals of marriage as generally espoused by today's society. Offered, therefore, is the following definition of the kinds of behavior desired of members of the intimate friendship group, evolutionary commune, or group marriage:

> Desired behavior, as evidenced in intimate friendship, evolutionary commune, or group marriage member, is behavior that permits and promotes the growth of the group in a shared direction. Growth of the member can be measured in terms of the degree and value of his active participation and demonstration of his capacity to cooperatively assist the group to successful achievement of its goals. Group achievement of goals must be measured by society.

Student communes were mentioned earlier in this paper but not discussed. Whether students call their shared living quarters a crash pad, a co-op, a nest, a commune, or simply a shared apartment, all these loosely organized coed living arrangements have one thing in common. They are temporary. They afford students an opportunity to experiment with a number of living modes of varying complexity, with the tacit understanding that they are not making permanent commitments. Under these circumstances free love, serial monogamy, and group sex can be fully explored without the pressure of value judgments with respect to success. Casual nudity, brother-sister type non-sexual intimacy, and celibacy all find acceptance in such a setting. Changes in the personnel of the group often lead to dramatic shifts in sexual practices, and the pill makes all of this investigation safe, within a loving, sharing, nonjudgmental setting that permits much freer expression and exploration of relationship potentials than is easily possible in the more structured adult society.

Although this is almost always uncommitted behavior with respect to the individual, it is most decidedly committed behavior with respect to the group search for a satisfying life-style in terms of equality of the sexes and critical examination of accepted societal marriage standards. These young people can be counted on to form pair-bonds based on equality. With their trial experience in more complex relationships, they can be expected to swell the ranks of intimate friendships, evolutionary communes, and group marriages, assuming they decide to cast their lot with existing society and work within existing social structures. This, in turn, should have a major impact on restructuring marriage in the direction of societal sanction of intimate friendship, communes, and group marriage.

REFERENCES

Babchuck, Nicholas and Alan P. Bates. The Primary Relations of Middle Class Couples: A Study in Male Dominance. *American Sociological Review,* 1963, **28,** 377–84.

Bartell, Gilbert, D. Personal conversation reported by Edward M. Brecher in *The Sex Researchers.* Boston: Little-Brown, 1969.

Bartell, Gilbert D. Group Sex Among the Mid-Americans, *Journal of Sex Research,* 1970, **6,** 113–130.

Bartell, Gilbert D. *Group Sex.* New York: Wyden, 1971.

Beigel, Hugo. In Defense of Mate Swapping. *Rational Living,* 1969, **4,** 15–16.

Bell, Robert R., and Lillian Silvan. Swinging: The Sexual Exchange of Marriage Partners. Mimeo. Read at annual meeting, Society for the Study of Social Problems, Washington, D.C. 1970.

Bird, Caroline. *Born Female: The High Cost of Keeping Women Down.* New York: Pocket Books, 1970.

Bott, Elizabeth. *Family and Social Network.* London: Tavistock, 1957.

Brecher, Edward M. *The Sex Researchers.* Boston: Little, Brown, 1969.

Breedlove, William and Jerrye Breedlove. *Swap Clubs.* Los Angeles: Sherbourne Press, 1964.

Buber, Martin. *Between Man and Man.* Boston: Beacon Press, 1955.

Carden, Maren L. *Oneida: Utopian Community to Modern Corporation.* Baltimore: Johns Hopkins, 1969.

Collier, James L. Communes: Togetherness Sixties Style. *True,* February, 1969.

Constantine, Larry L. and Joan M. Constantine. Where Is Marriage Going? *The Futurist* (Spring), 1970a.

Constantine, Larry L. and Joan M. Constantine. How to Make a Group Marriage. *The Modern Utopian,* 4 (Summer), 1970b.

Constantine, Larry L. and Joan M. Constantine. Report on Ongoing Research in Group Marriage. Presentation to January meeting, Society for the Scientific Study of Sex, New York, 1971.

Denfield, Duane and Michael Gordon. The Sociology of Mate Swapping: Or, the Family that Swings Together Clings Together. *Journal of Sex Research,* 1970, **6,** 85–100.

Farson, Richard Evans. *The Future of the Family.* New York: Family Service Association of America, 1969.

Gagnon, John H. and William Simon. *The Sexual Scene.* New York: Aldine, 1970.

Goodman, Paul. Interview with Paul Goodman, *Psychology Today,* 1971, **5,** 96.

Heinlein, Robert. *Stranger in a Strange Land.* New York: Avon, 1967.

Hine, Robert V. *California's Utopian Colonies.* San Marino, California: Huntington Library, 1953.

Hostetler, John A. *Amish Society.* Baltimore: Johns Hopkins Press, 1968.

Houriet, Robert. Life and Death of a Commune Called Oz. *New York Times Magazine,* February 16, 1969.

Huxley, Aldous. *Ends and Means.* Westport, Connecticut: Greenwood, 1937.

Kanter, Rosabeth M. Communes. *Psychology Today,* 1970, **4,** 53–78.

Kanter, Rosabeth M. Commitment and Social Organization: A Study of Commitment Mechanisms in Utopian Communities. *American Sociological Review,* 1968. **33.**

Komarovsky, Mirra. *Blue-Collar Marriage.* New York: Random House, 1962.

Krippner, Stanley and Donald Fersh. Mystic Communes. *The Modern Utopian,* 1970, **4** (Spring), 4–9. (Research report on 18 hip religious communes supported by Society for Comparative Philosophy)

Kriyanada. *Cooperative Communities.* San Francisco: Ananda Publications, 1969.

Lewis, Richard W. The Swingers. *Playboy,* 1969, **16,** 149–228.

Lynes, Russell. *A Surfeit of Honey.* New York: Harpers, 1953.

Marks, Paul J. *A New Community.* San Diego: Youth Resources, 1969.

Masters, William H., and Virginia E. Johnson. *Human Sexual Response.* Boston: Little, Brown and Company, 1966.

McLuhan, Marshall, and George B. Leonard. The Future of Sex. *Look,* 1967, **31** (July 25).

The Modern Utopian.
    1967 Vol. 1, Nos. 1–6
    1968 Vol. 2, Nos. 1–6
    1969 Vol. 3, Nos. 1–3
    1970 Vol. 4, Nos. 1–4

Nordhoff, Charles. *The Communistic Societies of the United States.* New York: Hillary House, 1961.

O'Neill, George C. and Nena O'Neill. 1969 Personal communication to the author.

O'Neill, George C. and Nena O'Neill. Patterns in Group Sexual Activity. *Journal of Sex Research* 1970, **6** (May), 101–112.

O'Neill, Nena and George C. O'Neill. *Open Marriage.* New York: Evans, 1972.

Osofsky, Howard and Joy Osofsky. Androgyny as a Life Style. *Family Coordinator,* 1972, **21.**

Palson, Chuck and Rebecca Markle Palson. *Swinging: The Minimizing of Jealousy.* Mimeo. Philadelphia 1970, **20.**

Pemberton, H. Earl. The Curve of Culture. *American Sociological Review*. 1936, 1, 547–556.

President's Commission on Obscenity and Pornography. *The Illustrated Presidential Report of the Commission on Obscenity and Pornography* San Diego: Greenleaf Classics, 1970.

Ramey, James W. The Relationship of Peer Group Rating to Certain Individual Perceptions of Personality. *Journal of Experimental Education* 1958, 27.

Ramey, James W. Diffusion of a New Technological Innovation. *Health Sciences TV Bulletin* (O.S.) 1963, 4, 2–3.

Ramey, James W. Conflict Resolution Through Videotape Simulation. Paper presented at annual meeting, American Psychiatric Association, Detroit, May 1967.

Ramey, James W. Teaching Medical Students by Videotape Simulation. *Journal of Medical Education* 1968, 48 (January), 55–59.

Ramey, James W. Group Marriage, Communes, and the Upper Middle Class. (in preparation) 1972.

Redekop, Calvin W. *The Old Colony Mennonites*. Baltimore: Johns Hopkins Press, 1969.

Riesman, David, Nathan Glazer, and Reuel Denney. *The Lonely Crowd*. Garden City, New York, Doubleday, 1955.

Rimmer, Robert H. *The Harrad Experiment*. New York: Bantam, 1967.

Rimmer, Robert H. *Proposition 31*. New York: Signet, 1968.

Rogers, Carl. *Client Centered Therapy*. New York: Houghton Mifflin, 1951.

Rossi, Peter H., W. Eugene Groves, and David Grafstein. *Life Styles and Campus Communities*. Baltimore: Johns Hopkins Press, 1971.

Scheflen, Albert E. Quasi-Courtship Behavior in Psychotherapy. Monograph. William Alanson White Psychiatric Foundation 28, 1965.

Slater, Philip E. Some Social Consequences of Temporary Systems. In W. G. Bennis and Philip E. Slater. *The Temporary Society*. New York: Harper and Row, 1968.

Smith, James R. and Lynn G. Smith. Consenting Adults: An Exploratory Study of the Sexual Freedom Movement. (to be published by Little-Brown in 1971) as discussed with Edward M. Brecher, *The Sex Researchers*. Boston: Little-Brown, 1969.

Smith, James R. and Lynn G. Smith. Co-Marital Sex and the Sexual Freedom Movement. *Journal of Sex Research* 1970, 6, 131–142.

Spiro, Melford. *Kibbutz, Venture in Utopia*. New York: Schocken Books, 1963.

Symonds, Carolyn. The Utopian Aspects of Sexual Mate Swapping. Mimeo. Paper delivered at the annual meeting, Society for the Study of Social Problems, Washington, D.C., September, 1970.

Stoller, Frederick H. The Intimate Network of Families as a New Structure. In Herbert Otto (Ed.). *The Family in Search of a Future*. New York: Appleton-Century-Crofts, 1970.

Toffler, Alvin. *Future Shock*. New York: Random House, 1970.

Twitchell, Jon. Unpublished research, as reported by Lynn G. Smith, Co-Marital Sex: The Incorporation of Extra Marital Sex into the Marriage Relationship, paper delivered at 61st annual meeting, American Psychopathological Association, New York, February, 1971.

U.S. News and World Report. How the Four-day Workweek Is Catching On. March 8, 1971.

Whyte, William H. Jr. *The Organization Man.* New York: Simon and Schuster, 1956.

Part
Four

Men's and Women's Roles

ALTHOUGH THE Women's Liberation Movement seems like a new phenomenon to the younger generation because of the renewed and increasing attention paid to it during the last five years or so, the movement to gain equal rights and alter the roles of women has been going on for quite some time. It might be said with some degree of accuracy that the women's movement started with Eve, but in our own culture, it is generally traced to the suffrage movements of the late nineteenth century. There were also some vestiges of the women's movement found in the abolitionist movements of the mid-nineteenth century, and some historians find the roots of women's liberation in the independence of and the need for the frontier woman. So this currently popular idea is by no means new.

The study of men's and women's roles in society and in the family and the ways in which their roles are related to each other is also not new. This topic is generally called the study of sex roles. The term *sex role* refers to the behavior which is expected of a person because of his sex. The term is most often used in discussions of the division of labor within the family, division of labor referring to the manner in which the various domestic tasks are allocated according to sex. Of course, the concept of sex role has application outside the family as well.

Western culture has traditionally viewed the different roles required of men and women as being based upon ascriptive qualities, that is, those qualities related to inherent or natural differences between the sexes. However, we are now being made increasingly aware through the findings of both biological and social research, that the two sexes may not be as different as formerly thought. Currently, in both the academic world as well as the popular media, the debate rages over just what differences actually do exist between the sexes and over the precise nature of these differences. One obvious difference is that women bear children and men do not. The extremists of the Women's Liberation Movement would have us believe that there are no important differences between men and women and that childbearing is a relatively minor one. Another less radical position views childbearing as being important, but that women should not be discriminated against because of it.

On the other hand, many of those who are opposed to changes in women's roles attribute a number of distinct psychological and emotional characteristics to women which are not seen as applying to men. Presumably, the truth lies somewhere in between these various points of view. In any event, the informed person today sees far fewer differences between the sexes than was traditionally the case, and this can only mean that many of the difference of the past were based upon social and cultural factors rather than upon biological or natural factors.

Most sociologists view roles, and especially sex roles, as being defined in terms of other reciprocal or complementary roles. For example, the husband role exists and is defined mainly in terms of its complement which is the wife role. This complementarity applies to almost all situations in which men and women interact because of the condition that, as with almost all social roles, the sex of the role player is assumed to be a part of the definition of the role. Thus, all social roles are colored by the sex of the person playing the role although one's sex may be of no intrinsic importance to the actual role performance. This is probably the most crucial issue being raised by contemporary women's libbers, and it is also the issue which makes the current movement different from the earlier women's movements. The concern now is with informal social customs which, for the most part, are unrelated to sex in the biological or physiological sense, while in the past the concern was more with legal restrictions and inequalities related to the more basic freedoms and activities of citizenship.

Many people, both men and women, understand the goals of those who are seeking change with respect to women's roles, and quite a few are also in sympathy with those goals. However, many of those who claim to understand and sympathize have not yet fully grasped all of the implications and ramifications of the proposed changes in women's roles. Perhaps the most important ramification is related to the complementary nature of roles. If all roles are in fact complementary, then it must follow that any change which occurs in any one role must also bring about a change in all of those roles which are reciprocal or complementary to it. Therefore, if the role of the wife changes, it necessarily follows that the role of the husband must also change in order to maintain some sort of accommodation or agreement between the two roles, and consequently between the persons playing the roles. The same would hold true for other basic female roles such as mother and daughter, as well as for their various role reciprocals. And what is more important, this same principle of related change would also apply to those roles which may have been traditionally held by one sex or the other, such as occupational or professional roles.

This situation, in which changes in one role affect the other roles related to it, is probably the reason why many men, even those in sympathy with Women's Liberation, find themselves a little bewildered by the changes. In the past, men and women were able to interact with each other in a fairly standardized and predictable manner. That is, most men reacted to most women in the same expected and predictable way. However, as more and more women are changing their own style of behavior (changing their roles), men find themselves in an increasingly ambivalent position, often not knowing precisely how to react to a specific woman because he is unable to determine whether she is liberated or traditional.

On the other hand, the new woman may have similar problems. If she treats all men as if they held what she considers to be the outdated traditional views of women's roles, she may create difficulties when she encounters a man who is in sympathy with her newer ideas. Eventually she would also reach a point at which she would have the same problem as the bewildered males, in that she would not know how best to react to or interact with a particular man until she had first ascertained his views with respect to women.

Thus, it becomes clear that solving the problems of discrimination and differential behavior toward women involves far more than simply having men change their basic attitudes about the ways women ought to behave. The solution actually requires, at least theoretically, four shifts with respect to sex role expectations. Just as both men and women must make shifts in the ways in which they view each other's roles, they also must make shifts in the ways in which they view their own roles. Interaction problems and social maladjustments arise out of the fact that we as a society are unable to make all of these shifts simultaneously. In a game of musical chairs, if no chairs are removed when the music stops, then there are no problems. But if one or two chairs are taken away, there ensues great confusion and maybe even some conflict. It is increasingly evident that our society is in for a period of confusion and conflict on the question of men's and women's roles as the uncoordinated shifting goes on.

One of the most often cited discussions of sex roles in the family, and especially concerning the roles of women, is one formulated by Clifford Kirkpatrick.[1] His view is that women have actually had a wider range in the choice of possible roles than have men. His explanation of this position is that men have had little choice about roles because our society has not allowed men to do anything other than hold jobs. Except for the very rich and the very poor, the only legitimate role for a man is his occupational role. On the other hand, says Kirkpatrick, many women have had a choice about the roles they may occupy as well as the option of changing their major roles at various times throughout their lives. Among these choices are the *housewife-mother* role, the *equal partner* role, and the *companion* role. The major distinction between these roles is the woman's degree of involvement with the home as opposed to her involvement with a career or with her husband's career.

This analysis of women's roles is not meant to imply that women have total or even very much freedom in their choice of roles, but rather that there is probably more latitude in women's roles than in men's, and of course, some women have more freedom than other women do. Kirkpatrick is certainly not complaining about the fact that women have greater freedom in their choice of roles, for he feels that this role flexibility creates problems for both men and women, similar to the interaction problems mentioned in the previous few paragraphs. He says that men tend to develop the expectation that their wives should be able to perform all of the various women's roles well. Rather than allowing her to choose only one of the possible roles, he feels that she should be able not only to hold a full-time job, but also to keep the house spotless as well as to take excellent care of the children. Of course the average woman cannot meet these expectations, so her husband berates her or withholds rewards.

With respect to the wife's own expectations about her roles, says Kirkpatrick, she tends to feel that she is adequately meeting the expectations of her husband and performing all of the roles well. Therefore, she is dissatisfied with her husband's response to her performance. The result of all this is a great deal of discord on the part of both men and women, but all centered upon the woman's role.

The conclusion must be drawn that the problems of determining the appropriate roles for both men and women, as well as the problem of changes in these roles, are issues which are very complex and which defy simple answers. The articles in this section which address these issues certainly do not contain all or even very many of the answers, but they express some interesting viewpoints and present some useful research findings.

The first article of Part Four subjects to critical scrutiny one of the major social and family roles of our culture: motherhood. In "Motherhood: Who Needs It?" Betty Rollin attacks what she refers to as the "Motherhood Myth." It consists essentially of that complex of cultural values, beliefs, attitudes, and, more than anything else, pressures which prevail upon young women to become mothers. According to the myth, motherhood is not only rewarding and fulfilling, it is the only real source of fulfillment and satisfaction for women. The myth additionally asserts that

motherhood is both a biological and psychological imperative.

The consequences of this fallacy, according to Rollin, are
multitudes of unhappy mothers with unhappy kids, not to
mention the problem of overpopulation. She says that just
because women are biologically capable of having children,
this is not sufficient reason why all women should do so;
many probably should not. But the myth places a variety
of sanctions on women who have no children, and especially on those women who have no children by choice.

The writer also has a few remarks with regard to the "Fatherhood Myth" as well, but as a role, fatherhood does not
have quite the social importance motherhood does; this
myth does not present us with nearly the number of problems of the motherhood myth. All in all, the article investi-
gates an unusual and relevant point of view, and is certainly applicable to the overall problem of changing roles
of both men and women.

The second article, "Women's Liberation and the Family,"
by Sylvia Clavan, is concerned with the impact of changes
in the roles of women upon the structure of the family,
and specifically upon the conjugal family unit. After a brief
review of the history of the current Women's Liberation
Movement, she examines the institutional bases for wom-
en's roles in society. These bases are found in the economic
institution and in the family. Most of the focus of women's
movements in the past have centered mainly upon upgrading the legal and economic positions of women. What is
significant about the current movement is that it is turning
its focus more upon the family, viewing present family
structure as the source of most of the modern woman's
problems and oppressions. The article raises some searching questions about what will happen to family structure
in light of the kinds of redefinitions of roles which women
are increasingly demanding, especially with respect to those
roles of women in the conjugal family. It certainly goes to
the heart of some of the questions raised earlier in this
commentary.

It was previously stated that it would be impossible for women's roles to change without causing changes to also come about in the roles of men. The more drastic the changes in women's roles, the more dramatic would be the changes expected in men's roles. This point of view is excellently illustrated in the final article in this section, "How Men Are Changing." It focuses upon some of the male reactions to changes in women, and also looks into changes that have been initiated by males themselves in efforts to begin a "men's liberation" movement, which would encompass more than just a reaction or backlash to the women's movement.

REFERENCES

1. Clifford Kirkpatrick, "The Measurement of Ethical Inconsistency in Marriage," *The International Journal of Ethics*, 46:444–460 (July, 1936).

10.

Motherhood: Who Needs It?

Betty Rollin

Motherhood is in trouble, and it ought to be. A rude question is long overdue: Who needs it? The answer used to be (1) society and (2) women. But now, with the impending horrors of overpopulation, society desperately *doesn't* need it. And women don't need it either. Thanks to the Motherhood Myth—the idea that having babies is something that all normal women instinctively want and need and will enjoy doing—they just *think* they do.

The notion that the maternal wish and the activity of mothering are instinctive or biologically predestined is baloney. Try asking most sociologists, psychologists, psychoanalysts, biologists—many of whom are mothers—about motherhood being instinctive; it's like asking department store presidents if their Santa Clauses are real. "Motherhood—instinctive?" shouts distinguished sociologist/author Dr. Jessie Bernard. "Biological destiny? Forget biology! If it were biology, people would die from not doing it."

"Women don't need to be mothers any more than they need spaghetti," says Dr. Richard Rabkin, a New York psychiatrist. "But if you're in a world where everyone is eating spaghetti, thinking they need it and want it, you will think so too. Romance has really contaminated science. So-called instincts have to do with stimulation. They are not things that well up inside of you."

Reprinted from *Look*, September 22, 1970 (Vol. 34, No. 19), pp. 15–17. Copyright © Cowles Communications, Inc. 1970.

"When a woman says with feeling that she craved her baby from within, she is putting into biological language what is psychological," says University of Michigan psychoanalyst and motherhood-researcher Dr. Frederick Wyatt. "There are no instincts," says Dr. William Goode, president-elect of the American Sociological Association. "There are reflexes, like eye-blinking, and drives, like sex. There is no innate drive for children. Otherwise, the enormous cultural pressures that there are to reproduce wouldn't exist. There are no cultural pressures to sell you on getting your hand out of the fire."

There are, to be sure, biologists and others who go on about biological destiny, that is, the innate or instinctive goal of motherhood. (At the turn of the century, even good old capitalism was explained by a theorist as "the *instinct* of acquisitiveness.") And many psychoanalysts still hold the Freudian view that women feel so rotten about not having a penis that they are necessarily propelled into the child-wish to replace the missing organ. Psychoanalysts also make much of the psychological need to repeat what one's parent of the same sex has done. Since every woman has a mother, it is considered normal to wish to imitate one's mother by being a mother.

There is, surely, a wish to pass on love if one has received it, but to insist women must pass it on in the same way is like insisting that every man whose father is a gardener has to be a gardener. One dissenting psychoanalyst says, simply, "There is a wish to comply with one's biology, yes, but we needn't and sometimes we shouldn't." (Interestingly, the woman who has been the greatest contributor to child therapy and who has probably given more to children than anyone alive is Dr. Anna Freud, Freud's magnificent daughter, who is not a mother.)

Anyway, what an expert cast of hundreds is telling us is, simply, that biological *possibility* and desire are not the same as biological *need*. Women have childbearing equipment. To choose not to use the equipment is no more blocking what is instinctive than it is for a man who, muscles or no, chooses not to be a weight lifter.

So much for the wish. What about the "instinctive" *activity* of mothering? One animal study shows that when a young member of a species is put in a cage, say, with an older member of the same species, the latter will act in a protective, "maternal" way. But that goes for both males and females who have been "mothered" themselves. And studies indicate that a human baby will also respond to whoever is around playing mother—even if it's father. Margaret Mead and many others frequently point out that mothering can be a fine occupation, if you want it, for either sex. Another experiment with monkeys who were brought up without mothers found them lacking in maternal behavior toward their own offspring. A similar study showed that monkeys brought up without other monkeys of the opposite sex had no interest in mating—all of which suggests that both mothering and mating behavior are learned, not instinctual. And, to turn the cart (or the baby carriage) around, baby ducks who lovingly follow their mothers seemed, in the mother's absence, to just as lovingly follow wooden ducks or even vacuum cleaners.

If motherhood isn't instinctive, when and why, then, was the Motherhood Myth born? Until recently, the entire question of maternal motivation was academic. Sex, like it or not, meant babies. Not that there haven't always been a lot of interesting contraceptive tries. But until the creation of the diaphragm in the 1880's, the birth of babies was largely unavoidable. And, generally speaking, nobody really seemed to mind. For one thing, people tend to be sort of good sports about what seems to be inevitable. For another, in the past, the population needed beefing up. Mortality rates were high, and agricultural cultures, particularly, have always needed children to help out. So because it "just happened" and because it was needed, motherhood was assumed to be innate.

Originally, it was the word of God that got the ball rolling with "Be fruitful and multiply," a practical suggestion, since the only people around then were Adam and Eve. But in no time, super-moralists like St. Augustine changed the tone of the message: "Intercourse, even with one's legitimate wife, is unlawful and wicked where the conception of the offspring is prevented," he, we assume, thundered. And the Roman Catholic position was thus cemented. So then and now, procreation took on a curious value among people who viewed (and view) the pleasures of sex as sinful. One could partake in the sinful pleasure, but feel vindicated by the ensuing birth. Motherhood cleaned up sex. Also, it cleaned up women, who have always been considered somewhat evil, because of Eve's transgression (". . . but the woman was deceived and became a transgressor. Yet woman will be saved through bearing children . . . ," I Timothy, 2:14–15), and somewhat dirty because of menstruation.

And so, based on need, inevitability, and pragmatic fantasy—the Myth *worked,* from society's point of view—the Myth grew like corn in Kansas. And society reinforced it with both laws and propaganda —laws that made woman a chattel, denied her education and personal mobility, and madonna propaganda that she was beautiful and wonderful doing it and it was all beautiful and wonderful to do. (One rarely sees a madonna washing dishes.)

In fact, the Myth persisted—breaking some kind of record for long-lasting fallacies—until something like yesterday. For as the truth about the Myth trickled in—as women's rights increased, as women gradually got the message that it was certainly possible for them to do most things that men did, that they live longer, that their brains were not tinier—then, finally, when the really big news rolled in, that they could *choose* whether or not to be mothers— what happened? The Motherhood Myth soared higher than ever. As Betty Friedan made oh-so-clear in *The Feminine Mystique,* the '40's and '50's produced a group of ladies who not only had babies as if they were going out of style (maybe they were) but, as never before, they turned motherhood into a cult. First, they wallowed in the aesthetics of it all—natural childbirth and nursing became maternal musts. Like heavy-bellied ostriches, they grounded their heads in the sands of motherhood, only coming up for air to say how utterly happy and fulfilled they were. But, as Mrs. Friedan says only too plainly, they weren't. The Myth galloped on, moreover, long after making babies had turned from practical asset to liability for both individual parents *and* society. With the average cost of a middle-class child figured conservatively at $30,000 (not including college), any parent knows that the only people who benefit economically from children are manufacturers of consumer goods. Hence all those gooey motherhood commercials. And the Myth gathered momentum long after sheer numbers, while not yet extinguishing us, have made us intensely uncomfortable. Almost all of our societal problems, from minor discomforts like traffic to major ones like hunger, the population people keep reminding us, have to do with there being too many people. And who suffers most? The kids who have been so mindlessly brought into the world, that's who. They are the ones who have to cope with all of the difficult and dehumanizing conditions brought on by overpopulation. They are the ones who have to cope with the psychological nausea of feeling unneeded by society. That's not the only reason for drugs, but, surely, it's a leading contender.

Unfortunately, the population curbers are tripped up by a romantic, stubborn, ideological hurdle. How can birth-control programs really be effective as long as the concept of glorious motherhood remains unchanged? (Even poor old Planned Parenthood has to euphemize—why not Planned Unparenthood?) Particularly among the poor, motherhood is one of the few inherently positive institutions that are accessible. As Berkeley demographer Judith Blake points out, "Poverty-oriented birth control programs do not make sense as a welfare measure . . . as long as existing pronatalist policies . . . encourage mating, pregnancy, and the care, support, and rearing of children." Or, she might have added, as long as the less-than-idyllic child-rearing part of motherhood remains "in small print."

Sure, motherhood gets dumped on sometimes: Philip Wylie's Momism got going in the '40's and Philip Roth's *Portnoy's Complaint* did its best to turn rancid the chicken-soup concept of Jewish motherhood. But these are viewed as the sour cries of a black humorist here, a malcontent there. Everyone shudders, laughs, but it's like the mouse and the elephant joke. Still, the Myth persists. Last April, a Brooklyn woman was indicted on charges of manslaughter and negligent homicide—11 children died in a fire in a building she owned and criminally neglected—"But," sputtered her lawyer, "my client, Mrs. Breslow, is a mother, a grandmother, and a great-grandmother!"

Most remarkably, the Motherhood Myth persists in the face of the most overwhelming maternal unhappiness and incompetence. If reproduction were merely superfluous and expensive, if the experience were as rich and rewarding as the cliché would have us believe, if it were a predominantly joyous trip for everyone riding—mother, father, child—then the going everybody-should-have-two-children plan would suffice. Certainly, there are a lot of joyous mothers, and their children and (sometimes, not necessarily) their husbands reflect their joy. But a lot of evidence suggests that for more women than anyone wants to admit, motherhood can be miserable. "If it weren't," says one psychiatrist wryly, "the world wouldn't be in the mess it's in.")

There is a remarkable statistical finding from a recent study of Dr. Bernard's, comparing the mental illness and unhappiness of married mothers and single women. The latter group, it turned out, was both markedly less sick and overtly more happy. Of course, it's not easy to measure slippery attitudes like happiness. "Many women have achieved a kind of reconciliation—a conformity," says Dr. Bernard,

> that they interpret as happiness. Since feminine happiness is supposed to lie in devoting one's life to one's husband and children, they do that; so *ipso facto,* they assume they are happy. And for many women, untrained for independence and "processed" for motherhood, they find their state far preferable to the alternatives, which don't really exist.

Also, unhappy mothers are often loath to admit it. For one thing, if in society's view not to be a mother is to be a freak, not to be a *blissful* mother is to be a witch. Besides, unlike a disappointing marriage, disappointing motherhood cannot be terminated by divorce. Of course, none of that stops such a woman from expressing her dissatisfaction in a variety of ways. Again, it is not only she who suffers but her husband and children as well. Enter the harridan housewife, the carping shrew. The realities of motherhood can turn women into terrible people. And, judging from the 50,000 cases of child abuse in the U.S. each year, some are worse than terrible.

In some cases, the unpleasing realities of motherhood begin even before the beginning. In *Her Infinite Variety,* Morton Hunt describes young married women pregnant for the first time as "very likely to be frightened and depressed, masking these feelings in order not to be considered contemptible. The arrival of pregnancy interrupts a pleasant dream of motherhood and awakens them to the realization that they have too little money, or not enough space, or unresolved marital problems. . . ."

The following are random quotes from interviews with some mothers in Ann Arbor, Mich., who described themselves as reasonably happy. They all had positive things to say about their children, although when asked about the best moment of their day, they *all* confessed it was when the children were in bed. Here is the rest:

> Suddenly I had to devote myself to the child totally. I was under the illusion that the baby was going to fit into my life, and I found that I had to switch my life and my schedule to

fit *him*. You think, "I'm in love, I'll get married, and we'll
have a baby." First there's two, then three, it's simple and romantic. You don't even think about the work. . . .

You never get away from the responsibility. Even when you
leave the children with a sitter, you are not out from under
the pressure of the responsibility. . . .

I hate ironing their pants and doing their underwear, and
they never put their clothes in the laundry basket. . . . As
they get older, they make less demands on your time because
they're in school, but the demands are greater in forming
their values. . . . Best moment of the day is when all the children are in bed. . . . The worst time of day is 4 p.m., when
you have to get dinner started, the kids are tired, hungry and
crabby—everybody wants to talk to you about *their day* . . .
your day is only half over.

Once a mother, the responsibility and concern for my children became so encompassing. . . . It took a great deal of
will to keep up other parts of my personality. . . . To me,
motherhood gets harder as they get older because you have
less control. . . . In an abstract sense, I'd have several. . . .
In the non-abstract, I would not have any. . . .

I had anticipated that the baby would sleep and eat, sleep
and eat. Instead, the experience was overwhelming. I really
had not thought particularly about what motherhood would
mean in a realistic sense. I want to do *other* things, like to become involved in things that are worthwhile—I don't mean
women's clubs—but I don't have the physical energy to go out
in the evenings. I feel like I'm missing something . . . the experience of being somewhere with people and having them
talking about something—something that's going on in the
world.

Every grownup person expects to pay a price for his pleasures,
but seldom is the price as vast as the one endured "however happily" by most mothers. We have mentioned the literal cost factor.
But what does that mean? For middle-class American women, it
means a life style with severe and usually unimagined limitations;
i.e., life in the suburbs, because who can afford three bedrooms in
the city? And what do suburbs mean? For women, suburbs mean
other women and children and leftover peanut-butter sandwiches
and car pools and seldom-seen husbands. Even the Feminine Mys-
tiqueniks—the housewives who finally admitted that their lives behind brooms (OK, electric brooms) were driving them crazy—were
loath to trace their predicament to their children. But it is simply a
fact that a childless married woman has no child-work and little
housework. She can live in a city, or, if she still chooses the suburbs
or the country, she can leave on the commuter train with her husband if she wants to. Even the most ardent job-seeking mother will
find little in the way of great opportunities in Scarsdale. Besides,

by the time she wakes up, she usually lacks both the preparation for the outside world and the self-confidence to get it. You will say there are plenty of city-dwelling working mothers. But most of those women do additional-funds-for-the-family kind of work, not the interesting career kind that takes plugging during childbearing years.

Nor is it a bed of petunias for the mother who does make it professionally. Says writer critic Marya Mannes:

> If the creative woman has children, she must pay for this indulgence with a long burden of guilt, for her life will be split three ways between them and her husband and her work. . . . No woman with any heart can compose a paragraph when her child is in trouble. . . . The creative woman has no wife to protect her from intrusion. A man at his desk in a room with closed door is a man at work. A woman at a desk in any room is available.

Speaking of jobs, do remember that mothering, salary or not, is a job. Even those who can afford nursies to handle the nitty-gritty still need to put out emotionally. "Well-cared-for" neurotic rich kids are not exactly unknown in our society. One of the more absurd aspects of the Myth is the underlying assumption that, since most women are biologically equipped to bear children, they are psychologically, mentally, emotionally, and technically equipped (or interested) to rear them. Never mind happiness. To assume that such an exacting, consuming, and important task is something almost all women are equipped to do is far more dangerous and ridiculous than assuming that everyone with vocal chords should seek a career in the opera.

A major expectation of the Myth is that children make a not-so-hot marriage hotter, or a hot marriage, hotter still. Yet almost every available study indicates that childless marriages are far happier. One of the biggest, of 850 couples, was conducted by Dr. Harold Feldman of Cornell University, who states his finding in no uncertain terms: "Those couples with children had a significantly lower level of marital satisfaction than did those without children." Some of the reasons are obvious. Even the most adorable children make for additional demands, complications, and hardships in the lives of even the most loving parents. If a woman feels disappointed and trapped in her mother role, it is bound to affect her marriage in any number of ways: she may take out her frustrations directly on her husband, or she may count on him too heavily for what she feels she is missing in her daily life.

". . . You begin to grow away from your husband," says one of the Michigan ladies. "He's working on his career and you're working on your family. But you both must gear your lives to the children. You do things the children enjoy, more than things you might enjoy." More subtle and possibly more serious is what motherhood may do to a woman's sexuality. Often when the stork flies in, sexuality flies out. Both in the emotional minds of some women *and* in the minds of their husbands, when a woman becomes a mother, she stops being a woman. It's not only that motherhood may destroy her physical attractiveness, but its madonna concept may destroy her *feelings* of sexuality.

And what of the payoff? Usually, even the most self-sacrificing maternal self-sacrificers expects a little something back. Gratified parents are not unknown to the Western world, but there are probably at least just as many who feel, to put it crudely, shortchanged. The experiment mentioned earlier—where the baby ducks followed vacuum cleaners instead of their mothers—indicates that what passes for love from baby to mother is merely a rudimentary kind of object attachment. Without necessarily feeling like a Hoover, a lot of women become disheartened because babies and children are not only not interesting to talk to (not everyone thrills at the wonders of da-da-ma-ma talk) but they are generally not empathetic, considerate people. Even the nicest children are not capable of empathy, surely a major ingredient of love, until they are much older. Sometimes they're never capable of it. Dr. Wyatt says that often, in later years particularly, when most of the "returns" are in, it is the "good mother" who suffers most of all. It is then she must face a reality: The child—the appendage with her genes—is not an appendage, but a separate person. What's more, he or she may be a separate person who doesn't even like her—or whom she doesn't really like.

So if the music is lousy, how come everyone's dancing? Because the motherhood minuet is taught freely from birth, and whether or not she has rhythm or likes the music, every woman is expected to do it. Indeed, she *wants* to do it. Little girls start learning what to want—and what to be—when they are still in their cribs. Dr. Miriam Keiffer, a young social psychologist at Bensalem, the Experimental College of Fordham University, points to studies showing that

> at six months of age, mothers are already treating their baby girls and boys quite differently. For instance, mothers have been found to touch, comfort, and talk to their females more. If these differences can be found at such an early stage, it's not surprising that the end product is as different as it is. What is surprising is that men and women, are in so many ways, similar.

Some people point to the way little girls play with dolls as proof of their innate motherliness. But remember, little girls are *given* dolls. When Margaret Mead presented some dolls to New Guinea children, it was the boys, not the girls, who wanted to play with them, which they did by crooning lullabies and rocking them in the most maternal fashion.

By the time they reach adolescence, most girls, unconsciously or not, have learned enough about role definition to qualify for a master's degree. In general, the lesson has been that no matter what kind of career thoughts one may entertain, one must, first and foremost, be a wife and mother. A girl's mother is usually her first teacher. As Dr. Goode says, "A woman is not only taught by society to have a child; she is taught to have a child who will have a child." A woman who has hung her life on the Motherhood Myth will almost always reinforce her young married daughter's early training by pushing for grandchildren. Prospective grandmothers are not the only ones. Husbands, too, can be effective sellers. After all, they have the Fatherhood Myth to cope with. A married man is *supposed* to have children. Often, particularly among Latins, children are a sign of potency. They help him assure the world—and himself— that he is the big man he is supposed to be. Plus, children give him both immortality (whatever that means) and possibly the chance to become more in his lifetime through the accomplishments of his children, particularly his son. (Sometimes it's important, however, for the son to do better, but not *too* much better.)

Friends, too, can be counted on as myth-pushers. Naturally one wants to do what one's friends do. One study, by the way, found a correlation between a woman's fertility and that of her three closest friends. The negative sell comes into play here, too. We have seen what the concept of non-mother means (cold, selfish, unwomanly, abnormal). In practice, particularly in the suburbs, it can mean, simply, exclusion—both from child-centered activities (that is, most activities) and child-centered conversations (that is, most conversations). It can also mean being the butt of a lot of unfunny jokes. ("Whaddya waiting for? An immaculate conception? Ha ha.") Worst of all, it can mean being an object of pity.

In case she's escaped all those pressures (that is, if she was brought up in a cave), a young married woman often wants a baby just so that she'll (1) have something to do (motherhood is better than clerk/typist, which is often the only kind of job she can get, since little more has been expected of her and, besides, her boss also expects her to leave and be a mother); (2) have something to hug and possess, to be needed by and have power over; and (3) have something to *be*—e.g., a baby's mother. Motherhood affords an instant identity. First, through wifehood, you are somebody's wife; then you are somebody's mother. Both give not only identity and activity, but status and stardom of a kind. During pregnancy, a woman can look forward to the kind of attention and pampering she may not ever have gotten or may never otherwise get. Some women consider birth the biggest accomplishment of their lives, which may be interpreted as saying not much for the rest of their lives. As Dr. Goode says, "It's like the gambler who may know the roulette wheel is crooked, but it's the only game in town." Also, with motherhood, the feeling of accomplishment is immediate. It is really much faster and easier to make a baby than paint a painting, or write a book, or get to the point of accomplishment in a job. It is also easier in a way to shift focus from self-development to child development—particularly since, for women, self-development is considered selfish. Even unwed mothers may achieve a feeling of this kind. (As we have seen, little thought is given to the aftermath.) And, again, since so many women are underdeveloped as people, they feel that, besides children, they have little else to give —to themselves, their husbands, to their world.

You may ask why then, when the realities do start pouring in, does a woman want to have a second, third, even fourth child? OK, (1) just because reality is pouring in doesn't mean she wants to *face* it. A new baby can help bring back some of the old illusions. Says psychoanalyst Dr. Natalie Shainess, "She may view each successive child as a knight in armor that will rescue her from being a 'bad unhappy mother.'" (2) Next on the horror list of having no children, is having one. It suffices to say that only children are not only OK, they even have a high rate of exceptionality. (3) Both parents usually want at least one child of each sex. The husband, for reasons discussed earlier, probably wants a son. (4) The more children one has, the more of an excuse one has not to develop in any other way.

What's the point? A world without children? Of course not. Nothing could be worse or more unlikely. No matter what anyone says in *Look* or anywhere else, motherhood isn't about to go out like a blown bulb, and who says it should? Only the Myth must go out, and now it seems to be dimming.

The younger-generation females who have been reared on the Myth have not rejected it totally, but at least they recognize it can be more loving to children not to have them. And at least they speak of adopting children instead of bearing them. Moreover, since the new nonbreeders are "less hung-up" on ownership, they seem to recognize that if you dig loving children, you don't necessarily have to own one. The end of the Motherhood Myth might make available more loving women (and men!) for those children who already exist.

When motherhood is no longer culturally compulsory, there will, certainly, be less of it. Women are now beginning to think and do more about development of self, of their individual resources. Far from being selfish, such development is probably our only hope. That means more alternatives for women. And more alternatives mean more selective, better, happier, motherhood—and childhood and husbandhood (or manhood) and peoplehood. It is not a question of whether or not children are sweet and marvelous to have and rear; the question is, even if that's so, whether or not one wants to pay the price for it. It doesn't make sense any more to pretend that women need babies, when what they really need is themselves. If God were still speaking to us in a voice we could hear, even He would probably say, "Be fruitful. Don't multiply."

11.

Women's Liberation
and the Family

Sylvia Clavan

The current efforts to win more equitable status on the part of many women in American society have emerged as a significant movement. Its potential for changing major social institutions, particularly that of the family, should not be underestimated. This paper is a statement on the present nature of the Women's Liberation Movement, the issues involved, and the implications it has for the future.

Transformation of the structure of the family as an institution in American society is underway. Changes in the role of the female, the role of the male, and the relationship between them are both cause and effect of the transformation. The potential for greater change in these areas is contained in the ideology and goals of the Women's Liberation Movement. An editorial from *Women: A Journal of Liberation* (vol. 1, no. 3) states, "Traditionally, women have been most oppressed by the institution of the family. . . . To be free, women must understand the source of their oppression and how to control it." Another editorial (vol. 1, no. 2) discussing the limited goals of earlier feminists states, "It is significant that the common phrase which describes the present women's movement is the word 'liberation.' This word implies a deep consciousness of the significance of our struggle: Women are asking for nothing less than the total transformation of the world."

Reprinted from *The Family Coordinator,* (Oct. 1970), pp. 317–323. By permission of the National Council on Family Relations.

Often it is the atypical or the deviant social phenomenon that points to future change. Jessie Bernard (1968, p. 6) suggests this when she writes:

> In discussing changes over time, it is important to remind ourselves of the enormous stability of social forms. The modal or typical segments of population show great inertia: they change slowly. . . . What does change, and rapidly, is the form the nontypical takes. It is the nontypical which characterizes a given time: that is, the typical, which tends to be stable, has to be distinguished from the characteristic or characterizing, which tends to be fluctuating. When we speak of the 'silent generation' or the 'beat generation' or the 'anti-establishment generation', we are not referring to the typical member of any generation but to those who are not typical.

It is suggested that some of the various actions and ideas of the Women's Liberation Movement might be considered as possible "nontypical behavior anticipating the norm."

The available material on the Women's Liberation Movement mainly consists of articles and journals prepared by women in the movement, a few studies underway, and recent coverage by the mass media including national magazines and local newspapers. The earlier feminist movements are part of history, and source materials pertaining to them are more readily available.

The literature dealing with the family does contain some reference to the relationship between a changing female role and possible changes in the present family structure. In general, these references have to do with the effects of role conflict on modern women in American society. Most often the role conflict is depicted as the outcome of antagonism between female needs and desires and the behavior expected of her. At other times the problem is presented as conflict inherent in the way modern women are socialized. That is, they are formally educated about the same as men, but are expected to assume the more traditional female roles of wife-mother-homemaker upon marrying. These types of references almost always apply to educated, middle-class women. They are mostly found in descriptive studies using general knowledge of role theory rather than in studies testing hypotheses. Dager's discussion (1964, pp. 757–759) of sex-role identification points to factors frequently alluded to in these studies. Other studies of the female role treat the effects of the working wife or mother on the family. One example would be Nye's (1967) discussion of possible changing trends in the family occurring because of women's increasing participation in the occupational world. Nye and Hoffman's (1963) *The Employed Mother in America* also looks at these effects. Goode's (1963, p. 373) *World Revolution and Family Patterns* touches on the possibility of the revolutionary idea of full equality for women, and he states: "We believe that it is possible to develop a society in which this would happen, but not without a radical reorganization of the social structure."

In general, the sociological literature does not seem to recognize any incipient and rapid change in the roles of women in American society as either an impetus for change or a predictor of change in other social sectors.

THE ISSUES INVOLVED

At the present point of its history, Women's Liberation Movement is an umbrella name covering a proliferation of women's groups, some more highly organized than others, but all dedicated to some aspect of improving women's status in this society. The current resurgence of active interest in the status of modern American women is often traced to the publication in 1963 of Betty Friedan's *The Feminine Mystique*. The book examined the post-World War II "back to the home" movement of American women and attacked as a myth the picture of the American woman as a fulfilled and happy housewife. Friedan established the National Organization for Women (NOW) in 1966 as a parliamentary style organization emphasizing improvement for women through legislative change.

Following the appearance of NOW, other feminist groups began to emerge. Among those frequently alluded to are the New York Radical Women, Women's International Terrorist Conspiracy from Hell (WITCH), Redstockings, the Feminists, and Female Liberation. Many of the young women comprising these groups came out of the civil rights and/or peace movements where, ironically, they found that they were treated as inferiors because of their sex.

For purpose of analysis, the Women's Liberation Movement may be conceptualized in two ways. First, it may be viewed as part of an ongoing process that results from industrialization or modernization of a soicety, of movement toward more equal status for men and women. Thus, in the United States, it may be seen as reactivation of the earlier feminist movement.

Second, the movement may be conceptualized in a more narrowly political sense as emerging out of the revolutionary spirit that characterized the 1960's. This view would hold that oppression of women is but one manifestation of a society that needs complete restructuring. Proponents of this view see female liberation as secondary to the primary focus of social revolution. Although the ideology of the political approach is still nontypical in the American social world, many of its ideas such as experiments with leaderless societies, rejection of traditional roles and institutions, self-determination, communal living, and shared responsibility for child-rearing, are pertinent to American family structure.

The aims of the different feminist groups are varied and often contradictory. The lack of an organized program can be attributed to newness of the movement, to organizational difficulties encountered at the outset of any new program, or probably most important, basic divisiveness as to an agreed upon goal or goals. It is possible, however, to pick out several ideas common to most groups.

All of the groups see the present conjugal family structure with its traditional division of labor as destructive to full female identity. Much of the focus has been on trying to alleviate the burdens of housework and to get help through free collective child care. The work world it attacked because of its sexual discriminatory practices. The traditional male-female relationship is viewed on a continuum ranging from a point that advocates some changes in sex roles to one that demands complete new definitions. For purposes of discussion, the areas generally considered by women liberationists to be in need of change fall roughly into economic and familial categories. Crossing both of these categories are questions of legal rights. Rights of women under law, however, have been and continue to be gained both worldwide and nationwide. Attempts to implement these rights are part of the feminist struggle.

THE ECONOMIC DIMENSION OF THE COMMON GOAL

Economic discrimination against women takes many forms, some overt and some covert. The argument for broader rights under the law overlaps the economic area, particularly for the single woman. The impetus for redress and amelioration is coming primarily from the highly educated, professional, semi-professional, or upper-ranked occupational segment of women in the labor force. Their particular situation can best be described as that of second-class citizens in a world of men, if they are permitted to enter that world at all. Although their grievances might appear strange to a female factory worker, they are visible and real and, to some extent, have been documented. (Rossi, 1970; Berman and Stocker, 1970) With an increasing number of women earning college degrees and seeking further professional training, action toward attaining a balance between men and women in the higher reaches of occupations will probably become intensified.

Two structural factors have been important in the increase of interaction of women and the economy, industrialization and the conjugal family unit. Goode (1963, p. 369; 1964, p. 110) has noted that with industrialization the family structure of a society tends toward a conjugal system. He suggests that both modern industrialism and the conjugal structure offer women more economic freedom. Some substantiation for this can be based on the figures given in the President's Commission on the Status of Women (1965, p. 45) to the effect that in 1962 there were 23 million women in the labor force. In 1967, the Federal Bureau of Labor Statistics (Report No. 94) reported that the number of women working was 27 million, and in the June, 1970 issue of the BLS *Employment and Earnings,* that the figure had grown to 30,974,000. Approximately three out of five women workers are married and among married women, one in three is working. While it is possible to infer from this that discrimination and prejudice against women in the world of work have lessened, the reality is that traditional women's jobs are accorded lower status, earnings are lower than those for men in equivalent jobs, many industries use women as an expendable work force, and men are given preference in hiring where qualified women are available, to name but a few common discriminatory practices. The complete disregard of the female as a member of the work force in her own right is underlined when one notes that they are rarely mentioned, if at all, in the literature dealing with work and occupations. When they are considered, it is almost always within the context of the family structure, i.e., characterized as *still single,* the secondary jobholder in an *organized* family, or the major jobholder in a *disorganized* family. Caplow and McGee (1958, p. 95 and p. 194) succinctly speak to the point:

> . . . women tend to be discriminated against in the academic profession, not because they have low prestige but because they are outside the prestige system entirely . . .

And:

> Women scholars are not taken seriously and cannot look forward to a normal professional career. This bias is part of the much larger pattern which determines the utilization of women in our economy.

— Johnstone (1968, p. 103), in considering what economic rights are for women, summarizes them as follows:

> . . . the right of access to vocational, technical, and professional training at all levels; the right of economic life without discrimination and to advancement in work life on the basis of qualifications and merit; the right to equal treatment in employment, including equal pay; and the right to maternity protection.

And Rossi (1970, pp. 99–102), exploring the problems of job discrimination suggests that women:

> . . . have numerical strength, and a growing number of women's rights organizations to assist them in tackling all levels of discrimination in employment.

She predicts that unless protections are forthcoming, there will be an increased militancy by American women. She suggests further that:

> . . . it must be recognized that such militant women will win legal, economic, and political rights for the daughters of today's traditionalist Aunt Bettys, just as our grandmothers won the vote that women can exercise today.

THE FAMILIAL DIMENSION OF THE COMMON GOAL

Although strengthening women's economic and legal positions would affect other changes in American society, social acceptance of Women's Liberation goals regarding the family has greater far-reaching implications. The assumptions underlying the President's Commission's Report on the Status of Women and its recommendations for improving women's economic, political, and legal positions presented only five years ago are summarized by Margaret Mead (1965, pp. 183–184) in an epilogue to that report. In part, they assume "that both males and females attain full biological humanity only through marriage and the presence of children in the home . . ." Americans feel that "a life that includes a legal and continuous sex relationship is the only good life." The typical woman is depicted as marrying early, having several children, and living many years after her children are grown. Mead goes on to say:

> Here it (the Report) makes the following assumptions: all women want to marry; marriage involves having (or at least, rearing) children; children are born (or adopted) early in marriage; the home consists of the nuclear family only and special attention must be given to women not in the state assumed to be normal—the single, the divorced, and the widowed.

Women's Liberation questions and challenges these traditionally held ideas about the ideal American woman. Not all liberationists favor destruction of the conjugal family system, but most view the expected role structure of the husband as provider and the wife as homemaker and child's nurse as the basis of their oppression. It is possible that the movement heralds a revolutionary change in the American family. The movement's proposals generate many questions and reconceptualizations of existing family organization. Some of these are suggested below:

1. The conjugal family system has often been presented as congenial to the mode of life in modern industrialized societies. However, some have suggested that American society has entered a new socioeconomic era. For example, a decade ago Galbraith (1958) spoke of the need for less emphasis on production, and the society is frequently referred to as a post-modern society. Within this context, it is possible to speculate that the conjugal unit may be outmoded. If upper strata women can be considered to have reached a post-modern economic level, then the traditional family arrangements may no longer suit their needs. This may partially explain the phenomenon of the protest coming from this socioeconomic level.

2. Change has occurred in the American family since the early Colonial period. There has been no serious suggestion, however, that child-rearing be made a public rather than a private responsibility so that women could pursue their own goals. In the past, instances of interest in public child-rearing have been closely allied to political and/or economic goals. The most frequently cited examples are the Hebrew kibbutz, the Chinese commune, and the Russian system of state nurseries for children. It may be argued that

the change to public responsibility has been going on with the transfer of the educational, religious, and recreational functions from the family to other social institutions. However, the functions of the family are most often stated to be the socialization of the child and the psychological function of providing emotional support for its members. Seen in this way, extended public child care would seriously weaken the basis for maintenance of a conjugal system.

Seeking an alternative mode of child care as a means of freeing women bears an inherent conflict. The basic premise is that the job is oppressive and demeaning. It is accorded low status and attracting competent men and women to the job might prove difficult. It is possible, however, that what is considered oppressive in private family settings may not be so considered should the task be accorded some professional ranking. Women in the movement are aware that a satisfactory solution to the problem will not be easy.

3. The institutionalized normative expectations of the female in American society today require that she regard her wife-mother-homemaker role as primary. Any employment that she may participate in is considered to be secondary to her basic role. A consequence of these prescribed behaviors is that an increasing number of women, particularly those who have enjoyed a higher education, find marriage and the home a source of discontent and unhappiness. They conform to expectations of them as women, but find that there is no social acceptance of their desire to participate fully in the world of work. The result is guilt on the part of those who pursue careers or unhappiness on the part of those who continue to conform. If, as Women's Liberation proposes, the career role moved to primary position and were socially sanctioned, would those women who find their present traditional roles acceptable become the new disaffected group? Put in another way, would exchange of one set of prescribed and proscribed behaviors liberate one segment of the female population but inhibit another segment?

4. If nothing else, the aims of Women's Liberation necessitate some degree of restructuring of the traditional roles of the male and female and the relationship between them. Jessie Bernard (1968, p. 14) described this problem area as somewhat like a "zero-sum game." For instance, on a material level when women are given rights such as the right to vote, men lose nothing. But when women are given property or employment rights, men are deprived of what was theirs. The same theory could be applied on a sociopsychological level. The emphasis on changes in the female role tends to hide the necessary corresponding changes in the male role. Bernard states, "For women, the relevant problems have to do with the implications of sexuality for equality; for men, with the implications of equality for sexuality." What is often referred to as the "emasculation of the male" has been given attention from time to time in both the professional literature and in fiction. This, of course, refers to emasculation within the context of the sociocultural defini-

tion of masculinity. Margaret Mead (1935) suggested that different definitions exist when she detailed different cultural manifestations of sexuality such as the unaggressive males and females of the Arapesh tribe, the "male like" males and females of the Mundu-gumor, and the reversal of sex attitudes that were found in the Tchambuli tribe, as compared to American sexual definitions.

The Women's Liberation Movement views men in varying ways. All of the views emphasize the present differences and the drive toward equality. This emphasis tends to obliterate the many attributes that men and women have in common, common needs, feelings, desires, emotions, etc. If society's prescriptions for approved female behavior have inhibited full realization of her potential, then those same prescriptions for the male have affected him similarly. The suggestion is that in a network of interdependent role relationships, it is unrealistic to emphasize one role over the other.

WHERE WILL IT LEAD?

As women begin to attain some of the goals toward which their efforts are directed, changes in family structure can be anticipated. The nature of the changes cannot be predicted with any degree of certainty. In general, the movement has emphasized the necessity for change in social expectations of the female without giving much attention to the attendant effects on the family that such change would bring. The exception to this is the stand taken by the most extreme liberationists who hold that the present family structure is not acceptable. If, however, the nuclear family unit is still viewed as functional and desirable, then efforts can be made toward accommodating future changes. While attention is focused on the demands for change in sexual roles, an opportunity exists also for bringing into closer correspondence the needs of both men and women for self-realization and the broader societal need for a healthy viable family form.

The kinds of action needed as steps toward this end open a new area of inquiry for those in the applied family services. It would seem that whatever the course the implementation takes, the underlying directional philosophy should be to permit choice. Oppression appears to exist where there is no choice of acceptable alternatives for the individual. It has already been suggested that freedom to choose a life style within marriage is an important indicator of happiness in that relationship. (Orden and Bradburn, 1969; and Janeway, 1970) The freedom to choose alternative patterns of behavior in the other role relationships within the nuclear family unit may well prove to be a source of strength for that unit.

Industrialization, advanced technology, and higher levels of education may spell the end of traditional division of labor by sex. Societal recognition and acceptance of variation in sex role patterns would be living proof of a societal revolution fashioned by the Women's Liberation Movement of the 70's.

REFERENCES

Beard, Mary. *Woman As Force in History*. New York: Macmillan, 1946.

Berman, J. and E. Stocker. Women's Lib in the American Psychological Association. *Women: A Journal of Liberation*, 1970, **1**, 52–53.

Bernard, Jessie. The Status of Women in Modern Patterns of Culture. *The Annals*, 1968, **375**, 3–14.

Caplow, Theodore and R. J. McGee. *The Academic Marketplace*. Garden City, N.Y.: Doubleday and Co., Inc., 1958.

Dager, Edward Z. Socialization and Personality Development in the Child. In H. T. Christensen (Ed.) *Handbook of Marriage and the Family*. Chicago: Rand McNally and Co., 1967.

deBeauvior, Simone. *The Second Sex*. New York: Knopf, 1953 (originally 1949).

Dunbar, Roxanne. Female Liberation as the Basis for Social Revolution. Boston: New England Free Press, 1969.

Engels, Friedrich. *The Origins of Family, Private Property, and the State*. New York: International Publishers, original date 1884.

Flexnor, Eleanor. *A Century of Struggle: The Women's Rights Movement in the U.S.A.* Cambridge: Harvard, 1959.

Friedan, Betty. *The Feminine Mystique*. New York: W. W. Norton, 1963.

Galbraith, John K. *The Affluent Society*. Boston: Houghton Mifflin Co., 1958.

Goode, W. J. *The Family*. Englewood Cliffs, N.J.: Prentice-Hall, Inc., 1964.

Goode, W. J. *World Revolution and Family Patterns*, New York: Free Press, 1963.

Janeway, Elizabeth. Happiness and the Right to Choose. *The Atlantic*, March, 1970, 118–126.

Johnstone, Elizabeth, Women in Economic Life: Rights and Opportunities. *The Annals*, 1968, **375**, 102–114.

Komisar, Lucy, The New Feminism. *Saturday Review*, February 21, 1970, 27–30 and 55.

Kraditor, Aileen S. *Ideas of the Woman Suffrage Movement*, 1890–1920. New York: Columbia University, 1965.

Mead, Margaret. *Sex and Temperament in Three Primitive Societies*. New York: William Morrow, and Co., Inc., 1935.

Mead, Margaret and F. Kaplan (Eds.). The Report of the President's Commission on the Status of Women and Other Publications of the Commission. *American Women*. New York: Charles Scribner's Sons, 1965.

Nye, F. Ivan. Values, Family, and a Changing Society. *Journal of Marriage and the Family*, 1967, **29**, 241–248.

Nye, F. Ivan and Lois W. Hoffman. *The Employed Mother in America*. Chicago: Rand McNally and Co., 1963.

Orden, S. R. and N. M. Bradburn. Working Wives and Marriage Happiness. *American Journal of Sociology*, 1969, **74**, 392–407.

Pitts, Jesse R. The Structural-Functional Approach. In H. T. Christensen (Ed.), *Handbook of Marriage and the Family*. Chicago: Rand McNally and Co., 1967.

Rossi, Alice S. Status of Women in Graduate Departments of Sociology, 1968–1969. *The American Sociologist,* 1970, 5, 1–12.

Rossi, Alice S. Job Discrimination and What Women Can Do About It. *The Atlantic,* March, 1970, **225**, 99–102.

U.S. Bureau of Labor Statistics. Employment and Earnings, June, 1970.

U.S. Bureau of Labor Statistics. Report Number 94, 1967.

Anon. Sisterhood is Powerful. *New York Times Magazine,* March 15, 1970.

Anon. The War on "Sexism." *Newsweek.* March 23, 1970.

Anon. *Women: A Journal of Liberation,* Winter, 1970, **1**; and Spring, 1970, **2**.

12.

How Men Are Changing

The Editors of *Newsweek*

O nce it was possible to define them by their advantages: physically superior to women, psychically more stalwart, men seemed to be predestined for dominance. They were the hunters and warriors, the bridge builders and lawgivers, the natural autocrats of the breakfast table and oligarchs of the bedroom. They worked and earned for their families, came home to hot meals and compliant wives, took their ease in the privileged fellowship of the locker room and the all-male club. And in the process, they suffered more heart disease, ulcers, alcoholism—and went to earlier graves—than women. Some advantage, some reward.

Men have always known it is a jungle out there, from which few breadwinners return intact. The cultural revolution of the '60s, with its attacks on the work ethic, set some of them wondering whether the game was worth the penalties. But it was women's liberation that first suggested how much the penalty lay simply in a man's need to act manfully. Many men have since come to recognize that, like women, they can be oppressed by their designated role—by the obligation to prove themselves as indomitable achievers and providers. In the middle-class havens where the feminist movement itself took root, there are signs that men are taking a hard look at the mixed blessedness of being male. They are reassessing their priorities, their ideas about success, their notions of them-selves as omnipotent husbands and lovers.

If nothing else, the growing presence of women at work is forcing men to revise their sexual stereotypes. One immediate result is that the earnings of working wives are allowing men to throttle down, work less and think more about the quality of their lives. They are turning down overtime, transfers and promotions in favor of more time at home and a stabler family life. They are making at least some gestures toward sharing the housework with their working wives. They are getting more involved as fathers, from the prenatal stage onward, and they are asserting their rights as fathers in di-vorce cases. "More and more fathers are demanding equality as a parent in custody battles," says Philip F. Solomon, president of the American Academy of Matrimonial Lawyers. "It is taking on the proportions of a revolution."

The very fact that fathers are showing what is invariably called a maternal impulse is the signpost of a larger breakthrough. Men are venturing to express emotions once anathematized as "feminine." They are finding it may be acceptable to confess fears, to touch other men, even to weep—a forbidden indulgence under the old rules of machismo. According to several recent surveys, men are far more concerned than has generally been assumed about satisfying women sexually. Some men admit they would like women to take more initiative in bed, and many seem newly willing to identify their problems in terms of sexual fears and frustrations.

The shift in male attitudes has scarcely reached phenomenal pro-portions. It is apparent mainly among younger, educated men in their 20s and 30s, the group usually quickest to respond to new social currents. The majority of older men have barely modified their views of male-female roles. Nor have the winds of change ruffled blue-collar communities, where wives have been working for years just to make ends meet, and a man's home—however humble —is still his castle. Even among the vanguard, the new attitudes are hedged with contradictions. Some experts doubt that anything is changing at all. "There is a certain awareness, maybe even a glim-mer, that men's roles need some improvement," says Princeton Uni-versity sociologist Suzanne Keller, "but I think it's at a very surface level."

The question is, what sort of changes are men capable of making? The habits of male supremacy are deeply ingrained. Some anthro-pologists maintain that historical evidence shows there has never been a society in which men did not dominate. Moreover, they con-tend, most men cherish their sovereignty. Virtually from birth, they are conditioned to believe that manhood is a prize to be earned.

Literature from Homer to Hemingway has exalted the male rites of passage on the battlefield, in the sports arena and in the boudoir. Hemingway virtually wrote the code of behavior for modern machismo. His protagonists did whatever is expected of a man— fought wars, bedded women, hunted lions—with a minimum of fuss. "Doesn't do to talk too much about all this," admonishes the white hunter in "The Short Happy Life of Francis Macomber" when the jittery Macomber begins babbling over his first kill. "No pleasure in anything if you mouth it up too much."

Even so, the strong, silent masculine types is scarcely in the classical mold. Historically, men have exhibited a full range of sensibilities. They could be romantic in the exquisite vein of Elizabethan poetry or flamboyant in the extravagant style of Regency period attire. And in the face of hardship, they could weep as copiously as their wives. It was the Industrial Revolution that separated the sexes into the tender and the tough. Where they had once shared work and child-rearing with their women, men acquired a lonely new authority as breadwinners in the harsh world of factories and foundries. But that authority and the status it conferred have steadily eroded. In recent decades, the status of men as sole providers for the family slipped as pensions, social security and college-loan plans took up some of the economic burden.

The counter-culture of the 1960s mounted the first overt challenge to male sovereignty. The hippies and flower children were a deliberate put-down of the gray-flanneled, success-driven organization man of the '50s. The new sexual candor scoffed at Victorian standards of feminine chastity. Vietnam protesters and draft evaders heaped scorn on the consecrated masculine proving ground of war.

Ultimately, the '60s embodied a revolt of people who wanted choices. First blacks, then youth, then women rebelled at being locked into the roles prepared for them by history. But most men were not yet prepared to acknowledge that they needed relief from manhood.

David Steinberg, a San Francisco-based writer and part-time carpenter, can talk about it in retrospect. "There's a greater expectation put on us of confidence and strength," he says. "Men have the problem that it's hard to admit we don't have it all together. If you get too emotional, people feel that's not manly in a dog-eat-dog world." Steinberg, 33, is the author of "Fatherjournal," an account of his awakening feelings of fatherhood toward his now 6-year-old son. He credits the awakening partly to his wife's involvement in feminist groups. "After she started going, she put it out to me strongly that she wasn't happy with my being distant," he explains. "At first it was scary, but then I broke through that with support from her, and I realized that I didn't want to be this way either."

It remains remarkably difficult for men to talk about their distress, but they are beginning to do something about it. And the change shows most in the world of work. Executive recruiters and corporate officials report that the upwardly mobile male workaholic of the past is harder to find. At California's Northrop Corp., workers who once demanded overtime opportunities as a consideration for taking a job are now rejecting late hours and weekend work, even at double pay. And fewer men are willing to take promotions to managerial spots from the production line if it cuts into their "discretionary time." "The values of the work force have changed," says a Northrop personnel officer. "A man may be just as dedicated to the company, but he wants more balance—his recreation, his family, his community activities."

Men are also balking at transfers and out-of-town travel assignments. Ten years ago, the rising young executive with 2.4 children and a captive wife stood ready to go anywhere, any time, for advancement. "Now I rarely see that man," says Robert Booth, head of Corporate Recruiters, which scouts personnel for the country's top corporations. "The new executive draws the line at uprooting the family." In a recent survey of 758 companies by Atlas Van Lines, 66 per cent reported that some employees were turning down transfers—nearly twice the 1973 percentage.

Part of the reason for the resistance is that spouses are demanding a bigger say in the decision. Companies now have to woo wives by taking them to lunch and answering pointed questions about a proposed move. And despite that, says top financial-executive recruiter Carl Miller, perhaps 25 per cent of his prospects are turning him down. Litton Industries says it is even having trouble hiring accountants who would have to spend two or three weeks each month out of town on regional audits. "Most of them say it would be too difficult on their wives," sighs personnel manager Nancy Thacker.

In large part, the wife's new veto power may be traced simply to the fact that she has her own job. Though the husband's income still largely determines the level at which the family lives, says MIT researcher Richard Coleman, the fact that the wife is working at all tends to strengthen her hand. According to Coleman, even if her income is only half that of her husband's, "the power relationship may be a one-to-one tie."

In the process of becoming stay-at-homebodies, men are also getting more involved with their children—and apparently liking it. Prenatal clinics have experienced a huge boom in male participation. Fathers are diapering babies without any notable rise in the incidence of pinpricks, and they are taking on more of the parenting as children grow older. There has been a sudden spate of books on the joys of male nurturing with such titles as "Tenderness Is Strength" and "Father Feelings." And there are latter-day life-with-father scenes of Dad dressing the kids for school in the morning, picking them up from band practice and bathing them before bedtime. "I know more and more men who are more involved with their children than with their wives," says New York novelist Anne Roiphe ("Up the Sandbox"). "At dinner parties the child calls out and it's the father who gets up to see what the child wants. *They* are the maternal person in the house."

Even when the family breaks up, men are asserting their parental rights. A series of breakthrough cases since 1970 has challenged the legal assumption that the mother is automatically "the appropriate custodian" for young children. So far, fifteen states have passed parental-equalizing statutes holding that both parents are to be judged on an equal basis in determining the custody of the child. And last month, a Missouri court of appeals upheld the rights of unwed fathers in custody cases, saying: "Today's sex roles are becoming more flexible, and unmarried fathers are both willing and capable of being competent parents." In his new novel, "Kramer vs. Kramer," Avery Corman deals with the growing love of a father for the son he wins in a custody battle. Corman doubts that the book could have been written ten years ago. "There was no forum then for a man to express loving feelings for a child," he says. "These things have been kept from us like a dark secret. We've been lean-jawed and macho all these years, and the women's movement has created a climate that allows us to express our feelings."

In an age when the strong, silent male prototype has come to seem as dated as a Valentino epic, men are becoming aware of how pointless and painful it can be to keep their emotions veiled. Steve Landsman, manager of a suburban Baltimore dry-cleaning business, found he couldn't deal with the complicated feelings aroused by the death of his father and decided to go through some group-encounter sessions. "I started opening up and feeling better about it," he recalls, "but I realized men don't express such emotions very well. They avoid extremes and try to stay in the middle of the road." Books and articles are beginning to probe the male mystery, focusing on how men are isolated by their stoicism. And editor Clay Felker, who has proved prescient in the past, is currently re-targeting Esquire magazine to talk about men's troubles, not just their conquests and couture.

Opening the sluice gates to expression has been the big push of male consciousness-raising groups. Men's liberation guru Warren Farrell, who claims to have launched about 300 such groups since the '60s, frequently alludes to the conversational "crutches" men lean on, such as sports, business and "things"—cars and stereo equipment. In consciousness-raising groups, he notes, men follow a pattern of avoidance that finally gives way to candor. "They begin by talking about themselves in the distant past—'When I was in the Boy Scouts'—then about a past problem—for example, 'I used to be too egocentric, but now, of course, I've changed that'." Gradually, says Farrell, they get around to talking about a problem in a relationship, but they put the blame on the woman. Finally, they come to acknowledge the problem as their own and ask the group for help. "It's a matter of learning how to be personal, and that's a very difficult thing for men," Farrell says.

Younger men are most at ease with the new openness. They are less obsessed, on the whole, with seeming masculine, and they accept as given what their fathers would not have dreamed of—the equal importance of women's goals. Many of them expect to share the breadwinning duties with their wives, and they emphasize family life more than work. Says University of Illinois junior Bruce

Zavon: "I hope the relationship would be more important than either of our jobs."

The real hallmark of the '70s may be the advent of "50-50" marriages among younger couples conditioned by women's liberation and the egalitarian house rules of coed dormitories. Greg and Karen Arenson, both in their late 20s, have taken turns accommodating each other's interests from the time they met as undergraduates at MIT. They moved to Chicago when Greg was accepted for law school there, costing Karen a chance for a full-time reporting job in Miami. Then, at the cost of Greg's position in a law firm, they moved to New York when Karen was offered a spot in the main office of Business Week magazine. They see their flexibility as a matter of "maximizing" the happiness of the household. They also divide housework on the basis of who is more competent or available to do what. "Partially, it's the milieu in which we went to college," reflects Greg, "and partly it was thinking about the world I wanted to live in. When I got married, I was aware of the expectation in our day and age that Karen would have her own career, her own decisions to make."

College students are conscious of the change that has come about in male expectations even in the course of their own brief experience. Harvard freshman Phil Bennett remembers high-school parties "with the boys all on one side, checking out the girls." At Harvard, he says, male students seek girls as friends, but not necessarily as "girlfriends." They are used to girls asking them out and tend to be eclectic about the rules of who pays for a movie or a meal. It is not uncommon for the more liberated women even to ask them to bed—a role reversal that makes male posturing a bit risky. "There are still some guys who go about flexing their biceps," says Harvard freshperson Melissa Franklin. "But the men don't bluster as much as they used to, because it's a distinct possibility that you're going to end up in the sack with them, and you're going to *find out.*"

In the long run, the social structure itself may be transformed by the evolving sex roles. Already there are fundamental changes in the relationships of men and women at work and at home. But in the process, the shift is creating some turmoil, especially among men who came of age with traditional assumptions of male primacy. Many of them are now confused to the point of anguish about what their roles should be. For all the changing perceptions of masculinity, there are still few models in popular culture for the sensitive, tender-minded male. In movies, television and advertising, machismo is still the message: men may be vulnerable occasionally, but they are seldom vincible.

Women themselves are apparently adding to the confusion. A 1977 nationwide survey by Psychology Today showed that a majority of women want their men to be tender and considerate, but at the same time they admire the familiar emblems of male bravado, including success at work. Reflecting later on the survey, one woman who had emphasized such preferred qualities as warmth and gentleness said she realized "it was the traits I had minimized on paper that aroused me in fact—pride in physical strength, competition in sports and his constant awareness of being masculine."

Because so much in the culture still tells them to be rugged achievers, men continue to define themselves by their work. But now they are also being told that success at work is not enough—they must be successful family men as well. Thus, says psychologist Robert Sayad of the American Institute of Family Relations, "they are caught in a cultural double bind. The trouble is, they're finding it impossible to be both." At the same time, men are encountering new threats to their sexual authority. Working wives are meeting other men at the office, forming relationships outside the surveillance of their husbands. And liberated single women, with an expanded frame of sexual reference, have taken to "rating" their lovers' bedmanship. "Men are aware they are being graded, and, by God, they try to measure up," says Catherine Kinsock, a 29-year-old Los Angeles feminist and TV director-in-training.

The aggressive new challenge is shaking up a lot of men. In increasing numbers, they are turning up at sex clinics and psychiatrists' offices with worries about impotence or premature ejaculation. "There's a new evaluatory atmosphere in the bedroom," says Nyles A. Freedman, director of Sexual Health Centers of New England, Inc. "Women have learned about orgasm, and there is a destructive emphasis on performance which can create anxiety and fear of functioning. Sexual impotence is increasing, at least partly due to what males expect females to expect."

Dena K. Whitebook of the American Institute of Family Relations puts the blame more squarely on the unreasonable demands of women. Especially since Shere Hite's 1976 "Hite Report" on female sexuality, says Whitebook, "women are coming in and saying, 'My husband is not sexy.' They ask me to fix their husband up and make him give them an orgasm." It is the women who are usually the troublemakers in the bedroom lately, agrees Dr. Herb Stone of the Atlanta Psychiatric Clinic. "If it's been a traditional marriage, he can't deal with the fact that his wife is no longer the sweet submissive girl he married," says Stone, a marriage counselor. "She talks back to him. She says, 'I want to have an orgasm. Don't just get it off quickly and leave.' That threatens his manhood, and they end up in my office—or they get divorced."

The threat is reverberating beyond the bedroom. One Georgia couple is seeing a marriage counselor because of the wife's frequent travel on the job. Los Angeles psychiatrist Roger Gould is treating a woman who began getting pathetic notes from a former lover when she was promoted over him at the office. The notes, Gould says, spoke of how the man was confused by their new relationship at work, and his belief that it could be worked out if they could only get back to bed. The woman began to feel it was impossible to deal with men at work without sex conflicts intervening. Things were less complicated in the bad old days, says Gould: "Some man would have been screwing the secretary, and there would have been no confusion where power and sex are concerned."

Detroit divorce lawyer Henry Baskin says his practice has changed over a fifteen-year period from a largely female clientele to roughly an even number of men and women petitioners. More men now come to his office fighting to keep wives who are having affairs or want to break out of the kitchen. "Now we're getting the dependent male," says Baskin. "They're losing the mother-wife combination and they can't accept the loss." The rapidity of the changes in women has left men behind. And instead of dealing with marital strife head-on, many of them go into emotional retreat. They refuse to discuss their problems and worries with their wives, for fear it might hurt their image.

Except for some refinements of etiquette and language that they have adopted almost as a survival technique, most men are not dealing very successfully with the importunings of women's lib. Many of them still regard work as a male prerogative, their careers as sacrosanct, and they guard the image of their competence in ritually circumscribed conversations with other men. Says New York Times cultural writer John Leonard: "The focus on sexual and money scoring, the intractability of sports statistics—all the stuff we talk about seems to say, 'I'm doing quite well, maybe better than you are'."

Even among the college males she interviewed for her book, "Dilemmas of Masculinity," sociologist Mirra Komarovsky found only around 10 per cent she considered to be real libbers. The majority were a study in contradictions. Typically, they would endorse the idea of working wives, then add the proviso that a wife's career should not rival her husband's or interfere with the smooth functioning of the home. They approved of women entering the professions, then disapproved of "aggressive, ambitious" women students. Though some men seemed genuinely committed to the goals of women's lib, "they have serious problems intergrating their new values with reality," Komarovsky concludes.

Feminist Catherine Kinsock finds that role-reversal situations make men uneasy. Once, she recalls, she asked out a man who immediately answered, "Matter of fact, I was just going to ask you out." The evening went smoothly, but he froze when she came on sexually. "I don't think he would have been as threatened if he had asked me out to begin with," she says. "I think it made him uncomfortable because he didn't have control of the situation."

Men struggle to adjust to the new rules, but their habitual need to dominate keeps breaking through. Michael Singer, 37, a West Coast writer and male therapist, says he went along with the ideas and rhetoric of the movement at first, mainly to avoid confrontations. But he realized his basic attitudes had not changed. "I still wanted to control, to have the power in every situation," he says.

Pushed by liberated wives, husbands are pushing back. Almost as a last line of defense, some men are beginning to portray themselves as the true victims in the war of the sexes. "My wife and I have gone to the wall, fought tooth and nail over whether men oppress women, or vice versa," says Allan Forman, a clinical social worker who has been married fourteen years. Forman, 36, is a member of Free Men, a group of largely upper-middle-class professional men organized in Columbia, Md., a year ago to ponder the male dilemma. The group considers itself the vanguard of a genuine men's liberation movement that will not "piggyback" on women's lib. Explains executive director Richard Haddad: "Feminism is fine for women, but it doesn't address my problem."

One of this group's inspirational texts is a book by psychologist Herb Goldberg called "The Hazards of Being Male," which insists a man cannot change meaningfully "until he experiences his underlying rage toward the endless, impossible binds under which he lives . . . and [toward] the guilt-oriented, self-denying way he has traditionally related to women . . ." Free Men urges that men by no means have it better than women—that many men are bored or trapped in their jobs and desperately want the option to develop the personal side of their lives.

Haddad believes male parenting is the coming issue for men's liberation. "Men are going to get more involved in raising their kids, instead of being just the other parent," he says. "Women may react the way men did when women entered the job markets. They may say, 'This is my turf, stay away'." Some of the Free Men feel men's liberation will be slow in developing because it lacks the immediate focal points that women's lib had. But others are convinced it will blossom into a full-fledged political movement within a few years.

Male backlash may be the inevitable next phase in the sex wars. It is a delayed reaction among men who have been on the defensive ever since women began calling them oppressors. "Men have been candy-assed in response to any comment that comes out of the women's movement," says psychologist William R. Phillips, president of the Georgia Association of Marriage and Family Counseling. "It's the same posture that Southern liberal Democrats were in for many years with regard to the civil-rights movement. I tell them not to fold, and try to help them separate what's chauvinistic in their behavior from what isn't."

The reaction coincides with a resurgence of scientific opinion which holds that men are biologically destined to remain aggressive and women are best suited for nurturing—an echo of the celebrated dictum attributed to Freud that "anatomy is destiny." "The evidence indicates that women should follow their own physiological imperatives and not choose to compete for men's goals," says Steven Goldberg, a sociologist at City University of New York.

Some psychologists warn that women, in fact, may be repeating the errors of men in their growing passion for work and professional achievement. One recently separated New York executive seconds that judgment from his own experience: "The women's movement helped to relieve men of some responsibilities they didn't want," he says. "But it also produced a demi-generation of very tough, defensive women who are suffering from some of the things that men are now trying to get over . . . I believe that love and work are the two most important things in life, but now everyone is superachieving at work and love is suffering."

At the core of male resistance, some social observers see a classic contest over the sharing of power. The crunch will come, they feel, as women gain something closer to equality in the office and men find their protected status eroding both at work and at home. "It is possible that in the end men will militantly oppose the redefinition of roles," speculates MIT psychologist Kenneth Keniston. "After all, they receive their power, authority and status from the traditional roles." Even so, Keniston is convinced that the redefinition is slowly coming about as women keep moving into the labor force. But others are equally certain that work will remain the top priority for men and thus their involvement at home will remain limited.

Brandeis University historian John Demos argues that fundamental change will have to come in the institutions of work itself, with employers easing their demands to afford both men and women the opportunity to live more balanced lives. Cornell University social psychologist Urie Bronfenbrenner agrees that the "millennium" will not arrive without legislative changes that will make employee time more flexible. For example, he suggests a "fair part-time employment participation act" that would guarantee improved benefits to part-time workers.

Whatever their differences over details, most experts tend to agree that something is changing in the roles of men and women. Women have clearly been in revolt, and men may now be in transition. The changes in men so far are shallow, but even the lip service they are giving to the changes in women is seen as important: the rhetoric can ultimately affect the reality. If men are also rebelling, it is understandable. Women may have to back off and give them time and terms on which they can accept a profound overturning of their self-image. "Partially because of the women's movement, partially because of Vietnam and partially because of a loss of faith in institutions," says psychiatrist Gould, "men are now having a far more difficult time defining precisely what their role is. The whole idea of machismo is in many places dead. But what will eventually replace it is not yet resolved."

Younger men have not quite resolved their roles either. They retain some of the imprint and impulses of the masculine mystique, and it conflicts with their perception of a changed sexual milieu. Yet they know they are different from their fathers. Rafael Suarez Jr., a soft-spoken New York University senior, worries about a career and about making more money than his wife, but he adds: "I'm in the first generation to grow up with feminism. We'll be the first to take it full cycle . . . Who needs the pressure of being a typical male? It's more fun being a human first."

That is a simple enough credo, and it has doubtless occurred to generations of work-worn men in the past. But it has taken a revolutionary age for men to be able to utter it, to contemplate living by it and to risk nothing of their manhood in the process.

Part
Five

To Have Children or Not?

*O*URS HAS always been a society which has encouraged, worshiped, and sometimes even demanded large families. Until recently, the idea that the wife should invariably bear children was taken as the normal course of events for a family. The only families who did not have children were those with medical problems and those with grave sexual incompatibilities. Even in the face of increasing levels of industrialization, it has only been within the last two or three decades that the trend to smaller families has taken hold in America. Most nations that experience high levels of industrial development almost always experience an immediate decline in the size of families. Some, like Japan, have even experienced slight declines in total population. But the United States was unusually slow in responding to industrialization in this particular aspect. Perhaps part of the reason was that while industry was expanding at a rapid pace, agriculture was also continuing to expand rather than to decline, at least up until the 1920's. The beginning of the trend toward smaller families seems to be concomitant with the decline in agriculture, both changes beginning in the 1920's.

There are perhaps a number of other reasons for the American tradition of large families, one of which is that it is not necessarily an exclusively American tradition. That is, many of the immigrants to this country brought with them their Old World tradition of large families. Also, much of the expansion of business was dependent upon an expanding population, so that the business world encouraged large families in any number of ways. Our society has always placed a great value upon population growth for the purpose of occupying the seemingly endless frontier. This emphasis upon growth had apparently gained so much momentum that it was not until several decades after the closing of the frontier that we began to have second thoughts about the value of growth.

Most of the major social institutions have done their part to encourage large families, either directly as has been the case with a number of our religious groups, or indirectly as was the case with education. Religions have encouraged having children for both ideological reasons, such as the admonition to "be fruitful and multiply," and for the practical reason of increasing the size of the religious body. Education has encouraged the bearing of children in a more indirect fashion by providing free public education for all children and requiring them to attend. This relieved the parents of constant child care responsibility, and assured to some degree that their children would be prepared to earn a living.

Until recent years, very few families ever explored their reasons for having children. Having children was as much a part of marriage as it was for the man and woman to live together. The question of whether or not to have children was rarely asked because few people ever thought to ask it, and those who did violated the prevalent norms. With the increased knowledge and effectiveness of contraceptives and the spread in their use during the 1920's and 30's, especially among the middle class, the idea of limiting family size began to be acceptable, and later on reached the point of being almost mandatory. However, it was not until the last decade that the idea of having no children at all began to gain some acceptance. Concomitant with and perhaps related to the Women's Liberation Movement is the present trend among more and more young married couples to at least ask questions of themselves about whether or not they want children, and to explore in depth just why they reach the conclusions they come to. Since it is the wife who has to bear and usually rear the child, women are demanding a larger role in the decisions about having children, with the result that in many cases they are having fewer children and occasionally they are deciding to have none.

Also having a tremendous impact upon families' decisions in this area have been the increased awareness of and sensitivity to the issues of overpopulation and environmental pollution, which have emerged as major social, political, and economic issues in the last few years. Concern over these issues has certainly made the choice not to have children a more socially acceptable one for many families.

Whatever the causes, there is no doubt that the average family size is decreasing as is evidenced by the decline in the fertility rate, which is the number of babies born to women of childbearing age. The decline in the fertility rate averaged 7 per cent per year between 1970 and 1973, and about 2 per cent between 1973 and 1976. Currently, the fertility rate is the lowest in history.[1] These rates are now so low as to be producing less than 2 children per family, which is also a record low. There are some indications, however, that this trend is bottoming out as evidenced by a slight increase in the birthrate during 1977.[2]

The population experts do not expect this trend to continue indefinitely, although most feel that the small family is here to stay and that more and more families will choose to remain childless. Since it is necessary for families to have an average of 2.1 children in order to maintain the population, the population would actually begin to decline in about 30 years if the current trends held. Most experts, however, do not think that this will occur because of what they believe to be the reasons for the extent of the current decreases, specifically the recent war and the current economic situation. They also feel that many young women who are not now having babies, will go ahead to have them later on, thus bringing things back a little more toward normal.

But the norm is still likely to be toward smaller families since some of the other factors that have contributed to the decline in births will remain. These are improved birth control techniques, liberalized abortion rules, and, as stated earlier, the increased acceptance and popularity of the childless marriage.

Another indication of the current trends is found in Census Bureau data concerning the expected number of children of young women. In 1967, wives 18 to 24 years of age expected to have an average of 2.85 children in their lifetimes. In 1976, wives in this same age category expected to have only 2.14 children.[3] An interesting sidelight is that in most of the similar studies done in the past, a majority of the women questioned ultimately had fewer children than they had expressed an expectation of having earlier in their marriages. It is probably safe to say, therefore, that at least for the immediate future the one- or two-child family will become the more prevalent family unit, with larger families becoming a rarity.

The question of family size, and specifically the trend toward the smaller family, is not really very much of an issue. What is much more at issue is the question of whether to have children at all; this question is dealt with in the first article of this section. In a journalistic style, this article looks into some of the ways of thinking that characterize many couples who are contemplating whether or not they want to "start a family." A number of the issues involved in such a decision are considered.

The second article in this section takes an altogether new approach to the question of whether or not to have children; it looks at the presence of children in purely economic terms, carefully analyzing the various monetary costs involved in bearing and rearing children. This approach may seem rather cold and objective, but there is no question but that a family's economic situation has an important influence on its decisions concerning children. Most readers will find the article interesting and informative if not startling.

The final article of this section is rather unusual and quite interesting in that it attempts to delineate and classify all of the various reasons why people might want to have children. And it succeeds admirably. The author, Bernard Berelson, constructs a taxonomy of reasons for wanting children that covers the biological, cultural, political, economic, familial, and, in greater detail, the personal reasons that might be seen as rationales behind procreation. The article concludes with a brief history of the differing evaluations that have been made of children.

REFERENCES

1. National Center for Health Statistics, *Monthly Vital Statistics Report, Annual Summary for the United States, 1976,* U.S. Department of Health, Education and Welfare, December 12, 1977, p. 2.

2. National Center for Health Statistics, *Monthly Vital Statistics Report*, U.S. Department of Health, Education and Welfare, January 6, 1978.

3. U.S. Bureau of the Census, *Current Population Reports*, Series P-20, No. 300, "Prospects for American Fertility: June 1976," U.S. Government Printing Office, 1976, p. 1.

13.

The Pros and Cons of Parenthood

The Editors of *Ebony*

Gilbert and Marsha Witherspoon have been married seven and a half years. They live in Chicago. Gilbert, 31, is a physical education teacher in a school for juvenile boys, and Marsha, 30, who quit her job as a public school teacher, stays at home to raise their sons, Ali, 2, Christopher, 3, and Ahsram (Marsha spelled backwards), 4. Proud poppa Gilbert says he has always wanted sons. A happy, healthy family, the Witherspoons have by now grown used to the changes necessitated by the births of their children. "The kids seem to have made the bond between Marsha and me stronger, more lasting," Gilbert says, cuddling Christopher. "I've built my life around my boys." Marsha always knew that she would eventually have a family. She prepared for a teaching career so that she would come in contact with youngsters every day. She was glad to leave teaching, however, when Ahsram was born. Now, with three boys, she says it is trying at times to attend graduate school part-time, teach and care for the boys, and, because of their small income, do without the time-saving conveniences that many families have. That will change, Gilbert says, when Marsha returns to work. Would they have done anything differently if they had the chance to start again? "No," came the reply, though perhaps they "might have established a better financial base" or "earned my master's degree" before starting the family. But nothing, they say, can top the joy of watching their youngsters grow.

Margaret and Jim Taylor knew even before they were married that children of their own would not be a part of their lives. Married four years, both for the first time, Margaret, 33, and Jim, 54, also live in Chicago. Like the Witherspoons, their work requires close association with young people. He teaches film production to young men and women in a community workshop; she works in the Chicago public schools and acts as a consultant to the film workshop's board of directors. Margaret, who holds a master's degree in social work, decided very early in life that she wanted a career, and by the time she was in college, was sure she would never have children of her own. "I'm just not a baby person," she candidly volunteers. "I work better with older children." Besides, coming from a family with eight children, she's had plenty of child-rearing experience with younger siblings. Jim insists that he is "too old" to start a family, and even confides that it was never his intention to get married. He changed his mind about matrimony when he fell in love with Margaret, but his determination to remain childless never wavered. Still, he enjoys kids, and perhaps they'll consider adopting a child "about eight or nine years old." Jim says he'd rather pass up the diaper and bottle stage. Doesn't he feel he's missed an important human experience by being childless? "Oh, no," he replies. "Actually, I have 40 kids," as he refers to his film students. The Taylors agree that children of their own would mean less time and effort devoted to their community activities.

It used to be that when a man or woman grew up, they'd get married, settle into a cozy place of their own, and start a family. Society didn't offer much of a choice. Sure, a man always had his job, and even a woman could distinguish herself in an ever-broadening array of fields. But the family, of course, reigned supreme; folks had their families even if all else failed.

Today, however, while men and women still triumph and fail at a number of careers and lifestyles, some people are having serious doubts about the one institution that heretofore went unquestioned (at least in public) : parenthood.

Unlike the Witherspoons and the Taylors, who are sure they have each made the right decision to become parents or not, thousands, maybe millions, are not sure which way to go. They are caught up in a web of options that point to happiness and self-fulfillment in ways that don't necessarily include childbearing. Still, societal pressures to reproduce weigh heavily upon healthy, fertile conscientious men and women.

Should we (I) have a baby? It is a question that can agonize even the most otherwise self-assured of potential parents. They dream, argue and compromise, they talk to counselors, they try parenting a niece or nephew for a weekend, they read books and compute costs, and still they wonder: Is it all right for us to have a baby? Is it all right for us not to?

Most "experts"—marriage and family counselors, psychologists, psychiatrists, clergymen, even advice columnists—agree that the choice today should be an individual one, untouched by traditional obligations to be fruitful and multiply.

"A young couple wrote to me and asked me whether or not I thought they should have a family," says columnist Ann Landers, whose advice is revered by millions coast-to-coast. "Well, you'd think that people would be making these kinds of decisions on their own—that what somebody else thinks wouldn't be very important." She proffers the simplest and most direct solution to the young couples who pop the question. "If you have to ask Ann Landers whether or not you should have a family," she says, "then I don't think you want a family bad enough. If you are undecided, my answer would be no. Children are work, they're expensive, they're energy- and time-consuming. Unless you really want to have a family, you shouldn't have one."

Ah, sound advice. Simple. But for many couples, the question isn't so easily dismissed.

Dr. Elizabeth Whelan and her husband Steve of New York City found themselves in a similar quandary nearly three years ago. She, an epidemiologist and specialist in public health, and he, a Wall Street attorney, had agreed that after their marriage they would wait about two years to begin a family. But when that time came, they realized that their agreeable lifestyle seemed threatened by the entrance of a baby. They had doubts about raising a child in New York City, yet didn't want to move to the gentler suburbs. They wondered how they could adjust without her income yet having another human being to provide for. In short, Dr. Whelan says, "We had a serious problem. For my husband, as with most men, time can just go on and on and maybe we'll have a baby someday, later. But I thought, with (age) 30 approaching, I'd better hurry up and make up my mind."

Determined to find an answer for herself, she began research that culminated in a book, *A Baby? . . . Maybe,* a pre-parenthood guide for the undecideds and ultimately a counseling service of the same name. "A Baby? . . . Maybe" services are a part-time endeavor for Dr. Whelan, a researcher in the Harvard University School of Public Health. Now, at age 31, she is expecting her first child in July.

"The key issue for the people who are undecided," Dr. Whelan says, "is personal freedom. The real hooker here is the woman's career. She's not sure what to do; he's become dependent on her income and doesn't want to lose it; she's wondering whether she can handle both (a career and a baby)."

One of Dr. Whelan's clients once remarked that the decision, ideally a mutual one between husband and wife, really boils down to the woman in the end because it is her life that changes most with the birth of a child. While the father continues in his normal routine for the most part, the mother has to fragment her activities, first "dropping out" to give birth, and then dividing her attentions between her baby, her outside activities and her husband.

The concerns are many. Some couples have been swayed by the exhortations of organizations such as Zero Population Growth and National Organization for Non-Parents, who contend every baby born is a threat to the world's precious resources. Others experience guilt feelings when, in the midst of a comfortable and satisfying lifestyle, they are pressured by their own parents and friends to reproduce, lest they be branded "too selfish" to rear children. Dr. Whelan has noticed that many young women who grew up with what she calls "super parents"—loving parents and a mother who stayed at home to provide for every child's needs—are feeling guilty because job commitments won't allow them to spend as much time with a child as their mothers spent with them.

Those who have chosen parenthood know well the inescapable sacrifice of time, money and personal freedom. Children, especially those under five years, require a tremendous amount of close supervision. The parent's time becomes his or her own only after the child has gone to sleep. Active parents who like to get away on weekends, attend a spur-of-the-moment social gathering, or run out to a restaurant in the middle of the night will find their movement restricted when they can't get a babysitter. Finally, the unexpected costs of rearing that first child have caught millions of parents by surprise. To be (a parent) or not to be is literally a $64,000 question, according to a recent study by an associate professor of economics. It costs a typical middle-income family that much to raise a first-born child to adulthood, including a college education at a state-supported institution, says Thomas J. Espenshade of Florida State University. Including data for "lost" wages if the mother leaves work to stay home with the child, the cost is pushed up to $107,000. The same costs to low-income families were estimated to be $44,000 or $77,000.

But the statistics don't end there. In 1974 researchers at the University of Michigan found that married couples aged 18 to 29 were happier with themselves and with their marriages than their peers who are parents. Moreover, couples with children under six years of age were not as happy as those with children over age six. Relative happiness increased as the children grew up and finally left home. And there's more: In Ann Landers' recent survey, in which she asked her readers: "If you had it to do over again, would you have had children?" about 70 percent of 40,000 responses answered no. Disgruntled parents fell into three categories: young couples who started families and resented the child's imposition on their freedom; middle aged couples whose teenagers were constantly in trouble; and retired couples who sacrificed to give their children every opportunity and comfort, only to be forgotten in their old age by their offspring. (Of course, it must be remembered that in most such surveys, more people who are dissatisfied will bother to respond than those who are content.)

And so on. The disadvantages continue to add up in favor of remaining child-free. Nevertheless, just a small portion of the population in the United States—under 5 percent—say unequivocally that they never want children of their own.

Why? The pro-baby reasons are less tangible than the con, but apparently no less important. "Many of the young unwed girls who come to Planned Parenthood want to have a baby because they need someone to love," says Beverly Crumley, a social worker at Planned Parenthood of New York City. Other advantages of child-bearing include establishing a closer bond with a spouse with the birth of a baby; the feeling of belonging to a complete unit, of being needed to keep that unit functioning; the pride and satisfaction that comes from molding a human life; the flattery of seeing oneself in one's child; the satisfaction of having an "heir" to continue one's blood line; the acceptance of love from a child; the personal growth one experiences in childrearing; feeling of prolonged youthfulness that comes with companionship with a child; and the belief one's children will prevent old-age loneliness.

For most of the population, these things outweigh the negative implications of raising a family. And soaring divorce statistics have had little effect on peoples' parental desires, even though there is now close to a 50–50 chance of either spouse raising a child alone following divorce.

To bear a child is one of the most critical decisions a human being can make. Still, for the vast majority of people, it is a decision made with little thought and preparation, says Jane Johnson, associate executive director of PPNYC.

"We make the assumption that everyone ought to be a parent. We ask little children, 'Now, when you grow up, how many children are you going to have?' We never say, 'When you grow up, *are* you going to have children? What are your plans for your life?' "

Mrs. Johnson believes there should be some kind of objective evaluation of prospective parents to determine whether or not they are parent material. "I know of nothing that takes more talent than being a good parent," she says. "I'm convinced that some people have oodles of it, and others have almost none of it. I don't think that is anything one ought to feel apologetic about, any more than the fact that they cannot play a violin. . . . What we are talking about is a capacity. Clearly, the great majority of human beings have the capacity to reproduce. We also have the capacity to commit murder. It does not follow that we will do that."

She agrees with most enlightened attitudes that not everyone is cut out for parenthood, or even marriage. For many couples, she says, parenthood was "thrust" upon them or was something they stumbled into with very little thought, though they believed they were doing what society expected of them. Some turned out to be miracle workers with kids, and others, total failures.

How do you know whether or not you're parent material? After all, if the partnership fails, you can separate or get a divorce; but if the man and woman fail as parents, the child cannot be sent back to from where it came. "People have to recognize that having a child requires giving up yourself, that you have to be able to love your child unconditionally, Mrs. Johnson says. "That's the most difficult kind of love—very few of us have gotten unconditional affection."

14.

The Cost of Children

Thomas J. Espenshade

Americans live in a consumption-oriented society. When we buy something we generally expect to get our money's worth. Rarely would we purchase anything without first knowing how much it costs; in fact, we often spend valuable time comparison shopping for the lowest possible price. Yet when it comes to children, parents have little or no idea of what they cost. One of the most expensive investments that couples can make is undertaken with only a meager amount of information. This chapter presents new evidence on the costs of American children. For those who are already parents, information about the expenses incurred in rearing a family can facilitate planning for the future. More importantly, it can guide prospective parents in making rational decisions about the number of children they want and can afford.

CONCEPT OF COSTS

Costs correspond to the disadvantages of children. In general, these refer to what parents must give up or sacrifice to obtain the benefits from children. Terms used for the costs of children include dissatisfactions, disadvantages, penalties, disvalues, and negative

From Thomas J. Espenshade, "The Value and Cost of Children," *Population Bulletin*, Vol. 32, No. 1 (April 1977). Abridged by the author and reprinted with permission of the Population Reference Bureau, Inc., Washington, D.C. 20036.

general values. As with values, both economic and noneconomic costs of children can be identified.

Under the heading of economic costs, two types are important:

1. *Direct maintenance costs.* These are the out-of-pocket expenses parents incur in bearing and raising children, and include such items as food, clothing, housing, education, and medical care.

2. *Opportunity costs.* The term "opportunity cost" reflects the opportunities parents forego when rearing children. Eva Mueller cites three categories of economic opportunity cost.[1] First, certain consumption expenditures may have to be relinquished, which could mean a lower standard of living. Second, children may reduce opportunities to save and invest. Depending on the circumstances, more children could mean less money to invest in the education of each of them, in a family-owned business or farm, or in house improvements. Third, the wife is giving up income-earning possibilities if the presence of young children at home causes a reduction in time spent in the labor force.

The relative importance of the three kinds of economic opportunity cost is likely to vary according to the level of economic development.[2] In the less developed countries, for example, there is a tendency to think that children scarcely affect consumption standards or the ability to save and invest. But whether or not this is actually the case depends on the level of aspirations among the population. Mueller reports that rising aspirations are a prominent source of opportunity cost in Taiwan, and that this in turn has affected fertility behavior. On the other hand, the importance of the third type of opportunity cost may be overemphasized. Especially in rural areas where women take their children with them into the fields or can care for them at the same time they are doing household chores, female roles of mother and worker are not incompatible. In the United States, studies by economists have focused almost exclusively on opportunity cost in the sense of income foregone. But even here, the concept is relevant only if women are prevented from spending more time at a job by the presence of young children.

Many of the costs of children are nonmonetary in nature. These include the emotional and psychological burdens children impose on parents such as the feeling of being "tied down," anxiety over the child's health and future welfare, frustrations over misbehavior, and the like.

Revised Estimates of Actual Economic Cost

It is important to distinguish clearly between *actual* costs and values and those that are *perceived* by parents to exist. Two couples can have different subjective perceptions of the same set of objective circumstances. While it might be argued that parents need to become better informed so that their perceptions are brought closer to actuality, as long as there is a discrepancy it is desirable to measure both. For example, a family allowance program would require data on the actual costs of bringing up children. On the other hand, fertility behavior is probably better understood in terms of parental expectations of how large the relevant costs and benefits will be. Here we are concerned with the actual cost of children.

Economists have attempted to quantify the *actual* economic cost that parents in the United States typically face. This cost is usually considered to have two components: *direct maintenance cost* which consists of out-of-pocket expenses for food, clothing, education, and the like, and *opportunity cost,* or the income that wives (principally) forego by staying home to raise children and by not participating in the labor force.

In a study for the U.S. Commission on Population Growth and the American Future, Ritchie Reed and Susan McIntosh prepared estimates of the size of the direct and opportunity costs confronting American families in 1969.[3] With more recently available data, I have estimated what these costs would be in 1977, based on the approach used by Reed and McIntosh.

Direct Maintenance Cost. The estimates that Reed and McIntosh supplied are for an average child in a family consisting of husband and wife and no more than five children. Separate calculations are made of the expenses associated with childbirth, other maintenance costs to age 18, and the cost of a four-year college education.

The largest of these three are the maintenance costs to the end of high school, excluding those surrounding birth. For these estimates, we rely on data provided by the U.S. Department of Agriculture (USDA), as did Reed and McIntosh, with Consumer Price Index Information from the Bureau of Labor Statistics used to update the picture to 1977. The results are shown in Table 1. Expenditures by type of residence, whether farm, rural nonfarm, or urban, do not vary consistently, though region of the country seems to make some difference: children are apparently more expensive to raise in the West. However, the family's standard of living is the important determinant of child-related purchases. To raise children at the level of the USDA's moderate-cost food plan costs approximately 50 percent more than their low-cost plan. (The USDA uses food costs to determine family living standards. The "low-cost food plan" corresponds roughly to family incomes after taxes of about $10,500 to $13,500, in 1977 dollars. Disposable incomes in the

TABLE 1   *Direct Cost of Raising a Child to Age 18 in the U.S. at 1977 Prices*[a]
(*By region, cost level, and type of residence*)

Region	Farm costs		Rural nonfarm costs		Urban costs	
	Low	Moderate	Low	Moderate	Low	Moderate
Total U.S.	$33,124[b]	$48,988[b]	$35,006	$53,830	$35,261	$53,605
North Central	31,764	47,046	31,675	47,237	36,849	50,671
South	35,365	52,617	34,415	55,173	34,654	54,863
Northeast	32,382	45,840	37,618	57,355	31,861	53,586
West	na	na	40,476	58,255	38,243	56,065

Sources: United States Department of Agriculture "Cost of Raising a Child," CFE (Adm.)-318, September 1971; Consumer Price Index data from U.S. Department of Labor, Bureau of Labor Statistics.

[a] Undiscounted figures

[b] West excluded

$16,500–$20,000 range identify families living at the moderate-cost level.)

With all these possible sources of variation considered, we estimate that the expense involved in raising a child to age 18 in the U.S. currently ranges from $31,675 for a low-cost-plan rural non-farm family in the North Central region to $58,255 for a moderate-cost-plan rural nonfarm family in the West. In 1969 the comparable range was from $19,360 to $35,830.

USDA data reveal that housing is now generally the leading item in child-rearing costs, followed by food and then transportation. For example, of the $50,671 it would cost a typical North Central city family to raise a child at a moderate standard of living, in 1977 prices, 32.3 percent would go to housing, 24.3 percent to food, 16.1 percent to transportation, 9.5 percent to clothing, 5.3 percent to medical care, 1.5 percent to education, and 11.0 percent to "all other" expenses.

Data on the cost of childbirth come from a 1976 report of the Health Insurance Institute, which pointed out that these costs were up by 40 percent over 1971.[4] The total cost of $2,194 for a first birth is broken down as: hospital costs (including four days at the national average cost of $128 per day, nursery, and labor and delivery rooms) —$782; medical expenses (including obstetrical and pediatric care) —$407; basic nursery supplies (a baby wardrobe, medical supplies, furnishing, utensils, and the like) —$741; and a maternity wardrobe for the mother—$264.

In computing the cost of higher education, it is assumed that a child from the moderate-cost standard of living would attend a four-year public university. This expense totaled $8,416 in 1975, according to the most recent data available from the Office of Education.[5] Educating a child from a low-cost background is presumed to cost somewhat less ($7,452 in 1975) since it is assumed that a person of this type would matriculate at a public four-year institution that was not a university. (Estimates of *future* college costs in the U.S. might be more relevant for prospective parents. The Oakland Financial Group of Charlottesville, Virginia, recently calculated that, by the 1990s when a year-old child of today would be ready for college, an annual inflation rate of 6 percent will have ballooned the costs for four years at a state university to $47,330 and to $82,830 at a private one.[6])

Summing these three expense categories as in Table 2 we obtain estimates of the total direct maintenance costs that range from $44,156 at the low-cost level to $64,215 at the moderate-cost standard. (When Reed and McIntosh made similar estimates for 1969, the range was from $27,109 to $39,924.) Actual expenditures by any particular family will, of course, deviate from these averages. The figures clearly would be reduced if, for example, children did not go to college or if part of their tuition, room, and board was covered by a scholarship or their own earnings from summer or parttime jobs.[7] Beyond that, expenses will depend upon the region of the

TABLE 2   *Total Direct Costs of a Child in the U.S., about 1977*
(By cost level)

Cost level	Childbirth	Costs to age 18[a]	4 years of college	Total
Low-cost	$1,443[b]	$35,261	$7,452	$44,156
Moderate-cost	2,194	53,605	8,416	64,215

Sources: *Health Insurance Institute News Data Sheet*, June 1976; W. Vance Grant and C. George Lind, *Digest of Educational Statistics, 1975 Edition*, National Center for Education Statistics, U.S. Department of Health, Education, and Welfare (Washington, D.C.: Government Printing Office, 1976); and Table 1.

[a] Based on U.S. average for urban areas.

[b] Assumed to be in the same proportion to the modern-cost childbirth figure as the respective costs to age 18.

country in which the family lives, the race of the head of the household, educational levels of the parents, and tastes and preferences for alternative life styles. Thus, the estimates in Table 2 are best interpreted as rough orders of magnitude, and should not be taken literally.

Opportunity Cost. Reed and McIntosh defined opportunity cost as "earnings that the women might have had, but had to forego because of the need to care for her children.[8] Two issues are involved. The first is to determine how many hours annually a wife loses from paid employment because of the presence of children of varying ages. Second, one must attach a price tag to the value of each hour that is lost. To measure the first of these, Reed and McIntosh adopted a methodology similar to the one that Glen Cain, a labor economist at the University of Wisconsin, used to estimate opportunity cost.[9] Using data on female labor force participation from a study by Bowen and Finegan,[10] Cain estimated that a typical wife in the childbearing ages who had no children would work an average of 1,000 hours per year, the equivalent of a halftime job, assuming that fulltime employment equals 2,000 hours (40 hours per week for 50 weeks). Next, data for labor force participation rates of wives with children of varying ages were used to construct the number of hours per year these women typically worked. The procedures adjusted for other differences between women such as level of schooling completed, race, age, amount of other family income, and employment status of the husband. Thus, differences in the number of hours worked reflected only differences in the ages of children.

Table 3 presents estimates of how much a first child could now cost a mother in "lost" earnings over the first 15 years of that child's life. Column 2 shows what Reed and McIntosh estimated to be the annual number of hours lost from work due to the presence of a child of alternative ages, using the behavior of childless women as the standard for comparison. Note that lost work time is greatest in the year following birth and declines as the child ages, with a

TABLE 3 *Average Opportunity Cost of a First Child for U.S. Wives, 1977 (By level of school completed)*

Age of child	Hours worked (1)	Lost worktime (2) = 1000[a] − (1)	All women (3) = (2) × $4.29[b]	Elementary (4) = (2) × $3.28[b]	High school (5) = (2) × $4.06[b]	College 4 years (6) = (2) × $5.29[b]	College 5 years and over (7) = (2) × $6.71[b]
<1 year	106	894	$3,835	$2,932	$3,630	$4,729	$5,999
1 year	191	809	3,471	2,654	3,285	4,280	5,428
2 years	219	781	3,350	2,562	3,171	4,131	5,241
3 years	237	763	3,273	2,503	3,098	4,036	5,120
4 years	279	721	3,093	2,365	2,927	3,814	4,838
5 years	289	711	3,050	2,332	2,887	3,761	4,771
6 years	620	380	1,630	1,246	1,543	2,010	2,550
7 years	620	380	1,630	1,246	1,543	2,010	2,550
8 years	620	380	1,630	1,246	1,543	2,010	2,550
9 years	620	380	1,630	1,246	1,543	2,010	2,550
10 years	620	380	1,630	1,246	1,543	2,010	2,550
11 years	620	380	1,630	1,246	1,543	2,010	2,550
12 years	620	380	1,630	1,246	1,543	2,010	2,550
13 years	620	380	1,630	1,246	1,543	2,010	2,550
14 years	620	380	1,630	1,246	1,543	2,010	2,550
Total:			34,742	26,562	32,885	42,841	54,347

Sources: Ritchie H. Reed and Susan McIntosh, "Costs of Children," in *Research Reports*, Vol. 2, Commission on Population Growth and the American Future (Washington, D.C.: Government Printing Office, 1972) Appendix Table 1; and U.S. Bureau of the Census. *Current Population Reports*, Series P-60, Nos. 75, 80, 85, 90, 97, and 101.

[a] Average hours worked per year by married urban woman with no children under 14 (based on their adjusted fulltime equivalent labor force participation rates).

[b] Adjusted hourly income estimated for 1977.

large reduction occurring when the child enters first grade. This pattern corroborates Bowen and Finegan's observation that "it can be misleading to speak of children in general as discouraging labor force participation—it is mainly the presence of children under 14, and especially children under 6, which seems to have this effect.[11]

Hourly market wage rates for women having attained alternative levels of education are computed by dividing the most recently available data on the median yearly earnings of wives who worked fulltime by 2,000 hours. The resulting dollar figures are assumed to represent the 1977 value of each hour lost from paid work. These are tabulated across the tops of columns 3 to 7 in Table 3, and when multiplied by the hours of lost work time, they yield the dollar opportunity cost corresponding to various ages of the child. Opportunity cost increases as education does, and when summed for 15 years rises from $26,562 for wives with only an elementary school education to $54,347 for those who have gone beyond their bachelor's degree.

Reed and McIntosh suggest that the rise in opportunity cost with education may actually be understated since the better educated she is the more likely a woman is to be working, whether or not she has a child under age 6. But the increase in labor force participation by education is less for mothers with such young children, which means that time withdrawn from the labor market is greatest for the best-educated women. Thus, they point out, "The highly educated woman has a much higher opportunity cost on both counts: she gives up more working time and higher wages by having a child."[12]

Reed and McIntosh also argue that the average participation rates for women without children used in their estimates (1,000 hours annually) are not relevant to all women. Certainly in 1977 many mothers would choose to work fulltime if they had no children under 15, and for them we should calculate opportunity cost by subtracting the number of hours worked by women with children from 2,000, not 1,000. Recomputing the data in Table 3 on this basis boosts the opportunity cost of a first child to about $75,000 for the least well-educated mothers, and to $155,000 for those with a post-graduate education, with an average value for all women of approximately $100,000.

These startling figures are up by more than half over Reed and McIntosh's estimates for 1969, which ranged from $44,121 to $103,000, with an overall average of $58,437. According to a March 1976 Census Bureau survey reported in a recent Bureau of Labor Statistics press release,[13] close to 40 percent of the some 14 million mothers of children under age six were in the labor force in 1975 as were 46 percent of the 25 million married women living with their husbands who had children under 18. Even if they include a high percentage of parttimers, the figures are strong evidence that potentially lost wages are an important factor in the thinking of many young U.S. women today.

There are some women to whom opportunity cost in the sense of lost earnings does not apply; they would not choose to work even if they had no children, and some allowances must be made for this fact in interpreting the overall figures on opportunity cost. Reed and McIntosh suggested that opportunity cost will be most relevant to the best-educated women, who derive not only the greatest money income from a career, but possibly also the greatest non-monetary rewards.

As a final comment on opportunity costs, it is important to recognize that using the going wage rate to put a dollar value on the wife's time computes gross opportunity cost, that is, income foregone before taxes. More relevant is net opportunity cost, or income foregone after taxes. The net figure could be substantially less than the gross because the extra family income contributed by the wife will be taxed at higher rates than the husband's income.

To summarize, these estimates indicate that direct maintenance costs and opportunity costs are roughly of equal magnitude. Assuming that the better educated a wife the higher her husband's income and adding direct and opportunity costs together, we obtain a total economic cost confronting American families in 1977 that varies on a per child basis from about $77,000 at the low-cost level to approximately $107,000 at the moderate-cost standard. (These figures are based on the data in Tables 2 and 3 and assume that wives in "low-cost-plan" families will be high school graduates, while those in "moderate-cost-plan" families have had a college education.)

Several additional aspects of the economic cost of children have been examined in studies by me and by Boone Turchi of the University of North Carolina.[14] My work is based on an analysis of the Survey of Consumer Expenditures conducted by the Bureau of Labor Statistics in 1960–1961, and deals with estimating what it then cost parents in urban areas of the United States to raise their children to the age of 18.

Although the dollars amounts are now, of course, gross underestimates, several conclusions of this study are still significant. Two of these are revealed in Table 4. Within each income level, real after-tax income was assumed to increase over time, from $4,564 to $5,860 at the lower level, from $6,326 to $8,111 for middle-class families, and from $9,007 to $11,692 for families with upper-level incomes. (All figures relate to 1960–61 levels.) Note first that as family income goes up so do money expenditures on children. This is not only because better-off parents have more to spend, but presumably also because the standards of what should be provided for children also climb with socioeconomic status. It is interesting, however, that, apart from college costs which are not explicitly accounted for here, child-related expenses rise proportionately *less* than income. For example, the combined expenditure on two children takes up half a lower-level family's income *over* 20 years but only one-third for families at the upper level.

TABLE 4   Direct Costs of a First and Second Child to Age 18 in the U.S., 1960–61

Costs	Income level		
	Lower	Middle	Upper
Total cost to age 18			
Combined	$55,583	$61,442	$71,644
	(2,779)[a]	(3,072)	(3,582)
First	37,655	41,119	47,045
	(2,092)	(2,284)	(2,614)
Second	17,928	20,324	24,599
	(996)	(1,129)	(1,367)
Ratio of cost to income earned in period[b]			
Combined	.5079	.4072	.3337
First	.3854	.3054	.2459
Second	.1790	.1472	.1252
Ratio of total cost of second to first child	.4761	.4943	.5229

Source: Thomas J. Espenshade, *The Cost of Children in Urban United States*, Population Monograph Series, No. 14 (Berkeley: Institute of International Studies, University of California, 1973) Table 9.

[a] Average annual cost, calculated by dividing combined total cost by 20 years and total cost of first and second child by 18 years.

[b] Length of time respective children are in the household extends for 20 years when two children are considered together and for 18 years each when they are considered separately.

Second, the eldest child in a family tends to be the most expensive. The data in Table 4 indicate that the marginal cost of the first child is roughly twice that of a second child. Second and third children in three-child families are about equally expensive.

Reed and McIntosh cited figures showing that maintenance costs in a child's 18th year were some 40 to 50 percent greater than during the year following birth.[15] My estimates indicate a somewhat greater variation. In 1960–61, expenditures on children aged 12 to 17 were approximately three times as large as those on a child under age 6.

A child's birth order (whether the eldest, second-born, etc.) and family income appear more important than family size in determining child costs. For example, as Table 5 indicates, expenditures on the first-born in a middle-income family are not substantially reduced when family size goes up from one to three children.

Finally, this study indicates that, as incomes rise, families tend to earmark more of their total savings for children, in both absolute and relative terms. It may be that some of this saving is done in anticipation of the costs of a college education.[16]

Boone Turchi's study contributes new information on the opportunity cost of having children. Of special interest is the oppor-

TABLE 5   Expenditures on First-Born by Family Size, United States, 1960–61
(Middle-income level)

No. of children in family	Expenditures on first-born to age 18
1	$42,565
2	41,119
3	40,156

Source: Espenshade, *op. cit.*, pp. 39, 46, 55.

tunity cost associated with successive children in the same family. Turchi interprets opportunity cost to mean the value of parental time spent in child care and rearing. Lacking direct information, he approximates the amount of time devoted to child care by the extra hours spent doing housework that are attributable to the presence of children under age 18. Data come from two sample surveys conducted by the Survey Research Center at the University of Michigan: the 1965 Productive Americans Survey and the 1970 Family Economics Survey.

To illustrate the magnitudes of time cost during the 18-year period each child is assumed to be in the household, Turchi constructs hypothetical examples corresponding to one-, two-, and three-child families, with births assumed to be spaced two years apart. Illustrative findings are tabulated in Table 6. The total cumulative hours of child care come to 9,274 in one-child families, 12,946 hours for families with two children, and 18,389 hours in three-child families. One can appreciate the significance of these quantities by realizing that fulltime employment entails 2,000 hours of work annually. Caring for three children until the last has graduated from high school is thus equivalent for the wife to a steady fulltime job for over nine years! It is little wonder that many women contend that raising a family is a fulltime occupation.

Turchi adds that some time costs are still excluded: "Note also that the decline in housework accompanying the growth of the family may be more than offset by increased claims on parental time for such child care activities as assisting with school work, PTA, Scouts, transportation and so on that are hardly captured by the housework measure."[17]

It is noteworthy that Turchi's estimate of time costs associated with the first child are generally consistent with those provided by Reed and McIntosh. What is especially significant, however, is the drop in extra time devoted to caring for second and third children, an average of approximately 4,500 hours in comparison to 9,200 for the first child. This decline matches the decline in the direct maintenance cost of successive children.

The dollar value attached to opportunity cost will depend on the price of time. In 1977, for example, the estimated average hourly

TABLE 6 Time Spent on Child-Generated Housework by U.S. Wives (Annual and total hours in one-, two-, and three-child families[a])

Event	First child born		Second child born		Third child born		First enters school		Second enters school		Third enters school			First enters grade 8
year	0	1	2	3	4	5	6	7	8	9	10	11	12	13
3 children	728	728	1072	1072	1525	1525	1275[b]	1275[b]	1075[b]	1075[b]	794	794	794	796
2 children	728	728	1072	1072	1072	1072	980[b]	900[b]	563	563	563	563	563	586
1 child	728	728	728	728	728	728	508	508	508	508	508	508	508	270

Event	Second enters grade 8		Third enters grade 8		First finishes high school		Second finishes high school		Third finishes high school	Total hours	Mean/ child	Incremental
year	14	15	16	17	18	19	20	21	22			
3 children	756[b]	756[b]	716[b]	563	265	265	270	270	270	18,389	6130	5443
2 children	586	265	265	265	270	270				12,946	6473	3672
1 child	270	270	270	270						9,274	9274	

Source: Boone A. Turchi, *The Demand for Children: The Economics of Fertility in the United States* (Cambridge, Mass.: Ballinger, 1975) Table 3–5.

[a] Children assumed to be born two years apart.

[b] Adjustments made for aging of children within an age group.

wage that women with a college education can earn if employed fulltime is $5.29. If we apply this to Turchi's data, this means an investment in terms of time of over $97,000 in the three-child family of Table 6, or an average of more than $32,000 per child. Total time cost in two-child families would amount to well over $68,000. One child involves close to $50,000 worth of a mother's time to age 18.

THE COST OF CHILDREN AND POPULATION POLICY

Statements concerning population policy must be tentative at this point. Policy conclusions should be firmly based on empirical investigations, and researchers have not yet explored fully, or with sufficient data, the ways in which the values and costs of children are related to fertility. With this in mind, it is sometimes suggested that the *actual* cost of children should be increased in order to lower fertility. One proposal, for example, is to put a tax on children.[18] To this there are at least two objections. The increase in actual cost may not always be perceived by parents, and if perceptions are really what matter as far as fertility behavior is concerned, then fertility would not be affected. Moreover, raising the actual cost of childbearing may have the unintentional effect of penalizing the children even more than their parents.

An alternative solution is simply to inform parents about how large the actual economic costs are, both direct costs and opportunity costs. This prescription has the double advantage that it affects perceptions and does not have adverse consequences for child welfare. Information programs to increase awareness of actual costs should have as their goal the eventual elimination of discrepancies between perceived and actual costs, and in order to have maximum impact, they should reach couples in the earliest stages of the family-building process.[19]

As a means of reducing fertility this proposal takes on added cogency, since there is some evidence to indicate that parents vastly underestimate the expenses involved in childrearing. For example, in the Value of Children pilot project in Hawaii, couples were asked, "About how much money in all do you think it has cost you to raise your children over the last twelve months?" The difficulty that parents had even in thinking about the problem is indicated by the fact that more than one-third of respondents were unwilling to attempt an estimate. The responses of those Caucasian parents who did answer are given in Table 7.

It is instructive to compare these perceptions with the estimates in Table 4. The amounts parents think they are spending are consistently below the estimates of actual direct cost. In Table 4, the middle-income parents are estimated to spend an average of 40.7 percent of annual income on their two children to raise them to age 18. By contrast, in Table 7, urban middle-class parents *perceive* that child-related expenditures account for only 14.7 percent of

TABLE 7   Perceived Economic Costs of Children, Hawaiian
Caucasians

Item	Urban middle	Urban lower
1. Average amount spent on all children	$ 2,266	$ 2,008
2. Mean family income	$15,393	$11,058
3. Percentage of mean family income spent on children ($\frac{1}{2}$)	14.7	21.9
4. Mean number of children	1.83	2.33
5. Average amount spent per child ($\frac{1}{4}$)	$ 1,238	$ 862
6. Percentage of mean family income spent per child ($\frac{5}{2}$)	8.1	9.4

Source: Fred Arnold and James T. Fawcett. *The Value of Children: A Cross-National Study, Vol. 3: Hawaii* (Honolulu: East-West Population Institute, East-West Center, 1976) Table 4.4.

yearly income. When broken down for individual children, the estimates of actual cost show that 30.5 percent of annual income is typically spent on the first-born, and 14.7 percent on the second child in middle-income families. Yet the amount middle-class Caucasian parents think they spend per child is just 8.1 percent of yearly income. Similar conclusions hold for lower-income families. As rough as these comparisons are, they do suggest that the perceived cost of children would probably increase if parents were made more aware of the actual economic costs their children entail.[20] Knowing, for instance, that one child could cost them on average between $77,000 and $107,000 might well cause young American couples to pause before embarking on parenthood.

FOOTNOTES AND REFERENCES

1.   Eva Mueller, "Economic Cost and Value of Children: Conceptualization and Measurement," in James T. Fawcett, ed., *The Satisfactions and Costs of Children: Theories, Concepts, Methods,* Honolulu: East-West Population Institute, East-West Center, 1972, (p. 215).

2.   *Ibid.,* pp. 183–184; and Mueller's comments to Paul Demeny's paper in the same volume (pp. 24–26).

3.   Ritchie H. Reed and Susan McIntosh, "Costs of Children," in *Research Reports,* Vol. 2, Commission on Population Growth and the American Future (Washington, D.C.: Government Printing Office, 1972) pp. 333–350. While most studies of the economic cost of children have focused on private cost, or the cost to families, there has been some interest in the cost to society. One investigation that attempts to quantity the federal subsidy that U.S. parents receive toward their child-rearing activities is Elliott R. Morss and Susan McIntosh Ralph, "Family Life Styles, the Childbearing Decision, and the Influence of Federal Activities: A Quantitative Approach," in

Research Reports, op. cit., pp. 351–368. The tentative conclusion is that the combination of federal activities has a significant pronatalist effect.

4. "Price of Having a Baby Bounces to $2,194," *Health Insurance Institute News Data Sheet*, June 1976.

5. W. Vance Grant and C. George Lind, *Digest of Educational Statistics, 1975 Edition*, National Center for Education Statistics, U.S. Department of Health, Education, and Welfare (Washington, D.C.: Government Printing Office, 1976) Table 121, p. 129. The data for public rather than private schools were used since, in the fall of 1975, enrollments in public institutions of higher education constituted 76 percent of the total (*Ibid.*, Table 79, p. 79).

6. Cited in *Parade*, February 27, 1977.

7. At the beginning of the school year 1974–75, 33.5 percent of the U.S. population aged 18–24 was enrolled in institutions of higher education. This was up from 30.3 percent in 1968 and 14.2 percent in 1940 (Grant and Lind, *op. cit.*, Table 78, p. 69).

8. Reed and McIntosh, *op. cit.*, p. 341.

9. Glen G. Cain, "Issues in the Economics of a Population Policy," Discussion Paper No. 88, University of Wisconsin, Institute for Research on Poverty, 1971, pp. 24–27.

10. William G. Bowen and T. Aldrich Finegan, *The Economics of Labor Force Participation* (Princeton, N.J.: Princeton University Press, 1969).

11. *Ibid.*, p. 99.

12. Reed and McIntosh, *op. cit.*, p. 343.

13. U.S. Department of Labor, Bureau of Labor Statistics, *News*, USDA 77–191, March 8, 1977.

14. Thomas J. Espenshade, *The Cost of Children in Urban United States*, Population Monograph Series No. 14 (Berkeley: Institute of International Studies, University of California, 1973); and Boone A. Turchi, *The Demand for Children: The Economics of Fertility in the United States* (Cambridge, Mass.: Ballinger, 1975).

15. Reed and McIntosh, *op. cit.*, Table 1, p. 338.

16. Espenshade, *op. cit.*, p. 43. See also Thomas J. Espenshade, "The Impact of Children on Household Saving: Age Effects versus Family Size," *Population Studies*, Vol. 29, No. 1 (March 1975) pp. 123–125.

17. Turchi, *op. cit.*, p. 89.

18. Joseph J. Spengler, "Population Problem: In Search of a Solution," *Science*, Vol. 166 (1969) pp. 1234–1238.

19. Fred Arnold et al., *The Value of Children: A Cross-National Study, Vol. 1: Introduction and Comparative Analysis* (Honolulu: East-West Population Institute, East-West Center, 1975) pp. 139 and 148; and Fred Arnold and James T. Fawcett, *The Value of Children: A Cross-National Study, Vol. 3: Hawaii* (Honolulu: East-West Population Institute, East West Center, 1976), p. 130.

20. More than ten years separate the two surveys on which Tables 4 and 7 are based, and income in Table 4 means after-tax income, whereas

before-tax income is apparently being used in Table 7. Moreover, Arnold and Fawcett, *op. cit.*, caution readers that most of the respondents' children in the Hawaiian sample were quite young (p. 91). Nevertheless, it does not seem reasonable to suppose that these factors could account for all of the discrepancies between the two tables.

15.

The Value of Children:
A Taxonomical Essay

Bernard Berelson

Why do people want children? It is a simple question to ask, perhaps an impossible one to answer.

Throughout most of human history, the question never seemed to need a reply. These years, however, the question has a new tone. It is being asked in a nonrhetorical way because of three revolutions in thought and behavior that characterize the latter decades of the twentieth century: the vital revolution in which lower death rates have given rise to the population problem and raise new issues about human fertility; the sexual revolution from reproduction; and the women's revolution in which childbearing and -rearing are no longer being accepted as the only or even the primary roles of half the human race. Accordingly, for about the first time, the question of why people want children can now be asked, so to speak, with a straight face.

"Why" questions of this kind, with simple surfaces but profound depths, are not answered or settled; they are ventilated, explicated, clarified. Anything as complex as the motives for having children can be classified in various ways so any such taxonomy has an arbitrary character to it. This one starts with chemistry and proceeds to spirit.

Reprinted from The *Population Council Annual Report—1972*, used by permission of the author.

Taxonomy

THE BIOLOGICAL

Do people innately want children for some built-in reason of physiology? Is there anything to maternal instinct, or parental instinct? Or is biology satisfied with the sex instinct as the way to assure continuity?

In psychoanalytic thought there is talk of the "child-wish," the "instinctual drive of physiological cause," "the innate femaleness of the girl direct (ing) her development toward motherhood," and the wanting of children as "the essence of her self-realization," indicating normality. From the experimental literature, there is some evidence that man, like other animals, is innately attracted to the quality of "babyishness."

> If the young and adults of several species are compared for differences in bodily and facial features, it will be seen readily that the nature of the differences is apparently the same almost throughout the phylogenetic scale. Limbs are shorter and much heavier in proportion to the torso in babies than in adults. Also, the head is proportionately much larger in relation to the body than is the case with adults. On the face itself, the forehead is more prominent and bulbous; the eyes large and perhaps located as far down as below the middle of the face, because of the large forehead. In addition, the cheeks may be round and protruding. In many species there is also a greater degree of overall fatness in contrast to normal adult bodies. . . . In man, as in other animals, social prescriptions and customs are not the sole or even primary factors that guarantee the rearing and protection of babies. This seems to indicate that the biologically rooted releaser of babyishness may have promoted infant care in primitive man before societies were ever formed, just as it appears to do in many animal species. Thus this releaser may have a high survival value for the species of man.[1]

In the human species the question of social and personal motivation distinctively arises, but that does not necessarily mean that the biology is completely obliterated. In animals the instinct to reproduce appears to be all; in humans is it something?

THE CULTURAL

Whatever the biological answer, people do not want all the children they can physically have—no society, hardly any woman. Everywhere social traditions and social pressures enforce a certain conformity to the approved childbearing pattern, whether large numbers of children in Africa or small numbers in Eastern Europe. People want children because that is "the thing to do"—culturally sanctioned and institutionally supported, hence about as natural as any social behavior can be.

Such social expectations, expressed by everyone toward everyone,

FIGURE 1. Comparison of visual features provided by morphological characteristics of infantile and adult forms of four different species: human, rabbit, dog, and bird. While the infantile characteristics release parental responses, the adult ones do not. (Drawing after Lorenz in Musser, op. cit.)

are extremely strong in influencing behavior even on such an important element in life as childbearing, and whether the outcome is two children or six. In most human societies, the thing to do gets done, for social rewards and punishments are among the most powerful. Whether they produce lots of children or few and whether the matter is fully conscious or not, the cultural norms are all the more effective if, as often, they are rationalized as the will of God or the hand of fate.

THE POLITICAL

The cultural shades off into political considerations: reproduction for the purposes of a higher authority. In a way, the human responsibility to perpetuate the species is the grandest such expression—the human family pitted politically against fauna and flora—and there may always be people who partly rationalize their own childbearing as a contribution to that lofty end. Beneath that, however, there are political units for whom collective childbearing is or has been explicitly encouraged as a demographic duty—countries concerned with national glory or competitive political position; governments concerned with the supply of workers and soldiers; churches concerned with propagation of the faith or their relative strength; ethnic minorities concerned with their political power; linguistic communities competing for position; clans and tribes concerned over their relative status within a larger setting. In ancient Rome, according to the Oxford English Dictionary, the proletariat —from the root *proles,* for progeny—were "the lowest class of the community, regarded as contributing nothing to the state but offspring": and a proletaire was "one who served the state not with his property but only with his offspring." The world has changed since then, but not all the way.

THE ECONOMIC

As the "new home economics" is reminding us in its current attention to the microeconomics of fertility, children are economically valuable. Not that that would come as a surprise to the poor peasant who consciously acts on the premise, but it is clear that some people want children or not for economic reasons.

Start with the obvious case of economic returns from children that appears to be characteristic of the rural poor. To some extent, that accounts for their generally higher fertility than their urban and wealthier counterparts: labor in the fields; hunting, fishing, animal care; help in the home and with the younger children; dowry and "bridewealth"; support in later life (the individualized system of social security).

The economics of the case carries through on the negative side as well. It is not publicly comfortable to think of children as another consumer durable but sometimes that is precisely the way parents do think of them, before conception: another child or a trip to Europe; a birth deferred in favor of a new car, the nth child requiring more expenditure on education or housing. But observe the special characteristics of children viewed as consumer durables: they come only in whole units; they are not rentable or returnable or exchangeable or available on trial; they cannot be evaluated quickly; they do not come in several competing brands or products; their quality cannot be pretested before delivery; they are not usually available for appraisal in large numbers in one's personal experience; they themselves participate actively in the household's decisions. And in the broad view, both societies and families tend to choose standard of living over number of children when the opportunity presents itself.

THE FAMILIAL

In some societies people want children for what might be called familial reasons: to extend the family line or the family name; to propitiate the ancestors; to enable the proper functioning of religious rituals involving the family (e.g., the Hindu son needed to light the father's funeral pyre, the Jewish son needed to say Kaddish for the dead father). Such reasons may seem thin in the modern, secularized society but they have been and are powerful indeed in other places.

In addition, one class of family reasons shares a border with the category below, namely, having children in order to maintain or improve a marriage: to hold the husband or occupy the wife; to repair or rejuvenate the marriage; to increase the number of children on the assumption that family happiness lies that way. The point is underlined by its converse: in some societies the failure to bear children (or males) is a threat to the marriage and a ready cause for divorce.

Beyond all that is the profound significance of children to the very institution of the family itself. To many people, husband and wife alone do not seem a proper family—they need children to enrich the circle, to validate its family character, to gather the redemptive influence of offspring. Children need the family, but the family seems also to need children, as the social institution uniquely available, at least in principle, for security, comfort, assurance, and direction in a changing, often hostile, world. To most people, such a home base, in the literal sense, needs more than one person for sustenance, and in generational extension.

THE PERSONAL

Up to here the reasons for wanting children primarily refer to instrumental benefits. Now we come to a variety of reasons for wanting children that are supposed to bring direct personal benefits.

Personal Power. As noted, having children sometimes gives one parent power over the other. More than that, it gives the parents power over the child (ren) —in many cases, perhaps most, about as much effective power as they will ever have the opportunity of exercising on an individual basis. They are looked up to by the child (ren), literally and figuratively, and rarely does that happen otherwise. Beyond that, having children is involved in a wider circle of power:

> In most simple societies the lines of kinship are the lines of political power, social prestige and economic aggrandizement. The more children a man has, the more successful marriage alliances he can arrange, increasing his own power and influence by linking himself to men of greater power or to men who will be his supporters. . . . In primitive and peasant societies, the man with few children is the man of minor influence and the childless man is virtually a social non-entity.[2]

Personal Competence. Becoming a parent demonstrates competence in an essential human role. Men and women who are closed off from other demonstrations of competence, through lack of talent or educational opportunity or social status, still have this central one. For males, parenthood is thought to show virility, potency, *machismo*. For females it demonstrates fecundity, itself so critical to an acceptable life in many societies.

Personal Status. Everywhere parenthood confers status. It is an accomplishment open to all, or virtually all, and realized by the

overwhelming majority of adult humankind. Indeed, achieving parenthood must surely be one of the two most significant events in
one's life—that and being born in the first place. In many societies,
then and only then is one considered a real man or a real woman.

Childbearing is one of the few ways in which the poor can
compete with the rich. Life cannot make the poor man prosperous
in material goods and services but it can easily make him rich with
children. He cannot have as much of anything else worth having,
except sex, which itself typically means children in such societies.
Even so, the poor are still deprived by the arithmetic: they have
only two or three times as many children as the rich whereas the
rich have at least 40 times the income as the poor.

Personal Extension. Beyond the family line, wanting children is
a way to reach for personal immortality—for most people, the only
way available. It is a way to extend oneself indefinitely into the
future. And short of that, there is simply the physical and psychological extension of oneself in the children, here and now—a kind
of narcissism: there they are and they are mine (or like me).

> Look in thy glass and tell the face thou viewest,
> Now is the time that face should form another; . . .
> But if thou live, remember'd not to be,
> Die single, and thine image dies with thee.
> —Shakespeare's *Sonnets,* III

Personal Experience. Among all the activities of life, parenthood
is a unique experience. It is a part of life, of personal growth, that
simply cannot be experienced in any other way, and hence is literally an indispensable element of the full life. The experience has
many profound facets: the deep curiosity as to how the child will
turn out; the renewal of self in the second chance; the reliving of
one's own childhood; the redemptive opportunity; the challenge to
shape another human being; the sheer creativity and self-realization
involved. For a large proportion of the world's women, there was
and probably still is nothing else for the grown female to do with
her time and energy, as society defines her role. And for many
women, it may be the most emotional and spiritual experience they
ever have, and perhaps the most gratifying as well.

Personal Pleasure. Last, but one hopes not least, in the list of
reasons for wanting children is the altruistic pleasure of having
them, caring for them, watching them grow, shaping them, being
with them, enjoying them. This reason comes last on the list but it
is typically the first one mentioned on the casual inquiry: "because
I like children." Even this reason has its dark side, as with parents
who live through their children, often to the latter's distaste and
disadvantage. But that should not obscure a fundamental reason
for wanting children: love.

There are, in short, many reasons for wanting children. Taken together, they must be among the most compelling motivations in human behavior: culturally imposed, institutionally reinforced, psychologically welcome.

HISTORY

What of the broad, historical trends in the evaluation of children? The central trend can be embodied in a conundrum: over the long run, as children have become less valuable they have become more valued. That is, as children have lost their economic value to the parents, under the impact of modernization, they have gained value in a qualitative sense—in the provision of health and particularly education and training. In this sense, the world seems to move from quantity to quality in the evaluation of children.

Surely the modern response—modern not simply in the chronological but in the social sense—is in this direction: the child as a consumption not a production good; the child as deserving consideration in his own right; what the parent owes the child rather than what the child owes the parent. That adjustment is currently being worked through, and on the whole it probably means less wanting of children and fewer children (particularly as the available technology for fertility control gets more evenly distributed). So under man's newly-emerging conditions, already realized in some parts of the world, wanting few children is as natural as wanting several: after all, people can satisfy the reasons for wanting children without having many.

In the classical literature of Greece and Rome there appears to be little serious reference to children and childbearing except for the continuation of royal lines. According to George Boas, in *The Cult of Childhood,* the "ancients had a low opinion of children if they appraised them at all." According to Philippe Aries in *Centuries of Childhood,* "in medieval society the idea of childhood did not exist"; only in the eighteenth century are "not only the child's future but his presence and his very existence . . . of concern: the child has taken a central place in the family." And according to Peter Coveney in *Poor Monkey: The Child in Literature,* the emergence of the child is sharply visible in English literature:

> Until the last decades of the eighteenth century the child did not exist as an important and continuous theme in English literature. Childhood as a major theme came with the generation of Blake and Wordsworth. There were of course children in English literature before the Romantics . . . But in the Elizabethan drama, in the main body of Augustan verse, in the major eighteenth-century novel, the child is absent, or the occasion of a passing reference; at the most a subsidiary element in an adult world . . . Within the course of a few decades the child emerges from comparative unimportance to become the focus of an unprecedented literary interest, and, in time, the central figure of an increasingly significant proportion of our literature.

Why does the child in literature emerge only then, with the romantic period? There were some great events at work—the industrial revolution was changing the economy, the French revolution was changing the politics. But there was another revolution going on in England at just this time, a vital revolution of lower death rates (especially of infants and children) and increasing population. There were thus more children around, simply on a statistical basis, and hence more visible and accountable for. Children were living who previously would have died. Is it only historic accident that the literary interest and the demographic trends came together in this way?

Over the succeeding century, one can identify a rough progression from the innocent child of Wordsworth through the child employed for the social criticism of industrialized institutions in Dickens, through the sentimentalized and redemptive child of *Silas Marner* and worse, to the realistic child (and family) of Butler and Lawrence. So in about a century, the whole literary position of the child changed from romantic glorification to realistic appreciation. What Rousseau and Wordsworth started, Freud and the post-Freudian writers finished.

Man has come a long way in a short time in his evaluation of children: from nonappreciation of childhood, through innocent primitive and social cause, to obsession and problem. Many have remarked on our own "child-centered society," our "cult of children," yet even that may now be changing in response to the three revolutions.

In the end, we may need to rely on those old standbys, rationality and responsibility: not everyone is equally talented to be a parent any more than a pianist or a mathematician or a tennis player, though the parental talent may not be as rare as those; and concern is owed the developmental possibilities for the individual child beyond the parental or social gratifications. If a society has full information on personal and collective consequences of childbearing, full opportunity to control fertility and thus divorce reproduction from sexuality, productive alternatives for women, no undue social pressures with regard to marriage or parenthood, and genuine concern for the produced child, that is about the best we can do.

The currency is not debased, though modern conditions affect both numbers and values. For whatever else it is, wanting children remains a re-start for man, and for individual men, another chance to try for "the good life," a revitalization in both the literal and the symbolic sense. On the title page of *Silas Marner*, George Eliot quoted these lines from Wordsworth:

> A child, more than all other gifts
> That earth can offer to declining man,
> Brings hope with it, and forward-looking thoughts.

REFERENCES

1. Eckhard H. Hess, "Ethology and Developmental Psychology," *in* Paul
    H. Musser, ed., *Carmichael's Manual of Child Psychology*, vol. 1 (New
    York: Wiley, 1970), pp. 20–21.

2. Burton Benedict, "Population Regulation In Primitive Societies," *in*
    Anthony Allison, ed., *Population Control* (London: Penguin, 1970),
    pp. 176–177.

Part

Six

Abortion Reform

*T*HE STATUS OF legalized abortion in the United States has changed considerably since the January 1973 landmark decision of the U.S. Supreme Court, which essentially prohibited state governments from outlawing abortions for women who wanted them, no matter what the grounds. This decision was a capstone in the recent trend toward increased liberalization of abortion laws, which had already been occurring in several states. Liberalization had been brought about in two ways: First, a few states had changed their laws away from the rigid stance taken in the past, to either allow more grounds for obtaining an abortion or to do away with the whole notion of grounds, thus allowing abortion on demand; second, the laws in a few states had been either changed or thrown out by both state and federal courts, and the laws of more states were undergoing litigation at the time of the Court's decision.

Coming as it did and saying what it said, the Supreme Court decision produced surprise among the pro-abortion forces and dumbfounded the anti-abortion groups, who were attempting to stem the tide of liberalization. The pro-abortion groups had not expected quite so sweeping a decision, and the anti-abortion groups, feeling that they had begun to slow the trend toward liberalization, were thoroughly shocked and dismayed by the extent of the decision.

Since this major Court decision there have been a series of supplementary decisions that have served to further clarify the exact meaning and extent of the original decision. A number of state laws passed both before and after the decision sought to place further restrictions on abortion and raised a number of side issues. For example, there was the question as to whether or not a minor female needed her parents permission to obtain an abortion. Another issue was whether or not a woman's husband had to comply with her decision to have an abortion. There are also questions as to the circumstances under which an abortion may be refused, and the hotly debated issue as to whether or not federal medicare funds should be used to pay for the abortions of poor women.

However, the major question, at least from a legal standpoint, has been settled by the Supreme Court. But the issue is by no means dead since the anti-abortion forces have now adopted the approach of supporting a constitutional amendment that would negate the Court's decision.

What makes the abortion issue such a heated one is the fact that it is actually a dual issue, or at least one with two or more facets that overlap in such a manner as to create a great deal of confusion and controversy. On the one hand is the legal question and on the other is the moral-religious one. The former has to do with privacy, civil liberties, and personal freedoms; the latter has to do with the question of when life begins and what constitutes a human being. Of course, the question of when life begins might be considered from a medical standpoint as well, an aspect which could be seen as a third side of the controversy. However, aside from this possibly unanswerable question, there is actually very little at issue with regard to the medical aspects of abortion except for the variations in degrees of danger related to the stages of pregnancy at which an abortion might be induced.

Those on both sides of this controversy, at least in extreme instances, rarely recognize or admit to the dual nature of the issue. Those in favor of liberalized abortion see it as being solely a matter of civil liberties and a private patient-physician decision. They feel that the whole question of whether or not a fetus is a human being with all of the rights of other citizens is an unanswerable one and probably an irrelevant one as well. In addition, they often take a point of view similar to the one held by those who favor liberalizing other types of laws—those laws concerned only with private behavior which poses no threat to others. For example, the argument is made that the use of marijuana in the home or homosexual behavior between consenting adults harms no one, does not threaten society, and that laws attempting to regulate such behavior are unenforceable anyway. Abortion is seen as a similar type of situation, and an often-heard statement from this side of the issue is that it is impossible to legislate private morality.

From the anti-abortion side, the most extreme view would totally reject the civil liberties argument with the idea that abortion is the same as murder and that there is certainly no question about the illegality of murder. At the point of conception there exists a human being who has an equal status with all other humans. Those with less extreme views simply state that the unborn child, no matter at which stage of development, is a potential person and that it therefore has a right to life. Those of this persuasion would also reject the private morality argument, again based upon the fact that the potential human life means that there is no longer just one individual, the mother, involved, but also the helpless fetus who has no one to turn to for protection but society.

Underlying the morality argument against abortion is the rarely spoken but widely believed view that pregnancy is a just punishment for illicit sexual behavior and that allowing easy abortion lets the "sinner" escape deserved punishment. Persons with this belief, however, fail to recognize that most illegal abortions were sought by married women rather than single women.

This presentation of two sides of the issue is admittedly sketchy and certainly oversimplified, but many of these arguments are further developed in the articles which follow, and no position is taken here with respect to the issue. However, one further bit of explanation should be offered at this point. It concerns the meaning and the usage of the term *legislation of morality*. From a sociological standpoint, all legislation is in fact the legislation of morality in that laws always reflect the basic norms of a society, and the norms in turn are the embodiment of the society's morality. Thus, when a state legislature tries to regulate drugs, abortion, prostitution, pornography, or other sexual behaviors, it is in fact attempting to inject into the law its own, or perhaps its conception of the society's moral viewpoints. This is the case no matter what the laws are attempting to ban or regulate. Therefore, it is important that those who use the term *legislation of morality* specify that they are referring to attempts to regulate private, consensual behavior involving adults, which does no harm to anyone else. Many lawmakers fail to make even these distinctions, however, feeling that any behavior which violates society's basic norms should be banned, no matter what the circumstances. Furthermore, this explanation does nothing to solve the question of whether or not abortion is a purely private matter.

One thing is certain: Laws which attempt to regulate or ban certain kinds of private moral behavior actually do a great deal of harm to individuals and to society and rarely accomplish the goals for which they are enacted. They more often drive the behavior in question underground, create a black market, and often make criminals of otherwise ordinary citizens. This was certainly the case with laws against easy abortion. And specifically with abortion, an indirect result of restrictive laws was the high mortality rate of those who were forced to seek out amateur practitioners for release from an untenable situation. One of the most significant changes that occurred in those states which liberalized their abortion laws prior to the Supreme Court decision was the sharp decline in fatalities related to abortion. In New York City alone, during the first year of the new liberal abortion law, there were only three deaths as a result of illegal abortions, and the overall maternal death rate declined 50 per cent to the lowest maternal death rate ever recorded in that city. Other locations with new abortion laws reported similar occurrences.[1] There have also been significant declines in the rates of illegitimacy, indicating that single women are taking advantage of the new laws just as are women who feel that their families are large enough or perhaps too large.[2]

Medical authorities indicate that an abortion up to the twelfth week of pregnancy is a relatively minor procedure which takes only a few minutes and does not usually require a hospital stay. The method most commonly used for this type of abortion is called *vacuum aspiration* because it employs the use of a small suction pump to remove the placental material which contains the fertilized egg. This recently developed method is far superior to the older *dilation and curettage* method, in that it is safer and much easier on the patient, usually requiring no general anesthetic.

For the period of 13 to 16 weeks of pregnancy, abortion is slightly more dangerous, and many doctors are reluctant to perform the operation during that period, preferring to wait until after the sixteenth week. Beyond the twelfth week the operation is also more difficult and more expensive. The method used for later abortions is generally the *saline* method, in which a salt solution is injected into the uterus, which causes it to reject the fetus within several hours in much the same manner as childbirth. For this procedure the patient usually has to remain in the hospital for two or three days. Because of its similarity to actual childbirth, many women find this method more traumatic, but it is still the safest method for later abortions.

As far as the safety factor is concerned, having an abortion is actually safer than going on to have the baby at full term. For example, New York recorded a death rate of 4.2 per 100,000 legal abortions;[3] on the other hand, the general maternal mortality rate (deaths resulting from childbirth) is around four or five times greater.

As stated earlier, there are basically two sides to the whole issue of abortion, the legal side and the moral-religious side. The major legal question has now been settled by the Supreme Court, although there will continue to be maneuverings on the part of state legislatures with respect to regulating and delimiting the circumstances of abortion, as well as the continuing push for passage of a constitutional amendment to outlaw abortion on demand. But over and above the legal maneuverings, there will probably continue to be a certain amount of controversy over the moral, religious, and to some extent, the psychological aspects of abortion. Therefore, the major emphasis in the articles included in this part is upon the nonlegal aspects of abortion. The first two articles present opposing viewpoints on the moral aspects of abortion, whereas the third departs radically from these themes. In a tone almost devoid of the legal or moral issues involved, a young woman relates her personal experiences in an abortion clinic.

The title of the first article, "Abortion and the Reverence for Life," sounds like an anti-abortion statement, but it is actually just the contrary. The article reviews some of the major religious arguments both for and against abortion and then moves on to build an argument in favor of abortion based upon some of the major tenets in the arguments of those who oppose abortion. Many who oppose abortion do so on the basis of their belief in the sanctity of life, but the author here feels that there are many situations in which abortion might serve to enhance and sanctify the lives of some who have already attained full humanhood.

Just as the first article presented a theological argument in favor of abortion, the second presents a secular argument against it. (Both articles, however, were written by persons in religious professions.) In "A Secular Case Against Abortion on Demand," Richard Stith argues, among other things, that abortion on demand would be very damaging to the nation and its citizenry because of the lack of respect for life in general which would occur if abortion became widespread. He develops a nonreligious view of personhood which he uses to support his point. These articles air many of the major arguments, both religious and secular, that are brought to bear on the abortion issue.

The third article is a first-person account of a young, unmarried woman's experience in obtaining a legal abortion in a well-run clinic. The article is amazingly neutral with regard to being either in favor of or against abortion. The writer is obviously in favor of having one herself, although her own feelings seem to be ambivalent.

REFERENCES

1. "Legal Abortion: How Safe? How Available? How Costly?" *Consumer Reports,* **37**:467 (July 1972).
2. Christopher Tietze, "Two Years' Experience with a Liberal Abortion Law: Its Impact on Fertility Trends in New York City," *Family Planning Perspectives,* **5**:39 (Winter 1973).
3. *Consumer Reports,* op. cit., p. 469.

16.

Abortion and the Reverence for Life: A Pro-Abortion View

Paul W. Rahmeier

The tendency toward polarization, all too common throughout society, is increasingly evident in the current discussion of abortion. Proponents and opponents of abortion-law reform or repeal seem to be escalating the rhetoric, flinging verbal missiles at each other. As the temperature of the argument rises, it becomes more and more difficult to consider carefully the basic question of abortion.

Curiously, a listener to the raging debate may reach a surprising conclusion: Beneath the rhetoric, both proponents and opponents of abortion share a commitment to a basic value, human life. Both sides claim to be (and in my judgment *are*) motivated by a profound reverence for human life. The end, I believe, is agreed upon. The argument begins with discussion of the means: What is the best way to practice and promote reverence for human life?

The opponents of abortion-law reform/repeal (and, obviously, of abortion) affirm that human life is ultimately a gift of God, that it begins at the moment of conception, and that any deliberate interference with or interruption of pregnancy is willful destruction of human life, in other words, murder. Men of high morals, especially Christians, must not permit human life to be violated or desecrated by an act of abortion.

The proponents of reform or repeal (who, obviously, would permit abortion) also affirm that human life is of the highest value, though some may question whether that value derives from God or from man, or from a combination of sources. More important, they claim that human life does not necessarily begin at the moment of conception. The trophoblast-zygote-embryo-fetus develops into human life; but throughout the early stages of pregnancy the fetus, while alive, is not necessarily *humanly* alive. Therefore abortion is not the taking of a human life. Moreover, some proponents claim that Christian concern is concern for the quality as well as the quantity of human life, and that reverence for human life should be promoted by careful birth and population control.

Both sides, then, intend to practice and promote reverence for human life. The crucial question is: Which side offers the most effective method for the attainment of that end? My own reading (a charitable one, I hope) leads to the conclusion that, while the opponents of abortion are sincere and admirably consistent, the proponents of abortion-law reform/repeal are in fact more careful, more thoughtful and more effective in promoting reverence for human life. This conclusion is reached in the light of three questions:

1. What is the source of reverence for life? God? Man?
2. What do we mean by *human* life? When does human life begin? Is a fetus human?
3. What are the options? If we accept the anti-abortion position, what follows? Similarly, if we accept the pro-abortion position, what follows? Which option seems more successfully to promote reverence for life?

What is Meant by the Sanctity of Life?

Consider first the source of our reverence for life. What do we mean when we talk about the sanctity of life? The Judeo-Christian tradition, in virtually all its historical manifestations, seems to agree that God is the ultimate source of the sanctity of human life. That is, we value life because God values it. In his essay "The Morality of Abortion"[1] Paul Ramsey puts the case clearly:

> One grasps the religious outlook upon the sanctity of human life only if he sees that this life is asserted to be surrounded by sanctity that need not be in a man; that the most dignity a man ever possesses is the dignity that is alien to him. . . . A man's dignity is an overflow from God's dealing with him, and not primarily an anticipation of anything he will ever be by himself alone.

Thus, ultimately, the value placed on human life is placed there by God, not by man.

Some Jewish and Christian thinkers, while agreeing with this traditional position, hold that human life is also revered because we human beings ourselves place high value on it. God's regard for man may be the ultimate source of man's dignity, but man's own respect for human life also contributes considerably to reverence for life. In other words: If God grants value to human life, but human beings themselves place a low estimate on it, then, practically speaking, reverence for life is in short supply. Moreover, many nonreligious thinkers profess profound respect for human life. Certainly their attitude must be cherished and honored, especially in a pluralistic society where the search for justice necessarily involves a harmonizing of disparate value systems.

Does it make any difference whether our reverence for life stems from God or from man? Some, but not much. The nonreligious thinker is left with the problem of articulating that respect in humanistic terms, without recourse to external authority. The religious thinker, even though he claims recourse to divine authority, is not left without problems: he must articulate the nature of the authority and reverence for life as it is revealed by the authority. My conclusion (I omit much of the argument) is that, though we Christians will continue to assert that man's dignity derives primarily from God's love for man, we must also admit that man's own valuation of human life is a significant source of reverence for life.

WHAT DO WE MEAN BY HUMAN LIFE?

Our second question is more difficult: What precisely do we mean by human life? Is *human* a quality that can be judged biologically? Or theologically? When does human life begin?

Most opponents of abortion assert that human life is present from the moment of conception. While they may recognize and admit the development that must occur before the fetus takes on fully human form, they will insist—and in support they muster some recent findings of biological research—that the very first joining of genes marks the beginning of a new human life. Thus *human* seems to be defined genetically. Each new trophoblast constitutes a new human being.

This position is admirable in its simplicity, and it makes for marvelous consistency. Even so, several complicating questions arise. First, a minute technical point: It is difficult to pinpoint a moment when conception occurs, in that the male sperm penetrates the female ovum in a relatively slow process. Moreover, the new genetic package, or trophoblast, goes through the first six or seven days of cell division while still in the tube, and does not begin to implant itself in the uterus until early in the second week, when it is called the zygote. Another week goes by before the implantation is secure enough, and the cellular division complex enough, to produce what is properly called an embryo. Embryologists point out that many such genetic packages—perhaps as many as one third of all those formed—are naturally miscarried. If we claim that every conception creates a human individual, then we must admit that perhaps one third of all human beings die and their remains are disposed of without benefit of medical care, legal rights, or religious concern. Indeed, the mother usually never even realizes she is (or has been) pregnant!

A second fine point: Twinning may occur by a split of the sphere of cells up until the fourteenth day of pregnancy, at which point conjoined twins can still be produced. That is, one human being can divide into two. But it is also true that through these first few days of cellular development a set of twins or triplets can be recombined into one single zygote. That is, twins or triplets can become one human being again.

André Hellegers, writing on "Fetal Development" in the Catholic periodical *Theological Studies,*[2] uses these points to demonstrate that the initial fertilization of an ovum and the creation of a new genetic package does *not* mean that the genetic package is finally fixed from the moment of conception. Indeed, not all genetic material is crucially activated at fertilization; a final irreversible individuality has not yet been achieved.

What does this mean for our question about the definition of human life? Simply this: the genetic definition of human life, though it seems simple and consistent at first, is in fact not so. Even if we did accept this definition, would we not need to take seriously the fact that one third of all such individuals die before their existence is noticed?

Hylomorphism

The question of the beginning of human life has been answered variously. Aristotle, of course, proposed that the fetus develops steadily and is endowed successively with three types of soul: At conception, a vegetative soul inhabits the embryo; soon thereafter an animal soul takes over; on the fortieth day of gestation a human soul moves in (in the case of a male fetus, that is; according to Aristotle, the female fetus does not receive its human soul until the eightieth day of gestation).

Much Christian thinking about fetal development has been influenced by Aristotle, and hylomorphism—the notion that matter and material forms account sufficiently for the universe—continues to have its champions. Thomas Aquinas, for one, taught that form and matter must correspond and coexist. Man is a real unity, constituted by the complementary causality of his soul and prime matter. Man's unity is not complete until form and matter correspond in the fully human fetus or infant. The early fetus, then, is not as "human" as the later fetus.

In his famous law of complexity-consciousness, Teilhard de Chardin taught a modern form of hylomorphism. Briefly, he asserted that there can be no human self-consciousness without an almost infinite centro-complexity; that is, an orderly arrangement of an immense number of cells in a closed whole. Here too, the early fetus is not a fully developed human. A complex human soul can live only in a complex human body, with a correspondingly complex consciousness.

Reviewing the history of Catholic teaching on this subject,[3] Joseph Donceel, a contemporary Jesuit, finds that Aristotelian hylomorphism has always had some influence within the church. Especially through Christianity's early years, and well into the 16th century, many theologians taught that in its early stages the fetus is animated but not yet endowed with a human soul. Ensoulment occurs later, perhaps at the time of quickening. So Donceel, along with a number of other Catholics, claims that a more traditional and responsible Catholic position would be to teach "immediate animation" and "delayed hominization."

The Jewish tradition offers another emphasis. Orthodox, Conservative, and Reform teachers all place a high value on the developing fetus, but practically never regard the fetus as a human person. The fetus is a dependent part of the mother's body until birth begins. Only after it has come into the world and drawn breath may it be considered a *nefesh adam*.

We see, then, that the question about the beginning of human life can be answered in several ways. Most would agree that *life* is present from conception on, but many contend that *human* life should not be defined so simply. (Indeed, biologists often assert that life is present continuously in reproductive cells, and that it is scientifically inaccurate to speak about the "beginning" of life— unless we are speaking about some long-ago point in evolutionary time.) Personally, I object to the simplistic genetic definition of life because it seems mechanical and impersonal. In fact, to talk about an early zygote as a human being is, in my judgment, to show small reverence for human life. Precisely because I profoundly respect a newborn human being in all its glorious complexity, and because I marvel at the incredible development that has taken place during gestation, I find it difficult to refer to an early embryo as "human life" in the same sense that I refer to a newborn babe as "human life." Human life develops from a simple cell sphere into a beautifully coordinated and complicated new human being. The process of development must not be underestimated. To label a zygote a "human being" is to define human life in genetic, mechanical, and impersonal terms.

Let's return to the original question for a moment: What precisely do we mean by a human life? Obviously, we mean more than mere biological event. From Aristotle on, philosophers and theologians have indicated that human life includes more than biology, that human nature is somehow special. Greek dualism and all its Christian counterparts have talked about the "soul" as an additive. Hebrew thought has preferred to speak of man as a psychosomatic unity. Without even touching on that classic debate, we may agree that there is something uniquely "human" about human life.

Max Stackhouse writes helpfully about "person-hood."[4] Christian concern, he says, is with persons, not with biological organisms.

> I should like to suggest that in order to be a person, an exist-
> ent must be (1) in the genetic continuity of *homo sapiens;*
> (2) in an organic or economic relationship that demands allo-
> cation of energy resources in the direction of the existent; (3)
> capable of interactive relationships with another; and (4) in
> a community context that can and does recognize the signifi-
> cance of the reality of the existent.

Thus Stackhouse combines biological and social factors. A human person is a unique biological organism in a unique social setting. One of the definitive characteristics of personhood is the ability to relate to other persons—indeed the necessity of doing so. The Christian emphasis on covenant and community depends on such an understanding of human nature. When we talk about human life we are necessarily talking about a quality of life together.

HUMAN LIFE BEGINS AT BIRTH

Back once more to the main question: What is meant by human life? When does human life begin?

Without attempting to trace all the travels of my mind on this subject, I shall simply state my own conclusion, which is so traditional and so biblical as to be uncomfortably radical. A new person begins, a new human being enters the world, at birth. Human life begins at birth. Before birth, the growing fetus is a constantly developing organism worthy of ever-increasing respect, but it is not yet a human being.

This position, of course, is very conservative in that it is virtually a restatement of traditional Jewish thinking. The fetus *in utero* is to be highly regarded as a potential human being. Its life may not be taken easily or lightly; to do so is to commit a crime, though not murder. But the fetus is not yet a person. The human being, *nefesh adam,* is present only after birth, after breath is drawn. Then the infant is welcomed into the family and into the larger family of faith. Soon thereafter the name is given, and the beautiful web of human relationships begins to unfold. Both the Jewish and the Christian traditions put powerful theological emphasis on the significance of breath and the importance of naming. And breath is not drawn and name not given until after birth. Personhood begins with birth. Life is present in the earliest union of reproductive cells, but human life begins with birth.

TO REACH THE COMMON GOAL

We move now to the decisive question: In the current debate over abortion, which side seems to offer the most effective method for attaining the common goal, the furthering of reverence for life? I shall try to answer this question by reviewing the options. What can we logically expect if all abortions are prohibited? What can we logically expect if abortions are legally permitted?

If we sustain laws that prohibit abortion, we could expect some or all of the following effects:

1. Legally, we will define the earliest conceptus as being of equal value with an adult human. If the conceptus is fully human from the moment the ovum is fertilized, then it merits equal protection before the law and, certainly, equal religious concern. Human life will be defined genetically, so that we will soon face legal and ethical questions about so-called "test-tube" babies. (*The New York Times* of November 1, 1970, reported that Dr. Robert G. Edwards of Cambridge has developed a human embryo *in vitro* well beyond the 16-cell stage. At what point is such a conceptus called human?) Further, if we accept this definition, it follows that we should be morally, religiously, and medically concerned about the estimated one third of all zygotes that are naturally miscarried very early in term. Even though we recognize that most of these miscarriages (which must then be called "deaths") are nature's own way of disposing of defective organisms, we should, if we are logically consistent, do everything possible to prevent the death of such a human being.

2. If the restrictive laws are effective, we should expect approximately one million additional births each year in the United States (since that many abortions are estimated to take place annually in this country) ; or, if the laws are as ineffective as they have been in the past, that many illegal abortions will be performed. In the latter event, many women will suffer from inadequate medical care and from inhuman emotional treatment. In the former event—that is, if the laws are enforced and the million additional babies are born—we should expect a steady increase in the number of children who are literally or symbolically thrown away because they are not wanted. Millions of such children already exist. They are fully human. How is our society going to offer humane life to them? How can we develop and practice reverence for life in regard to these unwanted children?

3. If all abortions are prohibited, we will be saying that every conception should produce a new human being, whether or not that conception is desired or intended. Involuntary pregnancy will necessarily lead to involuntary childbirth. We shall place a premium on quantity of life rather than quality of life. If we believe that each new life constitutes a significant increase in God's image, then the population explosion should be celebrated as a blessing. In short, we shall be saying that the more life there is on earth, the more reverence for life will there be.

If, on the other hand, we work to create laws which permit abortion, either in specified situations or on demand, we may anticipate some of these consequences:

1. Family planning will be encouraged and implemented. Birth-control measures will be expanded so that real birth control is possible. At the moment, what is called "birth control" is actually only conception control. Prospective parents will be led to compare

the value of the embryo with other values in their family life. Presumably, a higher percentage of the newborn will be truly wanted. In principle, we might hope that children will receive more tender loving care because their birth was consciously chosen. Quality of life may be stressed over quantity of life.

2. The population explosion will be checked, at least in part. We should be honest at this point: Laws that permit abortion will function as a form of birth and population control. Other nations have carefully and deliberately passed such legislation in order to produce such an effect. Clearly, conception control is a much more attractive method of population control, but abortion can be and is used where other methods have been ineffective. If we believe the ecologists—even the calmest of them—slowing the population explosion is the necessary first step in sustaining human life on this planet. What better way to promote reverence for life?

3. We must be honest and admit that, as some observers fear, a negative consequence may develop: namely, a calloused attitude toward fetal life. By defining birth as the beginning of a new human being, we will perhaps condone devaluation of the fetus. Also, as medical techniques for examining the fetus improve, we can expect a growing interest in "perfect" babies. Some parents may want to destroy a fetus of the "wrong" sex. Creation of a super race may actually be attempted.

Such negative consequences are possible. If they seem to be developing, we shall need to work vigorously to counteract them. Indeed, most proponents of abortion-law reform or repeal make it plain that they place a very high value on the fetus, especially the more advanced fetus. The embryo embodies potential human life and is therefore precious in the eyes of God and man. But, again, it is not yet a person. Great as its value is, it may honestly be considered to be of lesser value than another value which more effectively expresses reverence for human life.

Most proponents of abortion-law reform are not necessarily proponents of abortion. That is, we do not intend to suggest that abortion is an unqualified good which ought to be practiced. Rather, we recognize that there are situations in which women who are pregnant against their wishes should be permitted to terminate that pregnancy in the name of reverence for life. Simply put: Does the reverence for *fetal* life mean that we must insist on irreverently abusing the life of the would-not-be-mother? I think so.

To Enhance Human Life

In sum, I am quite persuaded that if our intention is to promote reverence for life, then we should allow abortions in situations where the termination of fetal life would enhance human life.

My concentrated study of abortion took place during the seventh, eighth, and ninth months of my wife's fourth pregnancy, which eventuated in the birth of our third child and first son. At no time during this study was the life of this particular fetus or of any fetus taken lightly. At no time was abortion looked on as a highly desirable good. Indeed, throughout much of my reading, talking, and thinking on the subject I was strongly attracted to the straightforward and simple position of the strict anti-abortionist. Intellectually, however, I was carried insistently to my present conclusion. Emotionally, meanwhile, my wife and I were experiencing once again the marvelous sense of the growing fetus, which seemed to multiply in value even as the cells multiplied. During the latter stages of pregnancy we grew increasingly eager for it to emerge, become a person, and join the family. Birth happened, he breathed, and was named Timothy Paul—all in a moment.

REFERENCES

1. Daniel H. Labby (ed.), *Life or Death: Ethics and Options* (Seattle: University of Washington Press, 1970).
2. André E. Hellegers, "Fetal Development," *Theological Studies,* **31:** 3–9 (March 1970).
3. Joseph F. Donceel, "Immediate Animation and Delayed Hominization," *Theological Studies,* **31:**76–105 (March 1970).
4. Max Stackhouse, "Abortion and Animation," *Abortion in a Changing World* (New York: Columbia University Press, 1970).

17.

A Secular Case Against Abortion on Demand

Richard Stith

The trouble with the debate over abortion laws is that it has really never begun. Both sides have from the start been blind to the possibility of a public discussion of moral values. They have instead seen values as a matter of private revelation or even taste, and *de gustibus non disputandum*. Thus political pressure rather than rational discussion of the issues has been characteristic of the recent legislative history of abortion reform. Not surprisingly, the "debate" has now culminated in pressure for abortion on demand, rather than abortion only with a reasonable justification. Abortion on demand is abortion given to anyone on request, provided only that it be medically feasible. The on demand means that abortion is considered a value-neutral technical operation which does not need justification. The public legal world of shared values passes away to leave behind agreement only on what is an efficient abortion. Even continuous debate over precisely *what* might justify abortion would tend to unite us as a community, if not in agreement at least in the hope of convincing each other of our arguments. Abortion on demand leaves us with nothing to say to each other as citizens.

Yet abortion need not have been considered a merely private or religious matter. I believe that the proponents (if I may be permitted an abbreviation for those who lobby for abortion on demand) have failed to see what is publicly at stake: respect for human life

Reprinted from *Commonweal*, November 2, 1971. Used by permission of Commonweal Publishing Co., Inc.

and for their fellow citizens. In giving some examples of what they do not see, I am not arguing for a specific kind of abortion law. I am only arguing that the whole matter is still worth debating, and therefore that reasonable men and women should oppose abortion on demand.

Proponents often dismiss the charge of homicide by asserting that the fetus cannot be proven to be a person. But of course it cannot be proven not to be a person either. Moreover, we agree that it is a person, entitled to legal protection, as soon as it is born. So the proponents would have to argue that some drastic change, from non-person to person, must have taken place at birth or at some earlier moment, unless they wish also to advocate infanticide. Medical evidence shows no such sharp discontinuity in the development of the embryo. Indeed, science could hardly begin to explain these developmental processes if it did not assume that the child is actually emerging in them, rather than that the fetus is a sort of blind growth which might by chance become a person. If the proponents wish to allege that the fetus is not a person before a certain point, the burden of proof is upon them. Let them make a convincing argument that there is a metaphysical difference between a fetus and an infant, in spite of physical similarity. For example, if they wish to make birth the decisive criterion of personhood, they must show some difference in kind between a premature infant and an infant in the womb at the same stage of development—or between a fetus destroyed within the uterus and a twin brother by chance viable upon ejection, whose life we try to save.

Why don't the proponents of abortion see the need to prove that the fetus is not a person in order to say that abortion is not killing? Ironically, the proponents themselves must be surreptitiously and perhaps unconsciously using a particular *theological* criterion of personhood. There just seems to be no secular reason why a being at an earlier stage of development should not be presumed to be the same individual as at a later stage, even if his appearance changes. Is the first sprout of an oak tree not the same plant as the fully developed tree? Only if they imagine that the person does not *grow,* but is somehow infused whole as a soul into a merely animal body, could they consider the fetus different in kind from some later stage of human development.

Why does the proponents' theology postpone "ensoulment" to some time near birth? I suppose that most of us treat other human beings as persons because we somehow see, or otherwise sense, their personhood. However, the unborn child is hidden from view—is neither readily seeable, nor even nameable (because its sex is unknown). Perhaps this hiddenness accounts in part for the proponents' abstract conception of the fetus as a body without a soul, as mere matter without a form and direction.

(Not that this hiddenness would be a *reason,* as opposed to a *cause,* for considering the fetus non-human—just as distance and skin tone should not be allowed to obscure the humanity of the Vietnamese. More education might help in both cases.)

Even if we did not consider the unborn child a person, it is clearly human life. ("It's not an Airedale," as a friend of mine has remarked.) All other human life receives legal protection. So far at least, we do not have minimum standards that life must meet. We protect the sick and the deformed from casual slaughter, although it might be argued that they have a far less human future before them than does a healthy fetus. Indeed, we even provide protection for *dead* human bodies. It is illegal to dig up and destroy dead bodies. Cannibalism is not something done on demand. Yet the fetus is disposed of in abortion as though it were cancer or excrement. If we safeguard the dignity of human flesh even in a dead body, a body without a future, how much more should we care for an unborn child, a child in whom a human future surges!

Sometimes the proponents will grant that if one begins with the value of the infant, one is logically forced to accord a similar value to the fetus. However, they argue, if one accords such a value to the fetus, then one is logically forced to accord it to the sperm and to the ovum, and then to the testes and to the ovaries, *ad infinitum.* Which supposedly goes to show that one shouldn't take logic too seriously. Yet the blindness in their argument is serious. To see no difference between an unfertilized and fertilized egg is to fail to distinguish *probability* from *potentiality.* The unfertilized ovum is incomplete. Its probability of development depends on the *chance* that another half will join it to determine its future form. The fertilized egg, however, contains *completely* its own genetic map for development. All it asks from its environment is, essentially, food rather than form. (The issue would be very different if the mother's body took an active part in shaping and organizing the fetus during pregnancy.) Unlike between a fetus and an infant, there is a qualitative difference between an unfertilized egg and a fertilized one. This difference might be summarized most succinctly in saying that the fertilized egg *grows,* while the unfertilized egg does not.

BODIES AS OBJECTS

The argument that every woman has a right to control over her own body seems likewise blind. This argument *begins* by viewing our bodies as objects to be controlled and by atomistically assuming that each object is separable from every other object. But we do not control our bodies. We *are* our bodies, and our bodies are constantly connected to the world by myriad needs and obligations. Insofar as we do not have a right to control over ourselves, because we are required to respond to the obligations of community life, we do not have a right to control over our bodies either. How else could we pay taxes, yield the right of way, or obey any other law if not with our bodies?

The law does, of course, prohibit assaults on a person's body. We do have a right to be let alone, which includes a right to protection, rather than control, of our bodies. But if the mother's body is let alone, she will give birth! It is abortion itself which is an intrusion upon the woman's body. Moreover, abortion is not even private in the sense that it is done by the woman alone against herself alone. Besides the unborn child, at least the doctor, the state, and the father are involved. Even if the woman were to have a right to mutilate her own body or the growing life within it, the doctor does not. He could be held liable if he were to cut off a woman's leg on demand, without medical necessity. Likewise he ought to be held liable for destroying the unborn without a reason. Even if we were to consider the fetus to be part of the mother, surely it should have the same protection from mutilation as does a leg. The state is also involved in abortions, at least insofar as it prescribes technical medical procedures, provides financial assistance, and repeals previously existing abortion laws. (Thus abortion on demand may well be unconstitutional, because the state is engaged in deprival of life without due process of law.) Finally, especially the father (and perhaps also society) has a very strong interest in the unborn child. After all, the child is his as much as it is the mother's. She has no right to kill it arbitrarily, any more than a trustee can arbitrarily destroy that with which he has been entrusted.

Now, both the father and society are often unconscionably negligent in protecting their interest. They entrust the bearing and rearing of the child solely to the mother and go on their merry ways. Yet they have the audacity to punish the mother for wanting the same freedom from the burdens of a child which they enjoy. No wonder proponents of abortion attack such a system as unfair! It is unfair. The father and society have been totally irresponsible in failing to aid and comfort the child and the mother, especially the unwed mother. But why not strive for equal responsibility rather than equal irresponsibility? Surely, "two wrongs don't make a right" is a most elementary moral principle. We should have, at least, tighter paternity laws, more part-time jobs so that husband and wife can share child-rearing, and severe penalties for any discrimination against unwed mothers. State and private agencies should also encourage and assist couples to adopt children rather than to have their own. By adopting children, we would open our private worlds to share the distress of our sister-citizens. And by *wanting* to adopt children, we would miraculously help to stop both population growth and the growth of that ethos which considers children burdens to be avoided. But instead of asking for these reforms, around which we could begin to build a true community, most proponents seem to tolerate and even encourage paternal and social irresponsibility, as long as the woman is likewise not made responsible for the child. Only an ideal of universal irresponsibility can account for the proponents' extraordinary answer to the fairness question.

Again, I am not arguing against more liberal abortion laws. I am saying only that the fetus has a public value, primarily as organized and growing human life, and therefore that its destruction requires a public justification. Abortion on demand should not be permitted. We ought not to imitate New York. However, given the extreme hardships which sometimes surround pregnancy, we might wish to legalize abortions in certain circumstances. Nor do I argue that the courts or a panel of doctors ought to be the judge of whether a particular woman's case fits the approved circumstances. Perhaps the woman alone should judge whether her case fits. Once we agree that abortion requires a justification, specifying both the justifications and the persons we would trust as judges would be the difficult task of public dialogue.

The first step to dialogue would be to treat seriously the opinions of those who oppose abortion. Most proponents act as though abortion on demand were just another political issue, like electing a President or building a new road. They seem to assume that once all the lobbying and voting are over, we will all go quietly home and carry on as usual. But many Americans consider at least some forms of abortion to be murder. *Murder!* It is not just another political issue, but is an assault on their most fundamental moral convictions. Many proponents say they consider an abortion not to be an issue of conscience at all, but a matter of what is convenient for the individual. Indeed, since liberalized but still restrictive abortion laws could presumably permit all morally appropriate abortions, the *only* additional abortions permitted by an on demand clause would be those done merely for convenience. Even someone who thinks that all morality is purely a subjective matter must see the subjective difference in intensity, in unselfishness, and in centrality to conscience, between the positions of those who oppose and of those who favor abortion on demand. Yet the opinions of those in opposition are not respected. These opinions are belittled as mere private religious beliefs, in spite of the fact that they are publicly understandable and have a longer sanction in public tradition than have those of the proponents.

Even if a majority of citizens did favor legalization, and I think it does not, convictions so deep as those of the opponents of abortion must be taken into account if they are not to be wholly alienated from the body politic. And the fact that no one who does not believe in abortion will be forced to engage in abortion (as yet) does not help. It is like telling someone in Nazi Germany, "Don't worry, your hands are clean. *You* don't have to guard the camps." In order to go on supporting a government which he thinks kills the innocent, a person must surely begin to lose whatever moral standards he has. A nation of amoral beasts may be the result— either that or revolt. At least one New York state senator refused to agree to any aspect of the new budget, as long as it contained money "to kill babies." Other citizens might begin a tax revolt, refusing to finance what they consider murder. For the same reason (murder), our government may already be losing its support among many good people because of the war in Vietnam. But at least there the government offers justifications which can be discussed and refuted.

Abortions on demand require no justification whatsoever in the eyes of the proponents. They are considered merely private affairs. How would we feel if President Nixon were to call the war his private affair, and to refuse to discuss it? Our alienation and frustration would then perhaps be equivalent to that which the opponents of abortion must feel when abortion on demand is legalized. Yet these feelings are ignored by the proponents as they maneuver toward legislative success.

It is sometimes argued that the population explosion is a justification for encouraging as many abortions as possible. Now, I assume that the proponents do not contend that anything that cuts down on population is *per se* good, since surely they would not approve of famine, war, or disease. Most people who make this argument, I think, mean that we should not get *more* people. They are for preventing human life rather than killing it. I certainly agree with them about the need for birth control of some kind. But in this essay, I have argued that in the unborn child we've already *got* human life. It's too late to argue for birth control!

Some may be so concerned about the population explosion that they really do favor killing existing human life in order to preserve the lives of the rest of us. They would favor killing the unborn because they are the least developed, and most easily disposed of, part of the human race. Such an argument is at least an honest one. But once we declare the unborn unworthy to live, would we necessarily stop there? Might we not eventually execute the deformed, the old, or the unintelligent?

The underlying assumption made by the proponents of abortion on demand appears to be this: dependency entails control. They seem to assume that if something is within our power, is dependent on us, then we have a right to total control over it, even to the point of destroying it. Now, the unborn child is clearly and inevitably totally dependent for nurture on its mother, so dependent that it cannot even be seen and grasped as a separate object. Therefore, the proponents can conclude that she has the right to destroy it. The same logic would make the proponents ignore the humanity of the destroyed unborn child. For if to be human is to have rights, and if to be dependent is to have no rights, then nothing which is dependent can be considered human. Humanity becomes characterized by individual independence or self-sufficiency. Indeed, the only argument which I have ever heard which sought to prove that the fetus is non-human is that it is not "self-sufficient" or "viable." I suspect that the proponents may think that since the unborn child cannot be independently seen and grasped, it simply does not exist, except perhaps subjectively.

Ordinary moral sensibility leads to a different conclusion. We generally feel that when someone is dependent on us, we are responsible for him. We do not thereby acquire rights over him. If anything, he acquires rights over us—not a right to just anything, but the right to be *cared* for, to be helped toward a healthy development. Dependency entails care, not control. Our arbitrary freedom is thus limited by having others depend on us. For example, a king ought to be far less free to follow his whims than are his subjects, insofar as they are dependent on him. Otherwise he is a tyrant. Precisely because the child is utterly dependent on the mother for its very existence, she has the greatest possible responsibility to care for it. And dependency does not make it less human. We are all dependent on others, although our dependency is not so focused as is the child's on its mother. And we, too, have a kind of right to be cared for by those on whom we depend. A pregnant woman may not have a right to total control over the child, but both she and the child have a right to care from those on whom they depend, the father and society. Being cared for by others does not degrade our humanity, but elevates it. If the unborn child depends on us to recognize its very existence, it, too, is made no less human. To be held in memory or in anticipation, to be *believed* in by other men from whom he is partially or entirely hidden—that is one of the greatest honors a person can receive.

Care rather than control is, of course, possible only if we believe that the future is not wholly our invention. The ultimate issue is not whether we believe in abortion but whether we believe in pregnancy. If things and people are "pregnant," if they have "promise," if they "grow"—in short, if they have *meaning*—then we have no right to impose our whims on them like tyrants. If we do interfere with them, we must at least have a justification. Such an attitude is no doubt difficult in a technological age bent on control of all things. Yet it is required not only for morality but for all understanding of nature. Hopefully the ecological issues are helping us realize that we cannot with impudence impose just any future on our natural environment. And if we can at least continue to believe that women can be pregnant, that they can carry the future within them, perhaps someday we may also see the "pregnancy," the meaning, of men and things.

18.

Inside an Abortion Clinic

Pamela Dillett

Once inside the waiting room, with Saturday Pittsburgh traffic rumbling several stories below and my legs tucked cozily under my long corduroy skirt, I felt nothing but detachment. Until I glanced up from the magazine I wasn't reading and found four pairs of terrified eyes staring at me: 14-year-old Negro eyes; the weary eyes of a wizened welfare recipient; the analytical eyes of a well-dressed young socialite with two children; the hostile eyes of an attractive college coed.

The room was more accommodating than the usual doctor's waiting room. Yosemite Sam was six-shooting out of a color-TV set. There were davenports and carpeting of a soporific blue. But this wasn't a typical waiting room, for the patients were waiting to have an abortion.

I was in my junior year and majoring in English at a large university when I suspected I was pregnant. I wasn't on the Pill, even though I had been having sexual relations. Yet I wouldn't call myself a "pregnancy prone" woman, that is, an emotionally distraught female who subconsciously wants to get pregnant to punish her parents, or for various other neurotic reasons.

I think my negligence was attributable to the fact that by getting a prescription for the Pill, I would have been consciously admitting to myself that I was freely offering a sacred part of myself to someone whom I didn't even particularly like. At that time it was easier to quash all reasoning, thereby salvaging my self-respect.

I went to the infirmary, where I was given a urinalysis and a thorough inspection of my uterus. My uterus was bluish—a sign of pregnancy—and my urinalysis read positive. "Oh, Pamela," moaned the doctor, shaking his head, "you're about seven weeks pregnant."

Stupefied, I managed only to peep a fragile, "Oh."

He referred me to CHOICE, a pregnancy-information organization that helps direct a woman when she has decided what route to follow. I knew abortion was my sole alternative, and the CHOICE representative gave me all the vital information. I would need a letter from the doctor certifying pregnancy. When we decided on Pittsburgh's Women's Health Services, an abortion clinic, I was told I would also need a sanitary belt, $140 by check or money order, and transportation. The representative weighted me with pamphlets and sent me on my way.

All this time I was an automaton. Some subliminal defense mechanism shielded me from the pain of feeling, allowing me only one evening's copious patronage of Kleenex. In bed I would press my disappointingly flat stomach, trying to feel, or at least fathom, what dwelled there. During class I would draw Punnett squares, trying to determine the chances of the child's eyes being blue or brown. Most of the time, though, I wasn't overly concerned.

I called Women's Health Services to set up an appointment. The arrangement making went smoothly—I had to wait only two weeks for my appointment, and no questions were asked. This surprised me, as I was still thinking in terms of illegal abortions and expected all sorts of complications and shady inquiries. I was relieved that they asked only how many weeks pregnant I was.

I confided my pregnancy to two or three girl friends, all of whom were horrified that I wasn't having an emotional earthquake or attaching a noose to my overhead light. But what could I do? My decision was firm, there were term papers to be written, and, anyway, I didn't want to torture myself with notions of murder and the implications of premarital sex.

The night before my abortion I stayed with a friend in Pittsburgh. We ate pizza, discussed men, and watched the late movie as though we were going to a Pirates' game the next day instead of to an abortion clinic.

Saturday, May 4, 1974, was sunny and cold in Pittsburgh. We took a bus from Oakland to the inner city, where, in the mammoth office building, someone was probably having the contents of her womb uprooted at that very moment. Feeling we were still adolescent rebels, we rode up the elevator muttering outrageous allegations about our mothers and the milkman—just loud enough to arouse snorts and averted eyes from the other riders.

We found our floor and an unassuming door with "Women's Health Services, Inc." on frosted glass. I guess I expected a fist-sized black widow to sail down a pole of silk, cackling, "Come in, little girl—we've been expecting you."

The spacious room was pulsing with activity and people of both sexes and assorted ages, races, and income groups. The amicable receptionist asked to see the doctor's written verdict, then gave me a formidable list to fill out of vital information, including address, age, and comprehensive medical history. After relinquishing this portrait, I was told to wait until my name was called for a blood-pressure reading, a blood test for VD, and a urinalysis.

While waiting, I noted sundry boy friends, husbands, and whole families clustered around the feminine jewel who had suffered so much. Some women, like myself, were with girl friends; a couple were alone. One little black doll who looked frighteningly young sat silently with her mother—both staring straight ahead.

A professional voice called my name and I was whisked to a treatment room for those boring sorts of tests that the doctor gives once a year. There were several nurses bustling about with crimson-filled test tubes and little containers of urine. They didn't speak much or joke around, so I ventured some lamentably inane statement like, "Boy, I hope this is one scraping I get through all right."

One nurse looked interestedly at me, one frowned, and the others ignored me. "Roll up your sleeve, please," ordered one. I wished I'd kept my incorrigible mouth shut.

Then back to the reception room, where the receptionist told me that next time I'd be called back to pay my bill. I didn't think it was quite civil of them to continue taunting me with suspense, but at the same time I was relieved that I was spared the unknown for a while.

NERVOUSNESS SETS IN

Ten minutes later I handed over my $140 money order to a matron and returned to my restless friend to await my final calling, which would involve counseling from one of the youthful staff members. This was the part I dreaded, for I expected a maternal lecture on what I had gotten myself into and an intrusive probing into my mental condition. I asked the receptionist if my friend might accompany me in the recovery room. She replied that friends weren't permitted because there would be others recuperating there and the presence of a stranger who did not share their plight might be discomfiting. I was very disappointed because I had thought I would at least get to nurse my humiliation in private.

I unshackled my friend and instructed her to return in an hour and a half, for I'd certainly be finished by then. She left with well-wishings. Now alone, I started feeling a bit nervous.

Sometime later an attractive girl in her 20s named Sally, with smiling face and sparkling eye, wandered among playing children and cigaret-puffing fathers and asked for me. She led me out the door I had first entered, down a narrow hall, in another door, and down another hall, so that when she finally showed me into a windowless, bathroom-sized room, I could have been in Outer Mongolia for all I knew.

THE PROCEDURE EXPLAINED

She sat down opposite me and began talking while my eyes kept slipping down to the prophylactics, IUDs, and birth-control pills on the table beside me. On the wall was a diagram of a woman's reproductive system—just like the one we used to chortle over in ninth-grade health class.

Sally gave a sketch of what happens to a woman when pregnancy occurs. Then she explained what was going to happen to me and about 900,000 others that year during the latest and safest method of abortion—vacuum aspiration.

The doctor makes four injections of a Novocain derivative, usually Xylocaine, on either side of the cervix. Called a paracervical block, this process anesthetizes the cervical area against the pain of what follows. These injections include medication that helps prevent hemorrhaging.

Next a plastic tube is inserted into the uterus, and a suction pump vacuums out the fetus and any other related tissue in the uterus. When the doctor sees that no more material is traveling through the tube, he turns off the pump. He then takes a curette and scrapes once around the uterus to make certain that the contents are removed. This is not the oft-used method of the past— D and C. D and C (dilation and curettage) involves scraping during the entire lengthy procedure. The vacuum-aspiration procedure takes no more than five to seven minutes.

Sally told me there was some danger of infection or hemorrhaging and (she hated to tell me, but) women have died from the effects of induced abortion. (At that date no woman had ever died from an abortion at Pittsburgh's clinic.)

My stomach danced a quick Charleston, but she reassured me that the chances of complications arising were fairly low and that infection could be readily detected if I took my temperature late every morning and early every evening for five days following the operation. If my temperature rose to 100.4 degrees or above twice in a row, a doctor should be called, as fever indicates infection may have occurred.

Profuse bleeding would be checked periodically during the recovery period, so any hemorrhaging that occurred would be treated right there in the clinic.

A month's supply of the Pill would be handed out. The first pill was to be taken the following day because a menstrual period would begin as a result of the abortion.

ANXIETY INTRUDES

I asked a bit incredulously if she wasn't going to test my emotional stamina. She laughed and showed me the place on my record where she was to check off whether I seemed anywhere from cheerful and self-aware to depressed and unconversant. She added that unless the patient showed all signs of unwillingness to abort, the abortion would be performed.

She took my doctor's verification, made sure I had a sanitary belt (because I'd have to wear a napkin afterward), and took me to the waiting room. I sat down among four other patients who didn't even smile in greeting.

I felt my first sense of anxiety when I noticed all those terrified eyes penetrating me as though I were either their savior or their executioner.

The least Sally could have done was to wait here with me. There's that black nymphet; why does she flog me with those monstrously huge eyes? That blonde must be six feet tall; I wonder how her boy friend . . . oh, stop it, Pam! What's on TV? Why do they have a TV? To placate us, I guess. Sally sure was nice. Here's an article on Easter dinners. A little late, isn't it? "Instead of the traditional ham and cabbage this Easter, why not dazzle them with an exotic . . ."

THE FACELESS DOCTOR

"Mary Ann, come with me, please."

Oh-oh, there goes the blonde; I wonder how she feels? ". . . dazzle them with an exotic . . ." I bet Orb Eyes is still watching me. I'll glance up now. Yes, she is! Why doesn't she stop haunting me? I should write an article about this. How big is this room? I have to give a speech for Speech 200: The digger wasp vs. the tarantula. I better turn the page. I'm dying to laugh. There are several species of digger wasp. Why are the blinds closed? Oh, Orb Eyes.

"Pam, do you want to come with me?"

Oh, Orb Eyes!

Another girl, smiling and chipper like Sally, brought me to a tiny green operating room and instructed me to go behind a partition, shuck my skirt and panties, and put on my sanitary belt. This being done, I put the tablecloth-sized covering around me—an effort at discretion that I felt was terribly ironic. I hopped onto the rectangular table and inserted my feet in stirrups: I must have looked like the hapless Thanksgiving bird about to have her cornbread stuffing ripped out of her. These preliminaries were nothing unusual; any woman who's had a pelvic examination has endured this somewhat mortifying position.

In stormed the doctor—faceless, voiceless, devoid of emotion. He didn't say hello or even glance at my face. While the assistant, Jean, made small talk with me, the doctor expertly injected the four anesthetizing shots where I never dreamed a shot could be given. I'm no stoic, and that certainly hurt, but I continued to talk with my new-found confidant while never taking my eyes off the wordless robot trespassing down there on private property.

Next he inserted the plastic tube, which Jean warned would hurt a bit. He turned on the suction pump and the room was filled with what sounded like a jackhammer and then like a dentist's drill once I got used to the sound. The accompanying pain was exactly like a severe menstrual cramp—a shrill, persistent clamoring in the abdomen that bites the lower back and thighs as well.

At the End, Tears

Jean took my hand, and I knew she was scanning her mind for something diversionary to talk about. To help her out, I told her about school through gritted teeth.

The infernal machine finally stopped. It probably took all of an eternal 120 seconds.

Next he scraped the cervical walls, and that hurt like blue blazes.* While I frantically wriggled my feet, I asked Jean if she had to go to college in order to do this (yes) and where did she go (Pitt) and what was her major (psychology).

Then I erupted into tears. Here I thought I had been utterly composed. I suppose the days of suppressed anxiety, the guilt, the remote possibility of death, combined with the sound of my innards changing from solid to liquid, and that villain languidly watching my blood and tissue scurry through a tube must have come to my conscious realization. And during all this, here I was discussing Jean's educational history as though we were sitting over coffee and pound cake in Stouffer's. And still that brute never looked at me.

The Recovery Room

After a few minutes the operation was over. The doctor left. I put my skirt and napkin on and hobbled with Jean to the recovery room.

The recovery room had an airy, sunny atmosphere of near gaiety, like the initial reception room. After I was checked for bleeding and temperature, I was placed on a couch next to a pleasant-looking girl my age. We took our choice of soda, juice, coffee, tea, and cookies that a jovial nurse offered us.

I spoke with the girl (a college junior from Delaware) about our pregnancies and abortions. She eyed me warily when I seemed jubilant at the fact that she cried during the vacuum pumping.

We were to stay in the recovery room for an hour, checking temperatures and the amount of bleeding every 15 minutes. If a woman felt well enough, she was permitted to leave in 45 minutes.

Assorted women around the room reclined or sat up, alone with

* Techniques vary from one clinic to another. Scraping of the cervix is sometimes omitted when vacuum aspiration is used.—Editor.

their thoughts. Almost everybody had hot water bottles on their stomachs because they had menstrual cramps. I saw a couple of women from the waiting room, including the older welfare case, who rocked alone in a corner. One girl writhed about, moaning pitifully. I didn't see Orb Eyes.

I was anxious to get back to my friend, so after 45 minutes I checked myself out and received a thermometer, birth-control pills, and a postabortion instruction sheet.

The reception room was twice as crowded as it was when I entered it the first time. I saw by my watch that I'd been gone for three hours. When I approached my friend I winked and said, "Sorry I took so long," to the horror of a middle-aged woman sitting nearby. As we pulled on our coats we watched two girls emerge from the recovery room, solemnly embrace solicitous boy friends, and leave, arms intertwined.

Homeward bound on the bus, I mused about abortion—about how in the reception room and the waiting room I felt hostile toward the other waiting women around me, but how in the recovery room and back in the reception room I felt kinship and understanding that arise only from mutual suffering and persecution.

I thought of the hoary legislators who flung women's lives around cigar-fumed board rooms, mindlessly condemning them to perdition for the unfortunate results of mankind's fondest pastime.

I was grateful that I had to endure only minimal psychological and physical pain rather than the torture of bearing a child that I would have resented. I was grateful, too, that I could have my abortion in a sanitary hospital environment rather than in the dusty back rooms that housed death beds for many victims. As if to purge myself at last of subjugation and three hours of a knowledge that shouldn't have had to be known, I leaned out the bus window and vomited.

Part
Seven

Divorce Reform

*O*F THE VARIOUS ISSUES dealt with thus far, none is likely to have a greater impact upon the American family and its individual members than the question of divorce reform. It is a crucial issue not only because of the numbers of persons involved but also because those who do become involved in divorce proceedings usually suffer a great deal, perhaps more even than those who are confronted with abortion. Approximately 2 million persons are involved in half that number of divorces each year at the present time. In addition to these adults, many of whom are parents, there are currently about 800,000 children affected by these divorces. The types of harm encountered range from the emotional and psychological on the one hand, to the financial on the other.

As an issue, divorce reform might be seen as having two basic sides: those for and those against changing or reforming current laws dealing with divorce. There are also varying shades of opinion within the two sides: the reformers disagree about how much change is necessary and about some of the specific details of needed changes, whereas those of the other side disagree as to whether or not the laws should remain the same or become even more stringent.

The whole area of the control of marriage and divorce is one of those areas left to the states by the U.S. Constitution. Thus each state has its own laws concerning divorce and the manner in which one might be obtained. Although there were a few significant differences from one state to the next, most state laws were basically similar until recent years, when a number of states changed their divorce laws. Some states have made significant reforms whereas others have made only minor changes in their divorce laws. However, most states, including many of those that have made reforms, still operate under the old type of legal structure, which requires an "adversary" proceeding in which one party to the divorce must sue the other party, based upon the misdeeds or "faults" of the party being sued. Thus, as in most of our court proceedings, there must be an innocent party and a guilty party, the two being adversaries. This term is simply a legal nicety for enemies.

Historically speaking, matters of divorce have not always been the concern of the courts. Most of our legal and governmental tradition comes from England, and in the Middle Ages and early Renaissance, divorce was a matter of concern for the state church, and persons seeking divorces had to obtain them from the religious authorities. But from the Reformation onward, there have been changes to the effect that the church and the state have become increasingly separated from each other, this separation culminating finally in our own Constitution. Divorce was, therefore, less and less a matter of official religious concern and was increasingly the concern of secular sources of authority. With the founding of the United States, the administration and jurisdiction over domestic matters was assumed by the various state legislatures, and in order to obtain a divorce, one had to have his local legislative representative introduce a special bill of divorcement to be acted upon by the entire legislature. Of course, given the difficulty of divorce under these circumstances, along with the fact that divorces were usually allowed only for extraordinary reasons, they were relatively rare, and then occurred only among the wealthy and influential members of society. From a different standpoint, however, this procedure was not too great a problem because of the ready availability of the frontier, which provided an easy means by which to escape an intolerable marriage. So the wealthy got their divorces while the poor simply deserted.

Coincidental with the decline of the frontier, divorce began to be an increasingly burdensome problem for state legislatures, so the states began writing statutes regulating both marriage and divorce, thus shifting the jurisdiction for these matters over to the courts. Since courts have always operated under the adversary system in which the state sued the accused criminal or one injured party sued another for damages, it seemed quite natural that divorce should also involve adversaries since at that time the major grounds for divorce were the crimes of adultery or desertion. Through the years, various additional grounds, such as drunkenness, cruelty, commission of a felony, insanity, and a few others, have been added in a rather inconsistent fashion by most of the states with the effect of slightly improving the laws, but the adversary system has still been maintained in most states.

Under adversary type divorce laws, to get a divorce one spouse must file a suit against the other spouse charging one or more of the grounds that are available according to the laws of the particular state of residence. In the eyes of the court, one of the spouses must be guilty while the other must be blameless. A couple may not get a divorce simply because both parties want one. Furthermore, if the accused spouse proves his innocence, or if the court finds that both spouses are guilty, the divorce may not be granted. If the laws in most states were strictly adhered to, it would indeed be difficult to obtain a divorce. In reality, however, most divorces are obtained through a system of collusion which has developed through the years. Here the two parties to the divorce privately agree, before beginning any proceedings, as to which of the two will sue and which will be the guilty party. Of course, collusion is illegal, but unless it becomes blatantly obvious, the courts usually choose to pretend that it does not exist. Along with the development of this system of collusion, the use of the grounds of cruelty began to include what is referred to as "mental cruelty," and courts have been increasingly lenient in the breadth of the acceptable meanings of this term.

Those opposed to any changes feel that most present systems are adequate, and that perhaps the courts should even be a little stricter in their administration of the divorce laws by not allowing the system to be made a sham through collusion. They feel that it may already be too easy to get a divorce, and that easy divorces just encourage more people to break up their marriages.

On the other hand, the reformers point out that the adversary system is simply not the proper way to go about dissolving marriages. Furthermore, they say that the present system does not produce the results or goals that are desired by both the society in general or by the individuals involved. For example, many couples enter a divorce with everything arranged and agreed upon, and determined to end their marriage with no bitterness or squabbling. But for most couples, upon entering the legal process they find that their previous argreements seem to disappear as lawyers point out to their clients ways in which each might gain an advantage financially or perhaps with respect to child support and custody. This is not to fault lawyers, for their duty is to get the best deal for their clients and to see that their rights are protected. Thus, a feud ensues where none was wanted or expected. Reformers point out that this tendency on the part of the present system to produce heartrending and sometimes bitter disputes is the chief fault of the current divorce laws and is the major reason why they should be changed, so that divorce need no longer be an adversary proceeding. A far better system would be one in which a couple, whose marriage is broken for whatever reason, could petition the court to dissolve their marriage based upon their own previously agreed-upon plan of settlement.

Those urging reform go on to point out that the old laws based upon proof of fault are unnecessary simply because it makes no difference what the reasons are behind a marriage breakup. What is important is that only those who are parties to the marriage can know when it is in fact no longer a viable one, and that subjecting the couple, and perhaps children as well, to a legal dispute produces only negative consequences for all involved. Marriages should be allowed to die in peace, which is better for everyone, especially the children who suffer a great deal when disputes arise.

Another point of contention for those seeking reform is that the old laws, and more particularly the manner in which judges administer them, are highly unfair and discriminatory toward men. In many states, for example, women may receive alimony, but men may not. Additionally, most courts tend to take a punishing attitude toward the husband when dealing out property settlements, alimony, or child support. This attitude is an outgrowth of both the traditional view of the divorcé as a philanderer and ne'er-do-well, and the guilt-finding of the adversary system which dictates that one party, usually the husband, must be guilty and therefore should be punished. Perhaps the most crucial manner in which men are discriminated against under the old system is in the matter of child custody. It is almost impossible for a father to gain the custody of his children unless his wife chooses not to keep them, and this seldom happens because the children are the wife's major means of maintaining the upper hand with respect to the husband. Some wives even go so far as to use children as pawns to gain various concessions from the husband, and they can make life miserable for him by withholding visiting rights or by downgrading him in the eyes of his children.

Most of the states that have revised their laws require that child custody be awarded without any regard to marital fault and in some cases, without any regard to the sex of the spouses. However, getting judges to operate without their traditional biases with respect to men and child custody will probably be far more difficult than getting legislatures to revise the laws.

One further goal of divorce reformers is the abolition of the whole concept of alimony since it is essentially seen as being a sort of punishment for the husband. New laws attempt to replace this idea with the concept of "maintenance," which implies that either party to the marriage may be required to help support the other members of the family according to which one was the breadwinner during the marriage and also according to the ability of the other spouse to support him- or herself. The awarding of maintenance is also related to who has custody of the children.

Just as abortion laws were changed by both the courts and the state legislatures, the same is happening with divorce laws. However, where reform has occurred, it has been the legislatures that have made by far the most changes. Since there is no federal jurisdiction in divorce matters, changes would have to come from state courts, and traditionally state courts have been very reluctant to deny the constitutionality of state laws. Recently, however, a few state courts have begun to question the legality of divorce laws which discriminate against one sex in the matters of alimony and child custody.

Major legislative changes have been brought about by two methods: either by adding the grounds of "incompatibility" which would not require either spouse to be at fault, or by completely rewriting the laws so as to institute the "no-fault" concept which allows the couple to petition the court for a "dissolution" of their marriage on the basis of their "irreconcilable differences." The first method keeps the old adversary system while the second abolishes it. At least sixteen states now allow divorce on the grounds of incompatibility. Other states have changed their laws so that the sole grounds for a divorce is the "irretrievable breakdown" of the marriage. Some of these states have also abolished the adversary system as well.

To the charge that laws making divorce easier would lead to an increase in divorces, the reformers have several answers. The first of these might be a simple "so what?" response, the argument being that laws which require two miserable people to continue living together are unjust, and that if a new law better serves the happiness and satisfaction of citizens then there should be more such laws.

A better answer, however, might be that the new laws do not actually cause a significantly large increase in the divorce rate. The laws in the states that have recently changed them are still so new that there is little evidence on which to make a judgment concerning the increase or decrease in the rates of marital breakup. However, some evidence has been gained which so far indicates that the new laws have very little effect upon the established trends in the frequency of divorce. The first article in this section speaks more directly to this whole question.

Regarding the question of whether or not divorce should be made easier, it is one thing to make the process itself easier but quite another to provide a process which is ultimately easier upon the involved individuals in terms of pain and suffering, while maintaining a viable procedure for the protection of both individuals and society. The new laws probably do not encourage divorce by making the process a great deal more simple or easy, but they do remove much of the conflict and anguish, so that compared with the old laws, the new ones have vastly more desirable consequences.

Part Seven of this book is somewhat one-sided in that all of the articles presented here essentially reflect a favorable view of divorce reform. This is not too surprising in that most informed opinion favors reform, whereas those against reform are represented by a few local politicians along with religious leaders of a fundamentalist persuasion. Thus, published articles are more likely to reflect the opinion that grows out of a critical investigation of the total divorce situation. Indeed, no suitable article arguing against reform was located for the purpose of inclusion in this volume.

The first article of this section, which was prepared especially for this book, is a systematic review of the changes in the laws in the various states. This article also discusses the various types of laws that have thus far emerged from the reform process. One concern of those both for and against divorce law reform is that of whether or not divorces will increase or perhaps decrease as a result of changes in the laws. This article presents the latest available data regarding this question.

The article by Paul Bohannan, "Some Thoughts on Divorce Reform," is one of the best developed and most thought-provoking articles in this entire collection. It seeks to go beyond the legal, technical, and procedural aspects of divorce to try and determine what really occurs when couples divorce and how these occurrences can best be dealt with. It delineates not only what a divorce ends but what it begins, and it is interesting to note that there are many unexpected things which are not ended by divorce and many others which are begun or set in motion. Bohannan goes on to argue that in order to be adequate, divorce reform must take into account these other aspects of the divorce situation which are not currently dealt with by either the old laws or the new laws.

The final article of this part presents a little drama of sorts. "An Amicable Divorce" is an example of one way in which divorcing spouses might relate to one another through a brief ceremony in which they acknowledge that they can no longer live together, but will not be spiteful and antagonistic to each other and will remain friends. One cannot, however, overlook the irony of this situation. If a married couple can reach such an accord as demonstrated by this ceremony, one wonders why the couple could not have reached the same accord in the marriage.

19.

Divorce Law Reform and Increasing Divorce Rates

Kenneth D. Sell

"Easy-Out Divorces Soaring" the newspaper headlines declare, implying a relationship between increasing divorce rates and easily obtained divorces. Not only journalists but legal scholars have speculated about the relationship between liberalization of the United States divorce laws and escalating divorce rates (Brody 1970; Anderson 1972; Goddard 1972; Honigman 1972; Lee 1972; Gallagher 1973; German 1973; Miller 1973; Sass 1973; Newbern 1974; Steinboch 1975). Some of these authors have attempted to find a relationship between the liberalization of divorce laws and increasing divorce rates using the very limited data that were available several years ago. Some have expressed a concern about the weakening of family structures and increasing social problems that might result from the liberalized divorce laws. These fears may have impeded divorce law reform in some states. Zuckman (1975) has been one of the few to express his belief that the no-fault trend is not the cause of increasing divorce rates in the United States. More data now exists to examine the relationship between divorce law reform and the increasing divorce rates, and it is one purpose of this study to examine this relationship for the period 1968 through 1976.

The year 1968 was the first year of rapidly accelerating divorce rates, which had only been slowly increasing since 1962. The year 1968 was also the time when divorce reform legislation was begin-

Prepared especially for this volume by Kenneth D. Sell.

ning to be considered by state legislatures. No-fault divorce began with the passage of the California Family Law Act of 1969 (effective January 1, 1970). Although a few states had some elements of no-fault divorce prior to 1970, the California Act was the first attempt to completely eliminate the fault concept from the divorce process.

The no-fault label has been used to refer somewhat indiscriminately to a broad class of divorce legislation. The term has also been used when a no-fault ground has been added to the traditional grounds for divorce (Reike 1974). In this article, no-fault divorce is used in a narrower sense as indicated in the following definition. After a careful study of the grounds for divorce in each state, the present divorce laws were categorized and defined as follows:

A. "No-fault" grounds only
   The statutes contain only one ground for divorce, worded either as irretrievably broken marriage, breakdown of the marriage relationship, or irreconcilable differences (sometimes insanity may be added as an additional ground). Guilty or innocent parties are not established in the divorce proceedings.
B. "Fault" grounds only
   The statutes allow divorce only when a guilty and an innocent party can be established in terms of specific acts such as cruelty, desertion, and adultery.
C. Mixed: "incompatibility" added to "fault" grounds
   The statutes have the usual fault grounds where guilt or innocence must be proven, but there are also no-fault grounds of incompatibility where guilt does not have to be established. The terms *irreconcilable differences* or *irretrievable breakdown* may be used by some states instead of incompatibility.
D. Mixed: "separation" added to "fault" grounds
   These statutes have the usual fault grounds in addition to the no-fault ground of voluntary separation for a specified length of time.

Five states (Connecticut, Idaho, New Hampshire, Rhode Island, and Texas) have both fault grounds and the no-fault grounds of incompatibility *and* separation.

Since 1968 there has been a rapid change in divorce laws with more than two thirds of the states liberalizing their laws. Sixteen states have changed their laws to no-fault grounds only, thirteen states have added incompatibility or irreconcilable differences to the existing fault grounds, and nine states have either added voluntary separation provisions to existing fault grounds or have decreased the length of the separation period. At the present time, only three states have retained fault grounds as the sole condition for divorce. (See Table 1 for data on the grounds in each state).

TABLE 1 *Types of Grounds for Divorce by States**

A. "No-fault" grounds only

States (16)	Effective
California	1-01-70
Iowa	7-01-70
Florida	7-01-71
Oregon	10-01-71
Colorado	1-01-72
Michigan	1-01-72
Kentucky	6-16-72
Hawaii	7-01-72
Nebraska	7-06-72
Nevada	4-21-73
Washington	4-23-73
Arizona	8-08-73
Missouri	1-01-74
Minnesota	3-14-74
Delaware	6-01-74
Montana	1-01-76

B. "Fault" grounds only

States (3)
Illinois
Pennsylvania
South Dakota

C. Mixed grounds: "incompatibility," etc.; separation; added to "fault" grounds

States (5)	No-fault grounds effective	No-fault ground
Texas[c]	1970	IS
Idaho[d]	1971	IRD
New Hampshire[b]	1971	IRD & IRB
Connecticut[a]	1973	IRB & IC
Rhode Island[e]	1975	IRD

D. Mixed grounds: "incompatibility," etc., added to "fault" grounds

States (11)	No-fault grounds effective	No-fault ground
New Mexico	1933	IC
Alaska	1935	IC
Oklahoma	1953	IC
Kansas	1969	IC
Alabama	1971	IRB & IC
North Dakota	1971	IRD
Georgia	1973	IRB
Indiana	1973	IRB
Maine	1973	IRD
Massachusetts	1975	IRB
Mississippi	1976	IRD

E. Mixed grounds: "separation" added to "fault" grounds

States (15)	Latest change effective	Years separation required
Arkansas	1937	3
Louisiana	1938	2
Wyoming	1941	2
Utah	1943	3
Tennessee	1963	2
North Carolina	1965	1
West Virginia	1969 new	2
South Carolina	1969 new	3
New Jersey	1971 new	1½
New York	1972	1
Wisconsin	1972	1
Maryland	1973	1
Vermont	1973	½
Ohio	1974 new	2
Virginia	1975	1

Source: Search of the statutes of the fifty states
*as of August 1977.

IC = incompatibility

IS = insupportable marriage

IRB = irretrievable or irremediable breakdown

IRD = irreconcilable differences

a 1½ years separation
b 2 years separation
c 3 years separation
d 5 years separation

Background of Divorce Reform

In Europe, prior to the twelfth century, the state took little interest in either the regulation of marriage or its dissolution. However, as the sacramental aspect of marriage gained increasing importance, the church became more concerned about the stability of marriage. From the twelfth to the seventeenth century, the ecclesiastical courts had jurisdiction over marriage and divorce, and generally maintained that marriage was indissoluble. However, in England by the end of the seventeenth century, divorce was available by a special act of Parliament (Lee 1972). Legal separations were granted when proof of certain wrongs such as adultery, cruelty, or unnatural acts had been committed. Thus, fault was admitted into dissolution proceedings. In 1857, the English government took over control of marital termination completely (Marital Causes Act), when the state decided that marriage was a civil rather than a religious act, and the fault system was adopted for the termination of marriage (Walker 1971).

In America, divorce gradually passed to the colonial and state legislatures, and then on to the courts. The fault system was adopted when the courts began granting divorces. Thus, fault was actually an attempt to humanize the divorce laws, and the recognition of fault could be characterized as a liberalization of the law (German 1973). Historically, granting a divorce has been predicated on the proof of misbehavior. Consequently, divorce became both the prize for good behavior and the punishment for misbehavior (Honigman 1972).

After more than a century of dealing with the fault system, it had become increasingly evident that fault divorce as it was currently practiced in the American system of jurisprudence had many undesirable side effects. Reppy (1970) cites four main objections to the fault system: (a) the fault concepts are unrelated to the actual causes of marital failure, (b) the fault system promotes hatred, bitterness, and acrimony by accentuating the aggressive forces in the family, (c) the fault system frustrates the state's interest in preserving marriages that are not irreparably broken, and (d) the fault concept often requires individuals to perjure themselves to maintain the legal fiction of fault. In addition, Furner (1972) noted (e) that the fault system is demeaning to the legal profession to mould dead marriages into the proper grounds and forms, and (f) that it consumes a great deal of court time and money. An article in the Connecticut Bar Journal (1973) opined that it is really an invasion of privacy for the couple seeking a divorce to have to reveal very private intimate details of marital discord in order to prove proper grounds for divorce.

Some of the objections cited are more applicable to contested divorces than to uncontested ones. About 90 per cent of all divorces are uncontested (Sass 1973). However, as some scholars maintain, even in an uncontested case divorce may be bought at a price.

Commonly, the spouse who yearned for divorce sought to avoid a contested hearing and had to barter for his freedom at the cheapest price obtainable. Buying one's freedom has often required submission to a form of blackmail by way of either excessive or inadequate alimony or property settlement, or in custodial rights not necessarily geared to the best interests of the child. . . . No-fault embraces the principle of individual freedom which calls for the same volitional right to get out of a marriage as to get into one. (Honigman 1972)

In recent years legal scholars have theorized about the improvements needed in our divorce laws. Some of the principles that have been suggested are that (a) the law should seek to preserve marriages that are in temporary difficulties, (b) the law should allow irretrievably broken marriages to be dissolved with a minimum of bitterness, (c) there should be adequate safeguards and support for minor children, and (d) there should be fair and equitable distribution of property and support of spouses if necessary (Anderson 1972). A Connecticut Bar Journal article (1973) included some additional requirements: (e) respect for the privacy and integrity of the marriage relationship, and (f) protection of the integrity of the bar and the judicial system and encouragement of respect for the law.

Honigman (1972) seemed to capture the spirit of no-fault legislation when he wrote:

At the base of the marital relationship is the willingness of the parties to live together. If they are not willing to do so for whatever reason or whoever is at fault, the marital relationship is in fact terminated and the 'objects of matrimony have been destroyed.' Why they are unwilling to live together need be of no interest to the law. . . . Nor does the law require that both parties subscribe to the conclusion that they are unwilling to live together. If either of the parties is convinced that this is so and acts accordingly, it becomes a fact that the marital relationship has terminated.

No-Fault Divorce

In the light of the aforementioned criticisms of the fault system, 16 states have revised their divorce laws in an attempt to eliminate the fault concept from the divorce process. Some states have also eliminated the terminology of the old fault system. Following California's lead, the phrase *dissolution of marriage* has been substituted for the word *divorce* in the statutes of Arizona, Connecticut, Indiana, Iowa, Kentucky, Minnesota, Missouri, Nebraska, New Mexico, Oregon, and Washington. The adversary role is downplayed in California and other states by the use of the neutral phrase *in re the marriage of Mrs. Smith and Mr. Smith* instead of *Smith vs. Smith* or such labels as *plaintiff* and *defendant*.

Under the fault system an *innocent* party could often benefit financially from alimony, property settlements, or both. The law added to the bitterness of contested cases by requiring the proof of guilt or innocence. In many no-fault states the defenses formerly used against a divorce action have been eliminated. This means, in some states, that the marriage can be dissolved at the request of either the "innocent" or the "guilty" spouse (Sass 1973).

Despite the elimination of fault, the same issues have to be resolved, namely, the custody of minor children, if any, alimony and child support, and the division of property. The no-fault states employ a variety of solutions to these matters. Even in no-fault states, fault may be considered in the resolution of some of these issues.

The custody of minor children is dealt with in a variety of ways. In Florida, the law decrees that the father shall be given the same consideration for custody as the mother (Church 1971). The divorce law of Kentucky explicitly states that custody shall be determined without regard to marital misconduct (Humphrey 1972). In Washington, the statute does not expressly prohibit the court from considering marital misconduct, but it does state that the court shall not consider the conduct of a proposed guardian that does not adversely affect the welfare of the child (Holman 1973). In both Washington and Iowa, the courts may appoint counsel to represent the interests of minor children with respect to custody, support, and visitation (Peters 1971; Holman 1973).

But fault may enter the custody proceedings in some no-fault states. In California, custody may be given to either parent according to the best interests of the child but with preference given to the mother's custody when the children are of tender age (Hayes 1970). Both California and Oregon state that evidence of acts of misconduct shall be improper and inadvisable, except where child custody is an issue and such evidence is relevant to that issue (Reppy 1970; Leo 1972).

The second area of concern, spousal support or alimony, is dealt with in a number of ways in the no-fault states. A general principle of fairness, rather than punishment, seems to be the goal of most states that have adopted no-fault divorce laws. For example, Iowa requires that persons seeking support for self or minor children must provide the court with a financial statement showing both income and normal expenses, as well as assets and liabilities. That report must be accompanied by an affidavit (Thayer 1973). In the no-fault states the laws generally state that alimony can be awarded to either spouse. But fault may affect granting alimony even in some no-fault states. Altough Michigan adopted a no-fault divorce policy, the statutes dealing with alimony were not changed (Snyder 1971), so that fault can be used in deciding alimony awards. In a recent Kentucky case, the court ruled that fault could not be considered in awarding alimony but that fault could be taken into account in determining the amount of alimony to be given (Miller 1973). Florida courts may consider the adultery of a spouse, and the circumstances thereof, in determining whether alimony shall be awarded to such spouse or not. This was a legislative compromise so that an adulterous wife would not necessarily be awarded alimony (Archbell 1972).

A third issue to be resolved during a divorce is the division of property. Under California's no-fault statute, all community property, e.g., property acquired by either spouse during the marriage, shall be divided evenly. However, not all no-fault states have followed California's example. For instance, although Washington does not recognize fault in the division of property, it does not require that the property be divided equally. Kentucky requires an even distribution of property and may even recognize the wife's contribution as a homemaker (Humphrey 1972). Missouri, on the other hand, retains fault (at judicial discretion) in the division of property (Thayer 1973). In Michigan, property settlements may take fault into account (Snyder 1971). However, in many divorces there is little property to be divided. Expert opinion is divided concerning the effects of the elimination of fault from property settlements. Cline (1970) believes that the wife will need more support since she can receive only one half of the property where an equal distribution is required, whereas Goddard (1972) believes that judges will be making smaller and shorter awards to women under California's equal division law.

Thus, in all three principal issues raised by divorce, the concept of fault may be used even in the no-fault divorce states. The issue of fault is still alive.

Fault Divorce

In 1968, 22 states granted divorces solely on the basis of fault. The traditional fault grounds of physical or mental cruelty, desertion, impotency, conviction of a felony, and so on, were in force. One spouse was required to prove that the other spouse had been guilty of one of these offenses. As of December 31, 1977, only three states, Illinois, Pennsylvania, and South Dakota, wholly retain the fault concept in granting divorces. Numerous bills have been introduced into the legislatures of these states in an attempt to change the divorce laws. It is expected that these states will eventually join the trend to some form of no-fault legislation.

Mixed: "Incompatibility" Added to "Fault" Grounds

Only three states had incompatibility as a ground for divorce in 1968. At the end of 1977, 16 states had added incompatibility as a ground, in addition to retaining some of the fault grounds. See Table 1. The wording of the statutes varies with such phrases as irreconcilable differences, and irretrievable breakdown which overlap with incompatibility, and in many instances these phrases may be almost interchangable.

Historically, incompatibility was the first of these three grounds to be developed. A century ago ten states adopted incompatibility of temperament as grounds for divorce. None of these grounds survives today (Kennalley 1975). Modern incompatibility statutes had their origin in the Virgin Islands. When these islands were acquired from Denmark in 1917, Danish law allowed divorce for reasons of incompatibility (Schulman 1972). Incompatibility was retained as a ground for divorce after the islands became a United States territory. In 1935, the territory of Alaska also adopted incompatibility as a ground for divorce. Among the states, New Mexico added incompatibility in 1933 and Oklahoma followed suit in 1953. Since no law defined incompatibility, the U.S. Third Circuit Court of Appeals decreed, in 1952, that incompatibility

> refers to conflicts in personalities and dispositions so deep as to be irreconcilable and to render it impossible for the parties to continue a normal marital relationship with each other. . . . If the parties are so mismated that their marriage has in fact endured as a result of their hopeless disagreement and discord the courts should be empowered to terminate it as a matter of law. (Ferguson 1973)

In 1966, the Third Circuit Court further expanded its interpretation by saying:

> In determining whether a married pair are so incompatible as to justify a divorce on that ground, the inquiry is not as to the fault of either or both but rather as to whether their marital barque has so far foundered upon the rocks of disharmony and discord as to be beyond the possibility of salvage. (Ferguson 1973)

In this interpretation fault is not considered. However, authorities disagree on this point. A leading domestic relations expert points out that the courts have been strongly influenced by fault in the past. Three issues continually surround the ground of incompatibility: (a) must the plaintiff prove that the incompatibility is the fault of the defendant or prove mutual hostility or lack of affection? (b) must both parties feel incompatibility? and (c) are there defenses to incompatibility? (Clark, quoted in Gozansky 1973).

Incompatibility has been interpreted differently in the states that have adopted it as a ground. Some states indicate that a divorce shall be decreed, irrespective of the fault of either party, on the ground of irreconcilable differences which have caused the irremediable breakdown of the marriage. In any pleadings, evidence of specific acts of misconduct are improper and inadmissible, except where child custody is an issue, and such evidence is relevant to establish that parental custody would be detrimental to the child (Anderson 1972). At the present time, in the no-fault states incompatibility is the sole grounds for divorce.

In these mixed states where incompatibility and fault grounds are both in the statutes, the fault grounds generally become less

TABLE 2 Percent Divorces Based on Incompatibility in Selected
States

Kansas	1970	39%	Idaho	1973	86%
(1969)	1971	58%	(1971)	1974	89%
	1972	69%			
	1973	79%	New	1972	72%
	1974	85%	Hampshire	1973	95%
			(1971)		
Alabama	1972	69%			
(1971)	1973	81%	Montana	1974	84%
	1974	84%	(1973)		

Source: Vital statistics reports from the various states.

used in favor of the no-fault grounds. The data that are available
show the increased use of the no-fault grounds (see Table 2).

The date below each state indicates the year the incompatibility
ground was adopted. The percentages on the right show the increased use of incompatibility instead of fault grounds. Other states
have had similar experiences. This decreasing use of fault as a basis
for divorce led Montana to drop the fault grounds entirely in 1976
and it became a pure no-fault state. Where both fault and no-fault
grounds are available, a vindictive spouse can still seek revenge by
using the fault grounds. It would seem reasonable to expect that
as more states experience the decreasing use of the fault grounds,
the fault grounds will be repealed.

MIXED: "SEPARATION" ADDED TO "FAULT" GROUNDS

Twenty states permit divorce after a specified period of separation, in addition to maintaining the fault grounds for divorce (see
Table 1). Separation is a ground that is easy to prove and usually
does not involve fault. Separation as a no-fault ground has had a
long history in the United States. In 1839, New Hampshire passed
a law that stated:

> Where either of the parties shall unnecessarily, without suffi-
> cient cause and against the consent of the other, leave the
> other or has heretofore left the other and shall unnecessarily
> and without sufficient cause refuse or has heretofore refused
> to cohabit with the other for the space of three years together
> is shall be deemed and taken to be a sufficient cause for di-
> vorce. (Anderson 1972)

The separation period was reduced to two years in 1967. Other
states that had separation as a no-fault ground for divorce for a
long period are Kentucky (1850), Wisconsin (1866), and Rhode
Island (1893) (Lee 1972).

The trend during the past ten years has been to shorten the time
required for the separation. Seven states have shortened the re-

quired time of separation; these states are Virginia (1964) from three years to two years, and (1975) from two years to one year; North Carolina (1965) from two years to one year; New York (1972) from two years to one year; Rhode Island (1972) from ten years to five years, and later to three years; Wisconsin (1972) from five years to one year; Maryland (1973) from one and one-half years to one year; and Vermont (1972) from three years to six months. In addition, five states added separation to their fault grounds: New York (1968) two years; South Carolina (1969) three years; West Virginia (1969) three years; New Jersey (1971) one and one-half years; and Ohio (1974) two years.

The use of separation as a ground for divorce follows a different pattern than the utilization of the incompatibility grounds. Generally, the shorter the period of separation required, the more the ground of separation is used. When the separation period is one year or less, the separation ground is likely to be used in preference to the fault grounds. Where the period of required separation is longer than one year, fault grounds are more often used.

Table 3 shows the percentage of divorces that used the ground of separation in a given year or the average for a number of years. The number of years of separation required is indicated.

States that have separation as a ground for divorce differ in their interpretation of this ground. The most restrictive states require that the parties obtain a separation agreement or separate maintenance decree first and then live apart for the required length of time. New York and Utah are examples of this type of interpretation. A second type allows divorce only when *the couple* has voluntarily agreed to live apart for the statutory period. A third modification allows divorce on the basis of separation only if the plaintiff is innocent of any wrongdoing. The least restrictive and most widely

TABLE 3 *Percent Divorces Using Separation as Grounds for Divorce in Selected States*

Rhode Island	*10 years required* 1968–71	4%	South Carolina	*3 years required* 1973–74	12%
	5 years required 1972	7%	Tennessee	*2 years required* 1972	2%
Wisconsin	*10 years required* 1968–72	3½%	Virginia	*2 years required* 1968–73	26%
Vermont	*3 years required* 1968–70	12%	North Carolina	*1 year required* 1967–69	99%
	2 years required 1972	17%			
	6 months required 1973	84%			

Source: Vital statistics reports from the various states.

used separation statute grants divorce on the mere proof that the couple has lived apart for the required length of time (Jones 1975).

Whereas separation is basically a no-fault ground, fault may be considered in alimony, custody, and property settlements where separation is used as a ground. For instance, of the 26 states having separation as a ground for divorce, in 12 states fault has some bearing on alimony, especially for the wife. In five of these states, fault may play a part in property settlements (Freed and Foster 1973).

In recent years, bills have been introduced into the legislatures of many of these states to shorten the period of separation required and/or to substitute no-fault divorce for separation and fault.

INFLUENCES OF THE DIVORCE LAW CHANGES

Having looked at the changes in divorce laws in recent years, what influence have these changes had on divorce rates? Most legal scholars and many family life specialists assume that increasing divorce rates are a consequence of the legal changes. It seems reasonable that as divorce becomes easier to obtain, more people will take advantage of these changes. However, this assumes (a) that people are aware of the changes in the law, and (b) that these changes influence their actions. Deckert and Langelier (1977) in a study of divorce in Quebec found that 42 per cent of their subjects were not aware of the changes in Canadian divorce laws, and of those that did know about the changes, 91 per cent were not influenced by the prospect of more liberal laws. The situation would probably be similar in the United States.

There are considerable difficulties in making a rigorous analysis of the increasing divorce rates. These legal changes have been occurring continuously from state to state rather than as one-time changes as in Canada and England. There is a lack of statistical tools for the analysis of these kinds of data. In addition, some states changed their grounds for divorce several times during this period making a typology of change somewhat difficult. In states that kept their fault grounds and added some no-fault grounds (probably a legislative compromise instead of adopting complete no-fault), the information is incomplete regarding the extent to which the no-fault grounds have been used. These data may be available but they have not been published in the state vital statistics reports. The divorce statistics are incomplete or unavailable for a few states. Finally, there are problems of selectivity. There may be some basic differences between states that have changed their laws and those that did not change. In the states that have the most restrictive laws, there may be more migratory divorces. Some of the increases in the divorce rates in the more liberal states may be the result of fewer migratory divorces. These are a few of the problems that make a clear-cut analysis difficult.

Yet it is precisely these kinds of analyses that are needed in order for lawmakers to know the probable outcomes of changes in divorce laws. In fact, the analysis of the outcome data on many social programs has been the point of discussion by a number of authors in the past decade. Much of the current thinking about social program evaluation focuses on the use of time series for the analysis of the data. However, an adequate analysis requires that repeated observations be made both before and after the intervention or change. At this time, there are enough after observations available because of the recency of the changes in the laws. However, rather than violate the assumptions of certain statistical tests, it has been recommended in cases such as this where no statistical tests of hypotheses can be legitimately carried out, that it is useful to plot the data and "eye-ball" any change or lack of change (Cook and Campbell 1976).

Table 4 shows the crude divorce rates (the number of divorces per one thousand population) for the 32 states that changed their grounds for divorce and the 15 states that did not change their grounds for divorce between 1968 and 1976. The states that changed their grounds had an average increase in the crude divorce rate of 2.16 for the period, whereas the states that did not change their grounds had an average increase of 1.85. Data were not avail-

TABLE 4   Increases in the Crude Divorce Rates of States Changing and Not Changing Their Grounds for Divorce

Grounds for divorce changed	CDR 1968	CDR 1976	Increase in CDR 1968–76
A. Fault only to no-fault (10)	3.53	5.72	2.19
B. Separation and fault to no-fault (5)	4.72	6.82	2.10
C. Fault only to incompatibility and fault (7)	2.89	4.87	1.98
D. Fault only to separation and fault (5)	1.58	3.72	2.14
E. Fault, separation, and incompatibility (5)	3.76	5.75	1.99
M₁ Mean, states changing	2.97	5.13	2.16
Grounds for divorce not changed			
F. Fault only (3)	2.29	3.70	1.41
G. Fault and separation (9)	2.61	4.76	2.15
H. Fault and incompatibility (3)	5.62	7.93	2.31
M₂ Mean, states not changing	2.63	4.48	1.85
Mean, U.S.	2.88	4.95	2.07

Sources: *Vital Statistics of the United States, Vol. 3, Marriage and Divorce.* U.S. National Center for Health Statistics, 1968. *Monthly Vital Statistics Report, Births, Marriages, Divorces, and Deaths for 1976.* U.S. National Center for Health Statistics, Vol. 25, No. 12.

able for three states. It should be noted that the rates in both groups of states increased, and that the rates increased for every state with the exception of Nevada where there was a substantial decline, probably as a result of the decline in migratory divorces. States that had only fault grounds increased the least but it cannot be ascertained whether their restrictive laws led to more migratory divorces or not.

The increasing divorce rates are graphed in Figure 1. A uniform upward slope is characteristic for all types of states. This would lead to the conclusion that changes in the grounds for divorce do

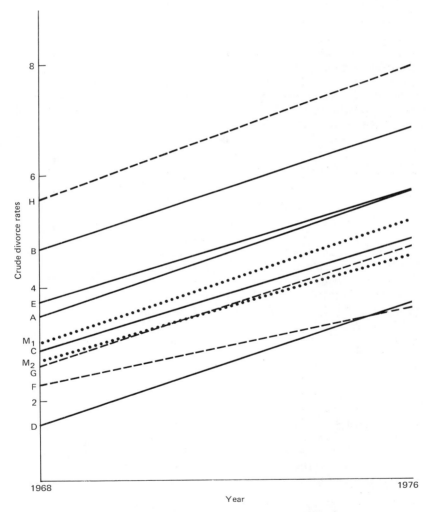

FIGURE 1. Increases in the crude divorce rates of states changing and not changing their grounds for divorces. (Key: see Table 4.)

not substantially increase the divorce rates. Subsequent analysis may be somewhat more precise, but from the current data available it does not appear that changes in the law have affected the divorce rates substantially. Persons who maintain the causal factor of legal changes fail to note that when states that have not changed their laws are used as a control group, these states also show substantial increases in their divorce rates. It should also be noted that the divorce rates began to increase some eight years before the first pure no-fault statutes went into effect.

At this point, alternate explanations can be made to account for the increasing rates of divorce without being able to quantify their individual effects. In the past, divorce rates have been higher in times of economic prosperity than in times of depression. The past decade has been relatively prosperous but even during the recession of 1973–75, the divorce rates continued to increase. Postwar periods have shown marked increases in divorce rates. Thus, the Vietnamese conflict probably has had some influence on recent divorce rates. Increased divorce rates may be a reflection of the general social disorganization of American society that is indicated by increases in crime, riots, and other forms of deviant behavior. Previous research indicates that children of divorced parents have had a somewhat higher rate of divorce and, since an increasing number of children from divorced homes are now of marriageable age, this could be another slight factor in the increasing divorce rates. Another demographic factor is that divorce occurs more often in early marriage than in later marriage. As a result of the baby boom, more persons are involved in young marriages at the present time, and hence there are more chances for divorce. With more women in the labor force and increased job opportunities available for women, women may now be less hesitant about dissolving an unsatisfactory marriage. In the realm of values there appears to be an increasing acceptance of divorce and less sanctioning of divorced persons, and thus social controls are less effective in deterring divorce. There appears to be a greater acceptance of divorce by religious institutions as indicated by more liberal annulments granted by the Roman Catholic Church, and increasing divorce among Protestant clergy. Finally, an unexplored factor may be the increased number of legal aid services that are made available to the poor who are now able to obtain divorces where desertion or separation would have been the outcome previously. The relative impact of all of these influences would be difficult to measure, but it appears that the sum of these factors is immeasurably more important than the sole factor of changing legal grounds for divorce in accounting for the increase in the divorce rates in the United States.

REFERENCES

Alabama's Vital Events. Montgomery, Alabama. Division of Vital Statistics. 1972, 1973, 1974.

Anderson, G. Wells
  1972 "New Hampshire Divorce Reform Act of 1971." *New Hampshire Bar Journal,* XIII: 4 (Spring) , 158–180.

Archbell, Roy A.
  1972 " 'No-Fault' Divorce—Iowa's Elimination of the Fault Concept Alimony Awards." *Wake Forest Law Review,* IX:1, 152–158.

Brody, Stuart A.
  1970 "California's Divorce Reform: Its Sociological Implications." *Pacific Law Journal,* I:1, 223–232.

Church, Virginia Anne
  1971 "Faults in Florida No-Fault Divorce." *Florida Bar Journal,* XXXXV: 9 (November) , 568–574.

Cline, Stephen R.
  1970 "California's Divorce Reform: Its Effect on Community Property Awards." *Pacific Law Journal,* I: 1, 310–320.

Connecticut Bar Journal
  1973 "Proposals for Revision of Connecticut Statutes Relative to Divorce." XXXXIV: 3 (September) , 411–437.

Cook, Thomas D. and Campbell, Donald T.
  1976 "The Design and Conduct of Quasi-Experiments and True Experiments in Field Settings." In Marvin D. Dunnette, ed. *Handbook of Industrial and Organizational Psychology* (Chicago: Rand McNally, pp. 223–326.

Cook, Thomas J. and Scioli, Frank P. Jr.
  1975 "Impact Analysis in Public Policy Research." In Kenneth M. Dolbeare, *Public Policy Evaluation* (Beverly Hills, California: Sage) , pp. 95–117.

Deckert, Pamela and Langelier, Regis
  1977 "A Comparative, Cross-Cultural Study of Divorced Canadians." Paper presented at the National Council on Family Relations annual meeting, San Diego, California, October 12–15, 1977.

Ferguson, Harold L. Jr.
  1973 "Incompatibility of Temperament and Irretrievable Breakdown —What Will They Mean in Alabama?" *Cumberland-Samford Law Review,* III, 3 (Fall) , 434–449.

Freed, Doris J. and Foster, Henry J. Jr.
  1977 "Family Law in the Fifty States: an Overview." *The Family Law Reporter,* III (September 6) , 4047–4052. Monograph no. 28.
  1973 "Economic Effects of Divorce (as of June 1, 1973) ." *Family Law Quarterly,* VII: 3 (Fall) , 275–343.

Furner, Joanne F. and Ohle, B. Robert.
  1972 "Fault or No-Fault Divorce for Alabama?" *The Alabama Lawyer,* XXXIII: 1 (January) , 46–57.

Gallagher, John T.
  1973 "No-Fault Divorce in Delaware." *American Bar Association Journal,* LIX: 13 (August) , 873–875.

German, Judith M.
  1973 "Dissolution of Marriage in Iowa: Collateral Determinations Under the No-Fault Concept." *Drake Law Review,* XXII: 3 (June) , 584–599.

Goddard, Wendell H.
 1972 "A Report on California's New Divorce Law: Progress and Problems." *Family Law Quarterly,* VI: 4 (Winter) , 405–421.

Gozansky, Nathan E.
 1973 "No-Fault Divorce Comes to Georgia?" *Georgia State Bar Journal,* X (August) , 9–15.

Hayes, James A.
 1970 "California Divorce Reform: Parting is Sweeter Sorrow." *American Bar Association Journal,* LVI (July) , 660–663.

Holman, Nancy Ann
 1973 "A Law in the Spirit of Conciliation and Understanding: Washington's Marriage Dissolution Act." *Gonzaga Law Review,* IX: 1 (Fall) , 39–56.

Honigman, Jason L.
 1972 "What 'No-Fault' Means to Divorce." *Michigan State Bar Journal,* LI: 1 (January) , 16–24.

Humphrey, Stephen L.
 1972 "Kentucky Divorce Reform." *Journal of Family Law,* XII (1972–73) , 109–127.

Idaho. Bureau of Vital Statistics.
 Report. 1973, 1974.

Jones, Robert B.
 1975 "The Ohio Divorce Reforms of 1974." *Case Western Reserve Law Review,* XXV, 844–875.

Kansas. Division of Vital Statistics.
 Kansas Vital Statistics: Annual Report. 1970, 1971, 1972, 1973, 1974.

Kennalley, John M.
 1975 "Domestic Relations: Incompatibility Divorce in Kansas—A Movement toward No-Fault Divorce." *Washburn Law Journal,* XIV, 349–354.

Kolb, Charles E. M.
 1977 "Vestigal Fault in No-Fault." *New Hampshire Bar Journal,* XVIII: 4, 238–249.

Lee, B. H.
 1972 "Divorce Law Reform in Michigan." *Journal of Law Reform,* V: 3 (Spring) , 409–425.

Leo, Roger J.
 1972 "Oregon's No-Fault Marriage Dissolution Act." *Oregon Law Review,* LI: 4, 715–726.

Miller, Thomas W.
 1973 "Kentucky's New Dissolution of Marriage Law." *Kentucky Law Journal,* LXI, 980–1002.

Montana. Department of Health and Environmental Sciences. Bureau of Records and Statistics. *Montana Vital Statistics.* 1974.

New Hampshire. Bureau of Vital Statistics.
 New Hampshire Vital Statistics. 1972, 1973.

Newbern, David and Johnson, Phyllis Hall.
 1974 "The Uniform Marriage and Divorce Act: Analysis for Arkansas."

Arkansas Law Review and Bar Association Journal, XXVIII: 2 (Summer) , 175–198.

North Carolina. Board of Health. Public Health Statistics Section. *Report.* 1967, 1968, 1969.

Peters, Jack W.
1971 "Iowa Reform of Marriage Termination." *Drake Law Review,* XX: 2 (January) , 211–226.

Reike, Luvern V.
1974 "The Dissolution Act of 1973: From Status to Contract?" *Washington Law Review,* IL: 2 (February) , 375–421.

Reppy, Susan Westerberg
1970 "The End of Innocence: Elimination of Fault in California Divorce Law." *UCLA Law Review,* XVII (June) , 1306–1332.

Rhode Island. Department of Public Health. Division of Vital Statistics. *Report of Birth, Marriage, Divorce and Death Statistics . . .* 1968, 1969, 1970, 1971, 1972.

Sass, Stephen L.
1973 "The Iowa No-Fault Dissolution of Marriage Law Action." *South Dakota Law Review,* XVIII (Summer) , 629–649.

Schulman, R. E.
1972 "Incompatibility: A 'New' Approach to the Dissolution of Marriage." *Kansas Law Review,* XX: 2 (Winter) , 227–237.

Scioli, Frank P. Jr. and Cook, Thomas J.
1973 "Experimental Design in Policy Impact Analysis." *Social Science Quarterly,* LIV: 2 (September) , 271–280.

Snyder, George E.
1971 "Divorce Michigan Style—1972 and Beyond." *Michigan State Bar Journal,* L: 12 (December) , 740–745.

South Carolina. Office of Vital Records. *South Carolina Vital Statistics.* 1973, 1974.

Steinbock, Delmar David Jr.
1974 "The Case for No-Fault Divorce." *Tulsa Law Journal,* X (1974– 1975) , 427–435.

Tennessee. Department of Public Health. *Annual Bulletin of Vital Statistics . . . 1972.*

Thayer, Charlotte P.
1973 "Introduction." *Journal of the Missouri Bar,* XXIX: 8 (November–December) , 496–500.

United States. National Center for Health Statistics.
1977 *Monthly Vital Statistics Report. Births, Marriages, Divorces, and Deaths for 1976.* Vol. 25, No. 12 (March 8) , p. 8.

United States. National Center for Health Statistics.
1971 *Vital Statistics of the United States.* Vol. III—*Marriage and Divorce.* 1968.

Vermont. Department of Health. Division of Public Health Statistics. *Annual Bulletin of Vital Statistics.* 1968, 1969, 1970, 1971, 1972, 1973.

Virginia. Department of Health.
 Statistical Annual Report. 1968, 1969, 1970, 1971, 1972, 1973.

Walker, Timothy B.
 1971 "Beyond Fault: An Examination of Patterns of Behavior in Response to Present Divorce Laws." *Journal of Family Law,* X, 267–299.

Wheeler, Michael
 1974 *No-Fault Divorce.* Boston: Beacon Press.

Wisconsin. State Board of Health.
 Public Health Statistics. 1968, 1969, 1970, 1971, 1972.

Zuckman, Harvey L.
 1975 "Recent Developments in American Divorce Legislation." *Jurist,* XXXV, 6–16.

20.

Some Thoughts on Divorce Reform

Paul Bohannan

What we ought to do about divorce depends not merely on our notion of divorce, but even more on what we think marriage ought to be. A divorce does not end everything about a marriage. It severs the legal contract between the husband and wife—but leaves a moral and emotional contract between ex-husband and ex-wife. It shatters the household that was based on the marriage. But it definitely does *not* break the kinship network that the children of the marriage create merely by their existence.

WHAT A DIVORCE ENDS AND HOW

Spouses do not simply cease to be associated at divorce; they become ex-husbands and ex-wives. Your wife cannot become your non-wife (as all the girls you never married might be considered); rather she becomes your ex-wife. Although it may not involve seeing her or doing anything to maintain a relationship, nevertheless the basis for a relationship and the history of a relationship are still there. It was DiMaggio who made the funeral arrangements for Marilyn Monroe. Your ex-wife or ex-husband may cease to be your responsibility in a legal sense—but in some attenuated sense or other, no matter how completely you have accomplished the psychic divorce, you choose autonomously to take a new kind of responsibility.

From *Divorce and After* copyright © 1970 by Paul Bohannan. Reprinted by permission of Doubleday & Company, Inc.

Divorce also shatters the household. This may be devastating if there are young children involved. It is the isolation of American and European households from stable and long-term association with the kinsmen of the spouses that leads to many of the sharpest problems at the time of divorce. Americans have a word for this shattered household—they need it. It is a "broken home." The single-parent household is understaffed, and hence the division of labor is altered. Our do-it-yourself world assumes both an adult male and an adult female in the household. When one or the other is not there, but children are, a harrowing lack of services results.

There is also a lack of role models for everyone in the household. The absence of father at home (no matter how present father is in every other sense) leads to a different structuring of a child's world. A good and workable relationship can be built, but it is not the same relationship. In many societies of the world, the married couple moves in with the husband's parents—and that, of course, may include all his brothers and their wives and his grandfather and his wife or wives. In these extended households, a divorce makes less difference. If the child goes with his mother at her divorce, he enters another large household—either her father's household, or that of her new husband. If he stays with his father, there are many adult females in the compound who are mothering their children, including him. He is not uniquely dependent on his very own father or mother in order to have a good idea of what fathers or mothers do.

Divorce, therefore, shatters the alliance between husband and wife—which can be rebuilt into a thinner compact between ex-husband and ex-wife. It breaks the household and so thrusts the family members into a condition in which the economic system of our society does not provide adequate services. It also disrupts the larger community in which the divorce occurs, but does not break it the same way it does the household. There is, in the community of friends nothing analogous to the kinship system which must be repaired and maintained at the time of divorce. Americans join and leave groups and communities—and divorce is just another time for regrouping, no matter how painful an experience it may be when one is undergoing the process.

What a Divorce Does Not End

Divorce never sunders a kinship relationship. And once a child is born, his parents are kinsmen to one another. Westerners have for centuries thought of kinship in terms of blood. This idea, under the pressure of modern science, has given way to the more correct expression in terms of genes, but has not changed in essence. Many other peoples of the world, however, trace kinship through descendants as well as through ancestors. Thus, through the mixture of their genes in a child, a man and woman become kinsmen—and all of their kinsmen become kinsmen of one another.

The most important thing that a divorce cannot cancel is the kinship. Moreover, if a ritual was performed at the time of marriage, no civil divorce can set it aside (although a church may choose to honor the divorce as tantamount to breaking the ritual, others do not).

Divorce does not break clean. There is always a residue to be dealt with.

What a Divorce Begins

Just as a wedding institutes a marriage, a decree institutes a divorce. The things about a marriage that a divorce decree does not end provide the basic content of the institution of divorce. Divorce is a social institution as much as marriage is. And it has a purpose, residual though it may be: the divorce must achieve the unfinished tasks of the broken family. Children must still be loved and educated; household tasks must still be done.

Divorce may be, for the participants, just as difficult an institution as the family it replaces. Although there is less pressure on divorcées today, and although divorced women are not unusual or unfairly treated (at least because of their divorces) in the labor market, there is still no public image of the way a divorce ought to be run. The divorce (like the marriage) devolves on the stability and organizing sense of the people concerned—everyone else is likely to stand back. After the searing experience of legal divorce, this new relationship will not be easy.

There is, moreover, no built-in sanction except the courts for ex-husbands and ex-wives to apply to one another. The parent-child relationships, backed by court orders when necessary, keep it together. Courts take a vast amount of time trying to make ex-husbands pay alimony and divorced fathers carry out obligations of support.

Thus, one of the areas in which we are weakest and in which a lot of social ingenuity must be put is into the contractual aspects of divorce. Our present system occupies judges, social workers, lawyers to an end for which a simpler solution would be cheaper and more comfortable. I do not know what that solution is, but we must search for one.

Divorce also begins a housing problem. The living arrangements that divorced persons must make all tend to be considered inadequate by them, unless they are single individuals with no dependents. Here are some of the solutions—most of them considered haphazard by the people who live in them.

The Bachelor Household. Bachelor apartments, for men or women, are part of the American scene and do not provide much difficulty. Therefore, the ex-spouse without the children passes into this category: "single householders." American culture provides adequate services to single householders.

The Mother-Centered Household. Just as a bachelor household can be called "individual centered" and the ordinary normal home can be called "couple centered," so the household of a divorced woman or widow is a mother-centered home. (Widows, however, do not run into the full range of complications.) We have seen that American tradition and economy are geared either to the individual-centered or the couple-centered households. The mother-centered household, on the other hand, has difficulty in carrying out the routine tasks of living, especially when children are young, because services are not provided except at the most exorbitant prices. Who does the man's job is always a problem; for children, there is a single source of both authority and affection—what we might call a direct current instead of an alternating current.

Obviously, there is a tendency in mother-centered households to search for a second adult. Several interesting forms have resulted.

The Bar-Bell Household. One not unusual form of household results from the compound of the mother-centered household with the bachelor household of the divorced husband/father. The bar-bell is composed of a house on one end, the apartment on the other, joined by an automobile. I know several instances in which reduction of interaction between spouses more or less cured their problems, so that they have been able to live for some years in these compound households. The ex-husband (and this form of household may of course occur without divorce) comes back to do some of the chores around the house—I have found no instance in which the ex-wife ever does any chores in the bachelor-household unit, but we have already seen that such services are available.

The bar-bell household offers maximum opportunity for a rapprochement between ex-spouses. I know instances in which the ex-husband sometimes eats with the mother-centered family and may ultimately come to spend two or three nights a week there, sleeping with his ex-wife.

This kind of household results when spouses are not ready to give up their associations with one another, but have never learned to live within the confines of a single house. Theirs is a tenuous solution, and this kind of arrangement is brittle, but it seems to occur with some regularity.

The Odd-Couple Household. Two men, one or both of them divorced, may try to move into a single apartment in order to save money. As Neil Simon's play, *The Odd Couple,* reported vividly, they react to one another just as they reacted to their spouses. This play is about roles, more or less independent of sex—some households (and therefore some marriages) fall apart because the close interconnection between people in a household is unbearable. Anyone who is not capable of close intimacy has trouble in an American household—it doesn't matter who the other people are.

The Inverse Odd-Couple Household. Sometimes two divorced women, both with custody, form a household. One takes care of the children of both, while the other works. Sometimes both women work, trying to dovetail their hours so that one of them is always home. They thus form a sort of dark image of the normal household. Sanctions are difficult—those based on love and kinship are seldom there, and hence one must fall back again on the weaker links of respect and good will; and the threat that if this household should break up, there is no ready substitute that provides any services at all. Not surprisingly, such households are full of tensions; they seem to be short-lived.

Sibling Households. Sometimes brother and sister, one or both with children from a broken marriage, live together in what they consider to be imitation of a normal household. Such households are usually full of tension, and there may be a great deal of guilt if there is unconscious sexual attraction between the siblings (and I venture that there often is). I have found no households made up of two sisters or of two brothers, but do not see why they should not exist. I have found one uncle-niece household that tried to imitate normal household patterns.

Grandfamily Households. Many divorced women take their children back to their own parents to form a three-generation household. I have known many who tried, few who were happy with the arrangement. The greatest difficulty is to be found in conflict for the woman between her daughter role and her mother role. Public opinion is also hostile: Her return may be interpreted (perhaps correctly) as her being tied to the apron strings. American values say very specifically that "you can't go home again."

Occasionally men are offered a place by their parents, and a few accept. My information on this type is limited—perhaps because such men do not join organizations, but I believe this is because of the rarity of the arrangement.

All these types of household have one thing in common: They show individual adaptation to an overall social situation that is poorly defined and morally unsolved. Every person in such a group feels that he has to make compromises in order to get along.

It makes little difference whether the mother-centered family is isolated in a mother-centered household or whether it is grafted onto some other form of household, the division of labor is at odds with that of the majority group. Husbands return to mow the lawn; children learn to iron shirts at a tender age; women become more or less adequate plumbers. And perhaps most important of all, they all resent it.

THE KINSHIP ASPECTS OF DIVORCE

Although divorce does not alter the relations in the kinship system, it necessarily has a great effect on the way they are carried out. The relationship between one parent and the children ceases to be any business of the other parent. If you are a man, it is now none of your business what their mother—your ex-wife—does with the children so long as she does not expose them to situations that the court (not you, the court) would consider physically or morally dangerous, and as long as you get your visitation rights. That is true even when the parents have joint legal custody.

Similarly, a divorced woman cannot control what her ex-husband does with the children when they go for vacations or visitations with their father. She cannot make issues about where they will or will not go, what he will or will not teach them to do, what influences he will or will not expose them to. Unless the court decides that what he does has a morally disruptive influence on the children, there is nothing she can do about it. It is officially none of her business. After divorce, being wife and mother no longer go together, because a man is no longer husband to the mother of his children.

Both parents have, of course, some say in the education of their children, and in some of their life decisions, but unless the ex-wife communicates about it with the ex-husband, and unless he is willing to discuss matters with her, such rights are difficult or impossible to enforce.

The difficulty shows up in many ways: the children either no longer want to stay with the mother, or they do not want ever to go with father at all, even for an afternoon. They may be grouchy and cranky, and perhaps physically ill. After such a visitation, their mother may try to stop all visitations. The father sees this as an infringement of his rights (which it is, unless she has done it with the consent of the court), and therefore uses the only weapon he has in the divorce institution—he stops child-support payments. The mother then has to go through legal channels to make him pay. It is difficult not to use the children as means of communication in all this—especially if direct communication leads to bitterness and recriminations.

The ideal of the mother image does not change on divorce. But the activities and practices of the mother must change. The responsibilities which the cultural tradition puts on a father do not change—but the means of meeting or compromising these responsibilities certainly do. The relationship among brothers and sisters may be altered—it may become more or less intense, either for good or ill.

The kinship aspects of divorce are even further complicated when remarriages ensue. Remarriage does not change divorce structurally, but only complicates it further. If marriage is not easy, divorce may be no easier. And divorce and remarriage may become almost impossibly complicated. Unless, of course, we laugh and turn it into farce—*Divorce, American Style.*

The Natural History of Divorce

It should now prove useful to create a chart of the problem areas of divorce. Some are adequately dealt with, others are dealt with badly, and some not at all. Just as some of the characteristics are accreted during courtship, others assumed at the wedding, and still others accreted during the marriage, so some of the aspects of divorce begin with erosion during marriage, some are canceled at the time of the decree, some more or less solved by the institution of divorce, and some are leftovers and not solved at all.

During courtship, the couple participate in what I have elsewhere called an adventure in intimacy,[1] as a part of which they work out an agreement to seek a major proportion of their companionship in one another, and to intertwine their lives in an emotional interdependency—what might better be called "interautonomy." Although both spouses can be independent if they like or if they are pushed to the point that they have to do so, they prefer to depend upon one another materially and emotionally. They therefore make a pact, in part presumed by the culture, in other part overtly stated. Although companionship and emotional interautonomy are subject to tremendous change and to ebb and flow during the course of a normal marriage, the foundations are usually in place before the wedding.

At the time of the wedding, a legal relationship between the spouses is cemented. This means, among other things, that in the eyes of the state and of its various communities, these two people have entered into the civil status of married people. They lose the legal right to marry again until the extant marriage is canceled, either by death or by divorce: They acquire some specific legal rights in each other.

The wedding establishes rights to form a financial unit composed of husband and wife. Many states in the United States create of this unit a property-owning corporation; all states regard financial cooperation as a requirement on the parties. In the ideal case, the husband is expected to support the wife, and the wife is expected to spend her portion of the husband's income (as well as any income of her own) wisely and judiciously.

Still at the wedding, the basis for a domestic union is recognized. The husband and wife now have claims on each other that a household will be established, and that together they will form a team to provide for the needs of one another and of their children. A choice must also be made by the spouses as to where the new household will be located. Most of the American states have laws stating that the husband has the ultimate right and duty to decide where the couple, and eventual family, shall live. The wedding also indicates community approval of sexual cohabitation.

In the course of the marriage, new characteristics are added. One of these characteristics can be called "coupleness." Coupleness is different from the emotional interautonomy that continues to grow throughout a successful marriage. Whereas emotional interautonomy is related to the psychic welfare of the two individuals and to their personal and private relationship with one another, coupleness is the way in which they function together as a unit, vis-à-vis third parties and the outside world. Many of us know of couples who function socially as a unit long after emotional interautonomy has been abandoned. These are the people who have experienced emotional divorce but have not proceeded through the rest of the stations.

With the birth of children, of course, the husband and wife take on obligations to children as well as kinship obligations to one another. Child support—both financial and emotional—is taken as a matter of course to be the responsibility of both parents.

Only two of these many aspects of marriage are unequivocally dissolved at the time of divorce. The legal relationship of spouses ends, and both are remarriageable. The law also says quite unequivocally that their legitimate sexual rights in one another are canceled. By indirection, the domestic rights are also canceled.

Though domestic rights may be canceled by a decree, domestic problems are not solved by it. The decree accomplishes only what we have called the legal divorce.

The institution of divorce is left with those problems the decree failed to solve. The institution of divorce involves a new form of financial cooperation between the ex-partners. Financial cooperation may be settled once and for all at the time of the decree, but if there are children, this financial cooperation is subject to reconsideration by the court. Child support remains the responsibility of both parents, but now their responsibilities are spelled out in somewhat greater detail—and therefore there are more loopholes. The normative sort of child support known in the course of the marriage is no longer enough to ensure the support of the children. The activities and expectations of coparents are greatly different in divorce from what they were during marriage.

Most divorcées change communities at the time of the decree, as they changed communities at the time of the wedding. Choice of community is now open to each, although the court may circumscribe the right of the parents to remove children from a specific state.

We are left with the residue—those aspects and factors of the marriage that have not been solved either by the decree or by the institution of divorce. The spiritual task of developing autonomy again; working out satisfactory emotional and training relationships with the children; creation of adequate domestic groups so that physical and emotional security of adults and children is assured; the community into which divorced people move.

DIVORCE REFORM

In discussing divorce reform, we must distinguish things we do badly and want to improve from the things we do not do at all.

Aspects of Divorce to Be Improved. The two main areas which we now deal with, but which could be improved, are the legal sphere and the psychological sphere. The legal reforms are being worked out by the Commission on Uniform State Laws, to make breakdown of the marriage replace the old idea of grounds and the adversary procedure. England adopted such a basis for divorce in 1969. California was only a few months behind. There seems today to be general agreement in a major part of the population that (without approving of divorce) we should have less painful ways of canceling those marriages that cannot be saved. The family court proposal for California is one of the most cogent of the movements in America. Here the "dissolution of the marriage" (rather than "divorce") would be heard by a court as a motion "in the interests of the John Doe family" rather than as *"Mary Doe* vs. *John Doe."*

We are also living in the midst of a growing set of programs to establish and improve mental health facilities. Some of them are turning to the problems of divorced people and their children.

Both the legal and the psychiatric professions have turned their attention to the problem. It is not primarily in the decree-granting that we are hung up—it is in the institution of divorce that follows on a decree. There less can be done because improvement demands fundamental social and cultural change. There is difficulty in financial cooperation of ex-spouses that is vastly wasteful of legal activities and the time and effort of highly trained people. And what we have is only a clumsy institution, involving the court as it does— clumsy when it works at all.

ASPECTS OF DIVORCE REFORM IN WHICH WE MUST START FROM SCRATCH

We must look to the residues on the chart—areas in which we do nothing. Americans badly need some kind of community campaign for understanding the problems that regaining emotional autonomy involve, for creating for divorced persons a positive role with a moral dimension, for creating a morality about the rights and obligations of divorced coparents that depends less fully on the courts for its sanctions and therefore is more likely to work.

Perhaps most important of all, we have to provide, hopefully through the private sector, the services required by households of divorce. If the private sector cannot do it, then government must. Both the psychic and the economic costs of running a single-parent household today are ruinous. Finally, we must deal with amending and improving the community life of divorced persons. There must be *something* besides Parents Without Partners to fill the gap between dating bars and solitude.

THE SHIELD OF IGNORANCE

The most discouraging factor for an investigator of divorce is the realization that large numbers of people, even divorced people, do not want to know anything about it. Yet, their number is, I think, dwindling. The first thing we must do to establish knowledge is to

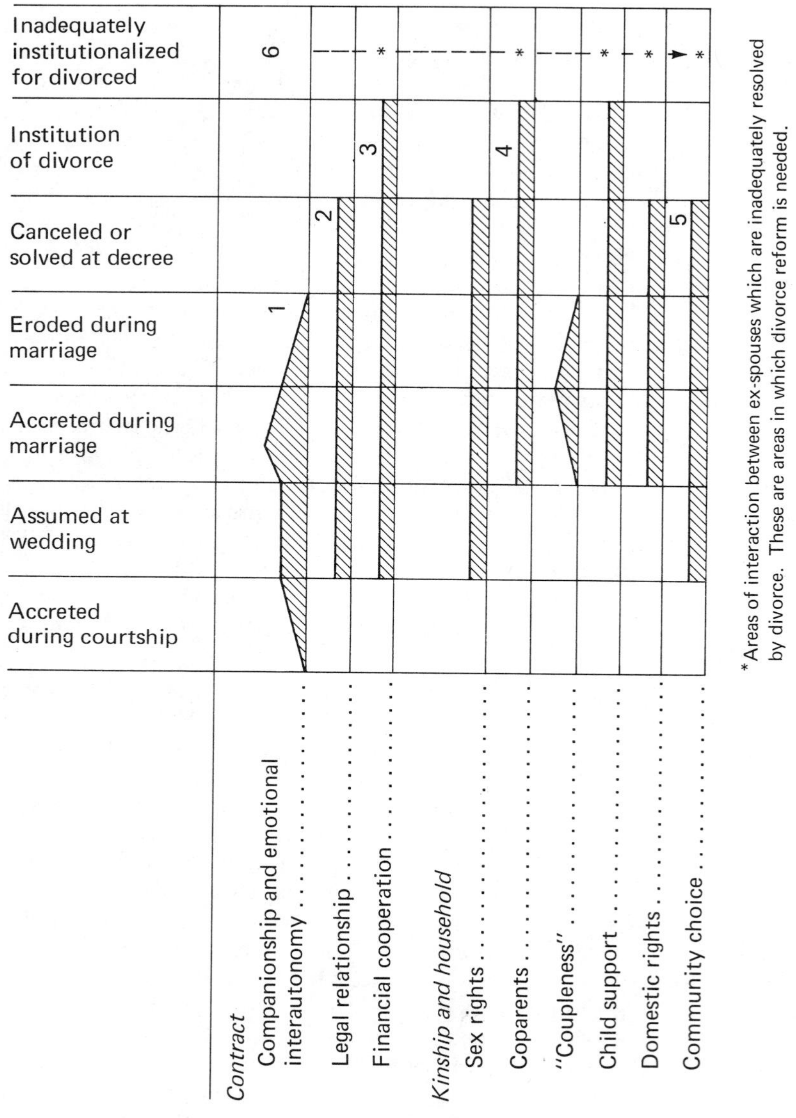

FIGURE 1. Areas of divorce reform: 1. The emotional divorce; 2. The legal divorce; 3. The financial divorce; 4. The coparental divorce; 5. The community divorce; 6. The psychic divorce.

question the trite proverb-like homilies: (1) Marriages should be saved. (2) When a marriage dies, its shell is insincere, hypocritical, or, what seems to be worst of all, cynical. (3) Easy divorce may lead to casual marriage and the demise of the family. (4) Difficult divorce may lead to unhappy and destructive marriages and the demise of the family. (5) Divorce is bad for children. Anybody who likes can add others—propositions that keep us from thinking; statements that block explanations because they masquerade as explanations.

Is Divorce Bad for Children? This is a silly question. Is polio bad for children? Of course divorce is bad for children—but living in the clogged atmosphere of emotional divorce may be worse than living in the cleared and knowledgeable atmosphere that can come with the completion of the six stations. Children need antidotes, not protection.

Although pediatricians, teachers, and psychiatrists have great funds of knowledge about the subject, little has been organized and published about the attitudes and ideas of the children themselves. The only shocking discovery of my study of divorce is the large number of divorced people who never give children any explanations, let alone adequate ones. "You can't kid kids—they know what is happening" is the refrain. The first half of the statement is undeniable—but the second half does not follow from it and is false. They know *something* is happening but, unless they are told, they seldom know what.

Easy and Difficult Divorce. I have never known a divorced person who got his divorce for silly or flimsy reasons. The grounds may have been trumped up and absurd—but the reasons were not. Ease and difficulty have little to do with grounds. Rather they have to do with the emotional tension and legal procedures that accompany divorce. Easing the grounds always follows wholesale dishonesty in using the grounds that were previously available—it is the law catching up with the community.

Although it is weakening, there is still an American penchant for resisting knowledge by claiming that it is inimical to good feelings. The homilies we have cited are old-fashioned. It is no news that new ideas are dominating the sexual, family, marriage, and divorce practices in this country. That being the case, we had better discover the new questions: How do we make the necessities of a full life available to people who happen to have failed at one of our favorite institutions? Moralize if we must—but we can no longer stop there. What is called for is massive community ingenuity. And the leaders in it will be—must be—intelligent and hard-working divorced people whose pain at their own situation has been turned to righteous wrath that society could make straightening out your life so difficult.

REFERENCE

1. Bohannan, Paul. *Love, Sex, and Being Human*. New York: Doubleday. 1969. pp. 88–91.

21.

An Amicable Divorce

Mary McDermott Shideler

Matthew and Anne Surrey
announce
an amicable divorce

Their friends and relatives
are invited not to take sides
and to keep in touch
with both of them

For the time being still
both at home at
1492 Columbus Circle
Middle City, Midwest

An amicable divorce sounds like a contradiction in terms. Usually we assume that either the couple was driven to that step by bitter conflict leading to permanent alienation if not violence, or else they had entered marriage so flippantly that its dissolution leaves them utterly indifferent to each other. Either way, the word "amicable" is not appropriate to describe the process or its aftermath.

Many people indeed, especially in our churches, are likely to feel that if the couple remains amicable, their marriage ought not to be dissolved. Marriage is too serious an affair, they believe, to be terminated unless it becomes intolerable; and when it has reached that stage, the break will necessarily be drastic. Other attitudes toward marriage and divorce are being developed, but are seldom enough understood to make it worth examining how the particular couple whom I have named Matthew and Anne Surrey approached their divorce and met certain of its problems, especially in the light of their Christian commitment and of their desire that the dissolution of their marriage, like its institution, should be solemnized with a religious ceremony.

In the dozen years of their marriage, Matt and Anne had separated twice—at least once for more than a year—in order to obtain for themselves and give each other the kind of breathing space they needed in their search for a way to solve their problems without violence. Each thoroughly liked and respected the other. They continued to share many interests. But now their relationship had become destructive of their individual selves and therefore of their union. The details do not matter. Here was simply the not uncommon situation where, in order to grow or even endure, each needed something that the other could not give without destroying his or her very identity as a person, and each was compelled to express in his or her own life something essential which undercut the other's well-being. They could laugh and weep together, but they could not build. The time had come for them to go their own ways, not bound and not keeping the other in bondage. "Nothing short of necessity," Anne told me, "could have pried us apart."

Those reasons did not satisfy the judge who presided over the final hearing. Apparently Anne's testimony that Matt had never physically abused her, that their previous separations had ended with reconciliations, and perhaps the fact that they had no children, conveyed to him an impression that they were treating the institution of marriage frivolously. And, since the divorce was not being contested, he was clearly shocked at Matt's presence in the courtroom—the more because he sat with Anne and her witness before the court was in session, the three of them conversing decorously but in as friendly a manner as if they were waiting for the curtain to rise at a theater. The judge plainly interpreted the case as one of "easy come, easy go," and his moral sensitivities were outraged. In conclusion, he said in so many words that he was exceedingly reluctant to grant this divorce, and did so only because the new laws in that state required him to.

For the legal making or breaking of a marriage, nothing more than such bare formalities is prescribed. The other rituals associated with marriage—the parties before the wedding, the ceremony in the presence of families and friends, the official announcements—are unnecessary. But they are notably enriching; they are means for initiating the couple and their associates into the new conditions of their lives. Far from being merely decorative, these rites of passage are psychologically and sociologically of great importance. Unfortunately, no such rites have yet been established for divorce, which is also the beginning of a new life. So the Surreys, recognizing their value and wanting them, improvised their own rites.

Because the Surreys are not only intelligent and perceptive but also imaginative, their rites accurately reflected their attitudes and convictions. Central for them was the affirmation that their divorce was not the cutting of a fabric but its unraveling. Their marriage was not a rag to be consigned to a trash can, but a network whose threads were to be disentangled and sorted out into those which could be used again and those which should be discarded. Moreover, they wanted to make their affirmation in both secular and religious terms. Between the time they filed for divorce and the time when Anne left town several days after it had been granted, two private and three public forms of expression emerged, not including their appearance in court.

First, together Matt and Anne told their closest friends of their intention. Together they received the brunt of the initial surprise and regret, answered any questions, and gave any explanations asked for. Whatever the procedure accomplished for them, it saved their friends from the considerable embarrassments which can follow when one party to a divorce confides individually in someone who has been close to both parties.

Second, the Surreys continued to inhabit the same house, to run their household as before, and to go places as a couple in their usual way. Partly this was because they were not financially able to maintain separate households. But also, throughout they remained friends—possibly better friends than while they were married; and the continuation of their domestic arrangements was a way of demonstrating publicly that extremely important fact. Let those who consider the Surreys' behavior another evidence of frivolity take note that, almost invariably, a request, a criticism, a gesture, will have a different impact if not a different meaning when it is made in the context of marriage and when it is made in the context of friendship or of a professional relationship (as with a priest or doctor or lawyer). Some people can be freer with each other and hurt each other less when they are not married than when they are, especially in the nuclear family where all one's emotional eggs are being carried by a single other person.

If marriage be interpreted narrowly as the licensing of sexual relations instead of broadly as the commitment to become a family, the Surreys' living together after they filed for divorce will appear scandalous. To the Surreys themselves, it was not only natural but right thus to affirm the mutual love and respect that endured even when they had discovered that the two of them could no longer constitute a family. To quote another woman, replying to her lawyer's expression of surprise that she should be so friendly with the man she was divorcing, "But I'm not married to all my friends!"

One view of marriage which is popular today says that friendship is (or should be) its basis. Another, falsely called "romanticism," says that love of a particular kind is enough for a successful marriage. Neither of these views, however, takes adequate account of the blazing truth that above all else, marriage in our society is a *working* relationship, a matter of building together a common structure by working toward a common goal: maintaining a household, bringing up children, serving the community, or whatever. In the absence of a working relationship, neither mutual love (romantic or other) nor friendship nor common interests will make a marriage more than tolerable. The essential is dedication to the same task. Husband and wife can have different vocations and occupations, and still be a family so long as their work is compatible and each is willing—and able—to serve the other in his or her vocation. But the exalted emotions are the icing on the cake, not the substance of the dinner.

The third of the Surreys' rites of passage was a party—today, the most pervasive and flexible of social rituals. Because the date of the hearing was postponed at the last minute, the observance preceded the event, but its character was in no way changed because of that dislocation.

Like all the Surreys' parties, this one was informal. Twenty or 30 people turned up in the course of the evening, many bringing contributions of beer, to sit on the floor of the tiny living room or gather where they could in the rest of the house. Many commented on how much they liked both Matt and Anne, and how sorry they were about the divorce. None in my sight or hearing criticized either by so much as a lifted eyebrow, or implied fault or blame, or seemed to think it out of place for them to announce the beginning of their lives apart with the same kind of fanfare that proclaims the beginning of a life together.

The high point of that party was the cutting of a wedding cake, complete with figures of a bride and groom on top. The company gathered about the table. Anne took the knife and Matt laid his hand on hers. They looked up to make sure that the friend who had brought his camera was ready to record the event. They brought the knife down accurately between the dolls, so that one fell over on each side. The noisy chatter started again, not quite drowning Anne's announcement that it was a spice cake, the flavor chosen for its symbolic meaning.

If the divorce had had bitter overtones, the party would have been unbearable for everyone. As it was, there was pain, but only the clean pain that characterizes even the happiest of weddings. The wound of separation is deep in marriage as well as in divorce, but it need not fester. And while its presence may give the festivities the tinge of a deeper color, it should not be allowed to dominate the pattern of rejoicing. Appropriately, emotions are mixed in an amicable divorce as well as in a happy wedding. But the priorities are kept clear, and private grief is expressed privately not because one is hypocritical, but from a sensitivity to the fitness of things. It is a grief too profound, too intimate, to be publicized.

The same intensity of feeling led the Surreys to make the religious ceremony a private one. Necessarily it was conducted in a home rather than in a church or chapel: what denomination today would sanctify a divorce? Nor has any denomination that they knew of provided such a liturgy as this, which they asked me to write for them, and which they and my husband amended slightly before it was performed on the evening of the day when their divorce decree was signed.

When Matthew and Anne arrived at our house with the two other friends they had invited, they were too keyed up from the hearing to do anything but tell their tale, with its funny moments as well as tense and sober ones. Bit by bit, the sharing of the narrative diminished their tension. When all of us were inwardly quiet, Anne put on the phonograph Egon Petrie's recording of his own transcription of "Sheep May Safely Graze." As it ended the Service for the Dissolution of a Marriage began.

> *Officiant:* Let us stand in a circle. [We did so, with Matt on his left and Anne on his right.]
>
> *All:* Oh Lord, our Lord, how excellent is thy Name in all the earth.
>
> *Officiant:* Dearly beloved, we have gathered here to solemnize the end of one time in Matthew's and Anne's lives, and the beginning of another. We are so made that we cannot live in isolation from our fellow men, but neither can we live too closely joined with them. We are social beings, but also individual selves, and it is the rhythm of union and separation that enables us to live in the communion which sustains our selves, and in the solitude which nourishes our community. As it is written: [Here he read Ecclesiastes 3: 1–8, 11–14.]
>
> Thirteen years ago, the time was right for Matthew and Anne to be joined in holy matrimony. Then they needed for their growth in grace and truth the visible bond of marriage. Now the time has come when that bond is hampering both their growth as individual persons, and their common life. They have resolved, therefore, to sever the ties of their marriage, though not of their mutual love and honor, and have asked us, their friends, to witness that affirmation of their new lives, and to uphold them in their new undertakings.
>
> Matthew Surrey, do you now relinquish your status as husband of Anne, freeing her from all claims upon and responsibilities to you except those that you willingly give to all other children of God?
>
> *Matthew:* I do.
>
> *Officiant:* Do you forgive her any sins she has committed against you, and do you accept her forgiveness, thus freeing her from the burdens of guilt and sterile remorse?
>
> *Matthew:* I do.
>
> *Officiant:* Do you release her with your love and blessing, in gratitude for the part she has played in your life, in knowledge that her part in you will never be forgotten or despised, and in faith that in separation as in union, you both are held in the grace and unity of God?
>
> *Matthew:* I do.

[The same questions were asked of Anne, and she replied in the same way.]

Officiant: Matthew, what sign do you give to Anne as a token of your forgiveness and your release of her?

Matthew: Her wedding ring reconsecrated to her freedom. [He placed it on the third finger of her right hand.]

Officiant: Anne, what sign do you give to Matthew as a token of your forgiveness and your release of him?

Anne: His wedding ring reconsecrated to his freedom. [She placed it on the third finger of his right hand.]

Officiant: Let us pray. Almighty and loving God, who has ordered that seasons shall change and that human lives shall proceed by change, we ask thy blessing upon thy children who now, in their commitment to thee, have severed their commitment to each other. Send them forth in the bond of peace. When they meet, sustain them in their liberty. Keep them both reminded that thy love flows upon and through them both. Sanctify them in their lives, deaths, and resurrections, by the power of thy Holy Spirit, and for the sake of thy Son, Jesus Christ our Lord.

All: Amen.

Officiant: The peace of God which passes all understanding keep your hearts and minds in the knowledge and love of God, and the blessing of God Almighty, the Father, the Son, and the Holy Spirit, be among you and remain with you always. Go in peace.

All: In the name of the Lord. Amen.

Spontaneously, each person put his arms around those closest him, and for several minutes there were tears and laughter, hugging and kissing, in a glorious affirmation. Awaiting them were home-made bread of that morning's baking, and wine that flashed red.

Two days later, the mail brought the last of their symbolic expressions, the notification printed in Gothic type: "Matthew and Anne Surrey announce an amicable divorce . . ."

Part
Eight

Marital Fidelity

*T*HE GENERAL PUBLIC as well as many popular writers seem to have a widespread knowledge about and understanding of marital infidelity in our society. Most believe that the majority of divorces are caused by adultery, usually on the part of the husband. Many further believe that undetected adultery, that is, undetected by the spouses of those involved, is rampant and increasing. Lurid stories concerning executives and their secretaries in the cities and lonely housewives in suburbia are widely disseminated and quite popular in the mass media.

On the other hand, social scientists, who should know whatever there is to be known about this topic, make no such claims of knowledge and understanding. Most admit that they have very few hard facts about such basic aspects of infidelity as, for example, what portion of married persons engage in it and how often. Furthermore, little is known about just what kinds of persons are most likely to be unfaithful to their spouses, what are the specific motivations for adultery, or at what points in the marriage life cycle is it more likely to occur.

Extramarital sex has traditionally been considered, both by sociologists and by the general public, to be a form of deviant behavior. Any sexual activity outside the marriage bond has been thought to constitute a threat either to the social order or to the family, or to both. However, extramarital sex has caused more concern than premarital sex, mainly because the former poses a direct threat to the family, our most hallowed institution, while the latter has threatened only virtue—as well as sometimes causing the real distress of an illegitimate pregnancy. Some states still have laws against adultery, although prosecutions under these statutes almost never occur. And, of course, adultery has been a grounds for divorce in every state, with the exception of those states which have recently revised their divorce laws to eliminate the whole concept of grounds.

Marital fidelity or infidelity really emerged as a full-blown concern in American society with the publication of the Kinsey sex studies of the late 1940's and early 1950's.[1] Until that time infidelity was thought to have occurred only rarely and the whole topic was both socially and scientifically taboo. Kinsey's findings showed that significant numbers of both men and women had engaged in extramarital affairs. Oddly enough, the Kinsey studies still continue to be the major source of social scientific data on this topic. No studies since that time have been as extensive so far as the size of the sample and the breadth of information uncovered.

According to the Kinsey data, by age 40 about half of all men and one-fourth of all women in the sample had engaged in at least one extramarital affair. These affairs were more likely to occur when the men were younger and the women older; that is, the affairs occurred early in the marriage for the men and later on for the women. This is contrary to the popular notion that men begin to wander upon reaching middle age. It also might be reflective of the fact that women usually reach their peak of sexual response about ten years later than do men. Kinsey also found that most of the affairs were sporadic adventures and one-time-only occurrences rather than the drawn-out, involved affairs of movies and fiction. Among the women who had engaged in extramarital intercourse, 41 per cent had committed adultery only once or with a single partner, another 40 per cent with from two to five partners, and the remaining 19 per cent with five or more partners.[2] It should be pointed out, however, that subsequent studies of Kinsey's sample indicated that it was likely to represent a more sexually active group than would a random cross section of the entire nation. Even so, the findings were and still are quite significant.

More recently, there have been a few studies which have focused less on determining frequencies of extramarital participation and more on the analysis of motivations, along with the uncovering of significant concomitant variables. For example, a study by Gerhard Neubeck and Vera Schletzer sought to determine the relationship between marital satisfaction and the extent of involvement in extramarital sexual relationships. Among the 40 couples studied, they found that spouses with low marital satisfaction tended to show a higher level of fantasy involvement, but when it came to actual involvement in sexual encounters, there was no relationship between satisfaction and extramarital involvement.[3] These findings, however, must be taken with caution because of the small size of the sample.

A later research study by Ralph Johnson[4] looked into the relationship between extramarital involvement (EMI) and a number of related variables such as (1) perceived opportunity, (2) desire for involvement, (3) potential for involvement, (4) justifications for involvement, (5) marital sexual satisfaction, and (6) marital adjustment. Among the findings were the facts that men perceived a much higher rate of opportunity for EMI than did women, and whether or not the woman worked outside the home made no difference with respect to her perceived opportunity. It was also found that, of those spouses who perceived an opportunity for EMI, only 40 per cent actually became involved in an affair. Of those without an opportunity, 48 per cent of the men and 5 per cent of the women said that they would like to have an affair. This does not mean, however, that they would actually become extramaritally involved if the opportunity presented itself.

Among the justifications given for EMI's were (1) spouse was handicapped, (2) spouse was having an affair, (3) spouse was unaffectionate or frigid, (4) obesity of spouse, (5) uncleanliness of spouse, (6) extended periods of separation, (7) sexually unsatisfied by spouse, (8) spouse would engage in intercourse only to get pregnant, and (9) spouse disliked sex.

With respect to the relationship between EMI and marital adjustment, Johnson's findings confirmed those of Neubeck and Schletzer noted above, that inclination to EMI did not differ among those with either high or low general satisfaction. However, those men with low marital sexual satisfaction were more often extramaritally involved than were those with high sexual satisfaction in their marriages. Care should be taken not to automatically assume that low sexual satisfaction in marriage is the cause of EMI; it may be that both are actually caused by some unknown third element. Among the women, there was no significant difference in the rate of EMI between those with high and low sexual satisfaction.

One of the most recent surveys of extramarital sexual activity is the one taken by *Playboy Magazine,* based upon a carefully selected sample of adults in the United States. In comparing their findings to those of the Kinsey studies of an earlier generation, the surprising result is the conclusion that there has been no increase in extramarital sexual activity, and some of the data indicate a possible slight decrease in extramarital sex among both men and women. Quoting from their report:

> The *Playboy* survey finds that, contrary to popular belief, sexual liberation has had little impact on traditional attitudes toward or adherence to the ideal of marital fidelity. . . . As for the new alternatives about which there is so much talk— open marriage, mate swapping, group sex, group marriage, etc.—the data suggest that they are mostly just talk.[5]

The survey also found that extramarital sex was reported by those who had engaged in it as being less satisfying sexually than their normal marital relations. It also found that the overwhelming majority of both men and women were against extramarital sex for people in general and for themselves in particular.

Without reference to further studies on the topic, a few tentative conclusions might be drawn with respect to current behavior and trends.

1. About twice as many men as women engage in extramarital affairs during married life, and for a large portion of both sexes, these are usually adventures which occur only once with one partner.

2. Adultery is rarely used as a legal grounds for divorce, and investigations of the causes of marital failure and divorce indicate that adultery is involved in less than 20 per cent of broken marriages.

3. Studies further indicate that, rather than causing marital breakups, adultery is more often simply a symptom of a sick marriage, or an indication that a marriage has already gone through the process of disintegration. One or both partners will sometimes engage in adultery as a means of subconsciously finalizing the conflict and bringing the marriage to an end.

4. There is some indication that more than in the past, spouses are willing to forgive infidelity, and there is less outside social pressure on the wronged spouse to divorce the wayward partner.

In the opening article of this part, Peter T. Chew takes a journalistic look at the topic of marital infidelity in "Charlie's Final Fling." The writer reviews some of the recent literature concerned with adultery, and then presents a hypothetical case example about "Good Old Charlie," a middle-aged man who suddenly sees life passing him by. Charlie answers the call to adventure, experiencing some of its rewards as well as its punishments of guilt and anxiety. The latter half of the article consists of analytical comments on Charlie's situation by several experts in the area of marital and extramarital behavior.

The second article takes a much more serious tone as it presents a partly historical, philosophical, and to some extent, religious point of view. In "Against Sexual Latitude," Stuart Babbage takes a consistent stance in opposition to most forms of what is often called "sexual freedom." He argues against such behavior as premarital sex, adultery, homosexuality, along with a few others, using arguments in both a moral as well as a practical vein. He takes a relatively traditional point of view, but in doing so he is aware that control of such behavior cannot be accomplished through laws passed for that purpose. As an example, he points to alcohol prohibition as well as attempts to control homosexuality, both of which have failed miserably. All in all, the article represents a summary of many of the best arguments against latitude in sexual behavior.

The third article of this part takes an unusual departure from the kinds of statements one usually hears or reads on the subject of adultery or infidelity. However, the author, Albert Ellis, is well-known for his innovative and sometimes radical ideas. In this article, called "Healthy and Disturbed Reasons for Having Extramarital Relations," he takes the position that there may very well be positive or healthy reasons for engaging in sexual relations outside of marriage, rather than viewing all extramarital sex as bad or damaging. Ellis states that the desire for sexual variety and adventure is a completely normal feeling, although he certainly does not suggest that all such desires should be followed. He feels that if one has the right motivations for extramarital sex, and if one handles the affair in such a manner as to do no harm to his marriage, then the situation might result in a healthy effect. The various motivations, psychological and social, are delineated, with some being seen as acceptable and others being deemed unacceptable. Finally, the attitudes and behavior patterns of the healthy adulterer are described. The arguments presented here are provocative and unconventional, but certainly they are worthy of full consideration.

It should be pointed out that all of the articles in this part assume, to one extent or another, that adultery is rampant and greatly increasing, contrary to some of the statistics presented earlier in this commentary. However, the majority of the comments, arguments, and opinions is not greatly affected by this particular shortcoming.

REFERENCES

1. Alfred C. Kinsey et al., *Sexual Behavior in the Human Female* (Philadelphia: Saunders, 1953).
   ———, *Sexual Behavior in the Human Male* (Philadelphia: Saunders, 1948).
2. Yoon Hough Kim, "The Kinsey Findings," *Extramarital Relations* (Englewood Cliffs, N.J.: Prentice-Hall, 1969), p. 60.
3. Gerhard Neubeck and Vera M. Schletzer, "A Study of Extramarital Relations," *Journal of Marriage and the Family*, 24:279–281 (Aug. 1962).
4. Ralph E. Johnson, "Some Correlates of Extramarital Coitus," *Journal of Marriage and the Family*, 32:449–456 (Aug. 1970).
5. Morton Hunt, "Sexual Behavior in the 1970's," *Playboy Magazine*, 21:60 (Jan. 1974).

22.

Charlie's Final Fling

Peter T. Chew

The Germans have a word for it: *Torschlusspanik,* "closed-door panic," the pursuit of younger women by middle-aged men seeking "the final fling before the gates close."

The *torschluss* syndrome is the most visible evidence of a larger psychological upheaval that overtakes all men in the middle age to some degree. Psychiatrists have only recently come to recognize the phenomenon as being as significant in its way as menopause is in women.

But if the dynamics of the final fling are only dimly understood as yet, science knows even less about its concomitant, adultery. The few studies done on infidelity agree that it is widespread in America and that its reality differs in many respects from our stereotypical conceptions. There agreement ends.

Some behavioral scientists see the extramarital affair as evidencing normal, healthy behavior. Others see it as an unhealthy symptom of deeper, unresolved conflicts with the spouse. Advocates of the situation ethic say that whether it is good or bad depends upon each individual circumstance. Still others see in our tolerance of adultery, pornography, and sexual obsessiveness of all sorts a clear threat to the institution of the family. And when the family disintegrates, they say, history has shown time and again that the civilization decays.

"The resolution of romantic love and lifelong sacramental mar-

Reprinted from *The National Observer,* September 9, 1972. Used by permission.

riage is a major clinical problem of middle-aged man," says geron-
tologist Robert Butler of Washington, D.C. "Amazingly, there is
little scientific literature available. There's no book that a man can
pick up to help him cope with his extramarital affair."

The late Dr. Alfred Kinsey's Institute for Sex Research shocked
many people in the late 1940's and early 1950's with the assertion
that at least 50 per cent of American men and at least 25 per cent
of American women engaged in extramarital relations. The foundation now believes that the post-Pill percentages are probably closer
to 60 for men and 40 for women—cause, if true, for many a side-
long glance in the nation's living rooms.

"I *know* my husband is having an affair," says a middle-aged
woman in a recent *New Yorker* cartoon. "All I want to know is
what she *sees* in him."

Kinsey was primarily concerned with the number of adulterous
episodes, perhaps because we Americans are almost as preoccupied
with statistics as we are with sex. Sociologists John F. Cuber and
Peggy B. Harroff, coauthors of *The Significant Americans: A Study
of Sexual Behavior Among the Affluent,* were more concerned with
the *context* in which adultery occurred. After interviewing nearly
450 upper-income Americans aged 35 to 55, they concluded that our
monogamous code was "a colossal unreality" based upon "common
pretense."

Virginia Satir, a marriage counselor and cofounder of the Esalen
Institute in Big Sur, Calif., has said that, "Almost every study of
sexual practices of married people today reports that the myth is
monogamy; the fact is frequent polygamy." Morton Hunt, author
of *The Affair: A Portrait of Extramarital Love in America,* considers adultery "the hidden reality" of American life. Says Hunt:

> The most common attitude toward the extramarital affair
> is somewhat like the American attitude toward paying one's
> income tax: Many people cheat—some a little, some a lot;
> most who don't would like to but are afraid; neither the ac-
> tual nor the would-be cheaters admit the truth or defend their
> views except to a few confidants; and practically all of them
> teach their children the accepted traditional code though they
> know they neither believe in it themselves nor expect that
> their children will do so when they grow up.

That Americans have a lip-smacking fascination with the Eternal
Triangle appears obvious from the public prints. The Seventh
Commandment has always been grist for the playwright and novel-
ist. Now it bids fair to replace the latest quick-weight-loss diet and
"Seven New Hairstyles for Fall" in the four-color slicks.

Thus *Town & Country* asks, "Is Infidelity a Sport?" *New York
Magazine* wonders, "Can Adultery Save Your Marriage?" and
Pageant weighs in with, "Affairs: Are More Women Having
Them?" *Lady's Circle* warns the housewife about "the other man."
Cosmopolitan encourages the "Cosmo girl" to have affairs with

married men—as long as she covers her emotional bets with a bachelor or two. *McCall's* chronicles "Husbands in Crisis." And *Washingtonian Magazine* serves up a juicy chronicle of past Presidential (and congressional) adultery.

Do the magazines truly reflect life around us? It's hard to say. But ask any attractive woman who works in an office among a lot of men. One married woman in her late 30's who went to work over a year ago for a scientific research group in a big Midwestern city says she's been propositioned by nearly every married man in her department. It would be more flattering, she added, if it weren't so routine.

> These guys are all pretty damn bright. They're tops in their fields, so they don't have the excuse of dull jobs. They all complain, "There's no excitement left with my wife any more." Then they've all gotten to this stage: "Well, do you want to go to bed or not?" At first I was shocked and disillusioned. But then I began to think, "I guess this is the way life really is!"

There is another side to that coin. One man who recently spent a year in Washington, D.C., between marriages says he was pleasantly dumfounded at the approaches he received—some oblique, some direct—from wives of friends.

Interviews about adultery with psychiatrists, marriage counselors, divorce lawyers, gynecologists, clergymen, and sexual therapists confirm that, as with a winter virus, "there's a lot of it going around."

Good Old Charlie, our middle-aged Casanova [*The National Observer,* April 5, 1971] would find—were he to seek it—widely conflicting advice from such experienced observers of human behavior.

Charlie is a stereotype. We all know him. He's not a bad guy. One day Charlie lifts his nose from the grindstone at Amalgamated Widget and says: "Hey, wait a minute. There's more to life than this damn stone!"

Shortly thereafter, *torschlusspanik* seized Charlie—in a dentist's chair while he is emerging from anesthesia. Even before his eyes open he senses her presence: a musky fragrance zephyring past his gently twitching nose; the starched rustle of her uniform . . .

Charlie phones her for lunch next day. To his amazement, she accepts. Charlie now dances from cloud to cloud bank, in his own eyes a romantic lover but in the eyes of society, an adulterer.

Charlie tells himself that he still loves his wife, Faithful Jane. He rationalizes his affair as "an escape valve" that will save his boring marriage. Yet Charlie wasn't born yesterday. "Charlie, old boy, if you've learned anything in your 40-plus years it's that you can't have it both ways in this life," says a recurrent whisper from within.

Or can he?

Some say he probably can. Dr. Albert Ellis, executive director of the Institute of Advanced Study in Rational Psychotherapy, said awhile back:

> The man who resides in a large urban area and who never once . . . is sorely tempted to engage in adultery for purposes of sexual variety is to be suspected of being indeed biologically and/or psychologically abnormal; and he who frequently has such desires and who occasionally and unobtrusively carries them into practice is well within the normal range. The good Judeo-Christian moralists may never believe it, but it would appear that healthy adultery, even in our supposedly monogamous society, *is* possible.

Prof. John Cuber of Ohio State University says (in *Extramarital Relations,* edited by Gerhard Neubeck) that we nourish, in our ignorance, many false stereotypes about adultery.

> We have inherited a morbid legacy which vigorously asserts that because of the guilt and deception involved for the participants and the feelings of humiliation and rejection experienced by the spouse, the net effect is necessarily negative to mental health. Our nonclinical sample would justify almost the opposite conclusion. . . . Overwhelmingly, these people expressed no guilt . . . although they sometimes acknowledged regret over practical consequences.
>
> The "offended" spouses were not often offended at all; sometimes they were even relieved to be out from under a relationship which was personally frustrating and, because of the adultery, they were able to maintain the marriage for other reasons.
>
> We were struck by the sizable group of people who were involved in adulterous relationships of many years standing, who were enriched and fulfilled through the relationship in much the same way that intrinsically married people are, whose health, efficiency, and creativity remain excellent. Many of these pairings are in effect *de facto* marriages.

Morton Hunt concurs. For *The Affair* he interviewed 85 unfaithful men and women. Some of the affairs proved disastrous all around; some proved benign; some proved felicitous and therapeutic to the adulterers' marriages.

Eleanore Hamilton, a Manhattan marriage counselor with a fashionable clientele, has advice for Charlie that would stun him:

> If Charlie had any guts he'd confront his wife with his sexual needs. He'd open up communications and let her see that this young woman is not a threat to her.
>
> Jane might react with hysterics. But after she's slept on the idea, she isn't going to throw Charlie out. The thing that frightens wives is that they'll be dislodged.

What is Charlie's young gal getting out of the arrangement?

> She's undoubtedly looking for instant knowledge, instant security, someone older who can introduce her to the ways of

the world. She might be looking for a surrogate father too, but most frequently I find in these cases it's strength and knowledge she's after. An older man like Charlie is much less impatient than a man her own age. He'll allow her to grow up; he'll be indulgent.

And Charlie?

A younger body, of course. He's afraid his masculinity is waning. Reassurance.

For months a book on this theme has been riding high on the best-seller lists. It is *Open Marriage: A New Life Style for Couples,* by George C. O'Neill, a City College of New York anthropology professor, and Nena, his wife of 26 years, also an anthropologist.

Man is not sexually monogamous by nature, evolution, or force of habit. In societies around the world in which he has been enjoined to become sexually monogamous in marriage he has failed. He may fail gloriously, impudently, nonchalantly, regretfully, or guiltily, but he always fails—in numbers large enough to make that failure significant. And that leads us to an inevitable question: Is it the "unfaithful" human being who is the failure, or is it the standard itself?

In open marriage you can come to know, enjoy, and share comradeship with others of the opposite sex besides your mate. These relationships enhance and augment the marital relationship in turn. These outside relationships may, of course, include sex. That is completely up to the partners involved.

Dr. Eric Riss, a Manhattan psychotherapist who has been counseling troubled married couples for more than two decades, considers the O'Neill book nonsense—dangerous nonsense. He explains:

I'm in favor of writing the popular book that explains to the layman psychological concepts that have been painstakingly arrived at through clinical work, but I get very upset by seemingly simple solutions such as this because people take them seriously—and then get very disappointed when they don't work.

For one thing, Riss says, such marriage styles have all been tried before—most notably during the moral decline of ancient Greece and Rome. For all its faults, he adds, the only form of marriage that has stood the test of time is one in which each party "can at least hope for permanence, hope for stability, hope for trust."

Riss considers the extramarital affair a symptom of

something going on in the marriage that the couple hasn't been able to deal with. The problem hasn't been talked about; it hasn't been resolved. When the degree of tension gets high enough, then one's love feelings go down. Then the fantasies start about an ideal love. The desire for extramarital sex is invariably the result of a high level of hostility.

When your friend Charlie says he's "bored" with Jane, it just isn't so. There has to be tension there—anger or rage—tension that he might not even be aware of. But this sort of thing *can* be dealt with if people are willing to work at it. So to say that extramarital affairs are desirable is to be completely oblivious to the complexities of marriage.

Many agree with Riss. "Few psychiatrists condone it [adultery] in spite of the popular mythology that psychiatry encourages sexual activity because the frustration and inhibition of sexual needs may produce mental illness," says New York City psychiatrist Leon Salzman in *The Psychodynamics of Work and Marriage,* edited by Jules Masserman.

> The concept of sexual etiology [origin] of mental disorder is often misrepresented by a greater emphasis on the adequate fulfillment of sexual needs than on the value of mature, loving relationship, both sexual and nonsexual. Some psychiatrists as well as patients who follow this notion presume that adequate treatment will free a person for a full, unrestrained, and uninhibited sexual life and justify infidelity. . . . Whether man is essentially monogamous or polygamous, there is sufficient evidence to bear out the contention that a direct relationship exists between love and the degree of fidelity in a relationship. Its [adultery's] presence, therefore, is always indicative of some degree of non-involvement or failure of commitment.

Psychologist Sallie S. Schumacher, director of the Human Sexuality Program at Long Island Jewish Medical Center in New Hyde Park, N.Y., says that few of us are emotionally equipped to swing. Even when marriage partners grant one another consent to have affairs, jealousy, envy, possessiveness, and deeper psychological difficulties invariably emerge to make life miserable for all concerned, she contends.

An attractive, socially prominent Washington, D.C., matron concurs. She has been happily married to her second husband for years, she relates, but during her unhappy first marriage, "I had a terribly wandering eye. I would lie to my husband and tell him I was going out to the movies with a friend. Then I felt so guilty about it—much as I hated him at the time—that I went upstairs to the bathroom and got violently ill."

"To most mature and loving husbands and wives, the thought of the other in another's arms is a stab of pain and fear," says Norman Sheresky, coauthor with Marya Mannes of *Uncoupling: The Art of Coming Apart.* "Right or wrong, this sense of exclusive possession is still a deep human need."

Sheresky, a lawyer, says that his experience with thousands of divorce cases has taught him that the honesty recommended by Eleanore Hamilton and the O'Neills can be a disastrous policy for Good Old Charlie. "His wife may forgive, but she will never forget," Sheresky explains.

As for the male, it's a rare bird indeed who will forgive his wife —even if he is having an affair himself. Finally, Sheresky says, most people "would be surprised to discover how many spouses simply do not want to know whether or not their mates are cheating." Jane O'Reilly, author of *The American Way of Love*, agrees.

> Some people confess their affairs because they want absolution from their mates. A wife comes home one night and confesses an affair, and her husband therefore feels justified in revealing everything he has looked at, thought, felt, touched, or had sex with for the last 15 years. That total candor can be just as damaging as Victorian secretiveness and lack of communication were.

Carle C. Zimmerman, author of the monumental history of the family entitled *Family and Civilization,* takes a poor view of schemes to loosen up the family structure. "The most prevalent idea," he wrote more than 25 years ago, "is that the family has merely to achieve the freeing of the individual to arrive at its ideal. The attitude is somewhat ambivalent: We want to retain the family but it must not interfere with our love affairs."

Indeed, Zimmerman takes an apocalyptic view of American society. He sees in our adultery, sexual obsessiveness, easy divorce, and other laxness clear historical parallels to societies when they are in moral decay. Ancient Greeks had their hetarae; the Romans had their concubines. "The question is no longer a moral one; it is social. It is no longer familistic; it is cultural. The very continuation of our culture seems to be inextricably associated with this nihilism in family behavior."

All of which should give Charlie something to think upon. As Morton Hunt concludes:

> The denial of polygamous desires will nearly always be somewhat galling, even when practiced in the name of love, while the indulgence of polygamous desires will nearly always incur some risks and costs.
>
> Yet how could it be otherwise? Any number of zealots, revolutionaries, poets, and philosophers have offered mankind Utopian solutions to its many dilemmas, but over the centuries not one of them, if put to the test, has proven ideal after all. For ideal solutions exist only in men's dreams; in their real lives, the best they can find are compromises among their warring desires.

23.

Against Sexual Latitude

Stuart Babbage

For centuries, the triple fear of conception, infection, and detection powerfully reinforced the traditional teaching of the Church that morality demanded continence before marriage, and fidelity within the marriage. Today, with the invention of the pill and the discovery of penicillin, conception has become a matter of private choice, and infection is a matter of simple remedy; while, given the freedom of modern society, the danger of being detected *in flagrante delicto* is slight, indeed.

In the 19th century, no well-brought-up girl of marriageable age would think of spending an evening alone in the compromising company of a person of the opposite sex without the discreet presence of a chaperone of unimpeachable respectability; today, society places few restrictions, if any, on what is permitted. In some men's dormitories, the rule may still be "the lights on, the door open, and both feet on the ground," but with a little ingenuity and some measure of determination, the effect of these regulations can easily be negated.

If a former generation relied heavily on the restraints of guilt and fear, these restraints have now lost much of their coercive power. Roger Shinn suggests that, if the slogan of the 19th century was "Beware of sex!" an appropriate slogan for the 20th century might be "Hurray for sex!"

Reprinted from *Sexual Latitude: For and Against,* Copyright © 1971 Hart Publishing Company, Inc.

One of the unhappy consequences of 19th century repression was, we know now, a great deal of hypocrisy and neurosis. The most innocent objects were endowed with a latent sexuality. Repression, however, is seldom successful: what is banished from waking consciousness erupts at another level in compulsive acts of morbid irrationality. Victorians found that the legs of tables and of chairs were excitingly and alarmingly erotic; the offending objects were carefully draped in the interests of decent modesty.

There was, the Victorians felt, something unclean about sex (we were born, someone noted with ill-concealed disgust, between feces and urine), and a good woman was one who was ignorant of sex and who knew nothing about the pleasures of sexual feeling. It is not surprising that there was widespread impotence on the one hand (Ruskin, Carlyle) and frigidity on the other (Charlotte Shaw). In this atmosphere of suppressed sexuality, it was widely believed that masturbation would result in curvature of the spine, insanity, and early death.

Towards the end of the century there was an increasing interest in, and attraction for, the subterranean world of sexual perversion. No doubt the public school practice of flogging contributed to the twin evils of sadism and masochism. "Who would have thought," one celebrated writer confided, "that this childhood punishment would have determined my tastes, my desires, my passions, for the rest of my life?" When the poet Coleridge heard of his old schoolmaster's death, he remarked that it was lucky that the cherubims who took him to heaven were nothing but faces and wings, or he would inevitably have flogged them on the way. Swinburne was preoccupied with the delights of flagellation; and whipping is prominent in much of the underground literature of the Victorian Era.

Oscar Wilde's notorious trial at the end of the century threw a lurid light on the ramifications of London's sordid homosexual underworld.

It would, however, be hypocritical for an age which finds an irresistable fascination in the bisexuality and predatory homosexuality of Myra Breckinridge and in Portnoy's compulsive masturbation to sit in smug and self-righteous judgment on the sexual activities of the Victorians. Like us, they were not innocent; like us, they had their hang-ups; but what, for them, was secret and always furtive is, for us, open and unashamed. The fear and anxiety of the Victorian Age is a thing of the past; what has taken its place is the uninhibited exuberance of the love generation ecstatically proclaiming the delights of polymorphous sex.

In the state of Illinois, homosexual acts between consenting adults in private are no longer a basis for criminal prosecution. In the state of New York, abortion during the first 24 weeks of pregnancy is a matter of personal decision. In relation to this tendency towards liberalization, the one exception is pornography. Rigid standards of censorship still apply for the most part.

We are discovering, however, that pornography is still a billion dollar business. The question is whether the problem can be solved by means of legal censorship. What is forbidden becomes, by that very fact, desirable. Augustine, in his *Confessions,* relates that, as a boy he delighted to rob orchards, not because he was hungry (in fact there were better apples in the garden at home) but because it was forbidden. The Apostle Paul says the same thing: "I had not known sin, except the law had said, thou shalt not covet."

The attempt to impose temperance on the American nation during the days of Prohibition was a calamitous and unhappy failure. Santayana rightly observes that those who refuse to accept the lessons of history are doomed to repeat them; with this recent example before us, we are seeking, once again, to prescribe, by means of the law, what is suitable reading for the public. Paradoxically, the attempt to suppress pornography by means of legal censorship is to guarantee its highly remunerative clandestine sale.

Denmark has already lifted its ban on the sale of pornography; and, according to reports, the result has been a dramatic slump in sales. There is no longer an inexhaustible demand for what is freely available, for in Denmark, pornography no longer has the attraction of the forbidden.

We need, of course, to protect minors from premature and undesirable exposure to what is salacious and obscene. There is, in America today, a great deal of what might be termed "sick sex." In relation to the sale of pornography, we need to do what we do in relation to the sale of alcoholic drinks: prohibit its sale to minors. Experience would suggest, however, that a normal child is not aroused but merely bored by sexual nudity.

The members of the commission responsible for the production of the Wolfenden Report made an important point which is relevant in this connection. They distinguished between what concerns the public welfare and what is more properly a matter of private morality. There are certain matters, they pointed out, which are not the law's business. Provided there is no public scandal, what happens in the bedroom is not the law's business. That is why they recommended that homosexual acts between consenting adults in private should no longer be regarded as a criminal offense. They pointed out that they were not concerned with the morality of such acts. They were concerned, not with sin, but with crime. They concluded:

> Where adultery, fornication and lesbian behavior are not criminal offences, there seems to us to be no valid ground, on the basis of damage to the family, for so regarding homosexual behavior between men.

They reiterated that they were not seeking to condone or encourage private immorality.

> On the contrary, to emphasize the personal and private nature of moral or immoral conduct is to emphasize the personal and

private responsibility of the individual for his own actions, and that is a responsibility that a mature agent can properly be expected to carry for himself without the threat of punishment from the law.

The compilers of this celebrated report rightly recognized that the best kind of morality is not that which is legally imposed but that which is freely embraced.

Christians gratefully acknowledge that sex is one of God's good gifts and that it has been given to us richly to enjoy. Sexual intercourse is an experience of the most intimate and intense kind. In the act of sexual intercourse two persons become, in a profound and mysterious sense, "one flesh." Intercourse, in relation to two persons who truly love one another, symbolizes and also seals an underlying unity of heart and mind. It is love which gives to intercourse its sanctity and significance; and within marriage, it is through repeated acts of intercourse that love is strengthened and renewed. Sexual intercourse, apart from love, is in Shakespeare's graphic words "lust in action."

Sex finds its proper fulfillment in marriage. According to the Judeo-Christian tradition, the institution of marriage predates the Fall. Traditionally, the Church has taught that marriage serves three ends:

1. It serves, in the first place, a biological purpose. It is the means by which children are propagated and the race is continued.
2. It serves as a means for the expression of sexual desire.
3. It serves the end of companionship.

God's first command was not, Milton notes, "Be fruitful and multiply," nor was it, "It is better to marry than to burn;" it was rather that "It is not good for man to be alone." And he observed *"Loneliness is the first thing which God's eye named not good."*

It is in the light of these purposes that we turn to a discussion of some of the controversial issues of our day.

PREMARITAL SEX

A distinction needs to be made between those who, anticipating marriage, participate in the act of sexual intercourse, and those who, being unmarried, practice promiscuity. Concerning the former, little needs to be said. The relationship, though lacking the full sanction and support of society, is nevertheless an expression of a real and prior commitment of heart and mind.

True love is always, by its very nature, exclusive. The phrase "free love" is a contradiction in terms: if it is free, it is not love; and if it is love, it is not free.

G. K. Chesterton makes the point that true lovers always use the language of eternity. That is why in the marriage service the promises are unconditional. The bridegroom, taking the right hand of the bride with his right hand, says:

> I . . . take thee . . . to my lawful wedded wife, to have and
> to hold, from this day forward, for better for worse, for
> richer for poorer, in sickness and in health, till death us do
> part, and thereto I pledge thee my troth.

There may be reasons why a couple, whose relationship is stable
and steadfast, should anticipate the marriage act. Marriage, however, has public consequences as well as private; that is why it is
fitting that those who intend to live together as man and wife
should publicly proclaim, by certain procedures, their willingness
to accept, not only the privileges, but also the responsibilities of
marriage.

For a couple for whom faith is meaningful there is, of course, a
more compelling reason: the desire to do that which is honorable,
not only in the sight of man, but also in the sight of God. For such
a couple there is something more important than the good wishes
and approval of society; there is the question of the blessing and
approbation of God.

Whether the ceremony is civil or religious, what is important is
the full and free commitment that each makes to the other. The
authentic language of true love is always: "My beloved is mine and
I am his."

If the marriage is not physically consummated, it is, in the eyes
of the church and of the state, null and void. It lacks the mutuality
of full and free surrender which constitutes the essence of marriage.
Without such physical consummation, the commitment of each to
the other is less than total. If coitus without co-existence is demonic
(Barth), co-existence without coitus is to invite certain temptation
by the devil (St. Paul).

True love is, by its very nature, self giving. In the act of intercourse the man gives himself to the woman, and the woman gives
herself to the man. For each, it is an act of joyous self-surrender: a
breathless dialectic of self-forgetfulness and self-fulfillment. For the
man, it is associated with a joyous sense of exhilarating achievement; for the woman, with an equally joyous sense of ecstatic
abandon. For both, the act of intercourse is the symbol and the
seal of co-existence; it is love's proper prerogative and supreme
privilege.

In relation to premarital sex, the important thing is the nature
of the relationship between the parties. In the case of an engaged
couple, there is already a real measure of public commitment; in
the case of the single person who is out to have a good time, what
we have is the selfish desire to enjoy love's privileges without accepting love's responsibilities.

CASUAL SEX

There could hardly be a greater contrast than that between an
authentic love relationship with its revolutionary consequences for
the life of each, and the fleeting coming together of two unrelated
persons in a relationship which is casual and often commercial.

Once, the pickup girl served the needs of casual sex; today, the needs of casual sex are served for the more sophisticated, by the call-girl system. The important thing about casual sex is that there are no strings attached. From the point of view of the fancy-free businessman, it has the additional (and vital) advantage of providing a convenient cloak of anonymity. One's identity can remain secret.

The basic presupposition of casual sex is that one does not get involved. There is no commitment beyond the fee. What, for true lovers, is an intensely personal relationship is degraded to the level of the commercial.

Geoffrey Gorer, the anthropologist, points out that there appears to be, in primitive society, a direct correlation between high rates of intercourse and lack of emotional interest or belief in love. For a society that believes in love (be it sacred or profane), the physiological aspect of love cannot be separated from the emotional, psychological concomitants without reducing it to meaninglessness. That is what casual sex does: it reduces love to meaninglessness. The act of sexual intercourse becomes a trigger mechanism divorced from genuine personal feelings of any significant kind.

If promiscuity is a poor preparation for the discipline and delights of marriage, casual sex is also incompatible with the institution of monogamous marriage. Kipling recognized this when he wrote:

> The more you've known of the many
> The less you will settle to one.

Adultery—to give casual sex its proper name—makes nonsense of the concept of marriage as "one flesh;" and in the expressive language of the Eastern Orthodox Church, is the "death of marriage."

GROUP SEX

The objection to group sex is that it makes sex cheap. It trivializes the nature of the sexual experience. It makes what should be private and holy, commonplace and ordinary. It robs sex of its mystery and sanctity. For true lovers, the act of sexual intercourse is something more than the experience of mutual orgasm: it is a vehicle for the expression of feelings which, in their emotional intensity, are too deep for words.

Group sex has nothing to do with love; it converts what should be private and holy into an occasion for voyeurism and exhibitionism and competitive rivalry.

There is something depressing as well as degrading about the concept of group sex: it irresistibly reminds one of a group of sweaty adolescents experimenting with group masturbation.

SEXUAL EXPERIMENTATION

There are some who argue that since sex is a personal matter, there are no limits to what an individual may do, except those limits the individual imposes on himself. This presupposes an individualistic, atomic view of society. We do not, in other areas of life, accept the view that a man may do what he likes; we insist that there are limits.

In this life, pleasure is always the by-product of something else: like the pot of gold at the rainbow's end, it eludes those who make it their goal. It is not by indiscriminate and inordinate indulgence, nor by desperate strategies of experimentation, that we heighten and intensify sexual feeling. It is by accepting the fact that there are limits, not only to what is possible but to what is permissible, that we enjoy Eros's elusive rewards.

What is possible is physiologically determined—there is, after all, a mathematical limit to the number of positions available for coitus. What is permissible is determined by our understanding of the place of sex in the life of man.

The normal avenue for the expression of sexual desire is marriage. There are a few who achieve the difficult art of self-control through sublimation: witness the life of Jesus. For the religious man, the goal is continence before marriage, and fidelity within marriage. For those who reject these traditional standards as normative, the alternatives, apart from self-control, are promiscuity and perversion.

Shakespeare aptly described the life of promiscuity as "a waste of spirit in a desert of shame." Norman Mailer speaks satirically of those who are forever seeking an orgasm more apocalyptic than the one that went before. They are set on a fool's quest. In this realm, as in all others, the law of diminishing returns applies.

HOMOSEXUALITY

The supporters of the "gay" revolution may argue that, under the Constitution, they have certain inalienable rights, among which are life, liberty, and the pursuit of happiness. Homosexuality, they say, is no more sinful than left-handedness. Admittedly, homosexuality, like left-handedness, is often a congenital condition, and therefore a matter for pity rather than blame. In a right-handed world, left-handedness is, nevertheless, a disability and a hindrance; in a straight world, homosexuality is undoubtedly an affliction and a handicap. We do not serve the needs of those who are homosexual by pretending that this is not so.

Homosexuality is an anomaly. There is, in the sexual realm, a difference between what is normal and what is abnormal, what is natural and what is unnatural.

Sexual differentiation serves a basic biological purpose. Gore Vidal argues that in the interests of population control, homosexuality ought to be encouraged rather than discouraged; but the question is whether he is persuading anyone other than himself.

Homosexuality may be a stage on the road to maturation: in an adult, it is invariably a sign of arrested psychological development.

Homosexuality is not admirable. The fact that a substantial minority of the population is, by choice or conditioning, homosexual is an eloquent witness to the tragic disorder of our society. The remedy is not in the threat of punishment; rather it is in the example of a more excellent way.

FETISHISM

What attitude are we to adopt in relation to the person who has made some non-sexual object or thing the object of his irresistible desires and sexual expression? Are we to adopt the view that, in the realm of human sexuality, all is permitted, or are we to say that there is a norm to which we ought to seek to conform?

The advocates of permissiveness argue that each man ought to do his own thing, and that we ought to establish commercial houses and social clubs to cater to the needs of those whose tastes are unorthodox and bizarre. Kinsey, in his classic studies on the behavior of the human male and human female, demonstrated that men and women are capable of a wide variety of sexual activities, from sexual contacts with animals to human heterosexual intercourse. There is, however, a qualitative difference between intercourse with an animal and intercourse with a human being.

The same considerations apply to fetishism. Fetishism undoubtedly represents a form of highly individualistic sexual activity; the question is the *quality* of the activity. The victim of fetishism is doing his own thing, but what he is doing is pathetic and pathological. Fetishism is a miserable and pitiable travesty of normal sexuality.

The advocates of an undiscriminating, non-judgmental permissiveness are not kind but cruel. By condoning behavior that is bizarre, grotesque, and patently absurd, they are condemning the unhappy victims of this perversion to perpetual servitude. The man who is a victim of fetishism needs help. It is hypocritical and grossly untrue to say that one thing is as good as another.

All great literature, whether drama or poetry or fiction, has as its theme the consuming experience of love. In the words of the *Song of Solomon,* love is not only "as strong as death, but a most vehement flame." Love finds its most perfect and classic expression, not in the twisted and tormented desires of the perverted and the promiscuous, but in the deep and abiding love of a man for a woman.

24.

Healthy and Disturbed Reasons for Having Extramarital Relations

Albert Ellis

Psychologists and sociologists, as Whitehurst points out, tend to look upon extramarital relations as an unusual or deviant form of behavior and to seek for disturbed motivations on the part of husbands and wives who engage in adulterous affairs. Although there is considerable clinical evidence that would seem to confirm this view, there are also studies—such as those of Kinsey and his associates (11, 12) and of Cuber and Harroff (1)—which throw considerable doubt on it. In my own observations of quite unusual adulterers—unusual in the sense that both partners to the marriage agreed upon and carried out extramarital affairs and in many instances actually engaged in wife-swapping—I have found that there are usually both good and bad, healthy and unhealthy reasons for this type of highly unconventional behavior (4) ; and if this is true in these extreme cases, it is almost certainly equally true or truer about the usual kind of secret adulterous affairs that are much more common in this country.

Let me now briefly review what I consider to be some of the main healthy and disturbed reasons for extramarital unions. My material for the following analysis comes from two main sources: (1) clinical interviews with individuals with whom I have had psychotherapy and marriage and family counseling sessions; (2) unofficial talks with scores of non-patients and non-counselees whom I have en-

Reprinted from Gerhard Neubeck, Ed., *Extramarital Relations*, © 1969. Reprinted by permission of Prentice-Hall, Inc., Englewood Cliffs, N.J.

countered in many parts of this country and who are presumably a fairly random sample of well-educated middle-class adults, most of whom have been married for five years or more. Although the first group of my interviewees included a high percentage of individuals whose marriages were far from ideal and were in many cases quite rocky, the second group consisted largely of individuals who had average or above-average marriages and who were, at the time I spoke to them, in no danger of separation or divorce.

From my talks with these individuals—some of which were relatively brief and some of which took, over a series of time, scores of hours—I am inclined to hypothesize the following healthy reasons for husbands and wives, even when they are happily married and want to continue their marital relationships, strongly wanting and doing their best to discreetly carry on extramarital affairs:

Sexual Varietism. Almost the entire history of mankind demonstrates that man is not, biologically, a truly monogamous animal; that he tends to be more monogynous than monogamic, desiring one woman at a time rather than a single woman for a lifetime, and that even when he acts monogynously he craves strongly occasional adulterous affairs in addition to his regular marital sex. The female of the human species seems to be less strongly motivated toward plural sexuality than is the male; but she, too, when she can have varietistic outlets with social impunity, quite frequently takes advantage of them (5).

A healthy married individual in our society is usually able to enjoy steady sex relations with his spouse; but he frequently tends to have *less* marital satisfaction after several years than he had for the first months or years after his wedding. He lusts after innumerable women besides his wife, particularly those who are younger and prettier than she is; he quite often enhances his marital sex enjoyment by thinking about these other women when copulating with his spouse; he enjoys mild or heavy petting with other females at office parties, social gatherings, and other suitable occasions; and he actually engages in adulterous affairs from time to time, especially when he and his wife are temporarily parted or when he can otherwise discreetly have a little fling with impunity, knowing that his spouse is not likely to discover what he is doing and that his extramarital affair will not seriously interfere with his marriage and family life. The man who resides in a large urban area and who never once, during thirty or more years of married life, is sorely tempted to engage in adultery for purposes of sexual variety is to be suspected of being indeed biologically and/or psychologically abnormal; and he who frequently has such desires and who occasionally and unobtrusively carries them into practice is well within the normal healthy range.

Love Enhancement. Healthy human beings are generally capable of loving pluralistically, on both a serial and a simultaneous basis.

Although conjugal or familial love tends to remain alive, and even to deepen, over a long period of years, romantic love generally wanes in from three to five years—particularly when the lovers live under the same roof and share numerous unromantic exigencies of life. Because romantic love, in spite of its palpable disadvantages, is a uniquely exciting and enlivening feeling and has many splendid repercussions on one's whole life, a great number of sensible and stable married individuals fall in love with someone other than their spouses and find, on some level, a mutual expression of their amative feelings with these others. To be incapable of further romantic attachments is in some respects to be dead; and both in imagination and in practice hordes of healthy husbands and wives, including those who continue to have a real fondness for their mates, become involved in romantic extramarital affairs. Although some of these affairs do not lead to any real sexual actualization, many of them do. The result is a great number of divorces and remarriages; but, in all probability, the result is an even greater number of adulterous love affairs that, for one reason or another, do not lead to legal separation from the original mate but which are carried on simultaneously with the marriage.

Experiential Drives. Loving, courting, going to bed with, and maintaining an ongoing relationship with a member of the other sex are all interesting and gratifying experiences, not only because of the elements of sex and love that are involved in these happenings but also because the sex-love partners learn a great many things about themselves and their chosen ones, and because they experience thoughts, feelings, and interchanges that would otherwise probably never come their way. To live, to a large degree, is to relate: and in our society intimate relationships usually reach their acme in sex-love affairs. The healthy, experience-hungry married individual, therefore, will be quite motivated, at least at times during his conjugal life, to add to the experience which he is likely to obtain through marriage itself, and often to return to some of the high levels of relating with members of the other sex which he may have known before he met his spouse. His desires to experiment or to re-experience in these respects may easily prejudice him in favor of adultery—especially with the kinds of members of the other sex who are quite different from his mate, and with whom he is not too likely to become closely related outside of his having an extramarital liaison.

Adventure Seeking. Most people today lead routinized, fairly dull, unadventurous lives; and their chances of fighting the Indians, hunting big game in Africa, or even trying a new job after working in the same one for a decade or more are reasonably slim. One of the few remaining areas in which they can frequently find real excitement and novelty of a general as well as a specifically sexual nature is in the area of sex-love affairs. Once this area is temporarily closed by marriage, child-rearing, and the fairly scheduled pursuits that tend to accompany domestic life, the healthy and still adventure-seeking person frequently looks longingly for some other outlets; and he or she is likely to find such outlets in extramarital relationships. This does not mean that all life-loving mates must eventually try to jazz up their humdrum existences with adulterous affairs; but it does mean that a certain percentage of creative, adventure-seeking individuals will and that they will do so for reasonably sensible motives.

Sexual Curiosity. Although an increasing number of people today have premarital sex experiences and a good number also have sex affairs between the time their first marriage ends by death or divorce and their next marriage begins, there are still many Americans, especially females, who reach the age of forty or fifty and have had a total of only one or two sex partners in their entire lives. Such individuals, even when they have had fairly satisfactory sex relations with their spouses, are often quite curious about what it would be like to try one or more other partners; and eventually a good number of them do experiment in this regard. Other individuals, including many who are happily married, are driven by their sex curiosity to try extramarital affairs because they would like to bring back new techniques to their own marriage bed, because they want to have at least one orgiastic experience before they die, or because some other aspect of their healthy information-seeking in sexual areas cannot very well be satisfied if they continue to have purely monogamous relations.

Social and Cultural Inducements. Literally millions of average Americans occasionally or frequently engage in adultery because it is the approved social thing to do at various times and in certain settings which are a regular part of their lives. Thus, normally monogamous males will think nothing of resorting to prostitutes or to easily available non-prostitutes at business parties, at men's club meetings, or at conventions. And very sedate women will take off their girdles and either pet to orgasm or have extramarital intercourse at wild drinking parties, on yacht or boat cruises, at vacation resorts, and at various other kinds of social affairs where adulterous behavior is not only permitted but is even expected. Although Americans rarely engage in the regular or periodic kinds of sex orgies which many primitive peoples permit themselves in the course of their married lives, they do fairly frequently engage in occasional orgiastic-like parties where extramarital affairs are encouraged and sometimes become the rule. This may not be the healthiest kind of adulterous behavior but it is well within the range of social normality and it often does seem to satisfy, in a socially approved way, some of the underlying sensible desires for sexual experience, adventure, and varietism that might otherwise be very difficult to fulfill in our society.

Sexual Deprivation. Many husbands and wives are acutely sexually deprived, either on a temporary or permanent basis. They may be separated from each other for reasons beyond their control—as when the husband goes off on a long business trip, is inducted into the armed forces, or is in poor physical health. Or they may live together and be theoretically sexually available to each other, but one of them may have a much lower sex drive than the other, may be sexually incompetent, or may otherwise be an unsatisfying bed partner even though he or she is perfectly adequate in the other aspects of marital life. Under such circumstances, the deprived mate can very healthfully long for and from time to time seek out extramarital affairs; and in many such instances this mate's marriage may actually be benefited by the having of such affairs, since otherwise acute and chronic sexual deprivation in the marriage may encourage hostilities that could easily disrupt the relationship.

The foregoing reasons for engaging in extramarital affairs would all seem to be reasonably healthy, though of course they can be mixed in with various neurotic reasons, too. Nor do these reasons exhaust the list of sane motivations that would induce many or most married individuals to strongly desire, and at times actually to have, adulterous liaisons. On the other side of the fence, however, there are several self-defeating or emotionally disturbed impulses behind adultery. These include the following:

Low Frustration Tolerance. While almost every healthy married person at times desires extramarital affairs, he does not truly need to have them, and he can usually tolerate (if not thoroughly enjoy) life very well without them, especially if his marriage is relatively good. The neurotic individual, however, frequently convinces himself that he needs what he wants and that his preferences are necessities. Consequently, he makes himself so desperately unhappy when he is sexually monogamous that he literally drives himself into extramarital affairs. Being a demander rather than a preferrer, he then usually finds something intolerable about his adulterous involvements, too; and he often winds up by becoming still more frustrated, unhappier, and even downright miserable and depressed. It is not marriage and its inevitable frustrations that bug him; it is his unreasonable expectation that marriage should not be frustrating.

Hostility to One's Spouse. Low frustration tolerance or unrealistic demandingness leads innumerable spouses to dislike their partner's behavior and to insist that the partner therefore ought not be the way he or she is. This childish insistence results in hostility; and once a married person becomes hostile, he frequently refuses to face the fact that he is making himself angry. He vindictively wants to punish his mate, he shies away from having sex with her (or encourages her to shy away from having sex with anyone who is as angry at her as he is), and he finds it much easier to have satisfactory social-sexual relations with another woman than his wife. He usually solves his problem only temporarily by this method, since as long as he remains anger-prone, the chances are that he will later become hostile howard his adulterous inamorata, and that the same kind of vicious circle will occur with his relations with her.

Self-deprecation. A great number of spouses are so perfectionistic in their demands on themselves, and so self-castigating when they do not live up to these demands, that they cannot bear to keep facing their mates (who are in the best positions to see their inadequacies). Because they condemn themselves for not being excellent economic providers, housekeepers, parents, sex partners, etc., they look for outside affairs in which fewer demands will be made on them or where they will not expect themselves to act so perfectly; and they feel more "comfortable," at least temporarily, while having such affairs, even though the much more logical solution to their problem would often be to work things out in their marriages while learning not to be so self-flagellating.

Ego-bolstering. Many married men feel that they are not really men and many married women feel that they are not really women unless they are continually proving that they are by winning the approval of members of the other sex. Some of them also feel that unless they can be seen in public with a particularly desirable sex partner, no one will really respect them. Consequently, they continually seek for conquests and have adulterous affairs to bolster their own low self-esteem rather than for sexual or companionship purposes.

Escapism. Most married individuals have serious enough problems to face in life, either at home, in their work, in their social affairs, or in their attitudes toward themselves. Rather than face and probably work through these problems, a number of these spouses find it much easier to run to some diverting affairs, such as those that adultery may offer. Wives who are poor mothers or who are in continual squabbles with their parents or their in-laws can find many distracting times in motel rooms or in some bachelor's apartment. Husbands who won't face their problems with their partners or with their employees can forget themselves, at least for an afternoon or an evening, in some mistress's more than willing arms. Both husbands and wives who have no vital absorbing interests in life, and who refuse to work at finding for themselves some major goal which would give more meaning to their days, can immerse themselves in adulterous involvements of a promiscuous or long-term nature and can almost forget about the aimlessness of their existences. Naturally, extramarital affairs that are started for these reasons themselves tend to be meaningless and are not vitally absorbing. But surely they are more interesting than mahjongg and television!

Marital Escapism. Most marriages in many respects leave much to be desired; and some are obviously completely blah and sterile and would better be brought to an end. Rather than face their marital and family problems, however, and rather than courageously arrange for a separation or a divorce, many couples prefer to avoid such difficult issues and to occupy themselves, instead, in extramarital liaisons, which at least sometimes render their marriages slightly more tolerable.

Sexual Disturbances. Sexual disturbances are rather widespread in our society—particularly in the form of impotence or frigidity of husbands and wives. Instead of trying to understand the philosophic core of such disturbances, and changing the irrational and self-defeating value systems that usually cause them (2, 3, 6, 7, 8, 9, 10), many husbands and wives follow the line of least resistance, decide to live with their sexual neuroses, and consequently seek out non-marital partners with whom they can more comfortably retain these aberrations. Thus, frigid wives, instead of working out their sexual incompatibilities with their husbands, sometimes pick a lover or a series of lovers with whom they are somewhat less frigid or who can more easily tolerate their sexual inadequacies. Impotent husbands or those who are fixated on some form of sex deviation, rather than getting to the source of their difficulties and overcoming them in their relations with their wives, find prostitutes, mistresses, or homosexual partners with whom they can remain comfortably deviant. In many instances, in fact, the spouse of the sexually disturbed individual is severely blamed for his or her anomaly, when little or no attempt has been made to correct this anomaly by working sexually with this spouse.

Excitement Needs. Where the healthy married person, as shown previously in this paper, has a distinct desire for adventure, novelty, and some degree of excitement in life and may therefore be motivated to have some extramarital affairs, the disturbed individual frequently has an inordinate need for excitation. He makes himself, for various reasons, so jaded with almost every aspect of his life that he can only temporarily enjoy himself by some form of thrill-seeking such as wild parties, bouts of drunkenness, compulsive moving around from place to place or job to job, or drug-taking. One of the modes of excitement-seeking which this kind of a disturbed person may take is that of incessantly searching for extramarital affairs. This will not cure his basic jadedness, but will give him surcease from pain for at least a period of time—as do, too, the alcohol and drugs that such individuals are prone to use.

If the thesis of this paper is correct, and there are both healthy and unhealthy reasons for an individual's engaging in extramarital sex relations, how can any given person's motives for adultery be objectively assessed? If Mrs. X, a housewife and mother of two children, or Mr. Y, a businessman and father of a teenage son, get together with other single or married individuals and carry on adulterously, how are we to say if one is or both are driven by sane or senseless motives? The answer is that we would have to judge each case individually on the basis of much psychological and sociological information, to determine what the person's true impulses are and how neurotic or psychotic they seem to be. To make such judgments, however, some kind of criteria have to be drawn up; and although this is difficult to do at present, partly because of our still limited knowledge of healthy individuals and social norms, I shall take a flyer and hazard an educated guess as to what these criteria might possibly be. Judging from my own personal, clinical, and research experience, I would say that the following standards of healthy adulterous behavior might be fairly valid:

1. The healthy adulterer is non-demanding and non-compulsive. He prefers but he does not need extramarital affairs. He believes that he can live better with than without them, and therefore he tries to arrange to have them from time to time. But he is also able to have a happy general and marital life if no such affairs are practicable.
2. The undisturbed adulterer usually manages to carry on his extramarital affairs without unduly disturbing his marriage and family relationships nor his general existence. He is sufficiently discreet about his adultery, on the one hand, and appropriately frank and honest about it with his close associates, on the other hand, so that most people he intimately knows are able to tolerate his affairs and not get too upset about them.
3. He fully accepts his own extramarital desires and acts and never condemns himself or punishes himself because of them, even though he may sometimes decide that they are unwise and may make specific attempts to bring them to a halt.
4. He faces his specific problems with his wife and family as well as his general life difficulties and does not use his adulterous relationships as a means of avoiding any of his serious problems.
5. He is usually tolerant of himself when he acts poorly or makes errors; he is minimally hostile when his wife and family members behave in a less than desirable manner; and he fully accepts the fact that the world is rough and life is often grim, but that there is no reason why it *must* be otherwise and that he can live happily even when conditions around him are not great. Consequently, he does not drive himself to adultery because of self-deprecation, self-pity or hostility to others.
6. He is sexually adequate with his spouse as well as with others

and therefore has extramarital affairs out of sex interest rather than for sex therapy.

Although the adulterer who lives up to these criteria may have still other emotional disturbances and may be having extramarital affairs for various neurotic reasons other than those outlined in this paper, there is also a good chance that this is not true. The good Judeo-Christian moralists may never believe it, but it would appear that healthy adultery, even in our supposedly monogynous society, *is* possible. Just how often our millions of adulterers practice extramarital relations for good and how often for bad reasons is an interesting question. It is hoped that future research in this area may be somewhat helped by some of the considerations pointed out in the present paper.

REFERENCES

1. Cuber, John F., and Harroff, Peggy B. *The Significant Americans.* New York: Appleton-Century-Crofts, Inc., 1965.

2. Ellis, Albert. *Reason and Emotion in Psychotherapy.* New York: Lyle Stuart, 1962.

3. Ellis, Albert. *The Art and Science of Love.* New York: Lyle Stuart and Bantam Books, 1969.

4. Ellis, Albert. *Suppressed: Seven Key Essays Publishers Dared Not Print.* Chicago: New Classic House, 1965 (especially Chap. 4).

5. Ellis, Albert. *The Case for Sexual Liberty.* Tucson: Seymour Press, 1965.

6. Ellis, Albert. *Sex Without Guilt.* New York: Lyle Stuart and Grove Press, 1966.

7. Ellis, Albert. *The Search for Sexual Enjoyment.* New York: McFadden-Bartell, 1966.

8. Ellis, Albert. *If This Be Sexual Heresy.* New York: Lyle Stuart and Tower Publications, 1966.

9. Ellis, Albert, and Harper, Robert A. *Creative Marriage.* New York: Lyle Stuart and Tower Publications, 1966.

10. Ellis, Albert, and Harper, Robert A. *A Guide to Rational Living.* Englewood Cliffs, N.J.: Prentice-Hall, Inc., 1967, and Hollywood: Wilshire Books, 1967.

11. Kinsey, Alfred C., et al. *Sexual Behavior in the Human Male.* Philadelphia: W. B. Saunders, 1948.

12. Kinsey, Alfred C., et al. *Sexual Behavior in the Human Female.* Philadelphia: W. B. Saunders, 1953.

Part
Nine

The Future
in Light of
the Issues

*E*ACH OF THE PRECEDING segments of this book has dealt with a specific family-related issue which is currently a point of contention in our society. This part will approach a summary of some of the consequences which might occur as a result of society's having to face some of these issues.

There are a few ways in which the future of the family might be considered a social issue. First, it might be an issue because of the fact that there are often heard, from various sources of public comment, statements to the effect that the family is disintegrating or disappearing. The sources of these types of comments are most often the political stump or the pulpit, but since such statements are usually either ignored or go unanswered, no real social issue is created on this topic. Another way in which the future of the family might be seen as an issue is within what might broadly be called the field of family studies. Among that group of sociologists, psychologists, lawyers, and doctors who refer to themselves as family specialists, there has been a continuing debate concerning the types of organization and structure the family will assume in the future. However, since this debate is very cool and academic in nature, it could hardly be seen as a full-blown issue, even within the family field. Furthermore, there is very little argument over the various views which are expressed; rather, experts simply present their own speculations without a great deal of agreement or disagreement from other professionals in the field.

But, with respect to the future of the family, there are rarely any significant political, legislative, or moral confrontations which relate specifically to the subject. Thus, there will be no attempt to present this topic as an issue, but rather to present two articles which speak of the future of the family in light of some of the issues which have been dealt with earlier. However, since the concern of this section is the future, it might be appropriate to summarize a few speculations concerning the outcomes of each of these previously discussed issues.

Regarding the issue of marriage versus nonmarriage, it appears likely that marriages will continue at a pace that will approximate the current high rate. Although the marriage rate declined steadily for several years through 1976, it again increased in 1977. Not only will most young people continue to marry, the rate of remarriage among the older widowed and divorced will probably continue to be high although this rate has also shown some recent fluctuations.

It is hard to predict whether or not the issues surrounding cohabitation will be quickly clarified or resolved. Both behavior and attitudes in this matter are still in a state of flux and could remain so for several years. However, present indications are that cohabitation will continue to be viewed with disdain by the older generations, while being increasingly accepted by the younger ones. On the other hand, as the picture clarifies, there could also be a sort of backlash against this sort of behavior by young people, especially if it comes to be seen as a type of exploitation on the part of one sex by the other.

The form of marriage will continue to be monogamy for almost everyone, both legally and otherwise. Experiments with communes and group marriages will further decline and probably disappear completely. There will, however, be some reinstitution of the common-law marriage as some of the states attempt to register and regulate informal living-together arrangements. With the failure of most attempts to change the structure of marriage, experimentation will probably be more along the lines of the development of informal, less structured types of variations of intimate relationships, and the development of family networks that approximate the older extended family.

Probably the most difficult area in which to make predictions is that of men's and women's roles. There is little doubt that significant shifts are now occurring and that more changes will occur as the Women's Liberation Movement runs its course. One likelihood, for which there is now some evidence, is that there will be some resurgence of a Men's Liberation Movement. An inevitable result of close scrutiny of the roles of women is the realization that there are also some major faults and inequities existing in the roles of men. However, there is likely to be little or no conflict between these two movements, as they are essentially after the same goals and represent the same views with respect to the redefinition of all sex roles in society.

Predictions concerning parenthood and nonparenthood were made in the commentary beginning Part Five, but to summarize, it appears that at least for those young couples who marry in the next decade, families will be smaller by one or two children than families in the previous two decades. The average family will have two children, whereas many will have only one and some will have none. In this regard, the status of nonparenthood will be further legitimized as more young couples follow that course.

Given the Supreme Court's decision on the right to abortion, it was expected that the anti-abortion individuals and organizations would cease to clamor over this question. However, this did not occur; they simply shifted their targets. Instead of trying to work through the courts or through the state legislatures, the opponents of abortion are attempting to have the Congress pass a constitutional amendment that would negate the Supreme Court's decision. So far they have been unsuccessful in these attempts, but they have demonstrated a high degree of tenacity in their efforts.

Eventually almost every state will pass some kind of divorce reform legislation, although in many cases the reforms will be piecemeal, simply adding grounds such as "incompatibility" and "irreconcilable differences" to the present laws. This procedure avoids dealing with the significant issues related to the adversary system and to sex discrimination. However, regarding sex discrimination, the courts will probably take an increased role in bringing about reform in the old laws which permit or encourage discrimination.

Finally, with respect to the issue of marital fidelity, just as the studies indicate that there has been little significant change in the last three decades, there is little reason to think that there will be much change in the next few decades. The increased openness in society concerning sexual matters has led us to an appearance of more infidelity, rather than the actual practice of such. Thus, there is likely to be a backlash of appearances as society moves toward a renewed repression in the area of sex, which may have already begun, resulting in an *apparent* decline in infidelity. However, just as there has been no increase in recent years, no real decrease is expected either.

The first of the two articles presented in this final section, "The Future of Marriage" by Morton Hunt, explores in some depth the proposition that marriage in modern society is dying out. To the contrary, the author concludes that marriage is not dying, but rather is going through evolutionary changes which will make it more responsive to the changed needs of modern men and women. He analyzes the effects upon marriage of such phenomena as divorce, infidelity, and living together, and concludes that, rather than threatening the institution of marriage, these are functional adaptations which allow marriage to continue in its basically monogamous form. He further considers the future of marriage as influenced by several of the issues presented in previous sections, such as parenthood and men's and women's roles. Although significant changes will occur with respect to marriage and the family, Hunt sees no major changes coming about in the basic structure of marriage so far as monogamy is concerned.

The final article closes out the book with a survey report similar to the article which began the book. In 1973, *Better Homes and Gardens* reported on a survey of over 300,000 of its readers concerning the state of the American family. In 1978 they conducted another survey which repeated many of the questions of the earlier one, but which was considerably more comprehensive. This new report deals with the attitudes and opinions of what might be considered a middle-class sample of the population, but being such a large sample it should certainly be considered as somewhat representative of the bulk of the population.

One of the general findings of the survey is that things may not really be as bad as most of us think that they are. As in the 1973 survey, large numbers think that the family is in trouble, but when asked about their own situation, the large majority feel that they are in pretty good shape. The article might be summarized as saying that the greatest thing wrong with the American family today is that everyone thinks that there is a great deal wrong with the American family today. That the family is in trouble is perhaps just one more of the many myths that plague our society. In fact, one of the purposes guiding the selection of all of the articles for this book, along with the commentary accompanying each section, has been to demonstrate that there is good reason to be optimistic about the future of marriage and the family in American society.

25.

The Future of Marriage

Morton Hunt

Over a century ago, the Swiss historian and ethnologist J. J. Bachofen postulated that early man lived in small packs, ignorant of marriage and indulging in beastlike sexual promiscuity. He could hardly have suggested anything more revolting, or more fascinating, to the puritanical and prurient sensibility of his time, and whole theories of the family and of society were based on his notion by various anthropologists, as well as by German socialist Friedrich Engels and Russian revolutionist Pëtr Kropotkin. As the Victorian fog dissipated, however, it turned out that among the hundreds of primitive peoples still on earth—many of whom lived much like early man—not a single one was without some form of marriage and some limitations on the sexual freedom of the married. Marriage, it appeared, was a genuine human universal, like speech and social organization.

Nonetheless, Bachofen's myth died hard, because it appealed to a longing, deep in all of us, for total freedom to do whatever we want. And recently, it has sprung up from its own ashes in the form of a startling new notion: Even if there never was a time when marriage didn't exist, there soon will be. Lately, the air has been filled with such prophecies of the decline and impending fall of marriage. Some of the prophets are grieved at this prospect—among them, men of the cloth, such as the Pope and Dr. Peale, who keep warning us that hedonism and easy divorce are eroding the very foundations of family life. Others, who rejoice at the thought, include an assortment of feminists, hippies, and anarchists, plus much-married theater people such as Joan Fontaine, who, having been married more times than the Pope and Dr Peale put together, has authoritatively told the world that marriage is obsolete and that any sensible person can live and love better without it.

Some of the fire-breathing dragon ladies who have given women's lib an undeservedly bad name urge single women not to marry and married ones to desert their husbands forthwith. Kate Millet, the movement's leading theoretician, expects marriage to wither away after women achieve full equality. Dr. Roger Egeberg, an Assistant Secretary of HEW, urged Americans in 1969 to reconsider their inherited belief that everyone ought to marry. And last August, Mrs. Rita Hauser, the U.S. representative to the UN Human Rights Commission, said that the idea that marriage was primarily for procreation had become outmoded and that laws banning marriage between homosexuals should be erased from the books.

So much for the voices of prophecy. Are there, in fact, any real indications of a mass revolt against traditional marriage? There certainly seem to be. For one thing, in 1969 there were 660,000 divorces in America—an all-time record—and the divorce rate seems certain to achieve historic new highs in the next few years. For another thing, marital infidelity seems to have increased markedly since Kinsey's first surveys of a generation ago and now is tried, sooner or later, by some 60 per cent of married men and 30 to 35 per cent of married women in this country. But in what is much more of a departure from the past, infidelity is now tacitly accepted by a fair number of the spouses of the unfaithful. For some couples it has become a shared hobby; mate-swapping and group-sex parties now involve thousands of middle-class marriages. Yet another indication of change is a sharp increase not only in the number of young men and women who, dispensing with legalities, live together unwed but also in the *kind* of people who are doing so; although common-law marriage has long been popular among the poor, in the past few years it has become widespread—and often esteemed—within the middle class.

An even more radical attack on our marriage system is the effort of people in hundreds of communes around the country to construct "families," or group marriages, in which the adults own everything in common, and often consider that they all belong to one another and play mix-and-match sexually with total freedom. A more complete break with tradition is being made by a rapidly growing percentage of America's male and female homosexuals, who nowadays feel freer than ever to avoid cover marriages and to live openly as homosexuals. Their lead is almost certain to be followed by countless others within the next decade or so as our society grows ever more tolerant of personal choice in sexual matters.

Nevertheless, reports of the death of marriage are, to paraphrase Mark Twain, greatly exaggerated. Most human beings regard whatever they grew up with as right and good and see nearly every change in human behavior as a decline in standards and a fall from grace. But change often means adaptation and evolution. The many signs of contemporary revolt against marriage have been viewed as symptoms of a fatal disease, but they may, instead, be signs of a change from an obsolescent form of marriage—patriarchal monogamy—into new forms better suited to present-day human needs.

Marriage as a social structure is exceedingly plastic, being shaped by the interplay of culture and of human needs into hundreds of different forms. In societies where women could do valuable productive work, it often made sense for a man to acquire more than one wife; where women were idle or relatively unproductive—and, hence, a burden—monogamy was more likely to be the pattern. When women had means of their own or could fall back upon relatives, divorce was apt to be easy; where they were wholly dependent on their husbands, it was generally difficult. Under marginal and primitive living conditions, men kept their women in useful subjugation; in wealthier and more leisured societies, women often managed to acquire a degree of independence and power.

For a long while, the only acceptable form of marriage in America was a lifelong one-to-one union, sexually faithful, all but indissoluble, productive of goods and children, and strongly husband-dominated. It was a thoroughly functional mechanism during the eighteenth and much of the nineteenth centuries, when men were struggling to secure the land and needed women who would clothe and feed them, produce and rear children to help them, and obey their orders without question for an entire lifetime. It was functional, too, for the women of that time, who, uneducated, unfit for other kinds of work, and endowed by law with almost no legal or property rights, needed men who would support them, give them social status, and be their guides and protectors for life.

But time passed, the Indians were conquered, the sod was busted, towns and cities grew up, railroads laced the land, factories and offices took the place of the frontier. Less and less did men need women to produce goods and children; more and more, women were educated, had time to spare, made their way into the job market—and realized that they no longer had to cling to their men for life. As patriarchalism lost its usefulness, women began to want and demand orgasms, contraceptives, the vote, and respect; men, finding the world growing ever more impersonal and cold, began to want wives who were warm, understanding, companionable, and sexy.

Yet, strangely enough, as all these things were happening, marriage not only did not lose ground but grew more popular, and today, when it is under full-scale attack on most fronts, it is more widespread than ever before. A considerably larger percentage of our adult population was married in 1970 than was the case in 1890; the marriage rate, though still below the level of the 1940's, has been climbing steadily since 1963.

The explanation of this paradox is that as marriage was losing its former uses, it was gaining new ones. The changes that were robbing marriage of practical and life-affirming values were turning America into a mechanized urban society in which we felt like numbers, not individuals, in which we had many neighbors but few lifelong friends, and in which our lives were controlled by remote governments, huge companies, and insensate computers. Alone and impotent, how can we find intimacy and warmth, understanding and a feeling of personal importance? Why, obviously, through *loving* and *marrying*. Marriage is a microcosm, a world within which we seek to correct the shortcomings of the macrocosm around us. Saint Paul said it is better to marry than to burn; today, feeling the glacial chill of the world we live in, we find it better to marry than to freeze.

The model of marriage that served the old purposes excellently serves the new ones poorly. But most of the contemporary assaults upon it are not efforts to destroy it; they are efforts to modify and remold it. Only traditional patriarchal marriage is dying, while all around us marriage is being reborn in new forms. The marriage of the future already exists; we have merely mistaken the signs of evolutionary change for the stigmata of necrosis.

Divorce is a case in point. Far from being a wasting illness, it is a healthful adaptation, enabling monogamy to survive in a time when patriarchal powers, privileges, and marital systems have become unworkable; far from being a radical change in the institution of marriage, divorce is a relatively minor modification of it and thoroughly supportive of most of its conventions.

Not that it seemed so at first. When divorce was introduced to Christian Europe, it appeared an extreme and rather sinful measure to most people; even among the wealthy—the only people who could afford it—it remained for centuries quite rare and thoroughly scandalous. In 1816, when president Timothy Dwight of Yale thundered against the "alarming and terrible" divorce rate in Connecticut, about one of every 100 marriages was being legally dissolved. But as women began achieving a certain degree of emancipation during the nineteenth century, and as the purposes of marriage changed, divorce laws were liberalized and the rate began climbing. Between 1870 and 1905, both the U.S. population and the divorce rate more than doubled; and between then and today, the divorce rate increased over four times.

And not only for the reasons we have already noted but for yet another: the increase in longevity. When people married in their late 20's and marriage was likely to end in death by the time the last child was leaving home, divorce seemed not only wrong but hardly worth the trouble; this was especially true where the only defect in a marriage was boredom. Today, however, when people marry earlier and have finished raising their children with half their adult lives still ahead of them, boredom seems a very good reason for getting divorced.

Half of all divorces occur after eight years of marriage and a quarter of them after 15—most of these being not the results of bad initial choices but of disparity or dullness that has grown with time.

Divorcing people, however, are seeking not to escape from marriage for the rest of their lives but to exchange unhappy or boring marriages for satisfying ones. Whatever bitter things they say at the time of divorce, the vast majority do remarry, most of their second marriages lasting the rest of their lives; even those whose second marriages fail are very likely to divorce and remarry again and, that failing, yet again. Divorcing people are actually marrying people, and divorce is not a negation of marriage but a workable cross between traditional monogamy and multiple marriage; sociologists have even referred to it as "serial polygamy."

Despite its costs and its hardships, divorce is thus a compromise between the monogamous ideal and the realities of present-day life. To judge from the statistics, it is becoming more useful and more socially acceptable every year. Although the divorce rate leveled off for a dozen years or so after the postwar surge of 1946, it has been climbing steadily since 1962, continuing the long-range trend of 100 years, and the rate for the entire nation now stands at nearly one for every three marriages. In some areas, it is even higher. In California, where a new ultraliberal law went into effect in 1970, nearly two of every three marriages end in divorce—a fact that astonishes people in other areas of the country but that Californians themselves accept with equanimity. They still approve of, and very much enjoy, being married; they have simply gone further than the rest of us in using divorce to keep monogamy workable in today's world.

Seen in the same light, marital infidelity is also a frequently useful modification of the marriage contract rather than a repudiation of it. It violates the conventional moral code to a greater degree than does divorce but, as practiced in America, is only a limited departure from the monogamous pattern. Unfaithful Americans, by and large, neither have extramarital love affairs that last for many years nor do they engage in a continuous series of minor liaisons; rather, their infidelity consists of relatively brief and widely scattered episodes, so that in the course of a married lifetime, they spend many more years being faithful than being unfaithful. Furthermore, American infidelity, unlike its European counterparts, has no recognized status as part of the marital system; except in a few circles, it remains impermissible, hidden and isolated from the rest of one's life.

This is not true at all levels of our society, however: Upper-class men—and, to some extent, women—have long regarded the discreet love affair as an essential complement to marriage, and lower-class husbands have always considered an extracurricular roll in the hay important to a married man's peace of mind. Indeed, very few societies have ever tried to make both husband and wife sexually faithful over a lifetime; the totally monogamous ideal is statistically an abnormality. Professors Clellan Ford and Frank Beach state in *Pat-*

terns of Sexual Behavior that less than 16 per cent of 185 societies studied by anthropologists had formal restrictions to a single mate —and, of these, less than a third wholly disapproved of both premarital and extramarital relationships.

Our middle-class, puritanical society, however, has long held that infidelity of any sort is impossible if one truly loves one's mate and is happily married, that any deviation from fidelity stems from an evil or neurotic character, and that it inevitably damages both the sinner and the sinned against. This credo drew support from earlier generations of psychotherapists, for almost all the adulterers they treated were neurotics, unhappily married, or out of sorts with life in general. But it is just such people who seek psychotherapy; they are hardly a fair sample. Recently, sex researchers have examined the unfaithful more representatively and have come up with quite different findings. Alfred Kinsey, sociologist Robert Whitehurst of Indiana University, sociologist John Cuber of Ohio State University, sexologist/therapist Dr. Albert Ellis, and various others (including myself) , all of whom have made surveys of unfaithful husbands and wives, agree in general that:

1. Many of the unfaithful—perhaps even a majority—are not seriously dissatisfied with their marriages nor their mates and a fair number are more or less happily married.

2. Only about a third—perhaps even fewer—appear to seek extramarital sex for neurotic motives; the rest do so for nonpathological reasons.

3. Many of the unfaithful—perhaps even a majority—do not feel that they, their mates, nor their marriages have been harmed; in my own sample, a tenth said that their marriages had been helped or made more tolerable by their infidelity.

It is still true that many a "deceived" husband or wife, learning about his or her mate's infidelity, feels humiliated, betrayed, and unloved, and is filled with rage and the desire for revenge; it is still true, too, that infidelity is a cause in perhaps a third of all divorces. But more often than not, deceived spouses never know of their mates' infidelity nor are their marriages perceptibly harmed by it.

The bulk of present-day infidelity remains hidden beneath the disguise of conventional marital behavior. But an unfettered minority of husbands and wives openly grant each other the right to outside relationships, limiting that right to certain occasions and certain kinds of involvement, in order to keep the marital relationship all-important and unimpaired. A few couples, for instance, take separate vacations or allow each other one night out alone per week, it being understood that their extramarital involvements are to be confined to those times. Similar freedoms have been urged by radical marriage reformers for decades but have never really caught on, and probably never will, for one simple reason: What's out of sight is not necessarily out of mind. What husband can feel sure, despite his wife's promises, that she might not find some other man who will make her dream come true? What wife can feel sure that her husband won't fall in love with some woman he is supposed to be having only a friendly tumble with?

But it's another matter when husband and wife go together in search of extramarital frolic and do their thing with other people, in full view of each other, where it is free of romantic feeling. This is the very essence of marital swinging, or, as it is sometimes called, comarital sex. Whether it consists of a quiet mate exchange between two couples, a small, sociable group-sex party, or a large orgiastic rumpus, the premise is the same: As long as the extramarital sex is open, shared, and purely recreational, it is not considered divisive of marriage.

So the husband and wife welcome the baby sitter, kiss the children good night, and drive off together to someone's home, where they drink a little and make social talk with their hosts and any other guests present, and then pair off with a couple of others and disappear into bedrooms for an hour or so or undress in the living room and have sex in front of their interested and approving mates.

No secrecy about that, certainly, and no hidden romance to fear; indeed, the very exhibitionism of marital swinging enforces its most important ground rule—the tacit understanding that participants will not indulge in emotional involvements with fellow swingers, no matter what physical acts they perform together. Though a man and a woman make it with each other at a group-sex party, they are not supposed to meet each other later on; two swinging couples who get together outside of parties are disapprovingly said to be going steady. According to several researchers, this proves that married swingers value their marriages: They want sexual fun and stimulation but nothing that would jeopardize their marital relationships. As sociologists Duane Denfeld and Michael Gordon of the University of Connecticut straight-facedly write, marital swingers "favor monogamy and want to maintain it" and do their swinging "in order to support and improve their marriages."

To the outsider, this must sound very odd, not to say outlandish. How could anyone hope to preserve the warmth and intimacy of marriage by performing the most private and personal sexual acts with other people in front of his own mate or watching his mate do so with others?

Such a question implies that sex is integrally interwoven with the rest of one's feelings about the mate—which it is—but swingers maintain that it can be detached and enjoyed apart from those feelings, without changing them in any way. Marital swinging is supposed to involve only this one segment of the marital relationship and during only a few hours of any week or month; all else is meant to remain intact, monogamous, and conventional.

Experts maintain that some people swing out of neurotic needs; some have sexual problems in their marriages that do not arise in casual sexual relationships; some are merely bored and in need of new stimuli; some need the ego lift of continual conquests. But the average swinger, whatever his (or her) motive, normal or pathological, is apt to believe that he loves his spouse, that he has a pretty good marriage, and that detaching sex—and sex alone—from marital restrictions not only will do the marriage no harm but will rid it of any aura of confinement.

In contrast to this highly specialized and sharply limited attitude, there seems to be a far broader and more thorough rejection of marriage on the part of those men and women who choose to live together unwed. Informal, nonlegal unions have long been widespread among poor blacks, largely for economic reasons, but the present wave of such unions among middle-class whites has an ideological basis, for most of those who choose this arrangement consider themselves revolutionaries who have the guts to pioneer in a more honest and vital relationship than conventional marriage. A 44-year-old conference leader, Theodora Wells, and a 51-year-old psychologist, Lee Christie, who live together in Beverly Hills, expounded their philosophy in the April 1970 issue of *The Futurist:*

> 'Personhood' is central to the living-together relationship; sex roles are central to the marriage relationship. Our experience strongly suggests that personhood excites growth, stimulates openness, increases joyful satisfactions in achieving, encompasses rich, full sexuality peaking in romance. Marriage may have the appearance of this in its romantic phase, but it settles down to prosaic routine. . . . The wife role is diametrically opposed to the personhood I want. I [Theodora] therefore choose to live with the man who joins me in the priority of personhood.

What this means is that she hates homemaking, is career oriented, and fears that if she became a legal wife, she would automatically be committed to traditional female roles, to dependency. Hence, she and Christie have rejected marriage and chosen an arrangement without legal obligations, without a head of the household, and without a primary money earner or primary homemaker—though Christie, as it happens, does 90 per cent of the cooking. Both believe that their freedom from legal ties and their constant need to rechoose each other make for a more exciting, real, and growing relationship.

A fair number of the avant-garde and many of the young have begun to find this not only a fashionably rebellious but thoroughly congenial attitude toward marriage; couples are living together, often openly, on many a college campus, risking punishment by college authorities (but finding the risk smaller every day) and bucking their parents' strenuous disapproval (but getting their glum acceptance more and more often).

When one examines the situation closely, however, it becomes clear that most of these marital Maoists live together in close, warm, committed, and monogamous fashion, very much like married people; they keep house together (although often dividing their roles in untraditional ways) and neither is free to have sex with anyone else, date anyone else, nor even find anyone else intriguing. Anthropologists Margaret Mead and Ashley Montague, sociologist John Gagnon, and other close observers of the youth scene feel that living together, whatever its defects, is actually an apprentice marriage and not a true rebellion against marriage at all.

Dr. Mead, incidentally, made a major public pitch in 1966 for a revision of our laws that would create two kinds of marital status: individual marriage, a legal but easily dissolved form for young people who were unready for parenthood or full commitment to each other but who wanted to live together with social acceptance; and parental marriage, a union involving all the legal commitments and responsibilities—and difficulties of dissolution—of marriage as we presently know it. Her suggestion aroused a great deal of public debate. The middle-aged, for the most part, condemned her proposal as being an attack upon and a debasement of marriage, while the young replied that the whole idea was unnecessary. The young were right: They were already creating their own new marital folkway in the form of the close, serious, but informal union that achieved all the goals of individual marriage except its legality and acceptance by the middle-aged. Thinking themselves rebels against marriage, they had only created a new form of marriage closely resembling the very thing Dr. Mead had suggested.

If these modifications of monogamy aren't quite as alarming or as revolutionary as they seem to be, one contemporary experiment in marriage *is* a genuine and total break with Western tradition. This is group marriage—a catchall term applied to a wide variety of polygamous experiments in which small groups of adult males and females, and their children, live together under one roof or in a close-knit settlement, calling themselves a family, tribe, commune, or, more grandly, intentional community, and considering themselves all married to one another.

As the term intentional community indicates, these are experiments not merely in marriage but in the building of a new type of society. They are utopian minisocieties existing within, but almost wholly opposed to, the mores and values of present-day American society.

Not that they are all of a piece. A few are located in cities and have members who look and act square and hold regular jobs; some, both urban and rural, consist largely of dropouts, acidheads, panhandlers, and petty thieves: but most are rural communities, have hippie-looking members, and aim at a self-sufficient farming-and-handicraft way of life. A very few communes are politically conservative, some are in the middle, and most are pacifist, anarchistic, and/or New Leftist. Nearly all, whatever their national political bent, are islands of primitive communism in which everything is collectively owned and all members work for the common good.

Their communism extends to—or perhaps really begins with—sexual collectivism. Though some communes consist of married couples who are conventionally faithful, many are built around some kind of group sexual sharing. In some of these, couples are paired off but occasionally sleep with other members of the group; in others, pairing off is actively discouraged and the members drift around sexually from one partner to another—a night here, a night there, as they wish.

Group marriage has captured the imagination of many thousands of college students in the past few years through its idealistic and romantic portrayal in three novels widely read by the young—Robert Heinlein's *Stranger in a Strange Land* and Robert Rimmer's *The Harrad Experiment* and *Proposition 31*. The underground press, too, has paid a good deal of sympathetic attention—and the establishment press a good deal of hostile attention—to communes. There has even been, for several years, a West Coast publication titled *The Modern Utopian* that is devoted, in large part, to news and discussions of group marriage. The magazine, which publishes a directory of intentional communities, recently listed 125 communes and the editor said, "For every listing you find here, you can be certain there are 100 others." And an article in *The New York Times* last December stated that "nearly 2000 communes in 34 states have turned up" but gave this as a conservative figure, as "no accurate count exists."

All this sometimes gives one the feeling that group marriage is sweeping the country; but, based on the undoubtedly exaggerated figures of *The Modern Utopian* and counting a generous average of 20 people per commune, it would still mean that no more than 250,000 adults—approximately one tenth of one percent of the U.S. population—are presently involved in group marriages. These figures seem improbable.

Nevertheless, group marriage offers solutions to a number of the nagging problems and discontents of modern monogamy. Collective parenthood—every parent being partly responsible for every child in the group—not only provides a warm and enveloping atmosphere for children but removes some of the pressure from individual parents; moreover, it minimizes the disruptive effects of divorce on the child's world. Sexual sharing is an answer to boredom and solves the problem of infidelity, or seeks to, by declaring extramarital experiences acceptable and admirable. It avoids the success-status-possession syndrome of middle-class family life by turning toward simplicity, communal ownership, and communal goals.

Finally, it avoids the loneliness and confinement of monogamy by creating something comparable to what anthropologists call the extended family, a larger grouping of related people living together. (There is a difference, of course: In group marriage, the extended family isn't composed of blood relatives.) Even when sexual switching isn't the focus, there is a warm feeling of being affectionally connected to everyone else. As one young woman in a Taos commune said ecstatically, "It's really groovy waking up and knowing that 48 people love you."

There is, however, a negative side: This drastic reformulation of marriage makes for new problems, some of them more severe than the ones it has solved. Albert Ellis, quoted in Herbert Otto's new book, *The Family in Search of a Future,* lists several categories of serious difficulties with group marriage, including the near impossibility of finding four or more adults who can live harmoniously and lovingly together, the stubborn intrusion of jealously and love conflicts, and the innumerable difficulties of coordinating and scheduling many lives.

Other writers, including those who have sampled communal life, also talk about the problems of leadership (most communes have few rules to start with; those that survive for any time do so by becoming almost conventional and traditional) and the difficulties in communal work sharing (there are always some members who are slovenly and lazy and others who are neat and hard-working, the latter either having to expel the former or give up and let the commune slowly die).

A more serious defect is that most group marriages, being based upon a simple, semiprimitive, agrarian life, reintroduce old-style patriarchalism, because such a life puts a premium on masculine muscle power and endurance and leaves the classic domestic and subservient roles to women. Even a most sympathetic observer, psychiatrist Joseph Downing, writes, "In the tribal families, while both sexes work, women are generally in a service role. . . . Male dominance is held desirable by both sexes."

Most serious of all are the emotional limitations of group marriage. Its ideal is sexual freedom and universal love, but the group marriages that most nearly achieve this have the least cohesiveness and the shallowest interpersonal involvements; people come and go, and there is really no marriage at all but only a continuously changing and highly unstable encounter group. The longer-lasting and more cohesive group marriages are, in fact, those in which, as Dr. Downing reports, the initial sexual spree "generally gives way to the quiet, semipermanent, monogamous relationship characteristic of many in our general society."

Not surprisingly, therefore, Dr. Ellis finds that most group marriages are unstable and last only several months to a few years; and sociologist Lewis Yablonsky of California State College at Hayward, who has visited and lived in a number of communes, says that they are often idealistic but rarely successful or enduring. Over and above their specific difficulties, they are utopian—they seek to construct a new society from whole cloth. But all utopians thus far have failed; human behavior is so incredibly complex that every totally new order, no matter how well planned, generates innumerable unforeseen problems. It really is a pity, group living and group marriage look wonderful on paper.

All in all, then, the evidence is overwhelming that old-fashioned marriage is not dying and that nearly all of what passes for rebellion against it is a series of patchwork modifications enabling marriage to serve the needs of modern man without being unduly costly or painful.

While this is the present situation, can we extrapolate it into the future? Will marriage continue to exist in some form we can recognize?

It is clear that, in the future, we are going to have an even greater need than we now do for love relationships that offer intimacy, warmth, companionship, and a reasonable degree of reliability. Such relationships need not, of course, be heterosexual. With our increasing tolerance of sexual diversity, it seems likely that many homosexual men and women will find it publicly acceptable to live together in quasi-marital alliances.

The great majority of men and women, however, will continue to find heterosexual love the preferred form, for biological and psychological reasons that hardly have to be spelled out here. But need heterosexual love be embodied within marriage? If the world is already badly overpopulated and daily getting worse, why add to its burden—and if one does not intend to have children, why seek to enclose love within a legal cage? Formal promises to love are promises no one can keep, for love is not an act of will; and legal bonds have no power to keep love alive when it is dying.

Such reasoning—more cogent today than ever, due to the climate of sexual permissiveness and to the twin technical advances of the pill and the loop—lies behind the growth of unwed unions. From all indications, however, such unions will not replace marriage as an institution but only precede it in the life of the individual.

It seems probable that more and more young people will live together unwed for a time and then marry each other or break up and make another similar alliance, and another, until one of them turns into a formal, legal marriage. In 50 years, perhaps less, we may come close to the Scandinavian pattern, in which a great many couples live together prior to marriage. It may be, moreover, that the spread of this practice will decrease the divorce rate among the young, for many of the mistakes that are recognized too late and are undone in divorce court will be recognized and undone outside the legal system, with less social and emotional damage than divorce involves.

If, therefore, marriage continues to be important, what form will it take? The one truly revolutionary innovation is group marriage —and, as we have seen, it poses innumerable and possibly insuperable practical and emotional difficulties. A marriage of one man and one woman involves only one interrelationship, yet we all know how difficult it is to find that one right fit and to keep it in working order. But add one more person, making the smallest possible group marriage, and you have three relationships (A-B, B-C, and A-C); add a fourth to make two couples and you have six relationships; add enough to make a typical group marriage of 15 persons and you have 105 relationships.

This is an abstract way of saying that human beings are all very different and that finding a satisfying and workable love relationship is not easy, even for a twosome, and is impossibly difficult for aggregations of a dozen or so. It might prove less difficult, a generation hence, for children brought up in group-marriage communes. Such children would not have known the close, intense, parent-child relationships of monogamous marriage and could more easily spread their affections thinly and undemandingly among many. But this is mere conjecture, for no communal-marriage experiment in America has lasted long enough for us to see the results, except the famous Oneida Community in upstate New York; it endured from 1848 to 1879, and then its offspring vanished back into the surrounding ocean of monogamy.

Those group marriages that do endure in the future will probably be dedicated to a rural and semiprimitive agrarian life-style. Urban communes may last for some years but with an ever-changing membership and a lack of inner familial indentity; in the city, one's work life lies outside the group, and with only emotional ties to hold the group together, any dissension or conflict will result in a turnover of membership. But while agrarian communes may have a sounder foundation, they can never become a mass movement; there is simply no way for the land to support well over 200,000,000 people with the low-efficiency productive methods of a century or two ago.

Agrarian communes not only cannot become a mass movement in the future but they will not even have much chance of surviving as islands in a sea of modern industrialism. For semiprimitive agrarianism is so marginal, so backbreaking, and so tedious a way of life that it is unlikely to hold most of its converts against the competing attractions of conventional civilization. Even Dr. Downing, for all his enthusiasm about the "Society of Awakening," as he calls tribal family living, predicts that for the foreseeable future, only a small minority will be attracted to it and that most of these will return to more normal surroundings and relationships after a matter of weeks or months.

Thus, monogamy will prevail; on this, nearly all experts agree. But it will almost certainly continue to change in the same general direction in which it has been changing for the past few generations; namely, toward a redefinition of the special roles played by husband and wife, so as to achieve a more equal distribution of the rights, privileges, and life expectations of man and woman.

This, however, will represent no sharp break with contemporary marriage, for the marriage of 1971 has come a long way from patriarchy toward the goal of equality. Our prevalent marital style has been termed companionship marriage by a generation of sociologists; in contrast to nineteenth century marriage, it is relatively egalitarian and intimate, husband and wife being intellectually and emotionally close, sexually compatible, and nearly equal in personal power and in the quantity and quality of labor each contributes to the marriage.

From an absolute point of view, however, it still is contaminated by patriarchalism. Although each partner votes, most husbands (and wives) still think that men understand politics better; although each may have had similar schooling and believes both sexes to be intellectually equal, most husbands and wives still act as if men were innately better equipped to handle money, drive the car, fill out tax returns, and replace fuses. There may be something close to equality in their homemaking, but nearly always it is his career that counts, not hers. If his company wants to move him to another city, she quits her job and looks for another in their new location; and when they want to have children, it is seldom questioned that he will continue to work while she will stay home.

With this, there is a considerable shift back toward traditional role assignments: He stops waxing the floors and washing dishes, begins to speak with greater authority about how their money is to be spent, tells her (rather than consults her) when he would like to work late or take a business trip, gives (or withholds) his approval of her suggestions for parties, vacations, and child discipline. The more he takes on the airs of his father, the more she learns to connive and manipulate like her mother. Feeling trapped and discriminated against, resenting the men of the world, she thinks she makes an exception of her husband, but in the hidden recesses of her mind he is one with the others. Bearing the burden of being a man in the world, and resenting the easy life of women, he thinks he makes an exception of his wife but deep down classifies her with the rest.

This is why a great many women yearn for change and what the majority of women's liberation members are actively hammering away at. A handful of radicals in the movement think that the answer is the total elimination of marriage, that real freedom for women will come about only through the abolition of legal bonds to men and the establishment of governmentally operated nurseries to rid women once and for all of domestic entrapment. But most women in the movement, and nearly all those outside it, have no sympathy with the anti-marriage extremists; they very much want to keep marriage alive but aim to push toward completion the evolutionary trends that have been underway so long.

Concretely, women want their husbands to treat them as equals; they want help and participation in domestic duties; they want help with child-rearing; they want day-care centers and other agencies to free them to work at least part time, while their children are small, so that they won't have to give up their careers and slide into the imprisonment of domesticity. They want an equal voice in all the decisions made in the home—including job decisions that affect married life; they want their husbands to respect them, not indulge them; they want, in short, to be treated as if they were their husband's best friends—which, in fact, they are, or should be.

All this is only a continuation of the developments in marriage over the past century and a quarter. The key question is: How far can marriage evolve in this direction without making excessive demands upon both partners? Can most husbands and wives have full-time uninterrupted careers, share all the chores and obligations of homemaking and parenthood, and still find time for the essential business of love and companionship?

From the time of the early suffragettes, there have been women with the drive and talent to be full-time doctors, lawyers, retailers, and the like, and at the same time to run a home and raise children with the help of housekeepers, nannies, and selfless husbands. From these examples, we can judge how likely this is to become the dominant pattern of the future. Simply put, it isn't, for it would take more energy, money, and good luck than the great majority of women possess and more skilled helpers than the country could possibly provide. But what if child care were more efficiently handled in state-run centers, which would make the totally egalitarian marriage much more feasible? The question then becomes: How many middle-class American women would really prefer full-time work to something less demanding that would give them more time with their children? The truth is that most of the world's work is dull and wearisome rather than exhilarating and inspiring. Women's lib leaders are largely middle-to-upper-echelon professionals, and no wonder they think every wife would be better off working full time —but we have yet to hear the same thing from saleswomen, secretaries, and bookkeepers.

Married women *are* working more all the time—in 1970, over half of all mothers whose children were in school held jobs—but the middle-class women among them pick and choose things they like to do rather than *have* to do for a living; moreover, many work part time until their children have grown old enough to make mothering a minor assignment. Accordingly, they make much less money than their husbands, rarely ever rise to any high positions in their fields, and, to some extent, play certain traditionally female roles within marriage. It is a compromise and, like all compromises, it delights no one—but serves nearly everyone better than more clear-cut and idealistic solutions.

Though the growth of egalitarianism will not solve all the problems of marriage, it may help solve the problems of a *bad* marriage. With their increasing independence, fewer and fewer wives will feel compelled to remain confined within unhappy or unrewarding marriages. Divorce, therefore, can be expected to continue to increase, despite the offsetting effect of extramarital liaisons. Extrapolating the rising divorce rate, we can conservatively expect that within another generation, half or more of all persons who marry will be divorced at least once. But even if divorce were to become an almost universal experience, it would not be the *antithesis* of marriage but only a part of the marital experience; most people will, as always, spend their adult lives married—not continuously, in a single marriage, but segmentally, in two or more marriages. For all the dislocations and pain these divorces cause, the sum total of emotional satisfaction in the lives of the divorced and remarried may well be greater than their great-grandparents were able to achieve.

Marital infidelity, since it also relieves some of the pressures and discontents of unsuccessful or boring marriages—and does so in most cases without breaking up the existing home—will remain an alternative to divorce and will probably continue to increase, all the more so as women come to share more fully the traditional male privileges. Within another generation, based on present trends, four of five husbands and two of three wives whose marriages last more than several years will have at least a few extramarital involvements.

Overt permissiveness, particularly in the form of marital swinging, may be tried more often than it now is, but most of those who test it out will do so only briefly rather than adopt it as a way of life. Swinging has a number of built-in difficulties, the first and most important of which is that the avoidance of all emotional involvement—the very keystone of swinging—is exceedingly hard to achieve. Nearly all professional observers report that jealously is a frequent and severely disruptive problem. And not only jealousy but sexual competitiveness: Men often have potency problems while being watched by other men or after seeing other men outperform them. Even a regular stud, moreover, may feel threatened when he observes his wife being more active at a swinging party than he himself could possibly be. Finally, the whole thing is truly workable only for the young and the attractive.

There will be wider and freer variations in marital styles—we are a pluralistic nation, growing more tolerant of diversity all the time —but throughout all the styles of marriage in the future will run a predominant motif that has been implicit in the evolution of marriage for a century and a quarter and that will finally come to full flowering in a generation or so. In short, the marriage of the future will be a heterosexual friendship, a free and unconstrained union of a man and a woman who are companions, partners, comrades, and sexual lovers. There will still be a certain degree of specialization within marriage, but by and large, the daily business of living together—the talk, the meals, the going out to work and coming home again, the spending of money, the lovemaking, the caring for the children, even the indulgence or nonindulgence in outside affairs—will be governed by this fundamental relationship rather than by the lord-and-servant relationship of patriarchal marriage. Like all friendships, it will exist only as long as it is valid; it will rarely last a lifetime, yet each marriage, while it does last, will meet the needs of the men and women of the future as no earlier form of marriage could have. Yet we who know the marriage of today will find it relatively familiar. comprehensible—and very much alive.

26.

What's Happening to the American Family?

By Gordon G. Greer
and Kate Keating

HOW'RE WE DOING? NOT SO HOT

I t's obvious in the answers to our very first question that most readers are disturbed by the present state of the family.

Do you feel that family life in America is in trouble?
Yes: 76%   No: 22%*

We wondered what readers viewed as the greatest threats to family life. In descending order, 37% said inattentive parents ("Parents don't want to be bothered anymore"); 36% said the absence of religious and spiritual foundation ("Living contrary to God's laws can only lead to great unhappiness"); 21% said materialism ("Necessities are confused with luxuries"); 18% said financial pressure ("It drives the mother and father out of the home to work, thus leaving the raising of children to other people and turning the home into no more than a motel for an overnight stay"); and 18% said divorce ("Obviously, the greatest threat to a family is having it broken up").

---

* Throughout this report, you may notice that the answers don't always add up to 100%. This is caused in some cases by multiple answers, and in others by rounding off decimal points or by omitting those respondents who "don't know" or didn't answer.

In their comments, many readers seemed especially distressed by the "me first" attitude they observed all around them (" 'Doing your own thing' is irresponsible and selfish"), the decline they perceive in adherence to religious credos ("Man has made a mess of his life without God"), and a widespread malaise and purposelessness they blame on a lack of worthwhile goals ("In our family we don't really know where we're at or where we're headed").

"People don't care enough" was a common lament. "They aren't willing to extend themselves for one another. We don't feel deeply enough about things—the family, the community, the inner cities, whatever—to give up our material comforts or our security to improve them."

Or, as a reader from Connecticut expressed it, "Every person who marries for any reason other than to love and to share; any person who has a child without committing 20 years or more to the nurturing and support of that child; any teacher who does not teach; any lawyer who is incompetent; any seamstress whose seams rip; any doctor who is too busy to heal; any clerk who is rude—all assault the community and its ability to exist."

How're You Doing? I'm O.K.

In their own pursuit of happiness and satisfaction, most readers say they put greater value on intangibles—raising kids, staying healthy, continuing to grow in mind and spirit—than on materialistic achievements, career success, or social status. When we asked what they considered "very important" to them personally, 86% said physical well-being, 77% said raising children, 65% said intellectual growth, and 55% said spiritual growth. Ranked lowest of the 11 items on our list were recognition by others (13%), influence over others (9%), and social status (5%). Sharing the middle ground were house and property (37%), financial achievement and salary (35%), job status and career (26%), and sexual attractiveness (22%).

And how are they doing? Quite well, on the whole. In only one of the 11 areas did even a third of our respondents report dissatisfaction with the progress they're making—39% listed themselves as "not satisfied" in the realm of intellectual growth.

> Are you better off materially than your parents were? Are you happier?
>
> Better off: Yes, better off 71%; About the same 20%; No, worse off 7%.
>
> Happier: Yes, happier 48%; About the same 42%; No, less happy 6%.

Some readers said they didn't feel as happy as they should: "I love my husband, we're very good friends, we love our son. But still there is something missing in my life. I just don't know anymore." Others seemed almost to purr with contentment: "After 26 years, if we had it to do over, we'd do it—hopes, fears, heartaches, joys, hardships and all. I'm a very happy woman today. Life has been good to me. I'm thankful for what I have."

KIDS: ARE THEY WORTH IT?

These are hard times for parents, our readers reported, but the rewards outweigh the difficulties in more than nine homes out of ten.

If you had it to do over, would you have children?
Yes: 91%   No: 9%

For many readers, their children are their greatest satisfaction: "They are people I like and enjoy as well as love." For a less lucky few, they seem a shattering disappointment: "Child rearing has to be the hardest, most demanding, most worrisome task there is—I don't know what happened to joyous, fulfilling, rewarding." Some parents say that if they were starting all over again, they'd have children but perhaps fewer of them: "We have three and find each well worth the effort—but the costs of feeding, clothing, lessons, camps, etc., are so high that two children are the most I'd consider if we had it to do over."

When we asked what they considered the ideal number of children for their own family, 47% said two; 23% said three; 11% said four; 8% said one; 5% said five or more; and 5% said none.

Arguments for childlessness were often well presented: "My husband and I have tried to analyze our relationship to discover why it only improves continually (into our 13th year) while others are failing. One conclusion is the fact that we are childless by choice."

How do readers feel about other married couples deciding not to have children? Only 15% disapprove. Another 43% checked "Not my concern," and 40% checked "Approve."

Asked if working parents spend enough time with their children, readers gave low marks to both sides of the family. Fathers drew a response of 86% "No." Working mothers did slightly better: 72% "No." "I'm glad you included fathers," wrote one woman, a doctor. "I'm often asked, 'Do you think you can be a good mother and wife and be a doctor, too?' My answer is usually, 'Are you a good father, husband, and doctor, too?'"

The issue of working mothers drew trenchant comments from all sides. "In my job as an adult counselor at our community college," said one letter from Illinois, "I encounter many working mothers and student mothers. They agree that the changes made in their families because of their working status have been good. Many report that their children's schoolwork has improved because of the example they set. Many become better organized and more efficient in housekeeping because they have less time to spend on it. Their children become more independent and resourceful because they.

are not always under the watchful eye. The children take their house responsibilities more seriously because they learn that Mom won't be there to pick up the slack. The mothers become more aware of the quality of time they spend with their children. In general, the families seem to take each other less for granted." Equally compelling comments expressed an entirely different view: "Some of my fondest childhood memories are when I would run in the house and tell my mother all about my day. I have always been thankful that she didn't work outside the home. It has made a real difference in my life."

The importance of the mother's remaining at home depends, our readers told us, on the age of their kids. For preschool children, 88% said it was important for the mother to stay home; for grade school kids, the figure dropped to 56%; for junior high students, 36%; and for high school youngsters, 24%.

GROWING UP: THE IMPRESSIONABLE YEARS

Second only to parents themselves, television emerges in our survey as the greatest influence on the general development of children under age 12—and by no means are all readers happy about it. ("Television is one of the worst things that has ever happened to family life. Next to that is interfering relatives.") After parents (84%) and TV (48%), readers see other important childhood influences as friends (40%), teachers (33%), church (19%), organized activities—scouting, sports, etc. (14%), books (8%), and other relatives (6%). The overall effect of these forces disturbs them.

Is America a better or worse place to raise children than it was ten or 15 years ago?
Better: 15%   Same: 26%   Worse: 58%

Not that parents got particularly high marks either. Nearly two-thirds of our readers (66%) said parents put too much pressure on their kids to achieve, and a whopping 87% think most parents are too permissive with their children—although only 26% of the parents answering recognized that fault in themselves. A higher number—33%—admitted to overindulging their kids' material requests. "Doesn't everybody?" one reader remarked.

Are readers having trouble communicating with their children? Only 3% of our parents said, yes, a great deal of trouble; 31% said some; 49% said very little; and 17% said none. Many suggested that our questionnaire had helped them find out. "I thought it might interest you to know," wrote a reader from California, "that my two teen-agers and I filled this out together using the majority rule law. It was surprising to us to find out how we differed on some subjects and had never even discussed them. We enjoyed doing it, and it did bring us closer to understanding one another."

THE TEEN YEARS: TRYING TIMES

"My psyche has holes in it from seeing our kids through their teens" is typical of the troubled comments this subject elicited. But, all in all, America's youngsters are judged as coping pretty well— maybe even upgrading the art of adolescence.

> **In your opinion, are teenagers today more qualified or less qualified to make independent value judgments than was true ten years ago?**
> More qualified: 37%
> Less qualified: 19%
> No change: 42%

Which better prepares youngsters for the future, a strict home environment or a permissive one? No contest: strict 73%, permissive only 20%. But many readers touted a combination: "Too much permissiveness leaves a child so confused and undisciplined that he is not desirable in an orderly society. Too much strictness can inhibit him so that his creativity is stifled and he is afraid to show initiative—thereby limiting his potential as a contributing member of the community."

Lack of communication is a widely felt concern. Asked if teenagers share their personal problems with either parent, a sobering 42% of our readers said no. Only 10% said yes, with both parents; 44% said mostly with the mother; and just 1% said mostly with the father. "Kids who come to see me," a social worker told us, "say there is no guidance in their life and that they're making decisions they're fearful of making alone. Parents in turn tell me they're afraid to offer advice, fearful that it will be wrong or turn their kids off. The parents' values are in turmoil, so they're having a hard time advising their kids. It's a dilemma—one generation seeking advice, the other afraid and unwilling to give it."

LOVE AND MARRIAGE: WHAT IT'S ALL ABOUT

We asked a lot of questions concerning marriage in our survey, and the answers showed respondents to be more satisfied than not.

Do you and your spouse share enough interests and activities? Among all married readers, 70% said "Yes."

Do you share an understanding about what you want from marriage? "Yes" said even more marrieds: 85%.

Do you share personal problems? "Yes" said nine out of ten.

Do you and your spouse talk to each other enough? "Yes" said 63%—and even some of the "Noes" made it clear they weren't complaining: "We could *never* talk enough. There's too much to say for just one lifetime." (There were curves on the other side, too: "Yes, we talk to each other enough. It's just that we sometimes don't listen enough.")

Do you and your spouse have enough time together? "Yes" answered 60%.

Within the marriage relationship, do you have enough time to yourself? "Yes" beat "No" by four to one.

Are most of your expectations of happiness in marriage being fulfilled?
Yes: 85%   No: 15%

When we asked for the strongest reasons why couples stay married, love triumphed over all with a score of 43%. Second came children (34%), then companionship (27%), security (24%), and the sharing of mutual goals (20%). Readers gave less importance in this regard to religion (12%), the comforts of home (11%), psychological dependency (11%), money (6%), material possessions (5%), and, last of all those listed, sex (4%).

How important is it that a husband and wife have separate interests and activities? "Very important" said 42%; "some importance" said 50%; "not important" said 8%. "After seven years of marriage," one reader told us, "I'm just now branching out on my own and doing things I want to do. It took me a long time to learn that you don't have to be together 24 hours a day." Another said, "I know of many husbands who seem to resent the fact that their wives cling to them so. It's not that they are not happy being married—just that they feel guilty if they continue with their own interests while the wife is left without anything to do. I do not believe it was intended for two people to come together in a unifying relationship of marriage just to be made exactly alike. Instead, they should complement each other."

Do you think an occasional big argument to "clear the air" helps the husband-wife relationship? "Yes" said 67%.

Would you consider a decline in the husband's dominance to be beneficial or harmful to family life? "Beneficial" said 45%; "harmful" said 52%. But many readers gently chided us for asking such a question: "A family is a unit; there should be no dominant partner."

THE NEW WOMAN: WHO IS SHE?

If we heard it once, we must have heard it from at least 1,000 women: "I'm a full-time homemaker and I'm proud of it! I love it!" And among all of our respondents 76% agree that the traditional role of wife and mother as a full-time homemaker can lead to a fulfilling life.

Does this mean that readers reject the women's movement? Not at all.

All in all, do you feel that the movement for women's rights is a force for the better?
Yes: 60%   No: 37%

The good thing, readers told us, is that women now have choices. And no stigma should attach to whatever choice they make. "Some women can fulfill their lives better by being fulltime homemakers; others find working outside the home helps satisfy their own needs, so they're better able to deal with the role of wife and mother, if they choose it. Women are individuals, too."

Most objections to the movement seem to center on its tactics ("too devisive for the overall good"), particularly the tendency among some of its leaders to belittle traditional points of view: "The women's movement has some good goals, such as equal pay for equal work, but I feel the bad effect of it all has been to downgrade the role of homemaker and mother. *There is no more important job!"*

In general, we asked, has the new awareness of women's rights altered the husband-wife relationship significantly? "Yes" answered 66%. For better or for worse, among the marriages you know? By nearly two to one, "good effect" beat "bad effect."

"I'm for equal rights and equal pay," one woman said, "but I still like to be treated like a lady by a gentleman."

The "new" American woman who emerges from our survey is no fiery-eyed radical set on making men knuckle under. Instead, she turns out to be the familiar "traditional" woman blessed with previously unheard-of opportunities and choices.

Money: Where Does it All Go?

As economic forecasters, the majority of respondents are cautious and sober, if not downright glum. For example, 77% think the rate of inflation over the next five years will increase (only 1% say it will decrease); 59% consider it likely that we'll have a major economic depression in the next decade; only 2% believe social security will provide enough money to live on when they retire; 87% think the single-family home will be priced out of reach of the average American family; and as a threat to the future of family life, they rank inflation second only to moral decay.

Yet in their own financial affairs they seem to be doing all right.

After meeting essential monthly obligations, is it possible for your family to make regular deposits in a savings program?
Yes: 64%   No: 35%

They think it's sound financial planning to put money in a savings account (by a margin of 87% to 12%), but they recognize (by 55% to 43%) that the importance of having a large amount of money stashed away has declined for most families in recent years.

What do they consider the best hedge against inflation? The majority (69%) said owning real estate. And they practice what they preach; 82% own their homes.

In the way they use credit, most respondents seem prudent. Only 11% regard the use of credit cards as essential (20% don't use them at all), and 66% feel that the ease of obtaining credit has not caused overspending problems for their family. Only 10% say having credit cards and charge accounts frequently causes them to make unnecessary purchases.

Departures from this conservatism were mostly among the young: "My generation wasn't scared by the Depression the way our parents were, so a big savings account isn't as important to us. We're accustomed to traveling and spending money."

THE ELDERLY: SANS EVERYTHING

Nowhere did respondents show more sadness or guilt than when describing what they saw as the neglect of America's elderly and their underutilization as a vital human resource. "Do you think it's important for a child's development that he or she have contact with the elderly?" The answer was a resounding 96% "Yes." But *do* most children have enough contact with the elderly? This time it was a resounding 87% "No."

Do you think the elderly are generally forgotten by their families?
Yes: 72%   No: 27%

A common observation was nicely phrased in a letter from Utica: "The elderly are not forgotten in thought, but the time actually spent with them is short."

Older people themselves did little complaining. Indeed, of those age 65 and over, only 64% answered the above question "Yes"—a significantly lower figure than that of any other age group. Sometimes the problems of aging appear more fearful from a distance. "It scares me to see myself lonely and forgotten," wrote a woman who gave her age as between 18 and 24. "That's why I volunteer at the psychiatric hospital and visit with the older patients. I just hope someone will reciprocate when I grow old."

One question on this subject split respondents right in half: Where is the best place for aging parents no longer capable of living alone? Half the respondents said "Retirement or nursing home"; the other 50% said "With their children."

The comments on this question were particularly poignant, obviously inspired by intense inner conflicts and the weight of emotional debts too enormous to repay. "I've worked in a nursing home and vowed I would *never* see my parents in a home like that," one young woman told us. "Even the good ones can't supply the love and care that a family can. My parents cared for my needs as a child, so I should do the same for them if they need it. I realize that saying and doing are two different things. I only hope to be able to live up to my ideals."

Not everyone of good intent is successful, of course: "I think it's wonderful when three or more generations can share the same household. However, my husband's grandmother lived with us for ten months and it didn't work."

Even apparent success can exact an extremely high toll: "My

husband's 91-year-old father has lived with us for the past five years at our invitation, and we wouldn't have it any other way. But when we are no longer able to maintain a home for ourselves, we are going to try at almost any cost to avoid living with our children."

In any case, the agony of decision is acute, the choice among the toughest a son or daughter ever faces. "The question can't be answered until a person has been through it. The reversal of roles— now I make the decision for Mom and Dad, when all my life it was the other way around—is terrible!"

SEX: TOO MUCH, TOO SOON?

A comparison with the results of our first family survey, which was published in 1972, shows that attitudes toward sex have relaxed since that time. For example, when we asked readers six years ago if they would approve or disapprove of two people living together for a while before making the commitment of marriage, 26% said "Approve." That figure has now risen to 41%.

But this is no wild embrace of the sexual revolution, no headlong rejection of responsible behavior. On the question of living together, only 22% approve when the arrangement is a substitute for marriage rather than a prelude to it, and even those who approve often insist on a mature relationship: "Living together is a cheap copout when it's simply 'playing house.'"

"I don't like the idea of my children living with someone," another reader said, "but neither would I approve of their rushing blindly into a marriage. To say it is not my concern is dodging the issue. Perhaps the best answer is that it depends on the maturity of the individuals."

Premarital sex was also viewed realistically. Although a majority of readers (57%) disapprove of premarital intercourse, 80% feel that birth control methods and information should nevertheless be available to anyone—including unmarried teen-agers. "I don't condone promiscuity," reasons one reader, "but withholding information on birth control doesn't help. And there are already too many unwed parents and unwanted kids."

> **Is there too much emphasis on sex in all aspects of our society today?**
> **Yes: 84%   No: 15%**

Some readers told us sex isn't all that important: "If couples would spend more time in conversation and less in bed before marriage they would make more rational choices in their selection of a person to spend their life with."

Others are offended by the tasteless distortions of sex: "I'm not a prude, but I'm sick and tired of being hit in the face with pornographic material in drugstores, shopping malls, bookstores, theaters, and on TV and record albums. How can children be expected to maintain high standards in a world cluttered by trash?"

Divorce: Fight or Flee?

Nobody feels very good about divorce, but most respondents accept it as sometimes the lesser of two evils. "Take it from me," one reader remarked, "it's better to come from a broken home than to live in one."

Do you think it's right or wrong for a couple who simply can't get along to get a divorce?
When no children are involved:
  Right: 84%   Wrong: 12%
When children are involved:
  Right: 75%   Wrong: 22%

Most readers who added comments lined up on two sides: "better to get divorced than to live together in misery" versus "quitting never solves anything." Of course, there were many less adamant remarks, too: "Sometimes the most loving solution to an unhappy marriage that has disintegrated because the lines of communication have been cut off is to divorce and give each other a chance to find a more fulfilling relationship. But this should not be done without much soul-searching and honest evaluation of the marriage."

We asked what readers considered the main reasons for failed marriages. Immaturity finished highest, checked by 61%. Next came selfishness (51%), followed by changes in or lack of mutual interests and goals (44%), financial problems (41%), third-party entanglements (24%), personality conflicts (22%), poor sexual adjustments (16%), job pressures (14%), and the burden of children (10%).

Whatever the particular problem, the prospect of divorce is always wrenching. "Truthfully," one reader confided, "having to raise my family without my husband, having to work to meet the financial burdens, and, most of all, not to have him with us, scares the life out of me."

Abortion: No Easy Answers

Most readers find the thought of abortion abhorrent. Yet the majority condone it under special circumstances—90% if the mother's health is in danger, 84% to abort a malformed fetus, 84% to end a pregnancy caused by rape. For an otherwise normal unplanned pregnancy, however, only 39% approve abortion for married women, 50% if the woman is unmarried. Readers were nearly unanimous in their strong disapproval of abortion as a means of birth control: "The use of abortion in 'family planning' is abominable—married or unmarried."

When we made the question personal, we got somewhat different answers.

Would you yourself consider an abortion for an unplanned pregnancy?
  Yes: 34%   No: 65%

Many comments we received were as personal as the question. "I fully support abortion in any case," said one reader. "I was an unwanted child and it's a hell of a life." A Michigan woman had a different perspective: "To consider abortion is one thing—to go through with it is another. I have considered it but didn't go through with it. An unwanted pregnancy can and usually does turn out to be a very wanted baby." A letter from Hawaii viewed the problem from another angle: "I have worked in both a state health department and a university hospital emergency room, where I encountered many tragic cases of child abuse and neglect from parents who did not want the children or who were too young to accept the responsibility of a child. If these unspeakable crimes can be eliminated or lessened by allowing abortions, then even though the thought is repugnant to me, abortions must have a real purpose in our society." Then, too, a cry we heard often is: "Abortion is murder!"

Assume a woman chooses to have an abortion. Should her husband have the right to prevent it? The majority of women readers (51%) said yes. On the other hand, the same percentage of men said no.

WORKING: JUST A GRIND?

The majority of our respondents (58%) think that most other people are unhappy in their jobs. They don't show much unhappiness themselves, however.

Do you like your job? Yes: 83%   No: 12%

Nor do they appear overeager to quit work at 65. Only 15% favor mandatory retirement at that age, and just 9% think forced retirement affects family life for the better. They also reject the idea of a shorter work week (by 66% to 31%) if it entails a reduction in family income.

On the other hand, many readers endorse split jobs: "For instance, two men could semi-retire and share a single position; or two women could share a job to have time for home responsibilities as well as a career."

"Fifteen years ago," another reader told us, "my husband and I would have been delighted to each have a half-time job. He was great with kids and enjoyed being with them. I was overwhelmed by the whole business of child care and total family responsibility and would have appreciated a chance to get out to a job and think about other things. But that kind of arrangement was an idea before its time, and so I was a full-time homemaker and my husband a full-time breadwinner. As retirement approaches, we hope half-time positions will be available. Perhaps we could share a job with a new parent."

What about the time not spent on the job? Nearly two-thirds of our respondents (65%) say they spend most of their evenings and weekends doing what they want to do, as opposed to the 32% who spend them on what they *have* to do. Only 18% say their life is "frequently" a rat race; 67% say "sometimes," and 14% say "never."

THE FUTURE: WHAT NEXT?

The naïve romanticism of American folklore has apparently yielded to a more realistic outlook that nonetheless is strongly laced with personal optimism. When we asked readers for their assessment of the American family's next ten years, only 18% checked "Things will be better"; 33% thought "Things will be worse," and the others said "Things will remain about the same"—not a particularly starry-eyed view. Yet when asked to predict their own fortunes in that decade, 53% said "My life will be better," and only 3% allowed as how "My life will be worse." ("My life will be the pits!" was one comment, but it was most unusual.)

Older people, of course, confront the fear of age and loneliness, and many readers added thoughtful comments on those subjects. "I don't dread growing old," a Wisconsin reader told us, "but I do worry about the financial hardships associated with old age in our country. The escalation of inflation, the devaluation of the dollar, and the meagerness of social security present a bleak retirement picture. The only encouraging aspect is that, by the time I reach old age, senior citizens will have a majority vote and, together, they can be a beneficial influence on the way our country is managed."

Statistically, however, other fears ranked much higher.

> **Are you seriously worried or fearful about any of the following?**
> **Possible harm to or death of a loved one: 46%**
> **Debilitating disease: 32%**
> **Financial hardship: 26%**
> **Being a victim of crime: 21%**
> **Loneliness: 19%**
> **Old age: 17%**
> **Failing to reach personal goals: 16%**
> **Failing to find a meaningful purpose in life: 13%**
> **Losing your youth: 10%**
> **None of the above: 23%**

Other woes were seen as serious threats to family life in general: moral decay (53%), inflation (41%), energy shortage (41%), crime (28%), pollution (28%), recession/depression (19%), food shortage (14%), changing weather patterns (10%), war (9%).

But even as they brooded on such ominous problems, most readers resisted the temptation to despair. Why? Because, for one thing, they have faith in the young ("There are so many outstanding young people around, the future surely has to be brighter"). For another, they show similar faith in themselves ("Our family will cope no matter what happens"). Also, as a reader from Washington put it, "There will always be a family—just as long as there is love."